Critical Pedagogies and Language Learning

THE CAMBRIDGE APPLIED LINGUISTICS SERIES

Series editors: Michael H. Long and Jack C. Richards

This series presents the findings of work in applied linguistics that are of direct relevance to language teaching and learning and of particular interest to applied linguists, researchers, language teachers, and teacher trainers.

Recent publications in this series:

Cognition and Second Language Instruction *edited by Peter Robinson*
Computer Applications in Second Language Acquisition *by Carol A. Chapelle*
Contrastive Rhetoric *by Ulla Connor*
Corpora in Applied Linguistics *by Susan Hunston*
Criterion-referenced Language Testing *by James Dean Brown and Thom Hudson*
Culture in Second Language Teaching and Learning *edited by Eli Hinkel*
Exploring the Dynamics of Second Language Teaching *edited by Barbara Kroll*
Exploring the Dynamics of Second Language Writing *by Barbara Kroll*
Exploring the Second Language Mental Lexicon *by David Singleton*
Focus on Form in Classroom Second Language Acquisition *edited by Catherine Doughty and Jessica Williams*
Immersion Education: International Perspectives *edited by Robert Keith Johnson and Merrill Swain*
Interfaces between Second Language Acquisition and Language Testing Research *edited by Lyle F. Bachman and Andrew D. Cohen*
Learning Vocabulary in Another Language *by I. S. P. Nation*
Network-based Language Teaching *edited by Mark Warschauer and Richard Kern*
Pragmatics in Language Teaching *edited by Kenneth R. Rose and Gabriele Kasper*
Research Perspectives on English for Academic Purposes *edited by John Flowerdew and Matthew Peacock*
Researching and Applying Metaphor *edited by Lynne Cameron and Graham Low*
Second Language Vocabulary Acquisition *edited by James Coady and Thomas Huckin*
Sociolinguistics and Language Teaching *edited by Sandra Lee McKay and Nancy H. Hornberger*
Teacher Cognition in Language Teaching: Beliefs, Decision-Making, and Classroom Practice *by Devon Woods*
Text, Role, and Context *by Ann M. Johns*
Understanding Expertise in Teaching: Case Studies of Language Teacher Development *by Amy B. M. Tsui*

Critical Pedagogies and Language Learning

Edited by

Bonny Norton
University of British Columbia

Kelleen Toohey
Simon Fraser University

PUBLISHED BY THE PRESS SYNDICATE OF THE UNIVERSITY OF CAMBRIDGE
The Pitt Building, Trumpington Street, Cambridge, United Kingdom

CAMBRIDGE UNIVERSITY PRESS
The Edinburgh Building, Cambridge CB2 2RU, UK
40 West 20th Street, New York, NY 10011-4211, USA
477 Williamstown Road, Port Melbourne, VIC 3207, Australia
Ruiz de Alarcón 13, 28014 Madrid, Spain
Dock House, The Waterfront, Cape Town 8001, South Africa

http://www.cambridge.org

First published 2004

Printed in the United States of America

Typefaces Sabon 10.5/12 pt. and Arial *System* LaTeX 2_ε [TB]

A catalog record for this book is available from the British Library.

Library of Congress Cataloging in Publication Data

Critical pedagogies and language learning / edited by Bonny Norton, Kelleen Toohey.
p. cm. – (Cambridge applied linguistics series)
Includes bibliographical references and index.
ISBN 0-521-82802-3 (hbk.) – ISBN 0-521-53522-0 (pbk.)
1. Language and languages – Study and teaching. 2. Language teachers – Training of. I. Norton, Bonny, 1956– II. Toohey, Kelleen, 1950– III. Series.
P53.C7 2003
418′.0071 – dc21 2003048557

ISBN 0 521 82802 3 hardback
ISBN 0 521 53522 0 paperback

Contents

Contributors

Elsa Auerbach, *University of Massachusetts/Boston, United States*

Inês Brito, *Jeremiah E. Burke High School, Boston, Massachusetts, United States*

Suresh Canagarajah, *Baruch College of the City University of New York, United States*

Tara Goldstein, *Ontario Institute for Studies in Education at the University of Toronto, Canada*

Roxy Harris, *King's College London, England*

Ryuko Kubota, *University of North Carolina at Chapel Hill, United States*

Constant Leung, *King's College London, England*

Ambrizeth Helena Lima, *Harvard Graduate School of Education, Massachusetts, United States*

Angel M. Y. Lin, *City University of Hong Kong*

Allan Luke, *Nanyang Technological University, Singapore*

Brian Morgan, *York University, Toronto, Ontario, Canada*

Bonny Norton, *University of British Columbia, Vancouver, Canada*

Aneta Pavlenko, *Temple University, Philadelphia, Pennsylvania, United States*

Alastair Pennycook, *University of Technology, Sydney, Australia*

Ben Rampton, *King's College London, England*

Elana Shohamy, *Tel Aviv University, Israel*

Sue Starfield, *University of New South Wales, Australia*

Pippa Stein, *University of the Witwatersrand, Johannesburg, South Africa*

Jane Sunderland, *Lancaster University, United Kingdom*

Kelleen Toohey, *Simon Fraser University, Burnaby, British Columbia, Canada*

Karen Vanderheyden, *YMCA International College, Vancouver, British Columbia, Canada*

Bonnie Waterstone, *Simon Fraser University, Burnaby, British Columbia, Canada*

Acknowledgments

This volume came into being as a result of the commitment and generosity of all the authors represented within, as well as that of others not listed as authors. It has been a pleasure to work with scholars in the field of second language education for whom we have the greatest respect. We would also like to express our appreciation to doctoral student Ena Lee at the University of British Columbia for her dedicated care in the copyediting process. Her attention to detail, insight, and good cheer were invaluable in the preparation of the manuscript. We thank as well series editor Jack Richards and editor Julia Hough for their confidence in the project and their excellent editorial advice. Funding from the Social Sciences and Humanities Research Council of Canada is gratefully acknowledged.

1 *Critical pedagogies and language learning: An introduction*

Bonny Norton
Kelleen Toohey

Advocates of critical approaches to second language teaching are interested in relationships between language learning and social change. From this perspective, language is not simply a means of expression or communication; rather, it is a practice that constructs, and is constructed by, the ways language learners understand themselves, their social surroundings, their histories, and their possibilities for the future. This collection assembles the work of a variety of scholars interested in critical perspectives on language education in globally diverse sites of practice. All are interested in investigating the ways that social relationships are lived out in language and how issues of power, while often obscured in language research and educational practice (Kubota, this volume), are centrally important in developing critical language education pedagogies. Indeed, as Morgan (this volume) suggests, "politically engaged critiques of power in everyday life, communities, and institutions" are precisely what are needed to develop critical pedagogies in language education. The chapters have varying foci, seeking to better understand the relationships between writers and readers, teachers and students, test makers and test takers, teacher–educators and student teachers, and researchers and researched.

The term *critical pedagogy* is often associated with the work of scholars such as Freire (1968/1970), Giroux (1992), Luke (1988), Luke and Gore (1992), McLaren (1989), and Simon (1992) in the field of education. Aware of myriad political and economic inequities in contemporary societies, advocates have explored the "social visions" that pedagogical practices support (Simon, 1992), and critiques of classroom practices in terms of their social visions have been common and longstanding in critical educational literature.[1] Feminist critiques have also considered classroom practice and have identified ways in which the relationships and activities of classrooms contribute to patriarchal, hierarchical, and dominating practices in wider societies (e.g., Davies, 1989; Ellsworth, 1989; Gaskell, 1992; Spender, 1982; Walkerdine, 1989). In second language education, critiques of classroom practices in terms of the social visions such practices support are relatively recent but are increasingly being published in major venues.[2]

All the chapters in this volume share this aim – that is, to consider how, in diverse sites of language education, practices might be modified, changed, developed, or abandoned in efforts to support learners, learning, and social change. At the same time, most of the authors here remind us that critical pedagogy cannot be a unitary set of texts, beliefs, convictions, or assumptions. Like Pavlenko (this volume), these authors describe *local* situations, problems, and issues and see responsiveness to the particularities of the local as important in the equitable and democratic approaches they are trying to develop. In seeking to resist totalizing discourses about critical teaching, subjects, and strategies for progressive action, we have used the term *critical pedagogies* in the title of our book.

While each of the authors represented here uses critical lenses to reflect on the teaching and research practices in her or his community, there are important differences of focus across the chapters. We have therefore decided to divide the book into four sections, each with a slightly different emphasis. In doing so, however, we recognize that the distinctions between sections are not clear-cut and that many overlapping themes emerge. Such themes are discussed in greater detail later in this introduction.

Organization of the book and chapter summaries

Reconceptualizing second language education

The first section of the book brings perspectives from four scholars in diverse contexts who consider the critical in language learning and teaching with foci on race, gender, pedagogy, and assessment. The first chapter, by Allan Luke, considers what can be meant by the term *critical* in language education. Reminding us of its roots in liberation movements and the politically engaged scholarship of the Frankfurt School, Luke argues that critical pedagogical approaches "call up for scrutiny, whether through embodied action or discursive practice, the rules of exchange within a social field." These entail (as described by Freire in 1970) externalization, naming, and questioning the world, to accompany action that resists the psychological and physical violence and material disempowerment that many language students have experienced. Noting "there can be no more overtly normative challenges to educational systems, educators, and the state other than how they manage their cultural and linguistic Others," Luke sees critical pedagogies as necessary to engage with the experiences of these marginalized learners.

The issue of cultural and linguistic disempowerment also engages Ryuko Kubota in a chapter that invites us to rethink notions of multiculturalism. Drawing on her experience in the North American context, she makes the argument that while most teachers in the field of language learning are sensitive to cultural and linguistic diversity among their students, many have not adequately recognized the extent to which power operates to reinforce inequalities in both classrooms and communities. She contrasts notions of *liberal multiculturalism*, which she maintains is a color-blind, relatively superficial conception of multiculturalism, with *critical multiculturalism*, which addresses in greater depth such issues as race, gender, and class. Critical multiculturalism, she argues, has an "intellectual alliance" with critical pedagogy in that it aims to raise student consciousness about unjust social practices and helps them to become active agents for social change. Further, because of the inclusive and antiracist orientation of critical multiculturalism, she examines issues of whiteness in educational debates. While arguing that discussions of whiteness should avoid essentialism, Kubota makes the case that white privilege is not normally viewed as a racial identity for whites just as male privilege is generally not recognized by males as part of male identity. She concludes that multicultural education needs to go beyond color-blind arguments of equality and inclusion to include a focus on social justice and transformation.

While Kubota's chapter addresses issues of race in language learning and teaching, Aneta Pavlenko turns her attention to questions of gender with a focus on both second and foreign language education. Her conception of gender, which extends beyond female–male divides, is understood to be a system of social relationships and discursive practices that may lead to systemic inequality among particular groups of learners, including women, minorities, elderly, and disabled. She argues, in essence, that to treat gender as an essentialized variable is to obscure other forms of oppression. We need to understand, for example, why it is that women who do not have access to educational resources are often immigrant women and that boys and girls who are silenced in the classroom are often working class. In developing this conception of gender, she draws on feminist poststructuralism and critical theory to understand the relationship between power and knowledge and to theorize the role of language in the production and reproduction of power. A central focus of the chapter is a discussion of gendered inequalities in regard to access to material and symbolic resources, the gendered nature of linguistic interaction, and discourses of gender and sexuality across cultures. The chapter concludes with a discussion of the way issues of gender and sexuality can be incorporated in classroom practice.

Providing another take on the critical, Elana Shohamy offers a comprehensive analysis of the way in which democratic principles can be applied to assessment practices in multicultural societies. In many multicultural societies, Shohamy suggests, minority groups struggle for recognition and respect from majority groups. While dominant groups may pay lip service to principles of equality, the de facto situation, in many societies, is that minority groups are expected to assimilate into the majority society. Evidence to this effect is frequently demonstrated in the forms of assessments that are used in education, where competing conceptions of knowledge vie for prominence. Drawing largely on assessment practices in Israel, Shohamy makes the case that tests (language tests in particular) can serve as tools to maintain and perpetuate the dominant knowledge of majority groups. In the interests of democratic assessment, Shohamy outlines five principles for more inclusive language testing. She makes the case that language testers need to (a) include the knowledge of diverse groups on language tests, (b) construct tests in collaboration with those tested, (c) recognize that tests are instruments of power that potentially discriminate against minority groups, (d) protect the rights of test takers, and (e) be accountable for the consequences of tests.

Challenging identities

The second section of the book focuses on the language learner and considers ways in which the learning of language engages the identities of language learners in diverse and complex ways. Pippa Stein's chapter on representation, rights, and resources, which invites us into a language and literacy classroom in postapartheid South Africa, draws on the innovative and increasingly influential work on multiliteracies associated with a variety of scholars, including those in the New London Group (2000). With reference to multiliteracies research as well as feminist theories of the body, Stein reflects on her classroom teaching with English language learners and develops a comprehensive blueprint for what she calls *multimodal pedagogies*. Such a blueprint, she argues, arises from the need to acknowledge the tensions between local forms of communication and the literacy demands of schooling as well as the recognition that representation occurs through a variety of modes, including visual, gestural, speech, writing, and sound. In outlining six assumptions that are central to her conception of multimodal pedagogies, Stein focuses on a conception of pedagogy as semiotic activity best understood in the context of identity, culture, and power. She draws on stories of learners to make the case that meaning making is bodily, that it is transformative, and that it involves "interested action." Because there are texts that exist predominantly in nonlinguistic modes, such as the visual and gestural, Stein argues that multimodal pedagogies recognize that language, as a linguistic system, cannot fully express the arc of human experience.

In exploring what he calls the *subversive identities* of language learners, Suresh Canagarajah addresses the intriguing question of how language learners can maintain membership in their vernacular communities and cultures while still learning a second language or dialect. He draws on his research with two very different groups – one in the United

States and the other in Sri Lanka – to argue that language learners are sometimes ambivalent about the learning of a second language or dialect and that they may resort to clandestine literacy practices to create what he calls *pedagogical safe houses* in the language classroom. His research in the United States draws on insights from African American students learning academic writing in English as a second dialect, while his research in Sri Lanka draws on insights from Tamil students learning English for general academic purposes. In both contexts, the clandestine literacy activities of the students are seen to be forms of resistance to unfavorable identities imposed on the learners. At the same time, however, these safe houses serve as sites of identity construction that allow students to negotiate the often contradictory tensions they encounter as members of diverse communities. Canagarajah makes the case that in adopting conformist identities for on-task activity while relegating critical learning to safe houses, students are developing *multivocal literacies*, which enable learners to cross discourse and community boundaries without getting penalized by the academy. A better understanding of such practices, Canagarajah concludes, will provide teachers with an enhanced estimation of the critical thinking and learning potential of students.

Sue Starfield, like Canagarajah, seeks innovative and empowering pedagogies that can expand the range of identities available to language learners. Her focus, however, is far from traditional as she draws on her experience with concordancing in academic writing at an Australian university. By way of introduction, she describes how computer technology has made possible the collection of huge electronic databases – or corpora – of spoken and written language. Concordancing programs can search through millions of words of text to find examples of a particular word in its immediate textual context. As a result, teachers have not only better grammars and dictionaries of actual language use, but a more rigorous basis for selecting which lexical items and grammatical structures to include in a language learning curriculum. Drawing on her teaching experience in an academic writing workshop, Starfield describes how she and her students used concordancing to examine the structure of academic writing and the ways in which authors use language to establish credibility and authority. One particularly successful exercise was designed with the specific purpose of better understanding how published authors report on the work of other researchers in their community. Over time, Starfield noted a marked improvement in the academic writing of her students. Her chapter thus provides a window into the possibilities that technology holds for helping students develop identities not only as accomplished writers, but as contributors to the larger academic community.

In a very different language learning–teaching context, Brian Morgan speaks as a teacher of adult newcomers in Toronto, Canada. He draws on the unlikely topic of a grammar lesson to explore questions of identity and critical pedagogy in a community-based program with predominantly Chinese language learners. The context is the 1995 Quebec referendum on sovereignty, which was taking place at the same time at which the learners' place of origin, Hong Kong, was undergoing momentous political change. Morgan's lesson seeks to achieve the goal of providing a practically oriented grammar lesson while simultaneously locating it in a broader sociocultural context. He achieves this by introducing a subset of grammar (i.e., modality) through which feelings of ambivalence, apprehension, and possibility regarding the future are expressed. As Morgan notes, the interweaving of the two historic events in the lives of these language learners encouraged students to explore the meaning potential available through the lexicogrammatical system. He also demonstrates how traditional language learning activities such as a grammar lesson can be organized in such a way as to explore larger questions of identity and possibility. In this regard, a grammar lesson can serve not only as a site of identity representation, but as a site of identity creation. Morgan concludes that the metalanguage associated with language learning provides exciting opportunities for linking the microstructures of text with the macrostructures of society.

Researching critical practices

In the third section of the book, focus shifts from questions of identity to a consideration of the ways in which innovative approaches to language education research can help to inform critical pedagogical practices in the language classroom. The four chapters included in this section offer different perspectives on second language research but are all centrally concerned with the ways in which classrooms and communities structure language learning possibilities for students of diverse histories and investments.

The first chapter, by Inês Brito, Ambrizeth Lima, and Elsa Auerbach, describes an innovative course in the Cape Verdean language, culture, and history, taught in a Boston, Massachusetts, high school. The collaboration, in which Brito was the teacher, was not framed as a formal research project but as action research and reflective inquiry in which goals and procedures emerged over time and analysis was formative rather than summative. The chapter provides a classic example of the way in which pedagogy can be enhanced through the collaboration of teachers-as-researchers and researchers-as-teachers. It also highlights the experiences of a little-researched community in the United States – that of Cape Verdean Creole (CVC) speakers – whose homeland off the west coast of Africa was colonized by the Portuguese. Bilingual programs in the United States that cater to this community frequently provide instruction in Portuguese rather than CVC, which, according to the authors, does little to enhance bilingual language development for these learners. It was for this reason that the authors developed a language course that focused not only on CVC, but on the goals of participatory democracy. While they consider the project a work in progress, the authors note that the learning that took place in the course, in which students became active and engaged participants, cannot be measured with traditional assessment instruments alone. At the same time, however, they highlight the challenges associated with the teaching of a language that has little legitimacy in the larger society.

Questions of legitimacy are central to the research of Bonny Norton and Karen Vanderheyden, who make the case that some of the literacy practices of language learners that may not be validated by language teachers may nevertheless have positive consequences for language learning. Norton and Vanderheyden, drawing on research with second language learners in a Vancouver, Canada, elementary school, investigate the multiple ways in which language learners engage with Archie comics in both classrooms and communities. They found that while teachers showed ambivalence toward Archie comics by dismissing the pictures and dialogue as "not real reading," second language learners found the pictures and comic book format helpful in meaning making. Also significant was the finding that many of the language learners read comics in their mother tongue. Perhaps most important, their data suggest that Archie comic readers constitute informal and loosely connected reading communities that cross ethnic and linguistic boundaries. Canagarajah (this volume) might call these communities, in which Archie readers are critically engaged in discussion and debate, safe houses. Nevertheless, the second language learners in their study had accepted the dominant view that comic book reading is not real reading and has little educational value. Norton and Vanderheyden, drawing on the multiliteracies research that Stein finds inspiring, suggest that both teachers and parents may need to rethink notions of literacy in a changing technological and social world.

With Jane Sunderland's chapter, we move from a North American context to foreign language education in the United Kingdom with a focus, in particular, on gender dynamics in classroom interaction: who talks most, to whom, and who says what. Sunderland reports on a study in a German as a foreign language secondary school classroom in which she observed and analyzed teacher-to-student talk and student-to-teacher talk. What she found was that male dominance does not necessarily surface in the language classroom, and to the extent that it does, the implications for language learning are not evident. Specifically, she found that although males dominated the classroom in terms of the amount of some types of teacher attention they received, girls dominated in terms of the academic nature of their specific contributions. The significance of this study, Sunderland argues, is that it identifies important subtleties in classroom interaction, helps researchers qualify their claims, and "rescues girls from a representational victimhood." At the same time, however, she notes that although boys' talk might be seen as disruptive and not necessarily equated with academic success, they may be developing confidence to speak publicly, seize the floor, and control topics of conversation. Studies of classroom interaction, Sunderland suggests, should be complemented by studies of a more ethnographic nature, which might help to identify the way gendered practices are structured both inside and outside the classroom.

The very complexity of ethnographic research, as advocated by Sunderland, is the topic of the chapter by Constant Leung, Roxy Harris, and Ben Rampton. Drawing on their research on task-based language learning in urban settings in the United Kingdom, they examine the inelegance of qualitative research and argue that the "epistemic turbulence" in second language acquisition qualitative research centers on the question of what constitutes or represents reality. In their study, naturally occurring data were collected with the use of video and audio recordings and were supplemented by field notes. An ongoing challenge was how to represent and account for data that did not fit neatly into the theoretical construct of task-based language use. In short, they found that student engagement and involvement with the tasks varied considerably and that there appeared a continuum of "on-taskness" – a situation that created a lack of fit between reality, theory, and data. To address this dilemma, the authors suggest that researchers interested in task-based learning need to seek a conceptual framework that acknowledges, rather than obscures, the messiness of data; further, these researchers might explore in greater depth – perhaps through innovative technology – the nontask-related interactions they observe in their research. Like Sunderland, they conclude that interaction is a multifaceted phenomenon in which institutional authority, friendship, social power, personal interest, and language all have a role to play.

Educating teachers for change

The final section of the book addresses the diverse means through which different educators working in Hong Kong, Canada, and Australia, respectively, seek to introduce innovation and social change in their teacher education practices. Their work is a reminder that innovations in teacher education practices that are centrally concerned with social change require sober reflection, thoughtful analysis, and creative action.

Angel Lin, as a teacher-educator, provides a comprehensive and rigorous account of her attempts to introduce a critical pedagogical curriculum in the Master of Arts in Teaching English as a Second Language (MATESL) program at the City University of Hong Kong. The challenges she experienced include student teacher frustration with the academic language of critical pedagogical texts as well as feelings of pessimism and powerlessness. She makes the argument, as Toohey and Waterstone (this volume) do, that schoolteachers, unlike academics, are situated in contexts in which cultural capital is determined not by mastery over academic language, but by the ability to make learning meaningful for students. In this context, the inaccessibility of some critical texts serves simply to alienate the very teachers who seek insight from these texts. Such frustration is exacerbated by pessimism arising from a teaching context that is largely undemocratic and in which labor relations are unfavorable to teachers. Lin sought to address these challenges, in part, by developing course assignments that were designed for a wider educational audience. This opportunity was well received by the student teachers, and their assignments, which incorporated an array of critical work, were published in a local professional newsletter. Lin concludes the chapter with a candid discussion of tensions arising from the unequal relations of power between teacher-educators and student teachers noting, in particular, the challenges faced by education workers in Hong Kong who are both junior and female.

An assessment of diverse sites of expertise in the educational community is also central to arguments made by Kelleen Toohey and Bonnie Waterstone in their chapter, "Negotiating Expertise in an Action Research Community." Toohey and Waterstone describe a research collaboration between teachers and researchers in Vancouver, Canada, with the mutual goal of investigating what practices in classrooms would make a difference to the learning opportunities of minority-language children. While teachers were comfortable discussing and critiquing their educational practices, they expressed ambivalence about translating their practice into publishable academic papers. Like the student teachers in Lin's study, the teachers in the research group felt little ownership over the academic language characteristic of many published journals. "It doesn't come from my heart," said Donna, one of the teachers, while another teacher, Marcy, raised the concern that a paper that is "too journalized up" would no longer be appealing to teachers. Toohey and Waterstone draw on this experience to suggest that writing that respects both teachers' and researchers' ways of knowing might artfully blend narrative with analysis and tell dramatic stories of classroom incidents enriched by a consideration of theoretical insights. The crucial question in collaborative research, Toohey and Waterstone conclude, is not, "Is power equitably shared among participants?" but "What should participants *do* with the diverse sources of power they have?" The acknowledgment of different sites of expertise renders collaborative research a powerful tool in teacher education.

Another powerful tool in teacher education, according to Tara Goldstein, is what she calls *performed ethnography*. In seeking to prepare student teachers to work across linguistic, cultural, and racial differences in multilingual schools, she has found that ethnographic playwriting and performed ethnography offer a unique set of possibilities for addressing learning and teaching challenges. To this end, Goldstein has written a play called "Hong Kong, Canada," which addresses some of the tensions that arise in multilingual–multicultural school contexts. Material for the play was drawn from a four-year (1996–2000) critical ethnographic case study of an English-speaking Canadian high school that had recently enrolled a large number of immigrant students from Hong Kong. Goldstein draws on this play to help student teachers explore issues associated with identity politics prior to confronting such issues in schools. The play also addresses the complex interplay between speech and silence in multilingual schools and offers the opportunity for student teachers to consider alternative endings to the play. Goldstein cautions that teacher-educators need to work actively and critically with student teacher responses to performed ethnography and draw attention to the linguistic privileges of target-language speakers. She concludes that ethnographic playwriting and performed ethnography will help student teachers engage in conflict resolution and antidiscriminatory education which will, in turn, help to create safe and equitable learning environments for language learners in multilingual schools.

The final chapter in the collection, by Alastair Pennycook, is a narrative account of his reflections as a teacher-educator observing a Teaching English to Speakers of Other Languages (TESOL) practicum in Sydney, Australia. He reminds us that a great deal of language teaching does not take place in well-funded institutes of education, but in community programs, places of worship, and immigrant centers where funds are limited and time is at a premium. Of central interest in his chapter is a consideration of the way in which teacher-educators can intervene in the process of practicum observation to bring about educational and social change. Pennycook's quest is for critical moments in the practicum – "a point of significance, an instant when things change." After the class is over, Pennycook and the student teacher, Kath, discuss three such moments that arise from (a) the actions of a disruptive male student, (b) the use of practice dialogues for calling technicians, and (c) the recognition of nonstandard English in the classroom. Each of these critical moments,

Pennycook argues, raises larger questions of power and authority in the wider society and provides an opportunity for critical discussion and reflection. In his after-class discussion with Kath, he examines these critical moments with respect to complexities of gender politics, authentic language, and the ownership of English. While analysis of critical moments may not change the world, he concludes, it does provide a window on what critical teacher education is all about.

Common themes

Along with their common interests in understanding power and contributing to social change in particular locations, as mentioned earlier, there are a number of overlapping themes running through the chapters of this book. All of the authors represented here seem interested in, and committed to, seeking critical classroom practices, creating and adapting materials for critical pedagogies, exploring diverse representations of knowledge, and exploring critical research practices. The following considers how these themes are manifested in the chapters.

Seeking critical classroom practices

These authors are struggling not only to find ways to teach language or language teaching methodologies, but to also make explicit, and sometimes to struggle against, the power relations embedded in this subject matter. Brito, Lima, and Auerbach's program, for example, was developed not only to teach Cape Verdean Creole, but also to engage the students in an analysis of the power relations that the usage of CVC, Portuguese, and English has indexed both in Cape Verde and in the United States. Morgan similarly has what might be seen as linguistic aims, but he also wishes to investigate with his students how uses of certain language forms are socioculturally and sociopolitically framed. As Freire, Dewey, and Luke (see Chapter 2, this volume) remind us, action on one's oppression comes only with naming, externalizing, and reading the world, including the causes of one's own oppression. These chapters describe experiences of naming and analysis that teachers and students have engaged in together.

Shohamy's critique of language assessment practices involves similar externalization and analysis. She shows how these practices disadvantage some learners and how dominant knowledges are maintained by such practices. Lin's teacher education course aims not only to "interrogat[e] . . . commonsensical notions about language, culture, and education, as well as their interrelations" but also to provide opportunities for her students to express "active, defiant, assertive subject positions through their writings for a wider audience" – that is, through a teacher journal. Pennycook, similarly concerned with teacher education, describes engaging a student teacher in discussion not only about her teaching practices, but also about how power was situated in what she taught. Goldstein describes activities she engages in with students in teacher education and shows how their participation in the production of her play, as well as in activities like forum theater (Boal, 1979), permits students to examine their own linguistic privileges and assumptions.

In all of the chapters, we see the authors describing and analyzing instructional situations in which they are, themselves, involved. These observers seem less interested in critiquing the practice of others than they are in attempting critical practices with their own students and turning critical eyes on their initiatives. Rejecting an authoritative stance with respect to students, critical pedagogy, or the material taught, these authors prefer, instead, to see critical instruction as coinvestigation with students of topics of importance to both students and teachers. The increased curricular control students have within these critical pedagogies is seen not only as a way to respectfully recognize students' backgrounds, but also as a way to ensure that critical language instruction has relevance to the issues and problems students face in their daily lives.

Creating and adapting materials for critical pedagogies

All of these authors report success as well as ambiguous results of their attempts to engage in critical instructional practices with students and discuss the use of instructional materials in classrooms and the need not only to create such materials, but also to broaden the range of what are considered appropriate materials. Sunderland observes that a major focus of much feminist work in language education has been to critique materials. Brito, Lima, and Auerbach report a paucity of materials written in CVC and report also that students' awareness of this limits their investment in CVC literacy. Lin reports that the materials she uses in a teacher education course are problematic, and she wonders how critical material resources relevant in particular contexts might be created and used with students. In another case, one in which relevance is not a problem, Norton and Vanderheyden discuss how Archie comics serve to engage second language learners in the culture of their peers. In this case, despite the comics' popularity and despite the evidence the authors present to show how preadolescent children read these texts critically, such materials are rarely seen as appropriate literacy materials by their teachers. Goldstein finds the material resource of an ethnographic play that she writes herself provides student teachers with new means to build bridges between their worlds and those of the adolescent students with whom they will work. Stein, working in postapartheid South Africa, explores how the material-culture products of classrooms can fully reflect the "diverse histories, multiple modes of representation, epistemologies, feelings, languages, and discourses" of school students. Pedagogies that elicit students' multimodal representations, she argues, provide a counter-discourse to the privileging of some means of representation over others and permit the opening of possibilities for meaning making in classrooms.

None of the authors concerned with changing instructional practices and materials in these chapters is unaware of the challenges there are to making such changes and countering previous means of educational rewards. (Shohamy, this volume, provides an important discussion of this.) Nevertheless, they are engaged in struggling to change both classroom practices and the material resources of classrooms as they work toward transforming pedagogical relationships. Their understandings of the complexities and resistance of systems to change established practices are articulated in those chapters of the book concerned with how research in classrooms and other sites of language might be addressed.

Exploring diverse representations of knowledge

In many of the chapters, attention is given to how students, teachers, textbook writers, researchers, and others involved in educational processes use language and other communicative means to represent knowledge. Lin aptly refers to the "diverse language games" of schoolteachers and university professors and points out that the teachers with whom she works are situated in a social field in which the ability to articulate stories from their classroom lives is prized above the ability to articulate theory. In the case described by Toohey and Waterstone, a teacher rejects the theoretical language offered to her as helpful to her in framing questions about events in her classroom although she *is* interested in theory and poses theoretical questions. This chapter also shows that despite participants' aims to provide for one another equitable and democratic opportunities for knowledge production and representation, traditional hierarchies are reinscribed when the group attempts to produce representations for academic audiences. Like students in classrooms who must transform their knowledge and understandings into material culture, the participants in this research group strive to find appropriate and critical ways to externalize their knowledge. Shohamy also discusses this matter of varieties of representational means as she considers how language assessments have served to reward learners differentially. Starfield's chapter, as well, considers how a specific genre of language – academic language – serves as a gatekeeper in postsecondary education, and she describes innovative means she has developed to aid learners in the accessing and controlling of this means of communication.

Stein considers linguistic and nonlinguistic representations that South African students in Johannesburg produce in classrooms. She maintains that restricting students to represent their knowing, feeling, remembering, and so on in the textually based genres familiar to the privileged, but unfamiliar to African students, guarantees that such students are restricted to making meanings that inadequately represent their knowledges, realities, understandings, and pasts. She argues that educators must join together with their students in refining, strengthening, and transforming these nontextual means of representation and that we must understand that academic language is just one (albeit the most privileged) way of representing, knowing, and speaking.

For many of the authors in this book, recognition of diverse genres has proved to be an important way of understanding more about how learners are subject to power and how learners might find ways to contest these power arrangements. For some, easing access to mainstream genres is seen as strategic in equalizing opportunities for learners; for others, a priority is to struggle for recognition of other genres and their potential power to represent realities that have not commonly been represented.

Seeking critical research practices

Leung, Harris, and Rampton present classroom data showing both the complexity of that data and the complexity of the decisions researchers must make in deciding which data to present in research reports. They argue that critical research cannot unproblematically present empirical data to support theoretical constructs and speculate, instead, that critical research practices may well "trouble" our received ideas about particular classroom approaches. Canagarajah similarly argues that language education researchers may well have missed important aspects of classroom discourses specifically with respect to student resistance to subordination in classroom "underlife" (cf. Gutierrez, Rymes, & Larson, 1995) and metaphorically with respect to the safe houses that subordinated peoples, including students, develop for themselves. Norton and Vanderheyden also argue that researchers might well examine the literacy practices of students outside classrooms to better understand the processes learners develop for themselves to learn new languages and cultural practices. Sunderland and Pavlenko make similar observations and note that previous research that has focused on language classroom interaction may well miss the meanings of that interaction if observers do not also examine gendered societal norms and expectations and their implications for gender in language education.

Conclusion

It is striking that most of the authors of the chapters in this book rely on aspects of feminist, poststructuralist, and critical theory in framing their research and instructional methodologies. We find here the consideration of culture, gender, race, instruction, assessment, and communicative practice, with each author stressing that identities and activities are historically constructed in diverse, dynamic, social, and political contexts and that politics will thus play a role in who is advantaged and who is disadvantaged with respect to these matters. These authors remind us that critical approaches to language education will require commitment to social transformation, justice, and equality. For them, it is essential that critical language education not only opens the door to new sources of knowledge and understanding, but that it also involves investigation of whose knowledge has historically been privileged, whose has been disregarded, and why. Luke speaks in effect for all in arguing there *must* be a critical approach to language education to resist prevalent technologies "for domesticating the Other into nation."

Finally, we note that the authors here seem interested not so much in telling readers, researchers, students, or teachers how to speak, write, read, listen, or engage in critical practice as they are in arranging possibilities for productive discussions about these matters. None propose orthodoxies of critical practice, but all articulate a stance toward intervention that aims at engaging participants in reflection and praxis. Lin cautions that the discourses of critical pedagogy can themselves run the risk of becoming authoritative. She, like the other authors represented here, aims at disrupting this authority so that teachers, researchers, teacher-educators, and students might assume agentive and active roles in, as Freire (1968/1970) outlined, "transforming the world."

Notes

1. See, for example, Apple, 1999; Carnoy and Levin, 1985; Cazden, 1980; Edwards and Westgate, 1994; Fairclough, 1992; Gee, 1990; Kress, 1989; Luke, 1996; Mehan, 1979; New London Group, 2000; and Varenne and McDermott, 1999.
2. Some recent volumes that reflect this trend include Benesch, 2001; Canagarajah, 1999; Corson, 2001; Cummins, 2001; Goldstein, 1996; Heller, 1999; Kramsch, 1993; Morgan, 1998; Norton, 2000; Pavlenko, Blackledge, Piller, and Teutsch-Dwyer, 2001; Pennycook, 2001; Phillipson, 1992; Rampton, 1995; Shohamy, 2001; Tollefson, 2001; and Toohey, 2000.

References

Apple, M. (1999). *Power, meaning, and identity: Essays in critical educational studies*. New York: Peter Lang.

Benesch, S. (2001). *Critical English for academic purposes: Theory, politics, and practice*. Mahwah, NJ: Lawrence Erlbaum Associates.

Boal, A. (1979). *Theatre of the oppressed*. London: Pluto Press.

Canagarajah, A. S. (1999). *Resisting linguistic imperialism in English teaching*. Oxford: Oxford University Press.

Carnoy, M., & Levin, M. (1985). *Schooling and work in the democratic state*. Palo Alto, CA: Stanford University Press.

Cazden, C. (1980). *Classroom discourse.* Portsmouth, NH: Heinemann.
Corson, D. (2001). *Language diversity and education.* Mahwah, NJ: Lawrence Erlbaum Associates.
Cummins, J. (2001). *Language, power, and pedagogy: Bilingual children in the crossfire.* Clevedon, England: Multilingual Matters.
Davies, B. (1989). *Frogs and snails and feminist tales: Preschool children and gender.* Boston: Allen & Unwin.
Edwards, A. D., & Westgate, D. P. G. (1994). *Investigating classroom talk.* Philadelphia: Falmer Press.
Ellsworth, E. (1989). "Why doesn't this feel empowering?" Working through the repressive myths of critical pedagogy. *Harvard Educational Review, 59*(3), 297–324.
Fairclough, N. (1992). *Discourse and social change.* Cambridge, England: Polity Press.
Freire, P. (1970). *Pedagogy of the oppressed* (M. B. Ramos, Trans.). New York: Continuum Books. (Original work published 1968.)
Gaskell, J. (1992). *Gender matters from school to work.* Philadelphia: Open University Press.
Gee, J. P. (1990). *Social linguistics and literacies: Ideology in discourses.* Basingstoke, England: Falmer Press.
Giroux, H. (1992). *Border crossings: Cultural workers and the politics of education.* New York: Routledge.
Goldstein, T. (1996). *Two languages at work: Bilingual life on the production floor.* Berlin: Mouton de Gruyter.
Gutierrez, K., Rymes, B., & Larson, J. (1995). Script, counterscript and underlife in the classroom: James Brown versus *Brown v. Board of Education. Harvard Educational Review, 65*(3), 445–71.
Heller, M. (1999). *Linguistic minorities and modernity: A sociolinguistic ethnography.* London: Longman.
Kramsch, C. (1993). *Context and culture in language teaching.* Oxford: Oxford University Press.
Kress, G. (1989). *Linguistic processes in sociocultural practice.* Oxford: Oxford University Press.
Luke, A. (1988). *Literacy, textbooks, and ideology.* London: Falmer.
Luke, A. (1996). Text and discourse in education: An introduction to critical discourse analysis. *Review of Research in Education, 4,* 107–29.
Luke, C., & Gore, J. (1992). *Feminisms and critical pedagogy.* New York: Routledge.
McLaren, P. (1989). *Life in schools: An introduction to critical pedagogy in the foundations of education.* White Plains, NY: Longman.
Mehan, H. (1979). *Learning lessons.* Cambridge, MA: Harvard University Press.
Morgan, B. (1998). *The ESL classroom: Teaching, critical practice, and community development.* Toronto, Ontario, Canada: University of Toronto Press.
New London Group. (2000). A pedagogy of multiliteracies: Designing social futures. In B. Cope & M. Kalantzis (Eds.), *Multiliteracies: Literacy learning and the design of social futures* (pp. 9–37). New York: Routledge.
Norton, B. (2000). *Identity and language learning: Gender, ethnicity, and educational change.* Harlow, England: Pearson Education.
Pavlenko, A., Blackledge, A., Piller, I., & Teutsch-Dwyer, M. (Eds.). (2001).

Multilingualism, second language learning, and gender. Berlin: Mouton de Gruyter.

Pennycook, A. (2001). *Critical applied linguistics: A critical introduction*. Mahwah, NJ: Lawrence Erlbaum Associates.

Phillipson, R. (1992). *Linguistic imperialism*. Oxford: Oxford University Press.

Rampton, B. (1995). *Crossing: Language and ethnicity among adolescents*. London: Longman.

Shohamy, E. (2001). *The power of tests: A critical perspective on the uses of language tests*. Harlow, England: Pearson Education.

Simon, R. (1992). *Teaching against the grain: Texts for a pedagogy of possibility*. New York: Bergin & Garvey.

Spender, D. (1982). *Invisible women: The schooling scandal*. London: The Women's Press.

Tollefson, J. (2001). *Language policies in education: Critical issues*. Mahwah, NJ: Lawrence Erlbaum Associates.

Toohey, K. (2000). *Learning English at school: Identity, social relations, and classroom practice*. Clevedon, England: Multilingual Matters.

Varenne, H., & McDermott, R. (1999). *Successful failure: The school America builds*. Boulder, CO: Westview Press.

Walkerdine, V. (1989). *Counting girls out*. London: Virago Press.

PART I: RECONCEPTUALIZING SECOND LANGUAGE EDUCATION

2 *Two takes on the critical*

Allan Luke

What has counted as the critical in recent years has focused on how people use texts and discourses to construct and negotiate identity, power, and capital. Critical approaches include political analyses of dominant texts and their social fields, textual production linked to identity politics, and the introduction of students to sophisticated linguistic and aesthetic metalanguages for talking about, critiquing, and reconstructing texts and discourses. These various takes on the critical do not share a common political stance. The term and its affiliated approaches have been enlisted on behalf of not only radical redistributions of power and capital, but also for liberal and neoliberal educational agendas to improve individual achievement and thinking, on behalf of postcolonial and ethnonationalist educational projects to recast the character of canonical text, knowledge, and voice in schooling, and to pursue agendas of text deconstruction and critique of master narratives.

As recently as a decade ago, for most language and literacy educators, the term *critical* referred to higher order reading comprehension and sophisticated personal response to literature. To this day, the term is a stand-in for a diversity of approaches to textual practice, each contingent on particular political and institutional fields where the teaching and learning of language resides. What has come to count as the critical, especially where there was no such marker before, depends on how the state, media, school, church, and other fields of institutional authority enable and disenable what can be said and done about texts and discourses and, as importantly, what can be said and done about identities, histories, and themselves as institutions.

Resourcing the critical

Critical education was formally framed in Paulo Freire's *Pedagogy of the Oppressed* (1968/1974), translated from the Portuguese in the midst of third world politics, the civil rights movement, and the international student movement. Freire's work has become a canonical example of what we might term *point of decolonization* educational theorizing about emancipation, consciousness raising, and education. I, like many, first read Freire in the early 1970s in the aftermath of 1968. This was not a moment of great hope and aspiration but one shaped by the Vietnam War and Watergate. I was enrolled in a summer school primary teacher education program at Simon Fraser University (before Kelleen Toohey joined the staff there) taught by Jonathan Kozol. Like many of my generation, I felt that Freire captured something about my own educational experience – as a cultural minority trained in a mainstream educational system. While works by Michael Young, Basil Bernstein, Pierre Bourdieu, and others were developing a nascent theoretical vocabulary for how the various message systems of education worked politically (Young, 1971), Freire, even in his most traditionally philosophic writings, spoke more directly to the psychic memory and bodily experience of being Other.

What is interesting in Freire is the degree to which the work speaks to what we could term, in hindsight, a *pre-poststructuralist* world – before the textual/linguistic/semiotic turn, a world that was not yet fully inhabited by wall-to-wall Nike, CNN, and franchised transnational capitalism. Freire's early work has two distinctive features that often are neglected in the push to postmodernize the critical educational project. First, it was theorizing done at the actual time of decolonization, when sophisticated textual self-consciousness, deconstructionist play, and skepticism towards metanarratives may not have been seen as particularly relevant. It was more an initial philosophic and political statement on behalf of a peasantry wholly economically and politically disenfranchised, physically battered, psychically and spiritually violated, and marginalized. Its concept of naming was much more akin to existential realization and ideological critique than to a complex understanding of how naming constitutes the world through text and discourse. The complexity and politics of truth in discourse now work in textual and semiotic designs and modalities that Freire didn't engage with. His work described and addressed a binary dialectical universe of oppression and liberation, hope and despair, a universe that has become immeasurably more complex and polysemous, not just in terms of an everyday life saturated by textuality and discourse, but also in terms of the complex material and ideological conditions of economic and cultural globalization. I'll return to this later. For it is the source of Freire's work's continuing power and strength, its relevance to some of the points and spaces of educational application described here, and its necessary revision in light of new economic and cultural conditions that have arisen some three decades later.

Second, Freire's work was an uncommon philosophical blend of Hegelian idealism, Marxist materialism, and Christian existentialism. It brought together Hegel's historical dialectics of consciousness and the negation of binaries as philosophical method and translated these into a pedagogy that stressed historical self-determination of individuals and communities through problem posing and solution, the latter recalling Dewey's (1958) aesthetic theory. At the same time, Freire's pedagogical model extended Socratic pedagogy and dialogue to a face-to-face externalization, naming, and questioning of the world. I think it is largely due to Freire's work that we've since turned the simple noun *problem* into the ubiquitous nominalizations of *problematic* and *problematicization* – all marking the critique of naturalization and common sense that is at the heart of critical pedagogies. But this has not occured without having formalized and nominalized it into a formal, replicable, analytic, intellectual "move." Freire's original focus on naming was grounded in a strong Marxian sense of historical self-determination by remediation of one's conscious relationship to the means of production. Finally, in Freire, we encounter a phenomenological and existential orientation toward the recollection and recovery of the self, with a focus on being and the ethics of care in the face of physical and symbolic violence, material oppression, and psychological repression – themes shared with his contemporary Christian philosophers such as Paul Tillich and C. S. Lewis.

There are, then, some powerful legacies of "being critical" from Freire. These were taken up in the diverse critical educational projects of the 1970s and 1980s that grew around first and second wave feminism and ethnic–cultural nationalist projects of minority consciousness and activism within and against Western and Northern educational systems. These include

- Activist critique and engagement with civil society, including a redefinition of the *political*, lobbying for legislative change, historical redress, and "apology" – beginning with the work of the New Left and 1968, pushed along by feminist theory, multiculturalists, and postcolonial critique, and now salient in defense of civic and democratic space post 9/11.
- A critique of political economy: understanding one's relationship – whether as peasant or intellectual or teacher – to the means of production, even as these shift toward service and semiotic economies or are rebuilt in the return to military industrial and energy economies.
- A critique of propaganda and ideology – beginning from the Frankfurt school critique of political oppression, sexual repression, and aesthetic commoditization and extending through Birmingham cultural studies' engagement with the codes of popular, contemporary, and youth cultures.
- A critical focus, often neglected, not on a romantic self or voice, but rather on the human psychologies of struggle and oppression – on strategies of silence, marginalization, and violence, and human responses to them.

This list isn't a further bid on what should count as the critical. Given the politically contextual and situated nature of struggle, theory, and educational practice, there are subtle dangers about canonizing Freire, dangers of plasticizing and marketing the critical – not the least of which is the risk of concealing its own historicity and necessary self-negation. Indeed, if we transpose this work field to field, we would find different versions of the critical emergent across curricular fields (e.g., in Queensland, Richard Tinning's and Doune MacDonald's approaches to critical health and physical education; in Canada, Tara Goldstein's move into the fields of performance ethnography), different national and regional inflections depending on extant political economies, and, as Pippa Stein's South African commentaries and Angel Lin's Hong Kong analyses in this volume would indicate, radically different salience of versions of the critical in North, South, East, and West. But beginning from Freire secures us a view of the available and, at times, contending approaches to the critical that run across this volume. It also suggests the extent to which the project of the critical is as yet open and unfinished in current educational, cultural, and geopolitical conditions. It is to this that I now turn.

The currency of the critical

Schooling and teaching remain technologies of a nation. As much as our efforts at antiracist and antisexist education might be successful and as much as several decades of research, social and political activism on language rights, and multilingualism and multiculturalism might have yielded legislatively, the situating of schooling and pedagogy within the project and construct of "nation" is an unspoken, yet powerful, residual force in our dialogue spanning a strange and ill-formed pan-Anglo/American/Commonwealth community of U.S., Canadian, E.U., UK, New Zealand, Asian, and Australian language and literacy educators. It would be interesting to run an index check on this volume to see where, how, and when the terms *nation*, *nationality*, and *nationalism* appear and to what extent they themselves are problematicized. Even within our attempts to develop pedagogical realizations and approximations of the critical, done meticulously across this volume, teaching remains about, within, and for the nation, tacitly about the protection and production of its Culture (and, by implication, its preferred ethnicities and races, languages, and codes) and committed to the production of its sovereign subjects.

It is in this context that we teach second and third languages and dialects – at times as the custodians of nation, at times as the technicians of empire, on behalf of the spread and multiplication of capital, or, perhaps as part of a larger project of the critical. It is a context of ethnic and national retribalization where there is talk of primordial "clash of civilizations" – a volatile moment of both unparalleled flows of bodies, discourses, and capital and a moment where such flows can face unpredictable stoppages, blockages, and collapses. What might this mean for the educational project of the critical for language and literacy education? How can we define it? What are its characteristics?

What exactly is the compelling reason for second language educators to engage with the critical? Is it because the traditional student bodies of such programs have historically been objects of colonial and imperial power or diasporic subjects living at the economic margins of Western and Northern cultures and economies? Is it because the work of second language education, notably Teachers of English to Speakers of Other Languages (TESOL), itself once a mixture of missionary work and orientalism, is now a transnational service industry in the production of skilled human resources for economic globalization, as Alastair Pennycook (1994) has argued? Is it because the identity politics and dynamics of power and patriarchy within the TESOL classroom in so many countries typically entail social relations between teachers and students that reproduce larger social and economic relations between economically mainstream and marginal, cosmopolitan and diasporic, and white and colored subjects? Probably all of the above. TESOL is a pedagogical site and institution for educating the racial and linguistic Other (Luke, 2003). If, as Bourdieu (1982/1991) argued, what is at stake is the construction of habitus, an identity, a sense of freedom and agency, with all that this construction might entail, TESOL as an educational practice and site differs from the training of the mainstream (if and where such an idealized, social class homogeneous, ethno-normalized student body might still exist). It is not a technology where teachers profess or enact the production of a class and ethno–racial habitus to a class of students already in prepossession of those constituent discourses, dispositions, and embodiments. Not only does this make teaching and learning less seamless, lacking in ostensive organicity (and perhaps therefore requiring a different kind of ideological suturing over possible difference and conflict), and all the more subject to surface compliance, passive resistance, disruption, misrecognition, and mismatch (of cultural practice, background knowledge, schemata, discourse style, genre, ideology, and bodily disposition): "When the objective conditions coincide with those that have produced it, the habitus anticipates the objective demands of the field" (Bourdieu, 1982/1991, p. 84).

There are several other implications. Where it is the case that language learners have already been the objects of mainstream power, whether symbolic, economic, or pedagogic, the result is likely to be a distorted doubling of the preferred production of the subject, generative of a normatively blended and hybrid habitus (Luke & Luke, 1999): that is, the self-reproduction of practice attempted by the teacher, by definition, will be inexact and imperfect, creolized and hybridized in some manner. Second, and more to the point here, is that the project of the critical will be fundamentally different and distinct from attempts at the pedagogical production of the critical in mainstream and economically class-privileged settings. In some ways, the critical will be easier.

Two takes on the critical

Time to show my hand on the critical. At least one of the characteristics of the critical is to engage in disruptive, skeptical, and "other" social and discourse relations than those dominant, conventionalized, and extant in particular social fields and linguistic markets. To be critical is to call up for scrutiny, whether through embodied action or discourse practice, the rules of exchange within a social field. To do so requires an analytic move to self-position oneself as Other even in a market or field that might not necessarily construe or structurally position one as Other (that is, on the basis of color, gender, class, etc.). This doubling and Othering of the self from dominant text and discourse can be cognate, analytic, expository, and hypothetical, and it can, indeed, be already lived and narrated, embodied, and experienced.

We can think of the critical, then, in at least two ways – as an intellectual, deconstructive, textual, and cognitive analytic task and as a form of embodied political anger, alienation, and alterity. In both senses, it entails an epistemological Othering and "doubling" of the world – a sense of being beside oneself or outside of oneself in another epistemological, discourse, and political space than one typically would inhabit. This is a kind of distantiation that entails the capacity to watch oneself watching without slipping into the infinite regress of ontologically ungrounded perception. James Paul Gee (1996) frames this facility in terms of the necessity of access to multiple discourses as a cognitive prerequisite to being able to hold any particular discourse up to scrutiny. But additionally, such multiplicity may also form a kind of abrasion, a kind of psychological and epistemological disconnection or suspension not only from what Gee calls one's "primary discourse," but from one's embodied experience and material conditions. Having access to multiple discourses, competing discourses, contending and abraiding discourses *may*, but will not necessarily, set the generative grounds for the critical. It may expand one's register capacity, expand the polyvocality of speech acts, and build a repertoire for practices for a broader array of social fields. But for the critical to happen, there must be some actual dissociation from one's available explanatory texts and discourses – a denaturalization and discomfort and "making the familiar strange," the classic ethnographic axiom suggests. Perhaps, as Freire would argue, this is easier for those who have been the objects of symbolic and physical violence, for those who have been materially Othered, for those for whom the normalized pedagogical site for the construction of the habitus feels unnatural.

Perhaps this is where the cognitive and discursive element of the critical can come into play. For the existential, phenomenological plight of being oppressed can become a place for basking in one's alterity – as those pedagogies that target and stay at the level of personal give space for, indulge, cultivate, and ultimately valorize the experience of Otherness and difference.

I am aware that these comments appear to privilege and romanticize the plight of the oppressed. But the question raised here is crucial, particularly as versions of the critical proliferate across educational systems. In order to practice the critical, must one have experienced the practices of embodied and physical, symbolic and cognitive oppression? In order to be the critical subject, must one have been the object of visible power? In order to analytically and discursively construct Otherness, difference and alternative pathways, strategies and schemata, must one have been Othered? Does having had the bodily experience of oppression, of alterity, enable a ticket to ride to the analytically, deconstructively critical?

What is needed here is an understanding of the reflexivity of these two modes of the critical. Freire's point was that the experience of oppression could only be translated into action through a process of externalization and analysis that began with naming and reading the world, including the sources and practices of one's own oppression. This entails what Dewey (1958) called the making of experience "cohate," or coherent, through expression, aesthetic, and design. So the bodily experience of having been the object of power remains just that until it is rendered coherent through naming, through problematicization, and, indeed, through textual analysis and the use of analytic metalanguage – the "doubling" discourses that name and rename experience and the social and physical world: indeed, that name and rename knowledge and social relations themselves.

By contrast, we can and should ask how and whether it is possible to teach the critical to those who have not had the experience of being Othered? Indeed, to what extent does the critical, without the biographical experience of having been the object of power and violence, become a pro forma or indeed formal analysis and renaming of the world, a parsing of design, or mastery of text deconstruction and reconstruction? To what extent does ideology critique stay, indeed, just that – an intellectual exercise lacking a translation into embodied action that might disrupt, interrupt, or transform the fields in question?

Marcuse (1969) argued that there were primordial demands of "species being" – needs for meaningful labor and caring social relations, needs for open communication and discourse, needs for physical sustenance and shelter. It is in violation and deprivation of these things that Freire's dialectics begin. This remains the basis for a very different sense of the critical: not one of abstraction, of distance, of doubling in a logico-analytic, scientific-expository sense, or of stepping back via complex linguistic metalanguage, but the out-of-body experience of watching oneself watch oneself as an object of power and naming oneself as such. Everyone who has been a relatively hapless object of racialized, colored and classed, and gendered and sexualized power knows this. What surprised me was just how physical and material the experience of being the object of discriminatory exclusion, racism, symbolic and physical violence was. Sheets of rage and fear, hot flashes, paralyzed in word and action, an absolutely disconsolate immobility in the face of power. This is not just a matter of moral outrage and critique or hapless martyrdom, however we may recount it as heroic resistance in our own communities' folk theories of oppression and liberation. But the pedagogic effect of such an experience cannot be undone.

It is for these reasons that I believe that there must be a critical approach to second language education. Each approach to the critical is normative, predicated on assumptions that the refashioning of language and literacy in this way will have an impact not just on individual capacities and life pathways, but also on the reshaping of institutions, of local cultures, of social lives, and of civic and political spheres. There can be no more overtly normative challenges to educational systems, educators, and the state other than how they manage their cultural and linguistic Others.

I am uncertain about whether second language education research is or should be about the desire for voice and identity, about the generation of new ways of being and communicating beyond the nation, or simply the wanting of the power to contest power. But the authors across this volume offer a convincing case that the field must do something other than what it currently does. Otherwise it will remain a technology for domesticating the Other into nation, whatever its scientific and humanist pretenses.

Acknowledgments

Thanks to Doug Kellner and Carmen Luke for ideas and Kelleen Toohey and Bonny Norton for editorial advice. The argument here is developed in Luke (in press).

References

Bourdieu, P. (1991). *Language and symbolic power* (J. B. Thompson, Ed.; G. Raymond & M. Adamson, Trans.). Cambridge, England: Polity Press. (Original work published 1982.)

Dewey, J. (1958). *Art as experience*. New York: Capricorn Books.

Freire, P. (1974). *Pedagogy of the oppressed* (M. B. Ramos, Trans.). New York: Seabury Press. (Original work published 1968.)

Gee, J. P. (1996). *Social linguistics and literacies* (2nd ed.). London: Taylor & Francis.

Luke, A. (in press). *Teaching and learning beyond the nation*. Mahwah, NJ: Lawrence Erlbaum Associates.

Luke, A. (2003). Literacy and the Other: A sociological approach to literacy research and policy in multilingual societies. *Reading Research Quarterly, 38*(1), 132–141.

Luke, C., & Luke, A. (1999). Theorising interracial families and hybrid identity: An Australian perspective. *Educational Theory, 49*(2), 223–49.

Marcuse, H. (1969). *Reason and revolution: Hegel and the rise of social theory*. Boston: Beacon Press.

Pennycook, A. (1994). *The cultural politics of English as an international language*. Harlow, England: Pearson Education.

Young, M. F. (Ed.). (1971). *Knowledge and control*. London: Collier-Macmillan.

3 *Critical multiculturalism and second language education*

Ryuko Kubota

It is commonly believed that ESL (English as a second language), EFL (English as a foreign language), or other second language educators are naturally sensitive to cultural and linguistic diversity. In educational institutions, they are usually regarded as liberal advocates for multiculturalism and diversity, striving to model for their colleagues and students. Qualities required for this liberal stance, which I shall call *liberal multiculturalism*, include open-mindedness and nonprejudiced attitudes in interacting with people with diverse racial, ethnic, and linguistic backgrounds. These qualities encourage acceptance of unfamiliar beliefs as well as appreciation of foreign customs and artifacts. In schools, liberal multiculturalism is manifested in annual cultural diversity events and fairs. In teacher training, the liberal approach to multiculturalism tends to focus on imparting information about the cultural values, customs, and way of life among various ethnic groups. While liberal multiculturalism values and appreciates cultural differences, it also supports the idea that all people, regardless of their backgrounds, are equal and should have equal opportunities in society. This egalitarianism leads to the view that each individual's academic and economic success is dependent upon his or her own effort. In short, liberal multiculturalism promotes tolerance, acceptance, and respect toward different cultures and culturally diverse people while supporting equality among them.

In my observations as a second language K–12 teacher-educator and researcher in the United States, second language educators often fit into the image of well-meaning liberal multiculturalists. Yet, I also notice that these culturally sensitive educators often revert to the blaming-the-victim, no-differential-treatment, or discrimination-is-everywhere arguments when confronted with such challenging questions as, Why are black and Latino(a) students underrepresented in certain educational programs? Should we provide native language support for Latino(a) students in schools? Why are some language minority students denied access to certain educational services? These questions involve issues of race, ethnicity, language, and power that challenge the taken-for-granted American ideology of individual meritocracy and egalitarianism. As this chapter illustrates, a liberal approach to multicultural education supported by many second language professionals actually exhibits limitations and has been criticized by a more radical politicized position that forms *critical multicultural education.*

This chapter demonstrates that issues in multicultural education are much more complex than simple respect for cultural difference, appreciation of ethnic traditions and artifacts, or promotion of cultural sensitivity. The chapter will first critique liberal multiculturalism and then introduce critical multiculturalism. Next, it reviews whiteness studies, which have recently attracted academic attention and have been discussed in the context of critical multicultural education. This academic focus further reveals the complexity and contentiousness of multicultural education. The final section will discuss implications for second language teaching. Most of the literature reviewed here comes from the U.S. context, including primary and secondary education. It is important to keep in mind, however, that the issues in multicultural education presented here may not universally apply to all parts of the world because each context has a different social and historical background (cf. Laine & Sutton, 2000). It is hoped that readers will explore implications in their own contexts.

Liberal multiculturalism – A critique

Philosophies underlying different approaches to multiculturalism have been discussed in the field of education (e.g., Kincheloe & Steinberg, 1997; McLaren, 1995; Nieto, 1995; Sleeter, 1996). Three broad perspectives on multicultural education have been identified: conservative, liberal, and critical. While a conservative critique of multicultural education overtly defends Eurocentric modes of thinking and educational practices and attacks multiculturalism as a cause of societal divisiveness, a liberal approach to multicultural education respects and appreciates various forms of differences. The following sections describe the characteristics of liberal multicultural education from the perspective of critical multicultural education.

Political correctness with little substance

A liberal approach to multicultural education is built upon superficial views of diversity of which everyone is expected to approve. It uses the term *multicultural* as a taken-for-granted label but often lacks serious inquiry into what the term actually means. A typical example occurred during a discussion to approve a new teacher education program in a faculty meeting I attended. In response to a description of the new program as being multicultural, a question was raised as to how multicultural the program would be. The response was "Well, we all support multicultural education, don't we?" There was no further discussion. Here, multicultural education is treated like a token social protocol that everyone has to endorse whether or not they agree. It echoes Nathan Glazer's (1997) grudging proclamation that "We are all multiculturalists now" – an unavoidable phenomenon that one can do nothing but accept. It is akin to an empty form of political correctness that silences both supporters and opponents in public dialogue while its substance or philosophical foundation is absent in the consciousness of the people who use the term. As an empty concept, liberal multiculturalism is often unable to elaborate on an actual vision of multicultural education.

Focus on commonality – Reinforcing color (difference)-blindness

A liberal view of multiculturalism often emphasizes common humanity and natural equality across racial, cultural, class, and gender differences. Liberal multiculturalists often express this concern by stressing that we should be working toward a society where there is only one race called the human race (Kincheloe & Steinberg, 1997). The emphasis on commonality among people is reflected in the U.S. mainstream liberal democratic philosophy of meritocracy, which endorses the idea that all individuals, regardless of their background, can socially and economically succeed as long as they work hard. In this logic, racial and other types of differences often get blinded and erased.

In the school context, this logic is played out as universal, neutral, and difference-blind institutionalism (Larson & Ovando, 2001). Educators often claim that in order to provide students and parents with equal access to services, it is best to avoid differential treatment of various groups and to remain neutral in terms of policies and practices. In daily instructional contexts, difference blindness is demonstrated in the following comments made by educators: "You have to treat all kids the same, white, black, red, purple: you can't have different rules for different kids" (Larson & Ovando, 2001, p. 65); "If I compare ... the foreign children to the English-speaking children, I don't see real big differences. It depends on each child.... Kids are kids" (Nozaki, 2000, p. 365). These comments also echo corporate discourse: "I don't care whether he is green or yellow ..., if only he has the capability to perform the labor for the price we are willing to pay" (van Dijk, 1993, p. 141) and white, middle class women's views about friendship: "... friends are people that you talk to ... it wouldn't make any difference if they were black, green, yellow, or pink" (Frankenberg, 1993). Some of the skin colors mentioned in these comments are ludicrous, and this linguistic strategy serves to make the racial difference seem insignificant, the race relation seem equal, and a color hierarchy seem nonexistent.

It is important to recognize that a focus on universality and nondiscriminatory practices has certainly mitigated racism and sexism to a certain extent. For instance, the equality argument endowed all women and racial minorities with the right to vote, which the liberal democracy of the United States historically denied for hundreds of years. Likewise, the civil rights movement fought against segregation and discrimination that have been part of American democracy for a long time (Larson & Ovando, 2001). Nonetheless, I contend that difference-blind institutionalism reinforces "power evasion" (Frankenberg, 1993). Instead of recognizing the power and privilege attached to whiteness, the power evasive position believes that "we are all the same under the skin; that, culturally, we are converging; that, materially, we have the same chances in U.S. society; and that . . . any failure to achieve is therefore the fault of people of color themselves" (Frankenberg 1993, p. 14). A difference-blind vision fails to recognize the social and economic inequalities and institutional racism that actually exist in schools and society.

Color blindness conveniently eliminates the possibility that racism affects the experiences of people of color. For instance, as a woman faculty of color in higher education, I sometimes face challenges in my interactions with white students and colleagues. My suspicion that the challenge has something to do with my Asian background is usually met with white women colleagues' reactions of "Oh no, that has nothing to do with it" or "He is sexist. He does it to every woman." In a color-blind vision, racism is completely denied and unnamed.

Color-blind vision among ESL professionals – An example of a political struggle

A good example of difference blindness is demonstrated in a position statement approved by the executive board of a local Teachers of English to Speakers of Other Languages (TESOL) organization in the U.S. Southeast. To give a brief background, several advocates for the growing Latino/a population in a Southeastern state recommended that the State Board of Education consider dual language (two-way immersion) education. They argued, drawing on research by Thomas and Collier (1997), that dual language education is an instructional model superior to the conventional pullout ESL program and that it can yield better long-term academic achievement. In the midst of the statewide effort to narrow student achievement gaps, the Board of Education became interested in the idea. This discussion, however, did not involve representatives from the local TESOL organization, which gave the TESOL board members a sense of alienation and fear of funding diversion from the existing pullout ESL programs to a new dual language initiative. In an effort to legitimate the current pullout ESL model, the local TESOL board issued its position statement.

The gist of the statement is as follows: There is a large diversity in native languages spoken by the LEP (limited English proficient) student population in the state. Because of the diversity, integration of LEP students through teaching English is critical for their success. ESL programs offer more exposure to English than two-way or transitional bilingual programs do. In school districts with a diverse and transient LEP population, the "ESL methodology" is more appropriate and vital for integration. Thus, it is important to allocate monies to strengthen current ESL programs.

On the surface, this text shows neutrality and calls for equal treatment of all English language learners (ELLs). However, it does not give adequate recognition of the specific needs of Hispanic students and assumes the maximum exposure hypothesis, which has been refuted by research evidence (Cummins, 2000). Although it is true that the ELL population in the state is not homogeneous, it is also the case that Spanish-speaking students account for 70 percent of this population and yet they are the lowest achieving group among them. Given the fact that a dual language or transitional bilingual program would most likely serve Spanish-speaking students, to caution against it due to linguistic diversity is to avoid exploring alternative instructional models for this underachieving and socially stigmatized population. It is important to note that the local TESOL board members are well-meaning liberal educators who promote multiculturalism. However, they fail to understand that this color-blind argument for treating all ELLs equally could actually serve to maintain the status quo by refusing to see the inequalities that exist among different ELL groups.

Focus on difference – Exoticizing and essentializing the Other

Along with the focus on commonality and universal humanity, liberal multiculturalism paradoxically also has a tendency to emphasize cultural differences and culturally unique characteristics. Kincheloe and Steinberg (1997) categorize this type of multiculturalism as "pluralist multiculturalism" as opposed to what they call "liberal multiculturalism," which focuses more on sameness than difference, although these two types share many features. In fact, these two views can coexist in classroom settings. In her ethnographic study, Nozaki (2000) observed that while elementary school teachers emphasized individual, rather than cultural, differences, they judged certain Japanese students' behaviors as abnormal based on their stereotypes of how Japanese students should behave. These stereotypes are shaped by a discourse of cultural difference that permeates various texts.

With its pluralist vision, liberal multiculturalism often celebrates cultural difference as an end in itself. However, what is celebrated tends to be superficial aspects of culture, such as artifacts, festivals, and customs, and they are treated in decontextualized and trivialized manners divorced from the everyday life of people and the political struggle to define cultural identity. Derman-Sparks (1998) calls this "cultural tourism" in the sense that tourists do not usually see the everyday life of people nor do they experience oppressive or unjust practices that locals may experience. The superficial and decontextualized treatment of culture can be often observed in school celebrations of Black History Month, Cinco de Mayo, or International Day, in which historical figures or cultural artifacts constitute the main focus of celebration. Here, very little attention is paid to issues such as the legacy of slavery, oppression, discrimination, inequality among people, exploitation in the global economy, international power relations, and so forth. In focusing on only the customs and traditions of different peoples, the culture of the Other is often exoticized and reduced to neutral objects for one to respect and appreciate. At the same time, the Other people and cultures are essentialized as something homogeneous, traditional, and authentic, despite the fact that culture is diverse and always shifting. This tendency is analogous to a museum display of non-Western artifacts that often represents the Western interpretation of them as having traditional, tribal, and primitive qualities (Clifford, 1988).

In teacher education, the exoticizing and essentialist tendency of liberal multiculturalism is demonstrated in the practice of discussing culturally unique behaviors, customs, values, and beliefs of different racial or ethnic groups. Here, "what is different from us" (i.e., middle-class white culture) is highlighted through explaining the characteristics of each group in static and essentialist terms. This essentialist group-based approach is also reflected in discussions about helping "at-risk" students – a group defined by their race, ethnicity, native language, and socioeconomic background. Despite well-meaning humanitarianism behind such efforts, this label defines students as uneducable based simply on their group identity (Nieto, 1999b), making it synonymous with the now politically incorrect term "culturally deprived" (Franklin, 2000).

Obscuring issues of power and privilege

Liberal multiculturalism, influenced by the dominant ideology of individualism and liberal humanism, tends to obscure issues of power and privilege attached to the white middle class. Liberal multiculturalism's focus on common humanity as well as its celebration of cultural differences places everyone on the same plate – everyone is presumably equal despite differences in skin color, language, culture, and so on. However, in reality, people occupy their space on different layers of plates garnished with different amounts of privilege and power. Putting everyone on the same neutral plate thus evades unequal relations of power and privilege. Furthermore, together with the commonality and difference arguments, evasion of power and privilege contributes to an implicit assimilationist agenda in liberal multiculturalism. In other words, the celebration of both individual differences and cultural differences is in a complicit relationship with the avoidance of power and privilege in creating illusionary equality while maintaining the existing power relations that the people on the margins are expected to assimilate into. To be discussed in more detail later, the underlying logic in power evasion is that white culture is the norm into which Others are expected to be assimilated.

One of the discursive strategies of power evasion is an insistence on the ubiquity of prejudice and discrimination. Van Dijk (1993) uses a sociology textbook written by Anthony Giddens to show how prejudice and discrimination are explained as universal phenomena and not limited to Western societies. Van Dijk argues that the notion that discrimination belongs to all societies "may provide argumentative fuel to the often-used excuse that our *own* white, European prejudice and discrimination are merely one of a type" and that "ethnocentrism and even racism are natural" (pp. 168–9). The ubiquity argument can be seen in the following example. In a conversation about some discriminatory practices I observed in a local high school against Latino(a) students, a white female second language teacher-educator commented to me, "But you see, discrimination is everywhere. Look how women are discriminated against." Here, the ubiquity argument makes all types of discrimination natural and functions as an excuse for not being able to solve the problem. At the same time, liberal egalitarianism equates the status of recently arrived Latino(a) students with that of white American women, neutralizing the privilege that white American women possess compared to Latino(a) students. According to Grillo and Wildman (1997), this kind of analogy between racism and sexism is often used among whites in an attempt to raise their own consciousness about racism. Nonetheless, comparing racism to sexism "perpetuates patterns of racial domination by minimizing the impact of racism, rendering it an insignificant phenomenon – one of a laundry list of isms or oppressions that society must suffer" (p. 621).

Critical multicultural education

The above critical examination of liberal multiculturalism provides a vision for critical multiculturalism. A number of publications have tackled challenging issues on race, gender, class, politics of language, and so forth that liberal multiculturalism has avoided (e.g., Banks, 1996, 1999; Kanpol & McLaren, 1995; Kincheloe & Steinberg, 1997; May, 1999a; Nieto, 1995, 1999a, 1999b, 2000; Ovando & McLaren, 2000; Sleeter, 1996; Sleeter & Grant, 1987; Sleeter & McLaren, 1995). Many authors have critiqued the limitations of conservative, as well as liberal, views of multiculturalism, calling for a more critical, transformative, liberatory, or social constructionist approach to multicultural education.

As a sociopolitical movement, critical multicultural education aims for social transformation by seeking social justice and equality among all people rather than merely celebrating differences or assuming a priori that all people are equal. It has an intellectual alliance with critical pedagogy that aims to raise students' critical consciousness about various forms of domination and oppression and to help students become active agents for social change (see, for example, Freire, 1968/1998; Freire & Macedo, 1987; Giroux, 1992; McLaren, 1989; Shor, 1992). As a social movement against the establishment, critical multicultural education is counterhegemonic and reflective in nature, demanding that "all knowledge, not only 'official knowledge,' be taught critically" (Nieto, 1999a, p. 207). In the following section, I will describe some basic principles underlying critical multicultural education.

Explicit focus on racism and other kinds of injustice at the collective level

While liberal multiculturalism focuses on universal commonality and natural equality among people, critical multiculturalism calls this assumption into question. It recognizes that social and economic inequality does exist and it critically examines how inequality and injustice are produced and perpetuated in relation to power and privilege. Here, rather than avoiding discussions of racism or mitigating it through euphemism by using the word *prejudice* (Frankenberg, 1993), critical multiculturalism confronts it.

A focus on racism and other kinds of injustice requires attention to collective, rather than individual, oppression. While liberal multiculturalism, based on liberal individualism, often explains prejudice in terms of individual perceptions and behaviors, critical multiculturalism examines how certain racial and other groups are systematically oppressed and discriminated against in institutions and society. Likewise, while liberal multiculturalism, influenced by difference blindness, attributes individual student achievement to individual effort and ability, critical multiculturalism focuses on how certain groups of students are disadvantaged in educational decisions such as tracking, testing, funding, curriculum, pedagogical approaches, and language of instruction. Nieto (1999b) convincingly states that "some groups have been the victims of widespread educational failure *not as individuals but because of their membership in particular groups*" and that "learning also is heavily influenced by social, cultural, and political forces that are largely beyond the control of individuals" (pp. 165–6). With its explicit focus on racism, critical multicultural education constitutes antiracist education.

Nonessentialist understanding of culture – Problematization of difference

As described, liberal multiculturalism often celebrates cultural or other kinds of differences as permanent, taken-for-granted social realities. In contrast, critical multiculturalism rejects neutrality and stability of difference. Rather, it explores such issues as why inequality among different groups of people exists and how various kinds of difference are produced, legitimated, or eliminated within unequal relations of power (Giroux, 1988, 1995). Appreciating diverse cultures, traditions, and people is certainly important, but it needs to be situated in the critical understanding of culture as a manifold living organism produced by, and influencing, political and economic relations of power. Critical multiculturalism problematizes, rather than presupposes, difference and explores a critical understanding of culture.

Contrary to liberal multiculturalism, which tends to represent the culture of the Other as homogeneous, traditional, and static, critical multiculturalism views culture as diverse, dynamic, and socially, politically, and discursively constructed. When one closely examines a certain nation, it is evident that people's ways of life exhibit diversity in regard to ethnicity, region, age, gender, class, sexual orientation, and so forth. Also, culture constantly shifts under the influence of political, economic, and technological developments as well as domestic and international relations of power. Moreover, recent scholarship in postmodernism and poststructualism has revealed the discursive nature of our knowledge about culture. In this view, images of a certain culture or language are neither neutral nor objective; rather, they are discursively constructed.

Culture as a discursive construct

Discourses in poststructuralism are "ways of constituting knowledge, together with the social practices, forms of subjectivity and power relations which inhere in such knowledges and the relations between them" (Weedon, 1987, p. 108). In this view, images of language and culture do not reflect objective truths inherent in the language and culture; rather, they are produced in political and ideological struggles of power that generate and transform their definition and reification. Thus culture and language are located in ever-shifting sites of struggle where different meanings are produced and challenged. Critical multiculturalism conceptualizes culture as dialectical and full of inherent tensions rather than as an orderly, coherent, and predictable system (Nieto, 1999a). The discursive construction of the images of language and culture has recently been discussed in the field of second language education. The following examples reveal that culture is indeed a site of struggle that involves competing images and contradictions.

Susser (1998), by drawing on a discourse of Orientalism (Said, 1978), examined the ways in which Japanese learners and culture are described in research on teaching and learning ESL and EFL. Susser argued that Orientalism, which draws a rigid conceptual distinction between the East and the West and constitutes "a Western style for dominating, restructuring, and having authority over the Orient" (p. 3), is manifested in Othering, stereotyping, and essentializing Japanese culture and learners. Similarly, I have argued elsewhere (Kubota, 1999) that the cultural dichotomy between Japan and the West manifested in applied linguistics reflects colonialism that produces and fixes cultural differences. Furthermore, the essentialized Japanese culture is appropriated by Japanese cultural nationalism epitomized by *nihonjinron*, which stresses the uniqueness of Japanese culture. However, this is contested by research findings on instructional practices in Japanese schools that contradict the stereotypes put forward by applied linguistics and *nihonjinron*.

Discourses of colonialism in relation to the images of English and the culture and people associated with it vis-à-vis the images of the Other constitute the main theme of Pennycook (1998). Pennycook argues that discourses of colonialism created and legitimated a colonial dichotomy between the Self and the Other in which the Self is conceptualized as civilized, rational, logical, and thus superior, whereas the Other is conceptualized as uncivilized, irrational, illogical, and thus inferior. Discourses of colonialism have produced European–Western images of the Self and Other as well as unequal power relations between them.

The discursive construction of images of the Self is manifested in the images of U.S. classrooms in scholarly writings (Kubota, 2001a). A literature review suggests that educational research, influenced by the discourse of the U.S. education crisis in the 1980s, generated negative images of U.S. classrooms that are quite similar to stereotypical images of East Asian classrooms (e.g., didactic teaching, passive students, lack of creativity). Conversely, positive images of U.S. classrooms appear when the United States is compared with other cultures (e.g., East Asian). This is observed in applied linguistics and in the recent "revisionist" discourse that critiques right-wing politics as manipulating international student achievement comparisons to undermine U.S. public education. Here again, positive images of the Self are produced within a discourse of colonialism that draws a binary distinction between the progressive Self and the backward Other.

As culture is a discursive site of struggle, multicultural education is a field where certain ways of thinking (color blindness, power evasion, etc.), educational practices (equal treatment of all students, celebration of ethnic festivals, etc.), and various texts (visual images, descriptions of different cultures, etc.) are constructed and contested. Multiculturalism as a discourse also reflects and produces certain power relations. There is an implicit assumption in liberal multiculturalism that whiteness is the norm against which all other racial groups are defined and is thus superior. Critical multicultural education deconstructs not only our knowledge of culture, but also the meanings of multiculturalism.

Critical multiculturalism is for all students and is pervasive throughout the curriculum

At a practical level, critical multiculturalism advocates multicultural education for all students rather than just for ethnic minority students who may need to raise their self-esteem. With its focus on demystifying hegemonic knowledge and dismantling a social, racial, and economic hierarchy, critical multicultural education involves all students, including those with racial and economic privileges. Critiquing white privilege as discussed below reflects the recognition that all individuals are participating in the cultural production of domination and subordination in one way or another.

Just as multicultural education should be inclusive in terms of participants, it should be comprehensive with respect to curriculum. Merely observing an annual celebration of Cinco de Mayo or International Day sends an implicit message to students that there is little need to think about diversity until that time next year (Warren, 1999). Critical multicultural education demands that curricula, materials, and daily instruction involve all students in critical inquiry into how taken-for-granted knowledge, such as history, geography, and lives of other people, is produced, legitimated, and contested in power struggles.

Whiteness studies

The inclusive and antiracist orientation of critical multiculturalism inevitably addresses issues of whiteness. As discussed above, critical multicultural education serves not just minority students or schools with minority students, nor does it serve as ethnic cheerleading or tolerance for an inevitable burden of diversity (Nieto, 1998); rather, it is for all students and teachers regardless of their background. Also, critical multicultural education explicitly addresses issues of racial domination and oppression that have both historically and contemporarily involved whites. In recent years, there has been a growing interest in whiteness in the field of education (e.g., Fine et al., 1997; Frankenberg, 1993; Haymes, 1995; McIntyre, 1997; McLaren & Muñoz, 2000; Sleeter, 1996). Many works have examined the complicity of whiteness in racism and hegemonic knowledge. Whiteness studies demonstrate an attempt to "study up" in the power hierarchy to address issues of domination and oppression instead of focusing exclusively on racially oppressed groups as heroic icons or racial victims (Roman, 1993).

Before discussing whiteness, it is important to keep in mind that just as in issues of culture in general, discussions of whiteness should avoid essentialism. Frankenberg (1993), based on her interviews with white women of varied ages and backgrounds, demonstrated that these women's views and experiences contain a great deal of diversity. As McLaren and Torres (1999) argue, white culture is not monolithic and fixed, but its borders are malleable and it is always in a state of flux. Differences in terms of class, sexual orientation, and so on certainly exist within white culture. Nonetheless, it is important to recognize whiteness as a racial category endowed with power and privilege and to avoid falling into color blindness.

Perhaps the first thing we realize when we think about whiteness is that it is usually not noticed or mentioned in our daily life. When our discussion is about culture, it usually refers to the culture of the Other rather than white culture. Thus, white culture is often made cultureless or invisible, yet it constitutes a hidden norm and universal standard against which all Others are racially and culturally defined and marked. The invisible nature of whiteness generates the power-evasive conception that "whites are *colorless*, and hence without racial subjectivities, interests, and privileges," and therefore that "whites are free of the responsibility to change racism" (Roman, 1993, p. 71). As Roman argues, it is important to recognize the fact that "white is color," but to not fall into white defensiveness that legitimates the privilege of whiteness or calls for inclusion as an equal member for the Other, further promoting color blindness. In other words, making whiteness visible just like other racial categories should not imply that all colors have equal power. Rather, it means to acknowledge the status that whiteness occupies in the racial power hierarchy and the privilege that whites possess.

White privilege constitutes an important focus in whiteness studies. Wildman and Davis (1997) argue that contrary to the experiences of nonwhites who constantly have to confront oppression, white privilege creates the invisible societal norm and the ability to choose whether to object to oppression. McIntosh (1997) defines white privilege as

> an invisible package of unearned assets which one can count on cashing in each day, but about which one was *meant* to remain oblivious. White privilege is like an invisible weightless knapsack of special provisions, assurances, tools, maps, guides, codebooks, passports, visas, clothes, compass, emergency gear, and a blank check. (p. 291)

As an invisible package that sets the norm, white privilege is normally not viewed as a racial identity for whites, just as male privilege is often not perceived by males as part of male identity. It is important to note that white privilege as well as the invisibility and normalcy of whiteness are not inherent in the white race. Rather, white race and privilege are a social and historical construction. McLaren and Muñoz (2000) review the historical studies on race in the United States by Allen (1994, 1997) and conclude that the concept of the white race was invented by the seventeenth-century ruling class as a social control to divide laboring classes in the colonial plantation economy – European Americans and African Americans – across racial lines. Giving European American bond-laborers and freemen privileges while denying the same privileges to African Americans, bond or free, and restricting their freedom enabled European Americans to take pride in being white and thus prevented them from uniting with African Americans in servile rebellion. This social control created a racial hierarchy that transformed class oppression into racial oppression with an interest in maintaining the order of plantocracy. The historical invention of white race and privilege confirms the notion in critical multiculturalism that our conception about race and racism as well as the social structures that sustain racism are implicated in political and economic struggles of power rather than natural racial difference or individual prejudice divorced from social, political, and historical contexts.

Critique of whiteness studies and critical multicultural education

Despite their transformative aim, whiteness studies and critical multiculturalism have been critiqued (e.g., Richardson & Villenas, 2000; Sheets, 2000). Criticisms reveal a risk of dislocating marginalized people in whiteness studies and a difficulty in moving against or away from the master narrative rooted in white supremacy in critiquing whiteness. Sheets reviewed three recently published books on issues of whiteness in education (Dilg, 1999; Howard, 1999; McIntyre, 1997). Drawing on Grillo and Wildman (1997), who critiqued the analogy often used between racism and sexism for awareness raising among whites, Sheets warned that these whiteness studies, despite their good intentions, could risk making issues related to whites central in the dialogue and dislocating people of color from center stage. Sheets also problematized the perceived role of teachers and students of color – they are often expected to serve as helpers or cultural bearers for white teachers and students striving to become social activists and change agents. In this relationship, people of color are lumped together as nonwhites who serve whites, further perpetuating their marginality and the binary picture of race relationships. Sheets worries that whiteness studies could empower only whites, displacing subordinate groups of teachers and students and bringing the attention back to the center (see also Warren, 1999).

Richardson and Villenas (2000) reviewed four books on multicultural education (Banks, 1996; Edgerton, 1996; Fullinwider, 1996; and McLaren, 1997). The authors' main concern centers around the Eurocentric and universalist nature of such notions as democracy, inclusion, pluralism, and equality that constitute underlying principles of these texts. The paradox of the reviewed texts is that while they critique power structures and promote transformative knowledge construction as well as democracy, pluralism, or revolutionary transformation of the capitalist world, their underlying perspectives are built upon white European notions of democracy, equality, human rights, Marxism, and so on. This problem echoes what Ellsworth (1997) calls the "double binds of whiteness" in which the definitional process of critiquing racism within white scholarship is rooted in the same process that has constructed and perpetuated racist relations of academic and other power. Richardson and Villenas caution against dancing with Eurocentric categories of meanings and they seek, instead, multiculturalism that resists oppression and white supremacy while creating a cultural integrity through solidarity and promoting "the maintenance of ... community-based traditions or 'cultural' ways and exercises in sovereignty" (p. 273).

In a way, their suggestions speak to identity politics, which promotes solidarity and a positive identity for marginalized groups and explores strategies for contesting oppression (Weedon, 1999). Despite its oppositional and liberatory aim, however, identity politics runs a risk of essentializing the marginalized group, restricting possibility for allowing divergent experiences and meanings within the group. The critique by Richardson and Villenas (2000) demonstrates a difficult challenge in dancing against whiteness and building oppositional cultural integrity outside the Eurocentric framework without totalizing the marginalized group.

Implications for second language teaching and learning

At the beginning of this chapter, I stated that second language educators are usually regarded as culturally sensitive and supportive of multiculturalism, yet they tend to treat multiculturalism as a token with little substance. However, as this chapter has demonstrated, multiculturalism involves highly complex and sometimes paradoxical conceptions. Multicultural education is clearly much more than including visual images and narratives of people with different skin colors in the curriculum or celebrating Black History Month once a year. It has to go beyond color-blind arguments of equality and inclusion while avoiding essentialization and romanticization of marginalized groups. As critical pedagogies seek social justice and transformation, critical multicultural education pursues oppositional politics with an antiracist aim through exposing issues of race and racism and critically examining discursive constructions of our knowledge on culture and language. At the same time, critical multiculturalism confronts contentious questions such as, What meanings are we confined to when we discuss democracy, rights, and equality? For whom do we advocate critical multiculturalism and to what end? In this sense, critical multicultural education is an open-ended project with ongoing praxis – that is, reflection and action (Freire, 1968/1998).

Throughout this chapter, I have presented some examples that apply to second language education. In this final section, I will explore more links between the issues raised in this chapter and teaching second languages.

Demystifying cultural essentialism and identity construction

One of the most problematic conceptions that second language educators need to debunk is cultural and ethnic essentialism and identity construction. As discussed earlier, it is important to understand that images of the Other and Self are neither natural nor neutral but are discursively constructed and are influenced by, and reinforce binary thinking within, unequal relations of power. The effort to understand the Other in relation to the Self or to allow the Others to express their *authentic* voice in educational settings includes good intentions. However, it often imposes an essentialized, idealized, or stigmatized identity onto the Other as documented by ethnographic research. For instance, Harklau (2000) observed that some high school teachers often viewed immigrant students as belonging to a fixed imaginary cultural group with hardworking, attentive, and diligent qualities, although others viewed the students as lacking cognitive abilities. These identities are reinforced by instructional practices in which students are encouraged to disclose their immigrant experiences through writing personal stories or they are rewarded for being hardworking and well-behaved. In contrast, in a community college ESL class where these same learners were positioned vis-à-vis newly arrived immigrant students, they were viewed as difficult students for their rudeness and lack of cooperation and academic skills. This study demonstrates that identity is neither neutral nor inherent but constructed by teachers' perceptions of the Other. Another example is a study by Nozaki (2000). The study revealed that, despite their emphasis on individual, rather than cultural, difference, elementary school teachers judged some Japanese students based on their preconceptions about what Japanese students should be like, and they failed to provide individualized support for those who did not fit into the stereotypes.

The pervasiveness of cultural essentialism seems to reflect discussions on cultural difference promoted by the field of intercultural communication. Intercultural communication presumes the existence of cultural differences between groups and explores how to bridge communication differences. As such, it assumes a homogeneous and stable culture that forms a unique communication style in each culture. Although the aim to promote better communication across cultures stems from humanitarianism, this approach ironically manifests a colonial legacy of drawing a rigid dichotomy between the culture of the center and that of the periphery. Cultural images of the Self and Other that are often produced and confirmed by writings in intercultural communication (e.g., Callis Buckley, 2001) need to be reevaluated through a critical lens.

It is important to note that contemporary racism is often culture based. Legitimation of racial differences is often disguised by descriptions of group differences in cultural terms (May, 1999b; van Dijk, 1993). In this respect, second language research fields such as contrastive rhetoric that investigates cultural differences of written text features, need to be reevaluated in light of their complicity with discourses of racial difference. An alternative approach to cultural difference would be to examine not only how cultures differ, but how cultural difference is discursively constructed and how such construction influences communication across cultures. This approach encourages us to make a connection between the formation of cultural and linguistic difference and societal forces including politics, economics, ideology, and international relations of power (cf. Kubota, 2002). In critical multicultural education, teachers and students need to critically reevaluate the taken-for-granted conceptions about cultural groups, Self or Other, and understand how these conceptions are produced and perpetuated.

Affirming multiplicity of perspectives and linguistic forms

As discussed earlier, liberal multiculturalism has an assimilationist agenda behind the celebration of individual and cultural difference. It is necessary to acknowledge that assimilation into the Eurocentric norm often underlies the superficial celebration of diversity preventing the diversification of worldviews and linguistic forms. In order to affirm genuine pluralism and multiplicity, it is necessary to interrogate existing power relations that sustain a hierarchy of multiple perspectives and linguistic forms and to explore possibilities for oppositional discourses.

Pennycook (1994) advocates a critical pedagogy in which English learners appropriate English to find oppositional views and voices that could broaden possibilities for thinking and communicating. One of the ways to amplify possibilities is through linguistic actions. Rather than avoiding the teaching of the standard forms of the target language, critical linguistic actions encourage students to learn the standard language critically, to use it to critique its complicity with domination and subordination, and to subvert the normative linguistic code. This view echoes Canagarajah (1999), who states, "whereas the uncritical use of English leads to accommodation or domination, and avoidance of English leads to marginalization or ghettoization, critical negotiation leads to [students'] empowerment" (p. 176). Pluralization of target language and cultural codes needs to be achieved through critical scrutiny of how the norm regulates and limits possibilities for marginalized people and how oppositional voices can create new possibilities.

Connection to whiteness studies

As discussed earlier, whiteness studies critically examine issues of white privilege and supremacy. In situations where a second language classroom involves white students (as in foreign language classes in Western countries) or white teachers (as in foreign language or ESL or EFL classrooms), issues of white power and privilege are directly relevant to the learners or teachers. But what about some EFL situations in which both students and teachers are non-white? It is important to note that whiteness and white supremacy are relevant not only to white people or societies inhabited by them, but also to other people and societies. As Shome (1999) puts it, whiteness is "more about the *discursive practices* that, because of colonialism and neocolonialism, privilege and sustain the global dominance of white imperial subjects and Eurocentric worldviews" (p. 108). Whiteness is indeed worldly in that it imposes the white norm and worldviews onto the ways that non-white people around the world think and communicate. Thus, it is necessary for teachers and students, white or non-white, to critically examine how their ways of thinking and communicating are regulated by Eurocentric norms in an imperialistic paradigm.

While critical scrutiny of whiteness is necessary, the critique can suffer from a double bind because the language of critique is usually embedded in the Western epistemology that whiteness studies critique. Also, a critique of whiteness could promote identity politics for a marginalized group, risking reductionist essentialism rather than promoting situated resistance. Critiques of whiteness offer second language education important insight, but they also exhibit complexity and challenges.

One point of connection between whiteness studies and the field of ESL and EFL is the tendency to associate whiteness with the notion of native speakers. ESL teachers of color often get constructed as nonnative speakers of English lacking credibility as legitimate instructors while white teachers are positioned as native speakers and normal instructors without an accent (Amin, 1997, 2000). There is indeed a similarity between whiteness and the native speaker construct in that both demonstrate an unmarked norm or privilege. Just as whiteness is viewed as colorless and yet normal, native speakers are regarded as having no accent and possessing normal linguistic ability. Nevertheless, the native speaker construct cannot be entirely conflated with whiteness because they manifest certain differences and the issues of race and language interact in a complex way. For instance, the way people react to racial biases or discriminations often differs from the way they react to any kind of differentiation of people based on their language ability or accent (see Lippi-Green, 1997). Also, not all white native speakers of English possess an equal amount of cultural capital; there are both prestigious and stigmatized varieties of English used among white people (Lippi-Green, 1997). Issues of whiteness in relation to the ideologies of the native–nonnative divide need to be further theorized in the field of applied linguistics.

Transforming outside the language classroom

Although oppositional pedagogy can empower students within a language classroom, it should also focus on dismantling the oppressive structure outside the classroom walls. Expecting students to become the sole agents of social transformation through creating alternative ways of thinking and communicating places too much of a burden on them. Social transformation involves a two-way process; that is, not only should the people on the periphery generate insurgent voices, but the center should also attend to such voices. In second language education, teachers and researchers need to advocate for the marginalized students in the mainstream society. They need to step outside the language classroom and attempt, for example, to engage mainstream students and teachers in critical learning about cultural and linguistic diversity as well as the importance of working with the marginalized students as equal partners (see Kubota, 2001b; Kubota et al., 2000; Kubota & Ward, 2000).

In foreign language situations, oppressive forces that demand linguistic and cultural norms and standards also operate in various spheres including educational institutions, textbook industries, and mass media. In teaching EFL, for instance, these norms are built upon particular worldviews that determine who are legitimate native speakers of English, what constitutes the legitimate form of English, and so on – norms that have been internalized locally by non-Anglophone people. Here also, teachers need to step outside the classroom and seek ways to broaden possibilities that allow hybrid forms of expression and worldviews.

In conclusion, second language classrooms can potentially provide learners with opportunities to understand and explore a multiplicity of expressions and interpretations. To the extent that second language learning offers learners some new possibilities beyond their abilities in their native language and culture, it does provide novel expressions and interpretations. This perhaps creates an illusion that second language learning inherently promotes multiculturalism and that second language teachers are born multiculturalists. However, as this chapter demonstrated, second language learning and teaching are often affected by liberal, yet difference-blind and Eurocentric, discourses that perpetuate racial and linguistic hierarchies. Second language education should critically examine the token status of liberal multiculturalism and redefine multiculturalism in light of power, domination, and oppression.

References

Allen, T. W. (1994). *The invention of the white race: Vol. 1. Racial oppression and social control.* London: Verso.

Allen, T. W. (1997). *The invention of the white race: Vol. 2. The origin of racial oppression in Anglo-America.* London: Verso.

Amin, N. (1997). Race and the identity of the nonnative ESL teacher. *TESOL Quarterly, 31*(3), 580–3.

Amin, N. (2000). *Negotiating nativism: Minority immigrant women ESL teachers and the native speaker construct.* Unpublished doctoral dissertation, Ontario Institute for Studies in Education, University of Toronto, Ontario, Canada.

Banks, J. A. (1996). *Multicultural education, transformative knowledge, and action: Historical and contemporary perspectives.* New York: Teachers College Press.

Banks, J. A. (1999). *An introduction to multicultural education* (2nd ed.). Boston: Allyn & Bacon.

Callis Buckley, L. (2001). Culture specific learning strategies. *Intercultural Communication Interest Section, 4*(4), 2–5.

Canagarajah, A. S. (1999). *Resisting linguistic imperialism in English teaching.* Oxford: Oxford University Press.

Clifford, J. (1988). *The predicament of culture: Twentieth-century ethnography, literature, and art.* Cambridge, MA: Harvard University Press.

Cummins, J. (2000). *Language, power, and pedagogy: Bilingual children in the crossfire.* Clevedon, England: Multilingual Matters.

Derman-Sparks, L. (1998). Educating for equality: Forging a shared vision. In E. Lee, D. Menkart, & M. Okazawa-Rey (Eds.), *Beyond heroes and holidays: A practical guide to K-12 anti-racist, multicultural education and staff development* (pp. 2–6). Washington, DC: Network of Educators on the Americas.

Dilg, M. A. (1999). *Race and culture in the classroom: Teaching and learning through multicultural education.* New York: Teachers College Press.

Edgerton, S. H. (1996). *Translating the curriculum: Multiculturalism into cultural studies.* New York: Routledge.

Ellsworth, E. (1997). Double binds of whiteness. In M. Fine, L. Weis, L. Powell, & L. M. Wong (Eds.), *Off white: Readings on race, power, and society* (pp. 259–69). New York: Routledge.

Fine, M., Weis, L., Powell, L., & Wong, L. M. (Eds.). (1997). *Off white: Readings on race, power, and society.* New York: Routledge.

Frankenberg, R. (1993). *White women, race matters: The social construction of whiteness.* Minneapolis: University of Minnesota Press.

Franklin, W. (2000). Students at promise and resilient: A historical look at risk. In M. S. Sanders (Ed.), *Schooling students placed at risk: Research, policy, and practice in the education of poor and minority adolescents* (pp. 3–17). Mahwah, NJ: Lawrence Erlbaum Associates.

Freire, P. (1998). *Pedagogy of the oppressed* (M. B. Ramos, Trans.). New York: Continuum Books. (Original work published 1968.)

Freire, P., & Macedo, D. (1987). *Literacy: Reading the word and the world.* South Hadley, MA: Bergin & Garvey.

Fullinwider, R. K. (Ed.). (1996). *Public education in a multicultural society: Policy, theory, and critique.* Cambridge, England: Cambridge University Press.

Giroux, H. A. (1988). Border pedagogy in the age of postmodernism. *Journal of Education, 170*, 162–81.

Giroux, H. A. (1992). *Border crossing: Cultural workers and the politics of education.* New York: Routledge.

Giroux, H. A. (1995). The politics of insurgent multiculturalism in the era of the Los Angeles Uprising. In B. Kanpol & P. McLaren (Eds.), *Critical multiculturalism: Uncommon voices in a common struggle* (pp. 107–24). Westport, CT: Bergin & Garvey.

Glazer, N. (1997). *We are all multiculturalists now.* Cambridge, MA: Harvard Educational Press.

Grillo, T., & Wildman, S. M. (1997). Obscuring the importance of race: The implications of making comparisons between racism and sexism (or other isms). In R. Delgado & J. Stefancic (Eds.), *Critical white studies: Looking behind the mirror* (pp. 619–29). Philadelphia: Temple University Press.

Harklau, L. (2000). From the "good kids" to the "worst": Representations of English language learners across educational settings. *TESOL Quarterly, 34*(1), 35–67.

Haymes, S. (1995). White culture and politics of racial difference: Implications for multiculturalism. In C. E. Sleeter & P. L. McLaren (Eds.), *Multicultural education, critical pedagogy, and the politics of difference* (pp. 105–23). Albany: State University of New York Press.

Howard, G. (1999). *We can't teach what we don't know: White teachers, multiracial schools.* New York: Teachers College Press.

Kanpol, B., & McLaren, P. (Eds.). (1995). *Critical multiculturalism: Uncommon voices in a common struggle*. Westport, CT: Bergin & Garvey.
Kincheloe, J. L., & Steinberg, S. R. (1997). *Changing multiculturalism*. Buckingham, England: Open University Press.
Kubota, R. (1999). Japanese culture constructed by discourses: Implications for applied linguistics research and English language teaching. *TESOL Quarterly, 33*(1), 9–35.
Kubota, R. (2001a). Discursive construction of the images of U.S. classrooms. *TESOL Quarterly, 35*(1), 9–38.
Kubota, R. (2001b). Teaching World Englishes to native speakers of English: A pilot project in a high school class. *World Englishes, 20*(1), 47–64.
Kubota, R. (2002). Japanese identities in written communication: Politics and discourses. In R. T. Donahue (Ed.), *Exploring Japaneseness: On Japanese enactments of culture and consciousness* (pp. 293–315). Westport, CT: Ablex.
Kubota, R., Gardner, K., Patten, M., Thatcher-Fettig, C., & Yoshida, M. (2000). Mainstream peers try on English Language Learners' shoes: A shock language experience. *TESOL Journal, 9*(4), 12–16.
Kubota, R., & Ward, L. (2000). Exploring linguistic diversity through World Englishes. *English Journal, 89*(6), 80–6.
Laine, S. W. M., & Sutton, M. (2000). The politics of multiculturalism: A three-country comparison. In C. J. Ovando & P. McLaren (Eds.), *Multiculturalism and bilingual education: Students and teachers caught in the cross fire* (pp. 83–103). Boston: McGraw-Hill.
Larson, C. L., & Ovando, C. J. (2001). *The color of bureaucracy: The politics of equity in multicultural school communities*. Belmont, CA: Wadsworth/Thomson Learning.
Lippi-Green, R. (1997). *English with an accent*. New York: Routledge.
May, S. (Ed.). (1999a). *Critical multiculturalism: Rethinking multicultural and antiracist education*. London: Falmer Press.
May, S. (1999b). Critical multiculturalism and cultural difference: Avoiding essentialism. In S. May (Ed.), *Critical multiculturalism: Rethinking multicultural and antiracist education* (pp. 11–41). London: Falmer Press.
McIntosh, P. (1997). White privilege and male privilege: A personal account of coming to see correspondences through work in women's studies. In R. Delgado & J. Stefancic (Eds.), *Critical white studies: Looking behind the mirror* (pp. 291–9). Philadelphia, PA: Temple University Press.
McIntyre, A. (1997). *Making meaning of whiteness: Exploring racial identity with white teachers*. Albany: State University of New York Press.
McLaren, P. (1989). *Life in schools: An introduction to critical pedagogy in the foundations of education*. New York: Longman.
McLaren, P. (1995). White terror and oppositional agency: Towards a critical multiculturalism. In C. E. Sleeter & P. McLaren (Eds.), *Multicultural education, critical pedagogy, and the politics of difference* (pp. 33–70). Albany: State University of New York Press.
McLaren, P. (1997). *Revolutionary multiculturalism: Pedagogies of dissent for the new millennium*. Boulder, CO: Westview Press.
McLaren, P., & Muñoz, J. (2000). Contesting whiteness: Critical perspectives on the struggle for social justice. In C. J. Ovando & P. McLaren (Eds.),

Multiculturalism and bilingual education: Students and teachers caught in the cross fire (pp. 22–9). Boston: McGraw-Hill.
McLaren, P., & Torres, R. (1999). Racism and multicultural education: Rethinking "race" and "whiteness" in late capitalism. In S. May (Ed.), *Critical multiculturalism: Rethinking multicultural and antiracist education* (pp. 42–76). London: Falmer Press.
Nieto, S. (1995). From brown heroes and holidays to assimilationist agendas: Reconsidering the critiques of multicultural education. In C. E. Sleeter & P. L. McLaren (Eds.), *Multicultural education, critical pedagogy, and the politics of difference* (pp. 191–220). Albany: State University of New York Press.
Nieto, S. (1998). Affirmation, solidarity and critique: Moving beyond tolerance in education. In E. Lee, D. Menkart, & M. Okazawa-Rey (Eds.), *Beyond heroes and holidays: A practical guide to K-12 anti-racist, multicultural education and staff development* (pp. 7–18). Washington, DC: Network of Educators on the Americas.
Nieto, S. (1999a). Critical multicultural education and students' perspectives. In S. May (Ed.), *Critical multiculturalism: Rethinking multicultural and antiracist education* (pp. 191–215). London: Falmer Press.
Nieto, S. (1999b). *The light in their eyes: Creating multicultural learning communities*. New York: Teachers College Press.
Nieto, S. (2000). *Affirming diversity: The sociopolitical context of multicultural education* (3rd ed.). New York: Addison Wesley Longman.
Nozaki, Y. (2000). Essentializing dilemma and multiculturalist pedagogy: An ethnographic study of Japanese children in a U.S. school. *Anthropology & Education Quarterly, 31*(3), 355–80.
Ovando, C. J., & McLaren, P. (2000). *Multiculturalism and bilingual education: Students and teachers caught in the cross fire*. Boston: McGraw-Hill.
Pennycook, A. (1994). *The cultural politics of English as an international language*. New York: Longman.
Pennycook, A. (1998). *English and the discourses of colonialism*. New York: Routledge.
Richardson, T., & Villenas, S. (2000). "Other" encounters: Dances with whiteness in multicultural education. *Educational Theory, 50*(2), 255–73.
Roman, L. G. (1993). White is a color!: White defensiveness, postmodernism, and anti-racist pedagogy. In C. McCarthy & W. Cricklow (Eds.), *Race, identity, and representation in education* (pp. 71–88). New York: Routledge.
Said, E. (1978). *Orientalism*. New York: Pantheon Books.
Sheets, R. H. (2000). Advancing the field or taking center stage: The white movement in multicultural education. *Educational Researcher, 29*(9), 15–21.
Shome, R. (1999). Whiteness and the politics of location: Postcolonial reflections. In T. K. Nakayama & J. N. Martin (Eds.), *Whiteness: The communication of social identity* (pp. 107–28). Thousand Oaks, CA: Sage.
Shor, I. (1992). *Empowering education: Critical teaching for social change*. Chicago, IL: University of Chicago Press.
Sleeter, C. E. (1996). *Multicultural education as social activism*. Albany: State University of New York Press.
Sleeter C. E., & Grant, C. A. (1987). An analysis of multicultural education in the United States. *Harvard Educational Review, 57*(4), 421–44.

Sleeter, C. E., & McLaren, P. L. (Eds.). (1995). *Multicultural education: Critical pedagogy, and the politics of difference*. Albany: State University of New York Press.

Susser, B. (1998). EFL's othering of Japan: Orientalism in English language teaching. *JALT Journal, 20*(1), 49–82.

Thomas, W. P., & Collier, V. P. (1997). *School effectiveness for language minority students*. Washington, DC: National Clearinghouse for Bilingual Education.

van Dijk, T. A. (1993). *Elite discourse and racism*. Newbury Park, CA: Sage.

Warren, J. T. (1999). Whiteness and cultural theory: Perspectives on research and education. *Urban Review, 31*(2), 185–203.

Weedon, C. (1987). *Feminist practice and poststructuralist theory*. Oxford: Basil Blackwell.

Weedon, C. (1999). *Feminism, theory and the politics of difference*. Oxford: Blackwell.

Wildman, W. M., & Davis, A. D. (1997). Making systems of privilege visible. In R. Delgado & J. Stefancic (Eds.), *Critical white studies: Looking behind the mirror* (pp. 314–9). Philadelphia: Temple University Press.

4 *Gender and sexuality in foreign and second language education: Critical and feminist approaches*

Aneta Pavlenko

Introduction

Over the years, a number of scholars have engaged in the study of how gender mediates second (L2) and foreign language (FL) learning in and out of the classroom. Several recent books and state-of-the-art reviews (Chavez, 2000; Ehrlich, 1997; Pavlenko, 2001a; Pavlenko et al., 2001; Sunderland, 2000a) provide a detailed discussion of these studies and do not need to be repeated here. Instead, in the present chapter, I will use a feminist poststructuralist framework to synthesize the findings of the recent studies and to discuss their implications for critical and feminist pedagogies in FL/L2 education.

Feminist poststructuralism and critical inquiry in FL/L2 education

While there are several approaches to feminist poststructuralism and critical inquiry, I see them sharing a common aim. Thus, I define *feminist poststructuralism*, outlined by Cameron (1992, 1997), Luke and Gore (1992a), and Weedon (1987), and *critical inquiry in applied linguistics*, outlined by Pennycook (2001), as approaches to language study that strive (a) to understand the relationship between power and knowledge; (b) to theorize the role of language in production and reproduction of power, difference, and symbolic domination; and (c) to deconstruct master narratives that oppress certain groups – be it immigrants, women, or minority members – and devalue their linguistic practices.

Similarly, recognizing differences between various pedagogical approaches, in the present chapter, I group together FL/L2 critical and feminist pedagogies that acknowledge and incorporate gender and draw on feminist poststructuralist thought in education (Davies, 1994; Jones, 1993; Luke & Gore, 1992a; Stanton & Stewart, 1995). These approaches are a relatively recent development that owes both to the pioneering efforts of Kramsch and von Hoene (1995, 2001), Nelson (1999),

Norton (2000), Norton Peirce (1995), Pennycook (1999a, 1999b, 2000, 2001), Schenke (1996), Sunderland (1994, 2000a, 2000b), and Vandrick (1994, 1995, 1997, 1999a, 1999b) and to the groundbreaking work of North American and Japanese feminists working in Japan (Casanave & Yamashiro, 1996; Fujimura-Fanselow & Vaughn, 1991; MacGregor, 1998; McMahill, 1997, 2001; Smith & Yamashiro, 1998; Yamashiro, 2000). The critical and feminist FL/L2 pedagogies developed by these and other scholars and teachers aim to demystify normative discourses of gender by clarifying the mechanisms of symbolic domination and to engage students with cross-cultural differences in the meanings of gender and sexuality.

Language is seen in this paradigm as the locus of social organization and power and a form of symbolic capital (Bourdieu, 1982/1991) as well as a site of struggle where subjectivity and individual consciousness are produced (Weedon, 1987). In turn, *gender* is seen as "a system of culturally constructed relations of power, produced and reproduced in interaction between and among men and women" (Gal, 1991, p. 176). This poststructuralist view of gender foregrounds sociohistoric, cross-cultural, and cross-linguistic differences in gender construction, emphasizing the fact that normative masculinities and femininities, as well as beliefs and ideas about gender relations, vary across cultures as well as over time within a culture (for an in-depth discussion of diverse meanings of gender across cultures, see Bonvillain, 1995; Ortner, 1996).

This view of gender is distinct from those espoused in other feminist frameworks such as cultural feminism, which inspires research on gender differences in language learning and use, and material feminism, embraced in research on male dominance in interaction (for an informative discussion of how different feminist theories approach language, see Gibbon, 1999). Both of these feminist frameworks often approach men and women as undifferentiated and unitary groups and, as a result, treat gender as an essentialized variable that influences language learning processes and outcomes (cf. Chavez, 2000). This view obscures oppression in terms of class and race and, consequently, the fact that it is *immigrant* women who do not always have access to educational resources, *working class* boys and girls who are silenced in the classroom, or young *black* men who do not have powerful role models in the school hierarchy (Jones, 1993).

In contrast, poststructuralist scholarship engages with full individuals who are positioned not only in terms of gender, but also in terms of age, race, class, ethnicity, national origins, immigrant status, sexuality, or (dis)ability. It also shifts the focus away from essentialist assumptions of "disadvantage" or "superiority" toward an exploration of multiple ways in which gender impacts the process of learning another language. I suggest that a feminist poststructuralist approach forces us to recognize a dual role gender plays in foreign and second language teaching. On the one hand, learners come into classrooms as individuals whose motivations, investments, choices, and options may be influenced by gender as a system of social relations and discursive practices. On the other hand, language classrooms introduce students to "imaginary worlds" of other languages where gender and sexuality may be constructed and performed differently than in their own culture.

The intersection of multiple individual trajectories and linguistic worlds offers a unique space for engagement with cross-linguistic differences in discursive and social construction of gender and sexuality, for exploration of oppression through dominant discourses of gender, and for production of discourses (and, thus, subjectivities) of resistance. The transformation commonly takes place through led discussions that provide students with multiple opportunities to locate their own personal experiences within larger social contexts and thus involve storytelling and autobiography as discourses of oppositional consciousness. In the words of Kramsch and von Hoene (2001), a feminist pedagogy puts the subject in the center: "It appeals not only to the learner's mind and behaviors, but to a subject's emotions, body, and his or her social and political habitus" (p. 297). In doing so, critical and feminist pedagogies do not neglect language. However, rather than organizing instruction around a fully predetermined curriculum, they advocate for instruction organized around daily experiences and needs of the students, acknowledging the students' complex and gendered realities and multilingual lives (Goldstein, 2001; Pennycook, 2001).

Pennycook (2001) emphasizes that while recent critical approaches to language education are fundamentally political, they distance themselves from the modernist liberalism and emancipatory assuredness of traditional leftist pedagogies that aimed to enlighten the unenlightened and to empower the disempowered. Instead, they explicitly question the key assumptions, goals, and pedagogical practices, such as empowerment, fundamental to earlier literature on critical pedagogy and embodied in the work of Paolo Freire and Ira Shor. Challenging the simplistic dichotomies between empowerment and oppression, or us (teachers) and them (students), feminist poststructuralist theorists call into question the privilege given to talk versus silence and to the public use of language versus private reflection (Kramsch & von Hoene, 2001). They also ask whether attempts to empower students to find and articulate their voices constitute, in themselves, a controlling process, one that demands verbal collaboration (Orner, 1992). Foregrounding difference, critical feminist approaches emphasize the impossibility of claiming "single-strategy pedagogies of empowerment, emancipation, and liberation" (Luke & Gore, 1992b, p. 7). Rather, they force us to challenge our own assumptions, to problematize our everyday practices, and to engage students in examining their own – and our – linguistic options, choices, and behaviors, developing, in the process, critical agency and "multivoiced consciousness" (Kramsch & von Hoene, 2001).

Gender in second and foreign language learning and teaching

My discussion of recent developments in feminist and critical research and praxis in FL/L2 education will touch upon three key areas where gender is central in language learning and teaching: (a) gendered inequalities in access to material and symbolic resources, (b) gendered nature of linguistic interaction, and (c) sexual harassment as a discursive and social practice. Then, I will discuss larger implications of this research for creation of critical feminist curricula. While not all of the studies I discuss below were conducted in the feminist poststructuralist paradigm, my analysis will be, at all times, explicitly situated in this framework.

Gendered inequalities in access to material and symbolic resources

The first issue addressed by critical and feminist pedagogies is systemic inequality: namely, the fact that gender, in conjunction with ethnicity, race, class, age, sexuality, or (dis)ability, may mediate individuals' access to material and symbolic resources, including educational and interactional opportunities. The key finding in the field of multilingualism, second language learning, and gender is that in contexts where a second or a majority language constitutes a valuable form of symbolic capital associated with social and economic benefits, some women – in particular, older immigrant and minority women from lower socioeconomic backgrounds – may face a number of gatekeeping practices that restrict their mobility and access to linguistic resources and learning opportunities (Corson, 2001; Goldstein, 1995, 2001; Heller, 1999, 2001; Kouritzin, 2000; Norton, 2000; Pavlenko & Piller, 2001).

Feminist and critical pedagogies address these inequalities in three ways: first, by creating language classes and programs responding to the needs of particular learners such as working class immigrant women; second, by acknowledging and exploring gender inequalities and discourses of resistance in classroom readings and discussions; and third, by examining access difficulties that prevent particular learners from taking advantage of educational opportunities. A case study by Rivera (1999) offers an excellent example of a program that helps working class immigrant Latina women acquire literacy skills, improve basic education, increase English proficiency, and prepare for the high school equivalency exam.

The curriculum and pedagogy implemented in the program build on the strength, survival skills, and linguistic and cultural resources of these women and question and challenge the social and economic forces that shape their lives. Several aspects of the curriculum make it particularly effective in bringing about change and helping participants to become partners in the educational process. To begin with, in order to acknowledge and incorporate the women's voices, the classes are conducted in both English and Spanish; this enables the students to participate more actively in the classroom and to share their personal experiences. The program helps the women realize that they had not learned to read as children because they were women who shared a certain cultural, social, and economic background and, in doing so, allows them to make links between their personal experiences and larger socioeconomic contexts. Students are also encouraged to conduct research in their own community on the topics they consider important (e.g., Latino immigration or the right to vote), to take action on issues, and to take up leadership positions in the community. The program also consciously blurs the line between teachers and students by continuously training some of the program's graduates to come back to the program as teachers.

Several studies also remind us that access problems may arise even in contexts where language classes, professional training, and other educational and linguistic resources are formally available to immigrants. Young immigrant women may be prohibited from attending classes where there are male students, as was the case with some Portuguese women in Goldstein's (1995, 2001) study. Mothers may be forced to stay home if the community culture mandates that only family should look after children, as was the case with a woman from India in Kouritzin's (2000) study. Other women may need to support their families and immediately go to work in the workplace that does not require high levels of majority language competence (Goldstein, 1995, 2001; Holmes, 1993; Norton Peirce, Harper, & Burnaby, 1993). Once working, women may be concerned that taking English classes may hamper their productivity and thus interfere with their employment (Norton Peirce et al., 1993). They may also be reluctant to attend classes due to lack of prior education (Tran, 1988) or because their husbands do not want the wives to become more educated than they are (Norton Peirce et al., 1993). Consequently, even the best of solutions, such as evening and weekend classes and externally funded daycare, may not help women who are culturally required to prioritize their roles as housekeepers, mothers, daughters, wives, or caretakers and economically forced to prioritize their employment. This situation is particularly troublesome in the case of refugees living outside of well-established immigrant communities in contexts where access to employment, health services, and education is predicated on the knowledge of the majority language.

The cases above remind us that in order to practice the pedagogy of inclusion and engagement, we need to think not only about the learners who are already in the classrooms but also about those who are excluded from access to symbolic resources. Gender as a system of social relations, in conjunction with race, ethnicity, class, and age, continues to play an important role in this exclusion as older immigrant women from lower socioeconomic backgrounds are often found among the most disempowered members of Western societies.

Gendered nature of linguistic interaction

Another important area of recent research addresses the gendered nature of linguistic exchanges suggesting that even when students make it to the classroom, interaction patterns may favor some over others. Two main approaches to the study of classroom interaction can be distinguished in the field of education (see also Sunderland's chapter, this volume). The first focuses on differences in the amount and quality of talk between boys and girls or men and women (cf. Sadker & Sadker, 1985), while the second asks whose discursive practices dominate the classroom and which particular men and women have the right to speak and to define meaning and which remain invisible (cf. Lewis & Simon, 1986).

The studies in FL/L2 education conducted within the first approach, typically inspired by material feminism, suggest that in some contexts, boys and men may dominate classroom talk and mixed-sex interactions through interruptions and unsolicited responses while girls and women profit more from same-sex group discussions (cf. Chavez, 2000; Shehadeh, 1999). These studies are deeply problematic for at least two reasons. First of all, they operate within essentialized gender dichotomies that do not consider either diversity in the classrooms or values assigned to different discursive practices in different contexts. Second, they make a problematic assumption that a high amount of interaction is, in itself, a positive phenomenon that leads to higher achievement. In reality, it is quite possible that some students may speak up quite frequently but progress very little, if at all, while others who contribute little to classroom discussions, for individual or cultural reasons, may succeed in accomplishing their own language learning goals. Most important, as pointed out by Lewis and Simon (1986) and Luke (1992), we should look beyond "donation" of equal classroom time as this focus "skirts the structural problematic of who, in schools or universities, has the authority to speak, to critique, and to judge what is worthwhile (student) speech and critique" (Luke, 1992, p. 39).

These concerns are heeded in the second approach, which examines classroom talk within a larger critical framework. An excellent example of how this can be accomplished is a classroom ethnography by Willett

(1995) that illuminates the fact that class and gender mediate learning opportunities even for the youngest L2 learners. In her examination of second language socialization of four seven-year-old English as a second language (ESL) children in a mainstream classroom, the researcher found that three middle class girls were treated differently from one working class boy. While the girls were allowed to work together, the boy was seated far away from his bilingual male friends and, as a result, had to rely on adults for help. Thus, even though the boy participated in numerous interactions, he earned a status of a needy child unable to work independently. As a result, when all four children scored the same on the Bilingual Syntax Measure, the three girls were allowed to exit the ESL class while the boy was told to stay. This and similar studies suggest that classroom interaction practices are assigned values in the context of local ideologies of language, class, and gender. Consequently, learners whose participation patterns are aligned with the dominant culture of learning may be evaluated higher than those who espouse alternative beliefs about appropriate classroom behaviors. In turn, students whose voices are not being acknowledged in the classroom may lose their desire to learn the language or may even engage in passive resistance to classroom practices and curriculum demands. Among these disenfranchised learners are both immigrant girls (Corson, 1998, 2001; Heller, 2001) and working class boys (Heller, 2001; Willett, 1995).

It is not surprising then that development of voice and authoritative means of self-expression, often termed "the right to speak" and the ability "to impose reception" (Bourdieu, 1982/1991), have become a central concern in feminist and critical approaches to FL/L2 pedagogy. Mere encouragement is no longer seen as sufficient – teachers need to provide the learners both with the safe space and with adequate linguistic resources for development of voices which can be heard. This development of a critical voice is often accomplished in feminist classrooms through the uses of personal narratives as a form of self-disclosure, knowledge, and authority.

Pioneering work on critical consciousness raising and voice development in foreign language education has been carried out by North American and Japanese feminists teaching English in Japan – most notably, McMahill (1997, 2001). McMahill's (2001) study of a feminist FL class suggests that the links perceived between feminism and English lead female Japanese learners to see English as a language of empowerment. The students state that the new vocabulary, the new themes, and the pronoun system of English allow them to position and express themselves differently as more independent individuals than when speaking Japanese. In turn, Frye (1999) examines implementation of feminist critical pedagogy in an L2 literacy class for immigrant low-income Latina women in the United States. Similar to the classroom described by McMahill (2001), the favorite forms of participation in this class were discussions and storytelling, where the women could share experiences, give each other advice, and explore differences in age, race, social class, religious background, sexual orientation, national origin, educational background, and the use of Spanish. It is these explorations that engendered most meaningful – albeit heated and, at times, even angry – conversations, discussions, and activities, through which the participants learned to negotiate differences and to practice their new voices. The comparison of their own stories to those of others allowed the women to see commonalities and disparities, to question the oppressive social and cultural forces that shaped their lives, and to perform new critical selves, constructing new possibilities and new visions for the future.

Of particular interest here are cases where resistance to the target language is prompted by the voice one acquires in it. For instance, Western women, at times, reject certain aspects of the Japanese female register, including gender-specific discourse markers (Siegal, 1996) or pitch, perceived by some as too "girlish" or "silly" (Ohara, 2001). Some choose to use more neutral discourse markers or maintain their English pitch – at the expense of sounding "less Japanese." Similarly, an American philosopher, Richard Watson (1995), justifying his reluctance to learn spoken French, comments tongue-in-cheek: "For American men at least, French sounds syrupy and effeminate" (p. 52).

Together, the studies above suggest that cross-linguistic and cross-cultural differences in gender as a system of discursive practices could be productively explored in the classroom. Learners could be encouraged to examine their language choices, perceptions, attitudes, and alternative selves offered to them by the new language, as well as decisions to adopt a voice that is less "native-like" but more acceptable in terms of their own gendered selves.

Sexual harassment as a discursive and social practice

To help learners develop new and powerful voices, teachers also need to acknowledge the gendered nature of linguistic interactions outside of the classroom. While textbooks typically offer learners texts and dialogues that are presumed to have stable meanings, in reality, utterances are interpreted in light of how the interlocutors are positioned with regard to each other in terms of gender, age, social status, or familiarity. The knowledge of discourses of gender and sexuality dominant in a particular culture could become crucial in deciding whether a particular utterance is a polite compliment, a light-hearted joke, or an attempt at sexual harassment. The lack of such knowledge may lead to miscommunication and negative attitudes toward the target language. It is not surprising then that recent research examines sexual harassment as a social and discursive practice that may restrict women's movement in the target language community, decrease the amount of interaction with target language speakers, and promote resentment and resistance to the target language (Ehrlich, 2001).

Complaints about behaviors perceived as sexual harassment have been documented in a wide range of contexts where American students travel to study – among them, Costa Rica, France, Japan, Russia, and Spain (Ehrlich, 2001; Polanyi, 1995; Siegal, 1996; Talburt & Stewart, 1999; Twombly, 1995). A particularly clear case for the link between differential language outcomes and sexual harassment is made in a study by Polanyi, which compares test scores on the Russian Oral Proficiency test by male and female American students prior to, and upon return from, study abroad in Russia. Before the trip, males and females achieved similar scores; however, upon return, male students showed greater gains and outperformed female students, in particular, on the listening test. The author links this differential achievement to sexual harassment experienced by American females, which, in turn, led to these women's growing reluctance to interact with Russians. Gender and race also appear to have limited the interactional opportunities of Misheila, an African American student on a study abroad trip to Spain (Talburt & Stewart, 1999). During the trip, Misheila had found herself consistently singled out by Spanish males: "When I walk in the streets I always receive comments on my skin and sexual commentaries, especially with old men and adolescents..." (p. 169). This sexual harassment, whether real or perceived, provoked a negative reaction in her toward Spanish and its speakers and may have curtailed any future investment in learning Spanish.

Consequently, Ehrlich (2001), Goldstein (1995), Polanyi (1995), and Vandrick (1995) call for more attention to the discursive practice of sexual harassment in the second and foreign language classroom. Ehrlich underscores that, as dispreferred responses, sexual refusals require much more linguistic and sociolinguistic interactional competence than sexual acceptances. Included among linguistic features that characterize competent refusals are delays (pauses and hesitations), hedges (e.g., *well*, *uh*), palliatives (e.g., apologies), and accounts (e.g., explanations, justifications). Ehrlich and Polanyi argue that refusals and other gendered speech acts should find a legitimate place in foreign language classrooms. In turn, Goldstein shows how issues of sexual harassment and assault can be incorporated in ESL classes and suggests ESL texts that provide women learning English with the language they need to respond to sexual harassment. Vandrick lists other useful resources that can be successfully incorporated in feminist ESL classrooms.

Notably, however, even when certain behaviors are commonly seen as unacceptable in the United States, this consensus cannot be easily extrapolated to other cultures. For instance, when inadvertent touching takes place, in particular between a male and a female, in many U.S.

communities, an apology is expected, while in Israel, China, or Japan, no apology is necessary. Sex-related joking, sexual banter, and catcalls are a legitimate means of performing masculinity in Eastern Europe, Spain, or Costa Rica (Pavlenko, 2001b; Pujolar, 2000; Twombly, 1995) but may be legally deemed sexual harassment in the United States. In contrast, while in many places in the United States it is considered to be a normal and friendly behavior for strangers of both genders to smile at each other, in other cultures, such behavior may be viewed as sexual and lead to miscommunication. Carroll (1988) points out that in France, nonverbal behaviors considered nonsexual in the United States may be seen as an invitation for a "pick-up" and constitute "a continual source of problems for unsuspecting American women" (p. 27). Similarly, Twombly (1995) and Talburt and Stewart (1999) argue that in order to avoid intercultural miscommunication, programs that send students to Spanish-speaking countries need to incorporate discussions of potential affective dimensions of the commonly used terms such as *negrita* [darkie] or *gordita* [fatso] and the multiple meanings of such common verbal behavior as *piropoing* [catcalling].

Interesting evidence of cultural and individual differences in definitions of what is seen as inappropriate behavior and sexual harassment comes from a study by Tyler and Boxer (1996) conducted within the context of International Teaching Assistant (ITA) training in a U.S. university. The researchers created twelve scenarios based on naturally occurring – and potentially problematic – interactions between ITAs and undergraduate students and asked forty-four U.S. undergraduates of both genders and twenty male ITAs for written interpretations, followed by in-depth interviews. Quantitative analyses of the results demonstrated that for five of the twelve scenarios, the responses of female undergraduates differed from those of male ITAs. A combination of quantitative and qualitative analyses identified both gender and cultural differences in student responses. In particular, several male ITAs found certain behaviors, such as putting an arm around one's shoulder, nonsexual and fully appropriate, while female and – to a lesser degree – male undergraduates found them unacceptable and sexually implicit. Tyler and Boxer point out that while younger Americans exhibit heightened sensitivity to the issue of sexual harassment, in other societies, the same verbal and nonverbal behaviors may be perceived as nonsexual in nature or, even when perceived as sexual, treated lightly. This disparity creates a range of problems for ITAs at U.S. universities that, at times, culminate in sexual harassment charges made against male ITAs by U.S. female undergraduates. This study in which ITAs were invited to discuss a number of potentially problematic and ambiguous scripts offers a promising direction for foreign and second language classrooms and for ITA and teacher training in cross-cultural contexts.

To sum up, recent research indicates that the social and discursive practice of sexual harassment may become particularly salient at the intersection of languages and cultures where second language users cannot competently participate in the gendered discursive practices of the other culture. To counteract both intercultural miscommunication and marginalization of particular learners, classroom discussions of competing conceptions of sexual harassment and other inappropriate forms of verbal behavior need, on the one hand, to acknowledge cross-cultural differences in discourses of gender and sexuality and, on the other, provide the learners with appropriate linguistic means of verbal self-defense.

Inclusivity, engagement, and authenticity in a critical feminist curriculum

This brief discussion of three strands of research on the role of gender in FL/L2 learning and teaching points to three key features of a critical feminist approach to language education: inclusivity, engagement, and authenticity (Nelson, 1999; Pennycook, 1999b).

Inclusivity here refers to acknowledgment of the fact that both students and target language speakers may have diverse ethnic, racial, and class backgrounds, sexual identities, and different degrees of (dis)ability. Goldstein (1995) and Vandrick (1995) underscore the need for inclusivity in terms of topics and argue that in adult ESL classes, discussions should embrace such important issues as sexual harassment, violence against women, pregnancy on the job, maternity leave, and the role of business and media in reproducing normative femininities and masculinities.

At the same time, many educators emphasize that inclusivity, per se, is not the ultimate goal in feminist praxis as it rarely goes beyond acknowledgment and the static sense of possibility (Nelson, 1999; Pennycook, 1999b). Sunderland (2000b) argues that even inherently biased texts could be put to good use by experienced teachers. Consequently, what is important in critical feminist pedagogies is the types of issues raised and the types of *engagement* offered in the classroom. The multiple forms of engagement should aim to offer a safe space in which students could learn to recognize and acknowledge existing gender discourses and explore alternative discourses, identities, and futures. Schenke (1996) argues that our understanding of *safe* should go beyond the trivial treatment of gender and encompass discussions that venture into the perilous domain of differences, even though "to unsettle familiar stories is, after all, to take risks with ourselves, our histories, and our feminist theories" (p. 157).

The key way to explore alternative discourses and possibilities is through *authenticity*, which involves recognition of cultural differences, of otherness, and of multiple interpretations and perceptions of gendered performances. This exploration, according to Kramsch and von Hoene (2001), has to move beyond standardized and generic authenticity of the language classroom to recapture the uniqueness of speech events and to make difference, rather than diversity, the key experience in language learning. Kramsch and von Hoene (1995, 2001) contend that FL instruction in the United States promotes a biased and ethnocentric knowledge, or "single-voiced consciousness," and does not allow the students to view themselves from the perspective of other cultures and thus acquire intercultural competence, or "multivoiced consciousness."

A case where such an opportunity was missed is illustrated in Durham's (1995) examination of the controversy over the alleged sexism of a French textbook and accompanying video, "French in Action." The students in a U.S. university classroom where these materials were used filed a complaint stating that both the text and the video were explicitly sexist and offensive. Durham's analysis shows that in their interpretation of texts and images, both professors and students imposed their own culturally informed beliefs and stereotypes on what could be alternatively perceived as an ironic postmodernist feminist critique of Hollywood's sexual romance narrative and of conventional discourses of masculinity. The researcher places this instance of intercultural misunderstanding within the larger context of differences between American and French feminist thought, arguing that the students' interpretations are fully consistent with the principles of American academic feminism but show complete lack of knowledge and understanding of French discourses of feminism, sexuality, and gender. This ideological position leads the students to equate sexism with the portrayal of sexuality and perhaps even with all instances of depiction of the female body. It also leads them to read female silence as negative and powerless (whereas it can also be seen as a culturally approved strategy in dealing with pick-up attempts) and male speech as positive and powerful (even when the male protagonist is actually portrayed as ineffectual and ridiculous). As a result, argues Durham, the students engage in an ethnocentric reading of the text and – since their teachers did not attempt to counteract such a reading – lose an opportunity to access important dimensions of French culture. Here, it is important to emphasize that recognition of multiple interpretations of certain verbal and nonverbal behaviors does not preclude us from seeing sexual harassment and violence against women as real issues. Yet it pushes students to consider alternative scenarios in order to avoid both ethnocentric biases and cultural stereotyping. To do so, however, requires them to suspend the familiar system of beliefs, which may be a daunting task in the confines of a foreign language classroom.

In contrast, in the context of English instruction, cross-cultural encounters appear somewhat more successful. Nelson (1999) offers an outstanding example of how to examine ways in which gender and sexual identities are constructed and legitimized linguistically, socially, and culturally. Her case study depicts an ESL lesson in which a teacher attempts to raise students' consciousness about cultural relativity in interpretations of same-sex affection displays. Going far beyond creating a gay- and lesbian-friendly environment, the teacher engages in an exploration of discourses of sexuality that normalize certain identities and behaviors and problematize others, and, as a result, frames the interpretive process, rather than particular behaviors, as potentially problematic.

Another example of successful introduction of the issues of sexuality in an English for Academic Purposes (EAP) class is offered by Benesch (1999). In this study, the teacher's initial attempts to talk about the murder of Matthew Shepard, an openly gay student, are initially met with negative or dismissive reactions from students. A shift in focus from some abstract gay issues to a discussion of their own experiences and reactions helped to initiate a deeper consideration of the roots of homophobic attitudes. The students, similar to those in Nelson's study, pointed to cross-cultural differences with regard to same-sex public affection displays, which are acceptable in many countries, but may be perceived negatively in the context of U.S. homophobia.

There is no doubt that classrooms where students come together from a variety of linguistic, ethnic, and cultural backgrounds to learn an additional language constitute a unique setting for exposing social and cultural underpinnings of identity categories – in particular, gender and sexuality. At the same time, and perhaps due to this multiplicity and richness, this environment is also fraught with problems. Among these problems are the possibility that authentic gender discourses of one culture may make learners from another culture extremely uncomfortable (as seen in Durham's [1995] study) and the fact that Anglo linguistic and communicative norms and cultural values are often imposed as universal (Cameron, 2002). It is this linguistic and cultural imperialism that best accounts for American students' reluctance to positively engage with alternative gender discourses and beliefs and for ESL students' willingness to learn about and, at times, to adopt new speech acts, behaviors, and values.

Vandrick's (1999a) personal reflections on growing up as a "missionary kid" point to ways in which some of the most progressive ESL teachers may still carry vestiges of the colonial past and use the West as the central reference point. In a similar vein, Asher and Smith Crocco (2001) remind us that "the Beijing Conference on Women's Rights in 1995 made clear that many non-Western women believe Western feminists are trapped within their own cultural paradigms and reflect the very forms of cultural imperialism and ethnocentric preconceptions for which the West is notorious" (p. 132). These authors examine the tensions faced by teachers who attempt to acknowledge cross-cultural differences in gender and sexuality and, in doing so, to search for a middle ground between ethnocentrism, which presents the experience of white, middle class, Western females as normative, and cultural relativism, which recognizes difference but offers no critique of practices such as suttee or genital mutilation.

An excellent argument for the need to look beyond Western conceptions of femininity is made by Abu Odeh (1997), who argues that in the context of Arab feminism, the contemporary veil is an empowering practice that seeks to address sexual harassment on the street. Abu Odeh reminds the reader that in the 1970s, many women walked the streets of Arab cities wearing Western attire, which may have positioned them as "civilized," but also as sexualized and objectified, making them, more than ever, victims of public sexual harassment. In the 1980s, the ambivalence the women felt about this clothing and public humiliation they experienced led them to revert to traditional Islamic dress. The veil shielded them from sexual harassment and empowered them to raise objections when such attempts took place; it did not prevent them from taking advantage of new educational and employment opportunities.

A similar argument comes from Kitetu and Sunderland (2000), who examine differential treatment of men and women in a Kenyan classroom, concluding that Western notions of women's rights, privilege, or disadvantage may not easily apply in that context. The authors argue that at this particular moment in Kenyan socioeconomic development, girls and women benefit less from an equal opportunities discourse and more from a privileged femininity discourse even though it may appear sexist from a Western perspective.

In sum, we can see that the field of FL/L2 education needs not only critical and feminist approaches, but also postcolonial theory that deconstructs Western ethnocentrism and recognizes important intersections between race, ethnicity, class, sexuality, geography, colonial tradition, and culture in the shaping of gender. This theory will allow us to challenge the assumption that all individuals share the same needs and desires as those of white, middle class, Western men and women and that the discourse of human rights can be uncritically applied to non-Western notions of gender without interrogating the Western values at the base of the system.

Conclusions

Together, studies investigating ways in which gender mediates access and interaction in the context of FL and L2 education suggest that more attention needs to be paid to locally constructed relations of power that are predicated not only on gender, but also on age, ethnicity, sexuality, class, and linguistic and cultural background. This complex approach should not, however, distract attention from the fact that it is female learners – and in particular, older immigrant women from lower socioeconomic backgrounds – that are still disadvantaged in the majority of contexts.

Critical feminist pedagogies respond to the research findings discussed above by incorporating the following distinguishing features into the FL/L2 curriculum (see also Mackie, 1999): (a) creation of programs suited to the needs of particular populations in order to ensure equal access and equal educational opportunities for all students; (b) acknowledgment of the students' multiple identities and multilingual realities; (c) incorporation of various forms of linguistic and cultural capital brought into the classroom by the students; (d) atmosphere of mutual respect, trust, and community that recognizes similarities and differences among the participants and allows for multiple viewpoints and positions; (e) personalization of instruction through incorporation of the students' own experiences; (f) shared leadership and presence of cooperative structures such as collaborative projects; (g) consciousness-raising with regard to how social contexts impact learning trajectories as well as with regard to researchers' and teachers' own subjective stances and involvements; and, finally, (h) continuous exploration of commonalities and differences in the discourses of gender and sexuality across cultures and communities in order to help students develop a "multivoiced consciousness."

References

Abu Odeh, L. (1997). Post-colonial feminism and the veil: Thinking the difference. In M. Gergen & S. Davis (Eds.), *Toward a new psychology of gender: A reader* (pp. 245–56). New York: Routledge.

Asher, N., & Smith Crocco, M. (2001). (En)gendering multicultural identities and representations in education. *Theory and Research in Social Education, 29*(1), 129–51.

Benesch, S. (1999). Thinking critically, thinking dialogically. *TESOL Quarterly, 33*(3), 573–80.

Bonvillain, N. (1995). *Women and men: Cultural constructs of gender*. Englewood Cliffs, NJ: Prentice-Hall.

Bourdieu, P. (1991). *Language and symbolic power* (G. Raymond & M. Adamson, Trans.). Cambridge, England: Polity Press. (Original work published 1982.)

Cameron, D. (1992). *Feminism and linguistic theory* (2nd ed.). London: McMillan.

Cameron, D. (1997). Theoretical debates in feminist linguistics: Questions of sex and gender. In R. Wodak (Ed.), *Gender and discourse* (pp. 21–36). London: Sage.

Cameron, D. (2002). Globalization and the teaching of "communication skills." In D. Block & D. Cameron (Eds.), *Globalization and language teaching* (pp. 67–82). New York: Routledge.

Carroll, R. (1988). *Cultural misunderstandings: The French-American experience*. Chicago: University of Chicago Press.

Casanave, C., & Yamashiro, A. (Eds.). (1996). Gender issues in language education [Special issue]. *Keio University Shonan Fujisawa Campus Journal.*

Chavez, M. (2000). *Gender in the language classroom*. Boston: McGraw-Hill.

Corson, D. (1998). *Changing education for diversity*. London: Open University Press.

Corson, D. (2001). *Language, diversity, and education*. Mahwah, NJ: Lawrence Erlbaum Associates.

Davies, B. (1994). *Poststructuralist theory and classroom practice*. Geelong, Australia: Deakin University Press.

Durham, C. (1995). At the crossroads of gender and culture: Where feminism and sexism intersect. *Modern Language Journal, 79*(2), 153–65.

Ehrlich, S. (1997). Gender as social practice: Implications for second language acquisition. *Studies in Second Language Acquisition, 19*, 421–46.

Ehrlich, S. (2001). Gendering the "learner": Sexual harassment and second language acquisition. In A. Pavlenko, A. Blackledge, I. Piller, & M. Teutsch-Dwyer (Eds.), *Multilingualism, second language learning, and gender* (pp. 103–29). Berlin: Mouton de Gruyter.

Frye, D. (1999). Participatory education as a critical framework for immigrant women's ESL class. *TESOL Quarterly, 33*(3), 501–13.

Fujimura-Fanselow, K., & Vaughn, D. (Eds.). (1991). Feminist issues in language teaching [Special issue]. *Language Teacher, 15*(7).

Gal, S. (1991). Between speech and silence: The problematics of research on language and gender. In M. Di Leonardo (Ed.), *Gender at the crossroads of knowledge* (pp. 175–203). Berkeley: University of California Press.

Gibbon, M. (1999). *Feminist perspectives on language*. New York: Longman.

Goldstein, T. (1995). "Nobody is talking bad": Creating community and claiming power on the production lines. In K. Hall & M. Bucholtz (Eds.), *Gender articulated: Language and the socially constructed self* (pp. 375–400). New York: Routledge.

Goldstein, T. (2001). Researching women's language practices in multilingual workplaces. In A. Pavlenko, A. Blackledge, I. Piller, & M. Teutsch-Dwyer (Eds.), *Multilingualism, second language learning, and gender* (pp. 77–101). Berlin: Mouton de Gruyter.

Heller, M. (1999). *Linguistic minorities and modernity: A sociolinguistic ethnography*. New York: Longman.

Heller, M. (2001). Gender and public space in a bilingual school. In A. Pavlenko, A. Blackledge, I. Piller, & M. Teutsch-Dwyer (Eds.), *Multilingualism, second language learning, and gender* (pp. 257–82). Berlin: Mouton de Gruyter.

Holmes, J. (1993). Immigrant women and language maintenance in Australia and New Zealand. *International Journal of Applied Linguistics, 3*(2), 159–79.

Jones, A. (1993). Becoming a "girl": Post-structuralist suggestions for educational research. *Gender and Education, 5*(2), 157–66.

Kitetu, C., & Sunderland, J. (2000). Gendered discourses in the classroom: The importance of cultural diversity. *Temple University Japan Working Papers in Applied Linguistics, 17*, 26–40.

Kouritzin, S. (2000). Immigrant mothers redefine access to ESL classes: Contradiction and ambivalence. *Journal of Multilingual and Multicultural Development, 21*(1), 14–32.

Kramsch, C., & von Hoene, L. (1995). The dialogic emergence of difference: Feminist explorations in foreign language learning and teaching. In D. Stanton & A. Stewart (Eds.), *Feminisms in the academy* (pp. 330–57). Ann Arbor: University of Michigan Press.

Kramsch, C., & von Hoene, L. (2001). Cross-cultural excursions: Foreign language study and feminist discourses of travel. In A. Pavlenko, A. Blackledge, I. Piller, & M. Teutsch-Dwyer (Eds.), *Multilingualism, second language learning, and gender* (pp. 283–306). Berlin: Mouton de Gruyter.

Lewis, M., & Simon, R. (1986). A discourse not intended for her: Learning and teaching within patriarchy. *Harvard Educational Review, 56*(4), 457–72.

Luke, C. (1992). Feminist politics in radical pedagogy. In C. Luke & J. Gore (Eds.), *Feminisms and critical pedagogy* (pp. 25–53). New York: Routledge.

Luke, C., & Gore, J. (Eds.). (1992a). *Feminisms and critical pedagogy*. New York: Routledge.

Luke, C., & Gore, J. (1992b). Introduction. In C. Luke & J. Gore (Eds.), *Feminisms and critical pedagogy* (pp. 1–14). New York: Routledge.

MacGregor, L. (Ed.). (1998). [Special issue]. *Language Teacher, 22*(6).

Mackie, A. (1999). Possibilities for feminism in ESL education and research. *TESOL Quarterly, 33*(3), 566–73.

McMahill, C. (1997). Communities of resistance: A case study of two feminist English classes in Japan. *TESOL Quarterly, 31*, 612–22.

McMahill, C. (2001). Self-expression, gender, and community: A Japanese feminist English class. In A. Pavlenko, A. Blackledge, I. Piller, & M. Teutsch-Dwyer (Eds.), *Multilingualism, second language learning, and gender* (pp. 307–44). Berlin: Mouton de Gruyter.

Nelson, C. (1999). Sexual identities in ESL: Queer theory and classroom inquiry. *TESOL Quarterly, 33*(3), 371–91.

Norton, B. (2000). *Identity and language learning: Gender, ethnicity and educational change*. Harlow, England: Pearson Education.

Norton Peirce, B. (1995). Social identity, investment, and language learning. *TESOL Quarterly, 29*(1), 9–31.

Norton Peirce, B., Harper, H., & Burnaby, B. (1993). Workplace ESL at Levi Strauss: "Dropouts" speak out. *TESL Canada Journal, 10*(2), 9–30.

Ohara, Y. (2001). Finding one's voice in Japanese: A study of pitch levels of L2 users. In A. Pavlenko, A. Blackledge, I. Piller, & M. Teutsch-Dwyer (Eds.), *Multilingualism, second language learning, and gender* (pp. 231–54). Berlin: Mouton de Gruyter.

Orner, M. (1992). Interrupting the calls for student voice in "liberatory" education: A feminist poststructuralist perspective. In C. Luke & J. Gore (Eds.), *Feminisms and critical pedagogy* (pp. 74–89). New York: Routledge.

Ortner, S. (1996). *Making gender: The politics and erotics of culture*. Boston: Beacon Press.

Pavlenko, A. (2001a). Bilingualism, gender, and ideology. *International Journal of Bilingualism, 5*(2), 117–51.

Pavlenko, A. (2001b). "How am I to become a woman in an American vein?" Transformations of gender performance in second language learning. In A.

Pavlenko, A. Blackledge, I. Piller, & M. Teutsch-Dwyer (Eds.), *Multilingualism, second language learning, and gender* (pp. 133–74). Berlin: Mouton de Gruyter.

Pavlenko, A., Blackledge, A., Piller, I., & Teutsch-Dwyer, M. (Eds.). (2001). *Multilingualism, second language learning, and gender*. Berlin: Mouton de Gruyter.

Pavlenko, A., & Piller, I. (2001). New directions in the study of multilingualism, second language learning and gender. In A. Pavlenko, A. Blackledge, I. Piller, & M. Teutsch-Dwyer (Eds.), *Multilingualism, second language learning, and gender* (pp. 17–52). Berlin: Mouton de Gruyter.

Pennycook, A. (Ed.). (1999a). Critical approaches to TESOL [Special issue]. *TESOL Quarterly, 33*(3).

Pennycook, A. (1999b). Introduction: Critical approaches to TESOL. *TESOL Quarterly, 33*(3), 329–48.

Pennycook, A. (2000). The social politics and the cultural politics of language classrooms. In J. K. Hall & W. Eggington (Eds.), *The sociopolitics of English language teaching* (pp. 89–103). Clevedon, England: Multilingual Matters.

Pennycook, A. (2001). *Critical applied linguistics: A critical introduction*. Mahwah, NJ: Lawrence Erlbaum Associates.

Polanyi, L. (1995). Language learning and living abroad: Stories from the field. In B. Freed (Ed.), *Second language acquisition in a study abroad context* (pp. 271–91). Philadelphia: John Benjamins.

Pujolar, J. (2000). *Gender, heteroglossia, and power: A sociolinguistic study of youth culture*. Berlin: Mouton de Gruyter.

Rivera, K. (1999). Popular research and social transformation: A community-based approach to critical pedagogy. *TESOL Quarterly, 33*(3), 485–500.

Sadker, M., & Sadker, D. (1985, March). Sexism in the schoolroom of the '80s. *Psychology Today*, 54–7.

Schenke, A. (1996) Not just a "social issue": Teaching feminist in ESL. *TESOL Quarterly, 30*, 155–9.

Shehadeh, A. (1999). Gender differences and equal opportunities in the ESL classroom. *ELT Journal, 53*(4), 256–61.

Siegal, M. (1996). The role of learner subjectivity in second language sociolinguistic competency: Western women learning Japanese. *Applied Linguistics, 17*, 356–82.

Smith, S., & Yamashiro, A. (1998). (Eds.). Gender issues in language teaching. [Special issue]. *Language Teacher, 22*(5).

Stanton, D., & Stewart, A. (Eds.). (1995). *Feminisms in the academy*. Ann Arbor: University of Michigan Press.

Sunderland, J. (Ed.). (1994). *Exploring gender: Questions and implications for English language education*. New York: Prentice Hall.

Sunderland, J. (2000a). Issues of language and gender in second and foreign language education. *Language Teaching, 33*(4), 203–23.

Sunderland, J. (2000b). New understandings of gender and language classroom research: Texts, teacher talk and student talk. *Language Teaching Research, 4*(2), 149–73.

Talburt, S., & Stewart, M. (1999). What's the subject of study abroad? Race, gender, and "living culture." *Modern Language Journal, 83*(2), 163–75.

Tran, T. (1988). Sex differences in English language acculturation and learning strategies among Vietnamese adults aged 40 and over in the United States. *Sex Roles, 19*(11/12), 747–58.

Twombly, S. (1995). *Piropos* and friendships: Gender and culture clash in a study abroad. *Frontiers: The Interdisciplinary Journal of Study Abroad, 1,* 1–27.

Tyler, A., & Boxer, D. (1996). Sexual harassment? Cross-cultural/cross-linguistic perspectives. *Discourse and Society,* 7(1), 107–33.

Vandrick, S. (1994). Feminist pedagogy and ESL. *College ESL,* 4(2), 69–92.

Vandrick, S. (1995). Teaching and practicing feminism in the university ESL class. *TESOL Journal,* 4(2), 4–6.

Vandrick, S. (1997). The role of hidden identities in the postsecondary ESL classroom. *TESOL Quarterly, 31*(1), 153–7.

Vandrick, S. (1999a). ESL and the colonial legacy: A teacher faces her "missionary kid" past. In G. Haroian-Guerin (Ed.), *The personal narrative: Writing ourselves as teachers and scholars* (pp. 63–74). Portland, Maine: Calendar Islands.

Vandrick, S. (1999b). Who's afraid of critical feminist pedagogies? *TESOL Matters,* 9(1), 9.

Watson, R. (1995). *The philosopher's demise: Learning French.* Columbia: University of Missouri Press.

Weedon, C. (1987). *Feminist practice and poststructuralist theory.* Oxford: Basil Blackwell.

Willett, J. (1995). Becoming first graders in an L2: An ethnographic study of L2 socialization. *TESOL Quarterly,* 29(3), 473–503.

Yamashiro, A. (Ed.). (2000). Gender issues in language education [Special issue]. *Temple University Japan Working Papers in Applied Linguistics, 17.*

5 *Assessment in multicultural societies: Applying democratic principles and practices to language testing*

Elana Shohamy

Introduction: The power of tests

This chapter will discuss dimensions of the power of language tests and their special roles in multicultural societies in which different groups are rejecting assimilative notions for the sake of recognition and interactive models. By discussing a number of language testing scenarios, the chapter will show how tests serve as tools to perpetuate de facto assimilative models. It will then propose a number of principles and assessment practices that better match democratic societies by giving voice to different groups, applying interactive assessment models, monitoring the uses of tests, protecting the rights of test takers, and recommending that language testers assume greater responsibilities for the tools they develop.

This chapter is contextualized within the framework of critical language testing (CLT) (Shohamy, 1998, 2001a, 2001b), an area that applies theories of critical pedagogy and critical applied linguistics (Kramsch, 1993; Pennycook, 2001) to the domain of language testing. CLT emerges from the need to examine, question, and monitor the uses of assessment tools in education and society, especially as they are used by institutions of power and authority. The need to examine, question, and monitor the uses of language tests is a result of growing evidence that tests are used in powerful ways in a variety of contexts. In this regard, Tollefson (1995) claims that tests represent three sources of power: state, discourse, and ideology. State power is understood in terms of bureaucracies, discourse power in terms of the imposition of tests by unequal individuals (the tester and the test taker), and ideological power in terms of the belief of what is right and what is wrong, what is good knowledge and what is not, what is worthwhile economically and what is not.

For a long time, language testers addressed mostly measurement issues while overlooking the social and political dimensions of tests. Recently, however, there has been an emphasis on the roles that language tests play in society. Following Messick (1981) and others, language testers have begun to view language tests not as isolated events, but rather as connected to psychological, social, and political variables that have effects on curriculum, ethicality, social class, politics, and language knowledge. The topics that are being addressed are test bias, the impact of tests on instruction, the use of tests for power and control, the responsibility of language testers, the conflict between professionalism and morality, washback, ethicality and fairness, the politics of gatekeeping, and the unequal power relations between test makers and test takers (Hamp-Lyons, 1997; Kunnan, 2000; Norton & Stein, 2001). While Davies (1997) observes this growing trend among scholars in language testing, he recognizes the challenges that language testers face from governments and bureaucracies:

> While the growing professionalization of language testing is perceived as a strength and a major contribution towards a growing sense of ethicality, the increase in commercial and market forces, as well as the widespread use of language assessment as an instrument in government policy, may pressure language testers into dangerous and (and unethical) conduct. (p. 236)

Shohamy (1998, 2001b) provides evidence showing that language tests are often introduced in undemocratic and unethical ways, mostly for disciplinary purposes and for carrying out the policy agendas of those in power. It is demonstrated that tests are used to redefine knowledge, change test takers' behavior according to the set agendas of those in power, and impose the values and knowledge of those in authority. It is also shown how tests are used by authoritative groups as disciplinary tools in covert ways for manipulating educational systems. The consequences of using tests in such powerful ways are that language tests narrow language knowledge and create contradictions with existing knowledge as expressed in official curricula. Such misuses are possible given the high stakes of tests, which cause those who are affected by them (i.e., individuals and educational systems) to change their behavior in accordance with the agendas of the tests, thereby maximizing their scores. The powerful uses of tests emerge also from the fact that tests have a strong appeal to the public, use the language of science and numbers, rely on documentation, and employ "objective" formats.

Bourdieu (1991) argues that there is an unwritten contract between those in authority and the subjects of power who are willing to be dominated by tests. He elaborates on the specific mechanism through which such domination continues to take place. Specifically, he writes about tests as tools for determining rites of passage, for creating dependence from an early age, and for establishing criteria of worth. In addition, he notes that the results of tests are endowed with economic value and can thus provide a means for controlling the knowledge of specific groups. For these reasons, tests are often used as ideological tools when – even in the absence of supporting evidence – those in authority claim that the introduction of tests will upgrade learning and improve achievements. At the same time, test takers, themselves, have no say about the content of tests or about the types of decisions that are being made based on their results. They have no channels to protect their rights; they are, in fact, rarely aware of these rights and therefore do not attempt to demand them.

It is argued here that the powerful uses of tests violate fundamental democratic values and principles in that the tests are in the hands of central organizations that are capable of controlling and defining knowledge on their own terms and in accordance with their own agendas. Thus, tests are often introduced not in order to assess knowledge, but rather to define it and to force test takers to master the knowledge that those who introduce the tests believe is important. The social and educational consequences of such powerful uses are of special significance in multicultural societies as tests are often used to force different groups to accept the knowledge of the dominant group and to serve as gatekeepers for groups such as immigrants and indigenous groups (Davies, 1997; Elder, 1997; Hawthorne, 1997; Shohamy, 2001a, 2001b).

Multiculturalism, education, and assessment

Multiculturalism is characteristic of most nations of the world today as they consist of different ethnic groups whether these groups have been residing in the country for some time or have recently arrived. These groups define themselves as different with respect to dimensions such as culture, language, religion, ideology, and politics and have begun to demand recognition of their differences. They are resisting pressures to conform to the dominant group and would rather preserve, maintain, and even enhance their uniqueness. In the past, however, these different groups were expected to conform to and assimilate with the dominant or majority group and assume its values and ideologies. With respect to language, in particular, Crowley (1996) notes that even in societies that insist on monolingual policies and ideologies as part of national identity, the reality is that there is constant influence and mixing with other languages, vernacular and global. Thus, the insistence of nations on negating foreign influences and viewing them as intrusions is successful only on the surface as many ethnolinguistic groups maintain their local identities and languages in nonpublic ways.

One important outcome of multiculturalism, with regard to education, concerns conceptions and definitions of knowledge. In earlier *assimilative* models, there was no appreciation of the knowledge that minority groups had; rather, they were expected to relinquish it and acquire the knowledge that is associated with the dominant group. A later model is referred to as *recognition*, implying that there is appreciation and acknowledgment of different forms of knowledge as valuable and important. In this model, different groups are granted credit for their knowledge and are often encouraged to maintain and cultivate it, at least for a temporary period. Current models are referred to as *interactive* in that the knowledge of the minority groups is seen to affect that of the dominant group and enrich it in a two-way interaction. Thus, the minority groups no longer simply accommodate and adjust to the majority. In this model, it is also not enough to *recognize* the knowledge; rather, the knowledge must be viewed as part of a new enriched knowledge, perceived as important funds of knowledge for the society as a whole.

Clearly, the two-way interaction model is not simple to apply as there is often resentment by the dominant groups who are eager to maintain and preserve their place in society and who view the other forms of knowledge as challenges to their values and existence. Thus, elite groups tend to deny interactive models in overt and covert ways and continue to perpetuate assimilative models by viewing the knowledge of the different groups as deficient. In most societies, it is still the assimilative model that is being practiced in which minority groups acquire the language of the dominant group, often with no encouragement to maintain their home languages. Tankersley (2001) notes that "the majority of people are of the opinion that minority language speakers in a country need to speak the language of the majority speakers in order to be seen as productive citizens" (p. 109). In some situations, the different groups are encouraged to maintain their languages, but it is rarely the case that the dominant group acquires the other languages spoken in the society.

This pattern is most apparent in schools where various types of mechanisms exist that allow for the perpetuation of policies in formal ways. In schools, the knowledge of minority students is not being acknowledged because immigrants and other groups are generally not granted any credit for it. Their different knowledge is viewed as deficient, and the knowledge of the dominant group is considered the only knowledge of value. Even in situations where multiculturalism is recognized, tokenism prevails and educational systems use a variety of overt and covert mechanisms to strive for homogeneous knowledge, which they believe should be owned by all. Thus, Tankersley (2001), for example, quotes a teacher who comments on the status of the Albanian language in Macedonia: "The majority in a country usually don't want to learn the language of the minority because they fear that the majority could be easily dominated that way. They would lose their superiority that way" (p. 120).

Tests provide effective tools for carrying out such assimilative agendas. Tests of language as well as of various school content play major roles in the process of maintaining and perpetuating the dominant knowledge.

They serve as tools to suppress and eliminate the unique knowledge of minority groups, eventually leading to its elimination. At times, curricula may contain statements that recognize diverse knowledge, yet the tests, which are based on homogeneous knowledge, represent the de facto educational policy. Minority groups rarely take part in the deliberations over the content of the tests and are not considered as partners in the decision-making process (Taylor, 1998). Further, in many cases, minority groups internalize and accept the domination and relevance of the dominant knowledge.

The scenarios described below illustrate how the knowledge of minority groups is often not valued and appreciated, and how tests – especially language tests – serve as tools to maintain and perpetuate the dominant knowledge of majority groups. Further details on these scenarios can be found in Shohamy (2001b).

Scenario 1: No recognition of previous language and content

Russian immigrant children arriving in Israel are proficient in the Russian language. In Israel, Hebrew is the dominant language and the avenue to success in the society. Since it takes immigrant students up to ten years to acquire a level of proficiency in the new language which is equivalent to that of native speakers, many of the Russian students fail the math tests. It is clear that the Russian students have to, and in fact do, acquire Hebrew, but they are not granted any credit for their knowledge of Russian. All the learning is taking place in Hebrew and the tests that determine their achievements and their entrance into higher education are conducted in Hebrew.

In the above case, the educational system does not recognize the knowledge that the immigrants possess. This is expressed in terms of both the language of instruction as well as the language of all the tests. Since the tests are conducted in Hebrew, a language that Russian immigrants are in the process of acquiring but are still not proficient in, the students cannot demonstrate the full range of their competence. In this scenario, the language and the knowledge that Russian students acquired in their home countries is not valued. It is clear that such a policy keeps the immigrants in a powerless position compared to the dominant group, and their unique knowledge is erased from the national repertoire.

Scenario 2: Language and content are recognized, but the testing policy is in contradiction

In Israel, both Hebrew and Arabic are official languages. Israeli Arabs study in their first language, so Arabic is the language of instruction. Israeli Arabs also learn Hebrew beginning in third grade, but as a second language. Yet the main criterion for entering Israeli universities is passing an end-of-high-school test that requires a high level proficiency in Hebrew. Clearly, the Arab students get no credit for their knowledge of Arabic, their language of instruction throughout their years of schooling.

In the above case, the dominant group recognizes the language of the minority group and, in fact, encourages it. In the Arab communities in Israel, Arabic is used as the language of instruction. Yet, without getting into the specific reasons for recognizing Arabic as the language of instruction (and not granting such rights to other groups such as the Russians), it is the performance on the Hebrew language tests (the dominant language) that serves as the main criterion for entrance into higher education. Language tests perpetuate the dominance of Hebrew and grant no value to Arabic, the language of instruction in schools. Clearly, such a situation is likely to result in low motivation on the part of the Arab students to maintain their home language because Arabic has no recognized status and no legitimacy as a rite of passage. In fact, there are already signs of this happening as more content areas in Arab secondary schools are being taught in Hebrew. Thus, the policy of maintaining the home language by using it as the language of instruction is in contradiction to testing polices; since tests are such powerful instruments, they create and dictate the de facto educational policies.

Scenario 3: The cultural interests of minority groups are not validated through testing practices

Israeli Arabs are required to study Jewish content such as Talmud, the Bible, and Hebrew literature; their studies contain very limited exposure to their own content areas, such as the Koran. The testing policy is in line with this. The final secondary school examination includes these content areas, and passing the test is a condition for entrance into higher education institutions. Interestingly, Jewish students are not required to study Arab content in school, and even the study of Arabic is not totally compulsory, although Arabic is an official language in Israel.

The above case indicates that some knowledge of minority groups can be recognized as important, such as the language but not the content. Regarding content, Arabs are required to study the dominant knowledge of the Jewish population. This is perpetuated even more through the tests that are a condition for entrance into higher education institutions. Here again, the tests serve as gatekeeping devices as those Arabs who do not master the knowledge of the dominant group will not be accepted to higher education institutions.

Scenario 4: Majority languages are enforced through testing practices

The Latvian language policy recognizes the existence of both the Latvian and the Russian languages as part of their language policy; yet, in order to obtain jobs as well as citizenship, Russians have to pass tests in the Latvian language.

In the above example, while there is recognition of the Russian language in policy documents, it is testing that creates the de facto policy of limiting opportunities for minority groups, in this case Russian speakers in Latvia. Here, the testing policy is in contradiction to the official policy: while the language policy seems to be that of recognition, the testing policy is that of assimilation.

Scenario 5: One size fits all

Arab students learn three languages in school: Arabic, Hebrew, and English. Jewish students learn two languages: Hebrew and English. Clearly, the proficiency of the Arab students in English is not as high as those of the Jews, yet the Arabs are being measured with the same tests and are evaluated by the same criteria. Not surprisingly, their scores in English are consistently lower than those of the Jews.

In the above case, which is norm referenced, all groups are being compared to the dominant group and success is measured by the same tools for all, although the conditions and learning experiences are entirely different. There is no recognition that English is a third language for Arabs but a second language for Jews. Using the same test means using the same criteria for both groups, which is bound to result in a situation in which the Arabs will generally get lower scores. In most societies that apply assimilative models, the same tests are used for all groups regardless of different backgrounds and experiences, thereby guaranteeing the superiority of the dominant group. Thus, by using a norm-referenced approach, various groups are compared to the dominant group. By applying criterion-referenced approaches, language proficiency is measured according to the experiences of each group.

The above scenarios describe how the linguistic and cultural knowledge of minority groups is often not recognized by majority groups and how tests are used as tools to perpetuate inequality. Furthermore, even in situations where knowledge is recognized as part of multiculturalism, tests serve as tools to contradict such policies and thus to homogenize knowledge so that assimilative models are carried out. Clearly, the testing policy is the de facto educational policy and standardized tests, which are based on homogeneous knowledge, serve as tools to standardize knowledge and negate existing differences. These tests serve as tools to gatekeep, exclude, and eliminate knowledge in covert ways, thus undermining multicultural practices that, in theory, recognize the voices of diverse groups as partners in multicultural societies. As Taylor (1998, p. 143) would argue, liberal democracies should apply philosophies of inclusion in which reference to "the people" is taken to mean everybody, without unspoken restrictions. J. Oller (personal communication, May 26, 1998) wonders whether it is possible to introduce language tests that follow more democratic practices and asks whether it is not possible "to have testing of the people, for the people, and by the people."

Principles for more inclusive language testing

In the next part of the chapter, a number of practices that can make language tests more democratic will be proposed based on a number of principles that adopt more inclusive models of assessment as well as monitor the misuses of tests (Shohamy, 2001a).

1. The first democratic principle is that of inclusion, which calls for a need to consider the voices of diverse groups in multicultural societies. In terms of applying this principle to assessment in multicultural societies, it suggests a need to recognize and include the knowledge of diverse groups in test design.
2. The second principle calls for citizens in democratic societies to play a participatory and active role and for elites to transfer and share power with local bodies. The application of the principle suggests the need to conduct and administer testing in collaboration and in cooperation with those tested.
3. The third principle is the need for those in democratic societies to monitor and limit the uses of tools of power, especially those tests with the potential to exclude and discriminate against minority groups. The implication for assessment is the need to apply CLT approaches to monitor the uses of tests as instruments of power, to challenge their assumptions, and to examine their consequences.
4. The fourth principle is based on the need for those in democratic societies to protect from powerful institutions the rights of citizens; the application of this principle to assessment is the need to protect and guard the rights of the test takers.
5. The last principle is the need for those who develop powerful tools of power to assume responsibility for their consequences. The implication is the need for those involved in testing to assume responsibility for the tests and their uses.

Each of these democratic assessment practices is discussed below:

Principle 1: The need to consider and include knowledge of diverse groups on tests

As discussed in the first part of the chapter, this refers to the principle of considering the voices of diverse groups as partners in multicultural societies. As was discussed with reference to the five scenarios, even in those societies that recognize multiculturalism, there is rarely recognition of the specific and unique knowledge of different groups in schools, and educational leaders continue to strive for homogeneous knowledge for all. There is often a gap between curricula and assessment in that curricula may contain statements and intentions recognizing diverse knowledge, yet the tests are based on homogeneous knowledge. The testing policy becomes the de facto educational policy as standardized tests based on homogeneous knowledge serve as tools to standardize certain knowledge and ignore other knowledge. This is especially the case in high-stake standardized tests, which are capable of affecting and defining knowledge; frequently, the unique knowledge of different groups in multicultural and multilingual societies receives no recognition and is eventually erased.

The application of democratic principles implies a need to consider different groups in the process of test construction and to consider their knowledge as legitimate knowledge. There is a need to reject the notion that the standards of performance of immigrants and other groups are derived from comparisons with the dominant groups (norm referenced) and viewed as deficient and a need to find ways to assess the existing knowledge of different cultural groups (criterion referenced). There is also a need to understand the politics of testing (the real intentions) and to reject situations in which testers are being used to carry out the orders of central agencies, which always attempt to perpetuate existing dominant views. There is a need, therefore, to carry out extensive research into the knowledge of different groups and to identify the specific areas in which these different groups have strengths, advantages, and problems.

This approach also suggests that there is a need to involve members of different groups as participants in the development and design of tests in order to identify and represent these forms of knowledge. In situations where different groups request rights and power, there is a need to move away from a model whereby the testing profession is involved in knowledge standardization. Instead, the goal should be to democratize testing so that it responds to the needs of many new multicultural–multilingual societies in which different groups demand recognition of their differences as they move away from the traditional nation-state model. Immigrants and indigenous groups need to be recognized for their differences.

Principle 2: The need to conduct tests in collaboration and in cooperation with those tested

This refers to the democratic principle whereby citizens need to play a participatory and active role in the democratic process so that power is shared and transferred from elites to local bodies (Taylor, 1998). According to Giroux (1994), democracy takes up the issue of

> transferring power from elites and executive authorities who control the economic and cultural apparatus of society, to those producers who wield power at the local level and is made concrete through the organization and exercise of horizontal power in which knowledge needs to be widely shared through education and other technologies of culture. (p. 36)

The new models of assessment follow principles of shared power, collaboration, and representation and can therefore be viewed as more democratic. In the power model, knowledge and values reflect those in authority with little attention given to the other agents, including test takers. Like Giroux, Freire (1985) rejects such power models and promotes democracy in which a meaningful dialogical relation exists between two partners: the evaluator – as opposed to the inspector – and the person being evaluated:

> Through inspection, educators just become objects of vigilance by a central organization. Through evaluation, everyone is a subject along with the central organization in the act of criticism and establishing distance from the word. In understanding the process in this way, evaluation is not an act by which educator A evaluates educator B. It's an act by which educators A and B together evaluate an experience, its development, and the obstacles one confronts along with any mistakes or error. Thus, evaluation has a dialectical character. (pp. 23–25)

Such approaches change the balance of power between the tester and the test taker and assume that the tester is no longer the one who owns all knowledge. Instead, knowledge is complex; testing professionals do not have all the answers.

Darling-Hammond (1994) argues that assessment needs to change from a sorting mechanism to diagnostic supports, from external monitors of performance to locally generated tools for inquiring deeply into teaching and learning, and from purveyors of sanctions for those already undeserved to levers for equalizing resources. Adopting democratic principles along these lines implies that the act of testing is the mutual effort of testers and test takers; other sources of knowledge – such as parents, teachers, and peers – are also important. Freedman (1993) argues for working collaboratively with schools and communities, involving teachers, administrators, students, and parents. Fetterman, Kaftarian, and Wandersman (1996) promote the notion of *empowerment evaluation* whereby collaborative approaches to evaluation are used to foster improvement in programs. A form of self-evaluation and reflection is used in which the evaluators act as facilitators and collaborators rather than as experts and counselors. The authors claim that such an approach is fundamentally democratic because it invites participation through which issues of concern to the entire community are examined in an open forum.

In some approaches, local groups – test takers, students, teachers, and schools – share power by collecting their own assessments and by using multiple assessment procedures (portfolios, self-assessment, projects, observations, and tests) that can provide evidence to properly reveal the knowledge of those who are being assessed. The professional tester serves mostly as a facilitator who assists in the strategies of collecting the information and in its interpretation. In other models, power is transferred from central bodies to local ones, such as when external examinations are abolished in favor of local and internal assessment. However, such an approach is often criticized on the grounds that the power relationship is simply being transferred to the teacher who, too, may engage in undemocratic behavior in the classroom. Broadfoot (1996) demonstrates how, in some situations, such approaches may lead to an illusion of democracy as teachers become the new servants of the central systems. She refers to this as "a new order of domination" (p. 87). Thus, the preferred model, in the classroom as well, is not a transfer of power, but the sharing of power with local bodies. It is collaboratively based on a broader representation of different agents, central and local, who together go through a process of contextualization of the evidence obtained from the different sources. Through constructive, interpretive, and dialogical sessions, each participant collects data and demonstrates it in an interpretive and contextualized manner. This approach can then be applied to the national, district, or classroom context. It suggests, therefore, that the assessment of student achievement ought to be seen as an art rather than a science in that it is interpretive, idiosyncratic, interpersonal, and relative.

There are a number of examples that demonstrate the use of models such as the one presented above. Moss (1996) gives the example of contextualization and shared authority with regard to certification. In this model, the decision about certification is made locally through dialogue among those professionals who are familiar with the candidates or with contexts in which the candidates work; thus, dialogue is based on portfolios as well as on documented observations and interactions over time with the candidate. In this way, triangulation of different methods strengthens the dependability and validity of decisions. The state or other outside evaluators assume more of an auditing role to ensure that the process is equitable, reflects state or professional standards, and is sufficiently rigorous to protect the public from the licensure of incompetent professionals. Shohamy (1996) reports on an assessment model where the language proficiency of the immigrant students is assessed by a number of agents: teachers, who collect data via tests and observations; the test takers themselves, who provide evidence of their language performance through self-assessment and portfolios; and a standardized diagnostic test, administered by a central body. The information obtained from all these agents through the various instruments is then gathered, processed, and interpreted in an assessment conference where language teacher, classroom teacher, student, and, occasionally, a parent discuss and interpret the information in order to arrive at meaningful recommendations for pedagogical and learning strategies for language improvement. Dialoguing has also been applied in the field of program evaluation by Nevo (1996). Such an approach can be used in the assessment of language; moreover, it is based on a two-way relationship and operates under the assumption that nobody knows everything, but both parties know something, and through dialoguing they will learn more. Dialoguing is a continuous process based on substantiated information that is data based and relevant. In such a form of evaluation, each party is responsible for the consequences and the impact.

One important component in the application of such democratic models of assessment is the consideration of multiple sources of evidence. The assumption is that tests are limited in what they can assess and that there is therefore a need for procedures to assess areas that cannot be tapped by tests. The application of collaborative and shared models is of particular importance in the classroom as it provides students with the experience of democratic assessment behavior from an early age; they become aware of the need to guard and protect their rights from the assessment machinery of centralized bodies.

Another dimension of shared power is based on the connection between testing and learning. Fredriksen and Collins (1989) introduced the notion of systemic validity, in which a closer connection exists between testing and learning. They contend that information obtained from tests can contribute to improved learning when tests are connected to the learning that takes place in the classroom. In systemic validity, the introduction of tests is a dynamic process so that changes in the educational system take place according to feedback obtained from tests. In systemic models, a valid test is one that brings about an improvement in the tested skills after a test has been in the educational system for a period of time. Thus, high systemic validity can only be achieved when a whole set of assessment activities foster it, such as direct tests, practicing self-assessment procedures, repeated testing, feedback on test performance, and multiple levels of success. Thus, tests that are used for the purpose of improving learning can be effective when they are connected to, and integrated into, other elements that are part of the educational system and not when they are used in isolation.

Principle 3: The need to apply CLT approaches to monitor the uses of tests as instruments of power, to challenge their assumptions, and examine their consequences

As noted above, CLT refers to the need to question the use of tests as tools of power, to examine their consequences in education and society, and eventually to monitor, control, and limit their powerful role. CLT originates from the need of those in democratic societies to question, monitor, and control powerful tools and institutions and to examine the ways such tools are being used by those in power. Below are examples of some of the issues that CLT can address (discussed in detail in Shohamy, 1998, 2001b):

- CLT examines the intentions of tests by asking whether they are meant to assess and negotiate knowledge or define and dictate it. It asks whether that knowledge is limited to those in power who want to maintain and preserve it or represents knowledge of diverse groups in society.
- CLT admits that as the knowledge of any tester is incomplete, there is a need to rely on additional sources in order to obtain more accurate, valid descriptions and interpretations of knowledge. This involves a variety of stakeholders, including policy makers, test writers, students, parents, and teachers.
- CLT challenges the uses of the test as the only instrument to assess knowledge and favors the use of multiple procedures, which together can provide a more valid picture for interpreting the knowledge of individuals and groups. In doing so, it challenges psychometric traditions and favors interpretive ones in which different meanings and multiple interpretations of test scores can be considered, rather than attempting to arrive at an absolute truth.
- CLT engages in a wider sphere of social dialogue and debate and confronts the roles that tests play and have been assigned to play in society by competing ideologies and the discourse that is thereby constructed. It draws testers toward areas of social processes and the power struggles embedded in democracies.
- CLT asks questions such as, Who are the testers? What are their agendas? Who are the test takers? What are their contexts? What is the context of the topics being tested? Who will benefit from the tests? Why are tests being given? What will their results be used for? What areas are being tested and why? What areas are not being tested and

why? What are the underlying values behind the tests? What are the testing methods? What additional evidence is collected? What kinds of decisions are reached based on the tests? Who else, besides the tester, is included in the design of the test and its implementation? What ideology is delivered through the test? What messages about students, teachers, and society do tests assume? What types of feedback are provided based on the tests and to whom is the feedback given? Can the tests and their results be challenged? What are the intended and unintended uses of the test? What are their impacts? What are some ways that test takers and others can challenge the test?

Thus, given the ease with which tests can be misused – often with the support of the public who may not be aware of the dangers and their consequences – CLT offers a mechanism that can challenge the powerful uses of tests.

Principle 4: The need to protect and guard the rights of test takers

This democratic principle refers to the rights of individuals in democratic societies to be protected from powerful institutions. The principle can be implemented through procedures such as a bill of rights, codes, and litigation. In a testing situation, the individual test takers should have mechanisms for protection.

The concept of the rights of test takers is relatively new. Traditionally, instead of having rights, the test taker has generally been viewed as a black box that has been important only in the context of computing the psychometric properties of the test. There is specific knowledge that the test taker is expected to know, and this is defined by those who have designed the tests; the test taker is expected to comply with this definition. As Shohamy (2001a, 2001b) argues, test takers are the true victims of tests in this unequal power relationship between the test as an organization and the demands put on test takers, who may have little access to testing information. It is rare for test takers to protest, complain, or claim that the test did not fit their knowledge. The authority of tests has been accepted without question. However, the growing involvement of the public in education throughout the 1990s and the increased power to legislate in a number of areas have been extended to the area of testing as well. There have been a number of court cases seeking legal redress for real and/or perceived violations of rights, and this, in turn, brings testing programs to court. Notable among legal issues are race or gender discrimination, unfairness, and the violation of due process, including failure to give sufficient notice for a test or failure to give opportunities for hearings and appeals. Among the educational testing practices brought to court are minimum competence standards, teacher certification tests (designed to control who is allowed to teach in a state), and college admissions testing. Applying this democratic principle can occur in a number of ways.

QUESTIONING THE USES OF TESTS

Test takers should view it as their civil right to question tests and the values inherent in them. Test takers can also question the test results and methods wherever there is concern that the rights of the tester have been violated. They may have been tested on unfamiliar materials or on using unfamiliar methods, or the test results may have been used for purposes for which they were not intended.

THE RIGHT NOT TO BE TESTED

Punch (1994) refers to whether the test takers have been clearly told that they are being tested, what they are being tested for, and what will be done with the results of the testing. Test takers, it is believed, should also have the right to refuse to be tested. Valdes and Figueroa (1996), arguing that the information obtained from tests used for bilinguals is not interpretable, propose the abolition of all testing of circumstantial bilingual persons when such tests are used to select, certify, or guide interventions for individuals. It is realized, however, that this is a long process. Given the present power of tests, which is in the hands of powerful institutions – whether testing organizations, schools, or teachers – it is difficult for individuals to question and protest. A strategy that is recommended is the establishment of advocacy groups, the role of which is to protect test takers from powerful organizations. This is no different from suing doctors for malpractice as a result of bad medical treatment.

LITIGATION

Rogosa (as cited in Rothstein, 2000), a well-known psychometrician from Stanford University, commenting on a specific widely used test used to determine promotion of students, noted that

> surprisingly, there has not yet been a wave of lawsuits by parents of children penalized largely because of a single test score. As more parents learn about the test's actual accuracy, litigation regarding high-stake decisions is bound to follow. Districts and states will then have to abandon an unfair reliance on single tests to evaluate students.

PRIVACY AND CONFIDENTIALITY

This refers to whether test takers are harmed by reports of their results from a test, reports that deny them entrance to institutions, or reports that prevent them from accessing social and economic resources. Lynch (1997) stresses that it is not the act of testing that is to blame, but the fact that certain realities in society call for selection based on merit; tests are efficient tools for such selection. The recommendation is that there should be accountability with regard to the purpose of the test, its practice, and its methods.

TEST DECISIONS: CONSEQUENCES AND FAIRNESS

This refers to the difficulty of deciding what constitutes fairness. While decisions may be based on equal opportunities and conditions of testing, they do not imply that all test takers have equal opportunity to obtain an equal education. The rights of test takers can therefore be violated by having different educational backgrounds; imposing tests that are based on one type of knowledge, decided by particular groups, may be a violation of the rights of those test takers who come from different backgrounds.

ALTERNATIVE FORMS OF ASSESSMENT

This refers to the fact that a test taker should be granted the possibility of being assessed via alternative forms of assessment, different from the traditional "test-only" ones. Such information can be used to counter evidence against decisions based on tests only, especially in testing immigrants who are not familiar with the formats used in the new country or in situations where the format of the item is more appropriate for one culture than another, gender included.

SHARING DISCOURSE

This refers to the need for a dialogue between the testing community and lay people and the need to create a common language with which persons of differing backgrounds can discuss matters of technology in thoughtful, critical terms. Specifically, there is a need to acquaint all groups who have concerns about tests and their use with the techniques and terminology of the testing community so that they can enter into the discourse without being dismissed as naïve. Testing cannot remain a field that belongs only to testers, but rather test takers and the public at large need to be part of a mutual discussion.

Principle 5: The need for those involved in the testing act to assume responsibility for the tests and their uses

Democratic assessment requires that those who develop powerful instruments be responsible for their consequences. The language tester, Davies (1997) argues, has both professional and moral obligations. No social science is immune from such obligations as it becomes less and less tenable for academic disciplines to allow their researchers the liberty to make up their own minds as to the conduct and practice of their professional research. He raises issues that can create conflicts, such as the relationship with stakeholders, the relationship between bias and fairness, washback, the politics of gatekeeping, and the conflict between fairness and face validity.

Once testers become aware of misuses of tests in society, they are faced with serious dilemmas regarding their professional roles and responsibilities. Is the test developer responsible for uses and misuses of tests? What is the role of the tester once he or she notices misuses? Is it his or her role at that point to warn against misuses or to take specific steps, such as using sanctions against misuses? Shohamy (2001a, 2001b) elaborates on these questions and issues by considering six views of the responsibility of the language testers:

(a) ethical responsibility,
(b) responsibility for making others aware,
(c) responsibility for all the language test consequences,
(d) responsibility for imposing sanctions,
(e) shared responsibility where the responsibilities for good conduct are in the hands of all those who are involved in the testing process (shared authority and shared responsibility), and
(f) responsibility to abide by Codes of Practice (ILTA, 2000).

Conclusion

Tests that were originally developed for democratizing purposes have been utilized in acts that are not democratic in that they have become tools used by centralized authorities to exercise power and control and to manipulate educational systems. Tests are central to a number of competing battles: between the need of central agencies for control and the desire for individual freedom; between the urge of groups for a common unifying knowledge and open, creative knowledge; between a monolingual "one language for all" policy and multilingual tolerance; between the public need for symbolic devices of social order and the need of individuals and groups for personal expression and freedom; between increased control in growing technological societies and fluid and relative knowledge; between resentment of control by centralized agencies and the need for control in order to maintain status and social order; between individual and group expression; and between practical concerns and ideological forces. There are, therefore, different views with regard to the current state and future prospects of tests.

On one hand, there are those who believe that the testing era is over, that there is no room for such authoritarian tools in postmodern, multicultural societies where knowledge is relative and fluid, and where diverse groups demand legitimacy and respect, identity and rights. Valdes and Figueroa (1996) argue for a radical yet equitable proposal in the context of the testing of bilinguals. They propose a declaration of a national moratorium and suspension of all testing of bilingual persons when such testing involves decision making about individuals. They claim that tests provide uninterpretable information and have far-reaching implications for these individuals in selection, certification, or intervention. They argue that instruments that are based on standardization of whole populations, where all people use the same yardsticks, pose major obstacles to self-expression.

On the other hand, there are those who think that tests should continue to exist and with more power and control than ever. After all, tests can be the most convenient tools for challenging those who demand to share power and to legitimize multicultural, postmodern agendas. For example, it may be easy to fight the proponents of Ebonics with standardized English tests. Similarly, it is possible to fight bilingual education by introducing uniform English tests as criteria for entrance and acceptance as part of the English-only agenda. Broadfoot (1996) is even more far-reaching in her view of the future of tests. She argues that it is the combination of technology and bureaucracy that will enable central groups to further increase their power as they legitimize policy decisions in terms of an objective, rational process of decision making, in turn, "leading to the growing powerlessness of the individual to resist the effects of an increasingly intrusive state machinery" (pp. 217–18).

There is also another view, which considers that tests are here to stay but in different shapes and forms. Such a view contends that the true power of tests is in the pedagogical benefits they offer in the form of feedback leading to more effective learning and teaching. Yet tests have emerged as powerful tools that violate important principles that must be safeguarded in democratic societies. The enormous power of tests has met very little resistance from those who are affected by the results of the tests. Thus, while tests can be used for beneficial and constructive purposes, at the same time, it is important to guard against central bodies and authoritarian agencies that seek ways to use tests in unethical and undemocratic ways for power and control.

This chapter has proposed a number of ways in which society can protect itself from undemocratic language testing. Specifically it has (a) recommended the inclusion of different voices in the assessment process, (b) offered a number of ways in which test takers can guard themselves from the misuses of tests, (c) examined the uses of tests from a critical language testing perspective, (d) considered the development of shared and collaborative assessment models, and (e) insisted on accountability from those who are engaged in test development. The message of this chapter is not a call for the abolition of tests, but rather a call for practicing democratic testing, which requires shared authority, collaboration, the involvement of different stakeholders (test takers included), and the monitoring of test use. There is a need for continuous examination of the quality of tests, for in-depth insight into how they are used, for the public exposure of test misuse, and for the education of the public regarding the motivation, harmful effects, and consequences of tests. The price of such democratic approaches is high as they take more time, involve more people, require greater resources, and involve compromise, as all democratic practices do. But if tests are so central and they represent such strong potential for misuse, the price is worth paying. This is the challenge that language testers need to face.

Language testers need to think of how such testing practices can be carried out, what new methodologies have to be developed in order to follow such practices, how more democratic testing can be pursued while at the same time guarding the validity of the tests, and how test users can be convinced not to use tests that do not meet equity standards. Testers, therefore, must become engaged in the discussion. They must assume an active role in considering the consequences and uses of tests, help guard against misuses, and offer assessment models that are more educational, democratic, ethical, and, at the same time, valid. Assuming tests are neutral only allows those in power to misuse tests with the very instruments that testers have provided them. Studies of the use of tests as part of test validation on an ongoing basis are essential for the integrity of the profession. Language tests fall in the crossroads of many conflicts and therefore should be studied, protected, and guarded as part of the process of preserving and perpetuating democratic cultures, values, and ethics.

References

Bourdieu, P. (1991). *Language and symbolic power.* Cambridge, MA: Harvard University Press.

Broadfoot, P. (1996). *Education, assessment, and society*. Buckingham, England: Open University Press.

Crowley, T. (1996). Signs of belonging: Languages, nations and cultures in the old and new Europe. In C. Hoffman (Ed.), *Language, culture, and communication in contemporary Europe* (pp. 47–60). Clevedon, England: Multilingual Matters.

Darling-Hammond, L. (1994). Performance-based assessment and educational equity. *Harvard Educational Review, 64*(1), 5–30.

Davies, A. (1997). Demands of being professional in language testing. *Language Testing, 14*(3), 328–39.

Elder, C. (1997). What does test bias have to do with fairness? *Language Testing, 14*(3), 261–77.

Fetterman, D., Kaftarian, S., & Wandersman, A. (1996). *Empowerment evaluation.* Thousand Oaks, CA: Sage.
Fredriksen, J., & Collins, A. (1989). A system approach to educational testing. *Educational Researcher, 18*, 27–32.
Freedman W. S. (1993). Linking large-scale testing and classroom portfolio assessments of student writing. *Educational Assessment, 1*(1), 27–52.
Freire, P. (1985). *The politics of education.* South Hadley, MA: Bergin and Garvey.
Giroux, H. (1994). Language, difference, and current theory: Beyond the politics and clarity. In P. McLaren & J. Giarelli (Eds.), *Critical theory and educational research* (pp. 23–38). Albany: State University of New York Press.
Hamp-Lyons, L. (1997). Washback, impact and validity: Ethical concerns. *Language Testing, 14*(3), 295–303.
Hawthorne, L. (1997). The political dimension of English language testing in Australia. *Language Testing, 14*(3), 248–60.
International Language Testing Association (ILTA). (2000). *Code of ethics for foreign/second language testing.* Hong Kong: Hong Kong International Language Testing Association.
Kramsch, C. (1993). *Context and culture in language teaching.* Oxford: Oxford University Press.
Kunnan, A. (Ed). (2000). Fairness and validation in language assessment. *Studies in Language Testing 9.* Cambridge, England: UCLES/Cambridge University Press.
Lynch, B. (1997). In search of the ethical test. *Language Testing, 14*(3), 315–27.
Messick, S. (1981). Evidence and ethics in the evaluation of tests. *Educational Researcher, 10*, 9–20.
Moss, P. (1996). Enlarging the dialogue in educational measurement: Voices from interpretive research traditions. *Educational Researcher, 25*(1), 20–8.
Nevo, D. (1996). *School based evaluation.* Oxford, England: Pergamon University Press.
Norton, B., & Stein, P. (2001). Why the "Monkeys Passage" bombed: Tests, genres and teaching. In S. W. Beck & L. N. Olah (Eds.), *Perspectives on language and literacy: Beyond the here and now* (pp. 419–34). Harvard Educational Review Reprint Series, No. 35. Cambridge, MA: President and Fellows of Harvard College.
Pennycook, A. (2001). *Critical applied linguistics: A critical introduction.* Mahwah, NJ: Lawrence Erlbaum Associates.
Punch, M. (1994). Politics and ethics in qualitative research. In N. K. Denzin & Y. S. Lincoln (Eds.), *Handbook of qualitative research* (pp. 83–97). Thousand Oaks, CA: Sage.
Rothstein, R. (2000, September 13). Lessons: How tests can drop the ball. *New York Times.*
Shohamy, E. (1996). Language testing: Matching assessment procedures with language knowledge. In M. Birenbaum & F. Dochy (Eds.), *Alternatives in assessment of achievements, learning processes and prior knowledge* (pp. 142–60). Boston: Kluwer Academic.
Shohamy, E. (1998). Critical language testing and beyond. *Studies in Educational Evaluation, 24*(4), 331–45.
Shohamy, E. (2001a). Democratic assessment as an alternative. *Language Testing, 18*(4), 373–91.

Shohamy, E. (2001b). *The power of tests: A critical perspective on the uses of language tests*. Harlow, England: Pearson Education.

Tankersley, D. (2001). Bombs or bilingual programmes: Dual-language immersion, transformative education and community building in Macedonia. *Bilingual Education and Bilingualism*, 4(2), 107–24.

Taylor C. (1998). The dynamics of democratic inclusion. *Journal of Democracy*, 9(4), 143–56.

Tollefson, J. (1995). Introduction: Language policy, power, and inequality. In J. Tollefson (Ed.), *Power and inequality in language education* (pp. 1–8). Cambridge, England: Cambridge University Press.

Valdes, G., & Figueroa, R. (1996). *Bilingualism and testing: A special case of bias*. Norwood, NJ: Ablex.

PART II: CHALLENGING IDENTITIES

6 *Representation, rights, and resources: Multimodal pedagogies in the language and literacy classroom*

Pippa Stein

Introduction

In this chapter, I explore the relations between modes of communication, communicative contexts, and practices in the language and literacy classroom. Through a focus on multimodality, multiple modes of communication such as language in its spoken and written forms, the visual, the gestural, and the performative, I discuss the insights that classroom-based research with diverse English as a second language (ESL) learners in Johannesburg offer in relation to thinking about representation: how sociocultural worlds and local knowledge come to be constituted in classroom spaces, the tensions between talk and silence in relation to the *unsayable* and *unthinkable* within the context of gendered identities and dominant culture, and the pedagogical and ethical dilemmas these issues pose for the language teacher. I advocate what I call *multimodal pedagogies* – pedagogies that position the body at the center of pedagogic activity. This act of repositioning the body as a multimodal sign and resource for meaning in the classroom challenges the hegemony of language, particularly written language, in the ESL classroom. Multimodal pedagogies allow for the expression of a much fuller range of human emotion and experience; they acknowledge the limits of language, admit the integrity of silence, and do not presume closure. I argue from an equity perspective that such pedagogies offer students a more representative base for representation. However, how representative such pedagogies become is inseparable from the inclusion of multimodal assessment as part of mainstream assessment practices in the language and literacy classroom.

Representation in diverse classrooms: A major pedagogical challenge

The exploration of conceptual and practical issues in relation to the activity of meaning making or representation in classrooms is central to our work as language and literacy teachers. A major pedagogical challenge is to bring knowing to the surface of consciousness, to help students render knowledge as material culture, and to transform what they know, remember, sense, hear, feel, and believe into a paragraph of writing, a lively dialogue, a scrapbook of images, or an academic essay. Much of our time involves designing classroom activities and assessment tasks that signify to us the extent to which *knowing* has occurred. And it is these signs that we use to make judgments about learners' competencies and potentials. Thus, the making of meaning in the language and literacy classroom can be seen as semiotic activity within a specific site of power and culture, for particular purposes and with particular consequences.

The politics and practices of representation in classrooms become particularly challenging in sites where learners and teachers come from very diverse historical, sociocultural, and linguistic contexts. This is the case in many urban classrooms in South Africa where learners are often multilingual code-switchers speaking a range of South African languages and where differences of class, gender, race, history, and culture are evident. The history of South Africa, with its apartheid divisions along the lines of race, language, geography, class, and culture, coupled with the history of patriarchy, has helped to naturalize divisions – among men and women, black and white, urban and rural, rich and poor. A major question is the extent to which teachers are prepared to actively work with difference. This is a complex political, as well as pedagogical, issue: What is the relationship between providing access to dominant discourses and resources and nation-building and reconciliation politics within the African, as well as global, context? In this post-apartheid period of reconstruction and transformation, issues of access to resources are central to any debate on education. However, dominant discourses are multiple and fluid: for example, a current dominant discourse of the new ruling elite is the African Renaissance vision of the African National Congress' (ANC) president Thabo Mbeki, which places African cultural revival at the center of the educational reconstruction debate. Whose discourses are dominant cannot be separated from ongoing struggles over nationhood and identity: who is an African, what it means to produce knowledge rooted in an African perspective, and how this works in relation to Western knowledge and hegemony.

In the realm of education, many urban multicultural schools in South Africa are working within assimilation models. In spite of a new language-in-education policy that actively promotes functional multilingualism, many black parents want their children to have access to one version of dominant culture that includes learning to speak English and being exposed to models of previously "whites-only" education (Heugh, 2002; Kapp, 2000; PanSALB, 1999). At the same time, the ANC government has introduced a new outcomes-based education (OBE) curriculum called Curriculum 2005, which has a nation-building and human rights agenda based on twelve critical outcomes. Critics of OBE in South Africa from an Africanist perspective maintain that the new curriculum has failed to integrate African culture within the schooling system (Nekwhevha, 2000).

My own position as an English teacher-educator and literacy researcher is to research pedagogies that can address the contexts of diversity in classrooms where students from multiple discursive and representational histories find themselves. How can the classroom as a space for meaning making be a complex, hybrid space founded on diverse histories, multiple modes of representation, epistemologies, feelings, languages, and discourses that can become harnessed for productivity and regenerativity? I argue that in the South African context, productive diversity can occur through (at least) two processes: (a) an engagement with contradiction and incoherence and (b) an acknowledgment of discontinuities and loss in relation to sociohistorical legacies of injustices, inequalities, and oppression.

Addressing the challenge: Multimodal pedagogies

Drawing on examples from local classrooms, I describe what I call multimodal pedagogies, which arise from a particular historical moment in South Africa. Post-apartheid conditions are highlighting the long-term damaging effects of apartheid on multiple aspects of people's lives, including fragmented experiences of education and literacy. The predominant modes of communication are oral. Radio, followed by television, is the dominant form of media communication. Print media have small readerships. This preference for nonwritten forms of communication presents teachers with particular kinds of challenges in relation to acknowledging the tensions between local forms of communication and the literacy demands of schooling.

Multimodal pedagogies: Basic assumptions

In this section, I explain a number of assumptions that form the basis of thinking about multimodal pedagogies. These ideas have been influenced by theorists working in multimodality and social semiotics (Hodge & Kress, 1988; Kress, 1993, 1997, 2000a, 2000b, 2000c; Kress et al., 2001; Kress & Van Leeuwen, 1996, 2001), "multiliteracies" (Cope & Kalantzis, 2000; New London Group, 1996), an anthropology of the senses (Seremetakis, 1994), and feminist theories of the body (Butler, 1990; Grosz, 1994).

Assumption 1: Pedagogy is semiotic activity within relations of culture, history, and power.
Assumption 2: Meaning making is bodily, sensory, and semiotic.
Assumption 3: Meaning making is multimodal.
Assumption 4: Meaning making is interested action.
Assumption 5: Language is limited.
Assumption 6: Meaning making is transformation, creativity, and design.

In the following sections, I explain these assumptions and explore their implications for multimodal pedagogies.

Assumption 1: Pedagogy is semiotic activity within relations of culture, history, and power

Multimodal pedagogies conceptualize pedagogy as semiotic activity that occurs in a particular site and within relations of power, culture, and history. Classrooms are semiotic spaces in which multimodal texts are constantly being produced and transformed by human beings who are the agents of their own meaning making. Each multimodal text can be viewed as a complex sign in response to, in resistance to, and in transformation of other signs. In the activity of learning and teaching, teachers and learners negotiate multiple signs within the boundaries and limits constituted within the discursive domains of the school and the broader social–political context. In this textual practice of reading other texts, learners and teachers are constantly involved in the making of multimodal texts in the form of written tasks, spoken and gestural explanations, and the use of questions and visuals, as well as in the activity of interpreting a multiplicity of texts across modes that learners constantly produce. This is in addition to teachers' work in interpreting the myriad of textual products that teachers and learners use in classrooms. Thus, multimodal pedagogy is fundamentally concerned with the use and effects of signs in different modes in classrooms.

All signs have roots. They have a history and identity in which is embedded the history of communicative practices within that domain or community. For example, literacy is an activity in which human beings create, use, and transform signs. Kress (2000b) talks about "the stuff" of literacy by which he means the forms, the texts, and the shapes of literacy. He argues for a dynamic relation between what this stuff is like and how people shape this stuff in different contexts and communities. So, for example, how we make photographs cannot be separated from what photography as a mode of representation and technology offers the photographer, as well as the particular photographer's relation to the culture and history of photography within specific communities and beyond.

> I think that *what people do with the stuff shapes the stuff*; but I also think the very materiality of the stuff, *what it is like as material*, what any one culture has done with it, how a culture has shaped it, has deep effects on what people may do with it. (Kress, 2000b, p. 1)

It is this dynamic relationship between human beings, the materiality of the stuff, and forms of culture that pushes the boundaries of possibility of representation forward.

Assumption 2: Meaning making is bodily, sensory, and semiotic

> The issue of multimodality reminds us forcefully that human semiosis rests, first and foremost, on the facts of biology and physiology. Human bodies have a wide range of means of engagement with the world.... These we call our "senses": sight, hearing, taste, smell, feel... that from the beginning, guarantees the multimodality of our semiotic world. (Kress, 2000c, p. 184)

MEANING MAKING IS BODILY

Multimodal pedagogies are concerned with the use and transformation of modes of communication in classrooms. Modes are produced in and by the body. The body articulates meaning. Multimodal pedagogies conceptualize human beings as embodied subjects, which posits an integrated relation, rather than a dualism, between the body and the mind. Feminists and political writers have sought to rethink the relations between the material body and consciousness in terms that avoid binaries and that place the individual within the social world of lived experiences. In this reformulation, the reflective individual is conceived of as an *embodied subjectivity*, part of, and inscribed by, the discursive and material practices of the social world. In the notion of the embodied subject, the body is neither brute nor passive but interwoven with, and constitutive of, systems of signification within the social world. As Grosz (1994) points out, what are regarded as fixed and unchangeable elements of facticity and biology are amenable to "wide historical vicissitudes and transformations" (p. 190). These reformulations have profound implications for multimodal pedagogies. The body is simultaneously a multimodal sign as well as a site of multimodal resources – meaning cannot occur outside of or without the body. Bodies hold history, memory, thought, feeling, and desires. Bodies hold language and silence. Our bodies are repositories of knowledge, but these knowledges are not always knowable in and through language – they can be felt, imagined, imaged, or dreamed.

Once there is an understanding that it is the body-subject that performs speech, reading, writing, drawing, or listening, teachers and learners can become aware of how different children enact their performances and how the differences between them are culturally marked. In reading these signs, teachers and learners are involved in forms of textual practice in which not only the sign itself but the conditions of embodiment of the sign maker are part of how the text is read.

AN EXAMPLE OF THE GENDERED BODY: LUNGILE'S STORYTELLING PRACTICES

Memorable instances of how bodies are inscribed with cultural and gendered relations occur when learners are engaged in any genre of performance work for it is in performance work that "the referent is always the agonizingly relevant body of the performer" (Phelan, 1993, p. 150). In a storytelling project on popular culture that I ran with multilingual preadolescents in a black state primary school on the outskirts of Johannesburg, I asked students to perform any stories that they knew or had heard. Many students chose to tell traditional African folkloric tales that they had heard through their families, communities, churches, or school, which they then overlaid with their own particular street culture in creative acts of reappropriation and transformation.

I was struck by the oral performances of one student, Lungile, a thirteen-year-old girl, who was labeled "the silent one" by her teachers, but who came into her own in the performative mode. Lungile navigated her way through the year telling different kinds of stories to her peers and her teacher, drawing on and redesigning the available resources of her history, culture, and community in ways which suited her shifting purposes as a performer. Here is a transcript, from one of her performances told in Zulu, of the mythic tale of Madevu Mbophe, a powerful chief. It contains a translation and commentary which describes her live performance:

'Mm! Lomuntu lona omude wayeyenza ukuthi imvula ine. Kade batshelene noMadevu Mbopha. Enza ukuthi imvula ine ishaye kakhula izindlu ziphephuke. Ayi! Manje kade kade kune lakuhlala khona izimvu. Lapho obekuhlala khona izimvu esibayeni sezimvu. Ayi-Wasuko lapho uMadevu Mbophe manje . . . imvula ine kakhulu . . . imvula ine. . . . ine kakhulu. Ayi! Abantu bagijima bangena endlini. Ine imvula ishaye izindlu zonke zilale phansi izindlu zonke. Abantu bazivale ngengubo. Bathathe amasenke bazivale ngawo.

[The tall man was the rainmaker. There was a lot of collaboration between him and Mbopha about rainmaking. The tall man used to make heavy rains. These rains were accompanied by strong winds which used to blow the houses away. . . . Now let me tell you what happened – Madevu then moved away. It rained heavily. It rained for a long time. Now let me tell you what happened. . . . The people ran into their houses. The rain continued, it demolished all their houses. The people covered themselves with blankets. They made shelters with "zincs" (corrugated iron).]

Commentary: In this section, the first important plot event takes place in the form of the devastating storm that destroys everything. Lungile's energy levels increase dramatically as she provides a densely animated description of the moments of the storm, repeating references to the rain and giving details of the people's responses to it. As she describes the storm, she uses her hands, body movements, and her eyes to give life to, and convey, the atmosphere of the storm. She puts her hands over her head to show people running for cover and mimes people gathering blankets and covering themselves. There is a softening of the voice. Her pitch and volume decrease as she tells of people covering themselves in blankets under their shacks of corrugated iron:

Bakike labantu abafishane. Kukhona labantu abafishane kade basebenzela lomuntu lo omunye. Bafike namabhakede. Bafike na . . . kade kukhone indawo . . . kade kuse kusemfuleni kunamafishi mhlawumbe kune lona . . . ixoxo zonke zihlala khona lapho. Mabafika khona bafika namabhakede baikhiphe bathi kunamofishi. Bakhiphe amafish bakhiphi amafishi ebhakedeni. Bawakhiphe bawafake emabhakedeni.

[Then the short people who had been working for the tall man arrived. . . . They came along with buckets. They came there, there was a place, it was a river, which was teeming with fishes and frogs. On their arrival there, they took out all the fish from the water. They filled their buckets with fish. They filled the buckets with fish . . . they filled the buckets with fish . . . they filled the buckets.]

Commentary: Her tone, pitch, and volume shift again with the next major plot event – the looting of fish from the river. She drops the volume and energy levels, picking it up briefly as she describes the looting process. As she describes the servants of the tall man-thief storming into the village and stealing the fish, her whole body starts to sway, a movement that is primarily located in her hips. Her body bends as the dwarfs take the fish out of the river and put them into the buckets. The force and pace of this activity is displayed through her swaying body, which enacts the movements of picking up and bending down, from the torso. Her voice deepens and the repetition of the lines picks up the pace and rhythm of the activity. As the tension and activity in the village increases, so do her body movements. It seems an unconscious response – in the sense that it is a natural activity, something she is used to and has done many times before. Up to this moment, it is as though she has been inhabiting two worlds, moving between the real world of the classroom and the imaginary world of the village. But at this point in the story, she shifts into a trance-like state as the story world holds sway over her. As she enacts again and again the filling up of the buckets, her audience enters into her story world and travels with her. In this state, she seems to forget – or is unable to retrieve – momentarily the word "river," so she uses a certain technique to remember it: She shifts her eye contact from her audience and looks to the side of the audience outside of the audience enclosure (an imaginary place) to recall it. This becomes her style of retrieval for geographical sites for the rest of the story.

What emerged after some months of witnessing her work in the performative, written, and visual modes was the extent to which Lungile inhabited each mode differently. The oral performative mode became her preferred mode for two main reasons. First, it offered an opportunity for imaginative play in which she is able to express pleasure and desire through the whole body. Lungile's storytelling performances were all body. Second, in African culture, the production of storytelling texts in the performative mode is fundamentally a social, community event that is constructed within and through the sets of relations that are established between performer and audience. Lungile's performances were sustained through the relations she established between herself and her peer group. What we witnessed as spectators, readers, and viewers of her various texts was a systematic shedding of parts of herself as she moved from elaborated oral performance, with all its attendant features of gesture, smile, body movement, audience response, and immediate feedback, to the private, individual, and solitary activity of writing and drawing. For her, transformations across semiotic modes from performance to writing were a struggle to work against loss – the loss of pleasure and control that comes with the shift from using the whole indivisible corporeal body within a living, present community, to the private, distant, solitary state of writing and drawing that materializes in the absence of community. These shifts involved a distancing from the object, a closing down of the performing body, and a loss of her smile. As Plato (trans. 1952) asks, how do you smile in writing? Lungile did not smile in writing.

Lungile told the class that she had been apprenticed into storytelling by her late grandmother. Storytelling as a cultural and social practice in African communities in South Africa is traditionally initiated, perpetuated, and performed by women (Hofmeyr, 1993; Scheub, 1975). Storytelling can thus be viewed as a gendered cultural practice within relations of male domination. The main aim of the female performer is to use her body movement, gesture, facial expression, and vocal dramatics to give the core image of the story a shape which pleases the audience so that they admire her and her work. Thus, female storytellers are culturally constructed as objects of desire within the gaze of (male) audiences.

Lungile's performance was a powerful example of how gender had been inscribed on her body; through her cultural apprenticeship with her grandmother, she had learned to use her mouth to pout and her smile and laugh to seduce. She had learned to move her hips and to sway in culturally defined ways which are, at times, sexual, and at other times, how women move when performing ordinary everyday tasks. One of these culturally defined hip movements is to disarticulate the torso from the hips so that the hips are moving almost independently of the rest of the body. This is a common use of the hips in traditional African women's dances.[1] However, the inscription of gender is not confined only to the enactment of femaleness but to all the other parts she plays within the performance, including young boys, older men, and chiefs. These are all overlaid with her overall desire to please her (male) audience.

The feminist philosopher Butler (1990) problematizes the materiality of the body in relation to gender and sex arguing that the classification of bodies into the categories of male or female in Western culture constructs gender as a discursive practice that constitutes bodies as sexed through a natural process. This "doing of gender" clearly manifests an embodiment of a "style of being" or set of strategies which are culturally and historically located (p. 272). Lungile's doing of gender in her performance manifests a style of being that arises out of a syncretic mix of her unique qualities as a performer in accordance with cultural and historical norms around what it means to inhabit femaleness – femaleness enacting maleness within female storyteller identities – within her particular context and community.

MEANING MAKING IS SENSORY

The senses of sight, touch, feeling, taste, and hearing are fundamental to our bodily engagement with the world. In the same way that speech and writing produce their own forms of thinking, Kress (2000a) suggests that sight, touch, taste, and smell also give rise to specialized forms of thought. Related to the senses is the fact of synaesthesia, which is the transduction of meaning from one semiotic mode to another: for example, the activity of transforming an image into a phrase into a sound.

Anthropologists researching the senses in everyday life have demonstrated the relationship among memory, the senses, and material culture. The senses are living, active things, repositories of history and memory. The Greek anthropologist Seremetakis (1994), in her work on perception and memory as material culture in modernity, explains how the senses represent interior states that cannot be displayed on the surface, thus transforming the senses into "meaning-generating apparatuses" that operate beyond consciousness and intention. What is being said may be "relativised, contradicted or confirmed by embodied acts, gestures or sensory effects" (p. 6).

When learners use their senses in touching objects, tracing shapes, drawing and responding to visual images, hearing sounds, and moving their bodies, they embody particular individual histories in relation to hearing particular sounds, images, tastes, and smells. What this might mean for teachers is a deepened awareness of the role of the senses in the everyday life of the classroom and a sensitivity as to how the senses as repositories of history, culture, and memory can be better used and more valued.

A few years ago, I had a postgraduate student from Lesotho who spent his childhood with his father, a migrant miner living in the single-sex male hostels on the mines on the Witwatersrand. He was taught the ritualized dances and songs the Lesotho miners performed as part of the cultural life of Lesotho migrants living in this context. When Keke performed these dances and songs for our Honors class as part of the literacy history performance course, most black members of the audience spontaneously responded vocally to these sounds as part of a ritualistic call and response that is expected when these particular songs and dances are performed. What was evident from the audience's response to the student's songs and dances is the extent to which black members of the audience embodied a history of particular sounds, songs, and dances, which, when evoked in this way, elicited a history: a memory, both visually (in terms of seeing Keke sing and dance in a particular style) and in sound that, in turn, produced from the audience a ritualistic vocal response full of force, pleasure, and solidarity.

MEANING MAKING IS SEMIOTIC

Semiotics is the general study of the variety of means used in human cultures to make meaning. In the making of meaning, human beings produce multiple signs in different forms. A sign is a combination of signifier and signified, a combination of meaning and form. Social semiotics is fundamentally concerned with the processes, effects, and practices of human semiosis within the social world, placing the human being as an active agent at the center of semiotic activity; it is human beings who have the capacity and will to negotiate their interests and change their social reality. A social semiotic theory is based on a theory of a motivated relationship between the signifier and the signified – in making meaning, human beings make choices from an array of different possibilities, and each choice is signifying of the interests of its maker (Kress, 1993).

Assumption 3: Meaning making is multimodal

One of the foundational issues in a theory of multimodality is that communication is structured through modes. A mode is defined as a fully semiotically articulated means of representation and communication: The visual, gestural, speech, writing, and sound are all modes through or in which representation occurs. A theory of multimodality is concerned with the properties, uses, and effects of different modes in different contexts as well as how modes are connected to one another and work together to make meaning. All texts are multimodal, although one mode can dominate in a communicational ensemble. A mode has materiality that refers to anything available in the world – the stuff – that can be worked on or in culture to make meaning. Modes carry memory, history, and affect. Each human being has a history in relation to how he or she has used modes in the past. These histories become part of the fabric of representational resources that individuals use in working with different modes. For example, if a person has had a negative association with talk or writing, this affects how the person engages with these modes. Relations to modes are fluid, however, and subject to change.

The focus on modes as the means through which representation occurs distinguishes this theory from mainstream language and literacy theories, which mark the linguistic as the central means through which representation occurs. The theory of multimodal communication marks a paradigm shift in language pedagogy from language, to mode, to exploring what modes are and how they can be used to maximize learning and assessment in ways that are equitable and beneficial to learners.

The making of meaning thus involves the use of several semiotic modes as resources, all working in conjunction to create particular communicative effects. Each semiotic mode has its own grammar and social languages – its own particular patterns that give it its coherence and cohesion in specific contexts. For example, the use of body gestures as a semiotic mode works to produce certain communicative effects, but the repertoire of gestures that the individual draws on might shift as he or she shifts social occasions. A good example from the South African context is the use of eye contact. For many black South Africans, not making eye contact shows respect for the person you are communicating with. For many white people, making eye contact shows respect and not making eye contact shows disrespect. How individuals navigate the use of eye contact as a gesture of respect or disrespect in diverse social settings is a question of power and context in the same way that language users shift their use of particular language practices across settings.

Local classroom-based research on multimodal communication has focused on the relations between modes of representation and the different takes each mode produces on the same subject (Archer, 1999; Beynon, 1999; Emanuel, 2001; Stein, 1999; Thesen, 1999). These studies show that learners inhabit different modes differently to produce different narratives and social identities in each mode. Emanuel worked in a convent and a remedial school to investigate how learners used the linguistic, visual, and performative modes to conceptualize their futures and their lives postschool. Learners were asked to write a response to the question, What do you want to do when you leave school? They were given disposable cameras to take a series of photographs that would address this question visually and to role-play a class reunion for the year 2010. In looking for similarities and differences in their use of different modes, learners at the remedial high school felt there were no differences, that their photographs and writing all tied in together. Learners at the convent felt that the photography had given them opportunities to extend their abilities and opportunities to communicate. In an analysis of the semiotic differences between the different modes of representation, Emanuel shows how learners provided different and sometimes contradictory responses across the different modes at the level of content. For example, in the case of a boy who wrote that his future desire was to "do art," his photographs were all of airbrush paintings of dolphins and whales. He used the visual mode to provide the more detailed, personal information about his interest in art, which was absent in the written mode, thus using different modes to express different social identities. In another example, a teenage girl used writing extensively to communicate her desire to be a pediatrician and work with HIV babies. Her photographs showed her embracing an HIV baby and changing her diaper. She associated the combination of using writing and taking photographs as a way to "know myself better." When asked how the use of different modes helped her with this knowing she said:

> I would like to become a doctor, but, you know, the photograph with that child, I was like very close to it, you know, it wasn't like I'm a doctor at that stage, but, um, holding the child, it was as if it's mine, or something, you know... [the photograph captured] the relationship between the doctor and the patient... the relationship that I have with that child. (Emanuel, 2001, p. 156)

For this teenage girl, she prefers to use the photograph as a form of bearing witness to her sensory appropriation of the child "as if it's mine." We develop different dispositions toward modes, but these dispositions are not fixed, and teachers can play a central role in their development.

Assumption 4: Meaning making is interested action

The notion of *interested action* is a key concept in Kress' (1993, 1997) framework for a theory of semiosis. Every sign produced is a representation of the sign maker's interest and this interest is a complex combination of the demands of the particular social occasion in which the text is being produced (including the interrelationship between genre, language, power relations, and contextual constraints of production) and the social, cultural, and historical characteristics of the individual maker of signs. Interests are personal, cultural, aesthetic, psychological, and political. They are entwined in relations of power and are often contradictory and hidden. In the making of meaning, the sign maker selects what she or he sees as the criterial aspect of the object that is being represented and this selection is made according to interests. The use of the term interested *action* in social semiotics is significant: Meaning making is an action in which human beings act out a fundamental aspect of humanness – their agency. In emphasizing agency in the processes of representation, Kress asserts that human beings have freedom to act, resist, and change their conditions of existence and participate in social transformation.

Assumption 5: Language is limited

The history of South Africa is a history of pain and violation. The effects of centuries of colonialism, apartheid, and human rights violations have penetrated the lives of every South African. We are all marked in different ways by this history. Since the first democratic elections in 1994, the people of South Africa have sought to rebuild this society based on principles of human rights and dignity. I stated earlier that I think that in the present historical moment, productive diversity can be realized through (at least) two processes: (a) an engagement with incoherence and contradiction, and (b) an acknowledgment of people's histories and loss in relation to the pain of the past.

The question of acknowledgment of people's histories and loss in relation to the pain of the past is an issue which South Africa as a new nation has put firmly into the national debate through the Truth and Reconciliation Commission (TRC). The TRC constructed itself as a public forum for breaking the silence around the past and giving victims of apartheid a voice in order to recount their experiences of harm and suffering. Through processes of amnesty and forgiveness, the TRC hoped to bring about national reconciliation and healing. There are many areas of social suffering in South Africa in which people choose to be silent rather than to speak. Many of these areas concern women and women's choices in relation to the recounting of experiences of harm, violence, abuse, loss, and pain. Ross (2000) has written about the marked absence of women testifying at the TRC. When women did come forward to testify, their narratives were silent in relation to recounting their own experiences of harm and violation. Ross demonstrates the extent to which women mostly spoke about others, usually men, whereas men testified about the harms they personally had suffered. Tracing the patterns of narrative forms in women's testimonies, Ross argues against a too easy acceptance of the need for voice; rather, she focuses on the intersection between voice and silence, suggesting that both are the results of social processes that give different weights to particular forms of experience (p. 205).

Henderson (1999) describes the silences surrounding boys' and girls' sexuality in New Crossroads in Cape Town, where silence in relating sexual experience and desire takes on differing inflections in relation to boys and girls. The silence of young girls surrounding sexuality are the most powerful in relation to rape, where girls remain silent because speaking about this violation turns the young girl into an object of titillation and curiosity. Speaking out about rape produces more rape. In these contexts, language is dangerous and can lead to further violation.

I have chosen to focus on the relationship between words and silence because it is an issue which touches our lives and work as teachers of language and literacy in South Africa. I am not advocating that the language and literacy classroom is primarily constituted around the recovery of "narratives of violence," but any meaningful engagement with issues of diversity and humanity cannot avoid the lived experiences of the participants who want their voices, histories, and experiences acknowledged. These experiences are often of anger, pain, and loss. If teaching for diversity is based on different forms of acknowledgment and tolerance of difference, then what is the place of the relation between pain and language that a culture has evolved? I have argued elsewhere (Stein, 1999) that it is not only the choice of signifiers within the texts themselves that are motivated choices, but that the choice of mode, itself, can be motivated by the constraints and possibilities that exist and are maintained within dominant culture. Thus, the choice of mode for representation, particularly in areas of cultural and social taboo, is determined within particular formations of power. Language, itself, as a mode of communication is subject to constraints around what is unthinkable and unsayable within the context of existing cultural forms. In areas culturally demarcated by silence, other semiotic modes are recruited for the exploration of experience and feeling that language cannot express. The current HIV/AIDS pandemic in South Africa exemplifies the tensions and contestations around modes of representation in relation to talk and silence about the disease. In many black families, the fact that someone has HIV/AIDS or has died from AIDS is unsayable within existing cultural frames. The naming of the disease through language is unacceptable. However, an alternative semiotic code in the form of a hand gesture has emerged within some communities to communicate that a person has died of an AIDS-related illness. In the Western-dominated media, the silence around the disease is constructed as denial as it pushes for the breaking of silence around the disease. Thus, the choice of mode around how to acknowledge the presence of HIV/AIDS has become a site of a struggle, signifying the tensions around the constraints and possibilities in relation to what constitutes the unsayable within particular social and cultural domains.

Suffering, like pain, exists beyond language. That is why I am proposing pedagogies that recognize the limits of language and the impossibility of language to express the arc of human experience. Multimodal pedagogies recognize a continuum of language that moves from silence to an economy of words, leading participants into modes that can make their meanings most powerfully.

THE RIGHT TO SILENCE

Who has a right to speak? Who has a right to silence? Multimodal pedagogies recognize participants' rights to silence. In language and literacy classrooms where talk and words are the focus of study and the means through which communication is achieved, an unproblematic relation exists between talk and authentic communication. Articulateness, volubility, and general eagerness to talk are perceived as positive and desirable qualities in learners (Jaworski & Sachdev, 1998). Silence and reticence are constructed as detrimental to learning. There are many textures of silence. There is an oppressive, dominating silence that is the result of tension and fear, similar to Freire's (1968/1970) culture of silence in which more powerful societies silence other less powerful societies. Breaking out of such cultures of silence means coming to a critical understanding of one's conditions of oppression. Another understanding of silence is of lack or absence – the spaces between talk that have no function. In multimodal pedagogies, silence as a mode of communication has the materiality of sound without volume; it has rhythm and variation. It is a mode that is participatory, affirmative, and productive rather than oppositional and resistant. Using silence in pedagogy is not to disadvantage any group. This is an inclusive silence, rather than excluding or threatening, allowing for a positivity and presence of being. This silence acknowledges learners as subjects of integrity who may want teachers to "hear" that there are things which are unspeakable, which cannot be said.

Valuing and acknowledging silence can be a dangerous feature of pedagogy that, if misunderstood, can foster oppression and marginalize the already marginalized and silenced. The kind of silence I am advocating here respects human beings' rights to silence in the context of the power exercised by teachers in placing learners under obligation to speak. In this sense, learners can be offered a choice of silence in the same vein as a choice to speak. What is being proposed is an ethics of pedagogy in relation to human beings' rights to dignity and choice in relation to language within the context of the language and literacy classroom.

Assumption 6: Meaning making is transformation, creativity, and design

This theory challenges theories of representation that conceptualize meaning making as transmission, reproduction, or personal interpretation. Introducing the concept of "designs of meaning," the New London Group (1996) recognizes how, in the activity of redesigning, the sign maker changes the available design and this action is transformative: it transforms both the object that is the focus of the redesigning *and the designer*. Thus, the act of redesigning is an act of creativity that effects change in the materiality of objects and the subjectivity of individuals.

A semiotic theory that does not have an account of change at its core is inadequate to account for the ways in which the new information technologies are changing the communication landscape. The act of designing is inseparable from cultural and social practices. Each individual has a particular representational history that includes the specific encounters and practices in meaning making that the individual has been exposed to in countless ways in the social world. In designing meaning, people draw on these representational histories in conjunction with what stuff is available to them in that moment of history. Through this process of designing, culture is both sustained and transformed.

These relations between culture, transformation, and design can be illustrated with reference to an early years literacy research project in multimodality, creativity, and story that was carried out recently in a local primary school on the West Rand of Johannesburg.[2] The school serves children from poor families living in informal settlements on the outskirts of Johannesburg. The children, aged between seven and nine, are multilingual, speaking at least Zulu or Sotho as their primary language, plus English and another South African language. The aim of the project was to work with Grade 1 and Grade 2 teachers of literacy and language in an attempt to generate what became known as "fresh stories" (i.e., original stories) as distinct from traditional folkloric stories which are part of the oral cultural heritage of many South African children. The pedagogic focus of the project was to work with the children across different modes of communication in a sequenced, scaffolded set of steps that began with the visual mode and ended with writing in any language they chose. The first stage was to work visually to construct a cast of characters based on real people from the children's homes, streets, and communities. This was done through asking each child to choose someone they came across regularly in their neighborhoods – for example, soccer players, spaza shop owners (street hawkers), sangomas (traditional healers) – and to draw this character. The children were then shown in class how to make papier mâché figures of these characters. The idea was that these figures would form the basis of the play-making and storytelling process in which the children could play with these figures and invent fresh narratives around them. The teachers, who had never worked with papier mâché before, made a flour and newspaper mixture which turned into a kind of porridge, and the figures "turned into a puddle" as the children put it. The children then told their teachers that they would make their own figures at home and bring them to school. Within a few days, the children had brought in an extraordinary collection of handmade dolls, sculptures, and figures that had been constructed from various forms of waste material: plastic bags in different colors, Coke bottles filled with stones and sand, pieces of dishcloth, scraps of materials, cardboard, paper, buttons, wire, and stockings.

On closer examination, many of these dolls and figures were transformed traditional objects where the children had drawn on materials and designs that are part of the African fertility doll making culture. These fertility dolls, as they have come to be called in the literature, are usually small, anthropomorphic figures fabricated by women for young girls and women. Such dolls have specific cultural, symbolic, and identity functions in different regions relating to women's fertility and marriage

Figure 6.1 Traditional child-doll figures (left, center) made from grasses, glass beads, leather, and stuffing. Child-doll figure made by child (right) using a plastic bottle, stockings, stones, twigs, and soft cloth.

rituals. A common use of such dolls is in the adolescent initiation ceremonies for young girls, and they are still used today in many rural villages in South Africa. What was so interesting about the children's doll-like figures, however, is how they had at their disposal (through their families, histories, and available people in the community) a range of representational resources for constructing these figures (the available designs) within an urban informal settlement and how they had redesigned these figures to suit their own needs (to make characters for a story to be told at school). These textual products illustrate the hybridity and fluidity of contemporary urban cultural life and the degree to which cultural and generic transformation has taken place at multiple levels including materials, purpose, design, structure, and context. It is traditionally women who make such dolls, but in this project, boys participated in the making of their own dolls. The traditional boundaries around what constitutes fertility dolls within ethnic and gender classifications have collapsed and what we witness in this process is the redesigning of the traditional (in all its multiplicity of forms) and the transformation into contemporary dolls using available contextual materials. Examples of Southern African traditional child-doll figures and a doll made by a child in the 'fresh stories' project are shown in Figure 6.1. The children's child-doll figures illustrate the extent to which individuals have many layers of representational resources available to them, not only from one culture, but from many cultures. This process of remaking is not reproductive, but innovative and transformative, extending the range of doll-making culture and of the childrens' subjectivities. By choosing to take agency when they realized that their teachers' designs were not working, the children have shown themselves to be active and creative transformers of culture, asserting their understanding of the historical–cultural world in and with which they live.

Multimodal pedagogies and assessment practices

We choose the most apt forms for our meanings, but what happens if those apt forms are not allowed, made invisible, or excluded from our realms of possibility? I have argued elsewhere (Norton & Stein, 2001) that in post-apartheid South Africa, the Constitution and the ANC educational policy frameworks (embodied in Curriculum 2005) promote fundamental principles of antiracism, antisexism, democracy, and redress. Such principles are inseparable from the promotion of equity and justice in assessment and pedagogical practices. If students live within communities and cultural contexts that value spoken language, performance, dance, craft, and music more than writing, then how can the worldview of the school integrate these multiple modes of representation to give students the best opportunities to demonstrate their abilities? Are students not succeeding because they do not share the worldview of their assessors or because they do not have the potential to succeed? I have argued so far that the key issues for language and literacy teachers are issues of representation and that written representation in English is the most privileged mode. I am not suggesting that writing is not important; however, in many of the research projects described above, the only work that would have counted for assessment would have been the written stories as the outcome of the creative work that preceded it.

I argue that multimodal pedagogies have the possibility of broadening the base of representation in classrooms. In other words, multimodal forms of communication in classrooms can constitute a more representative base for representation. Multimodal pedagogies, with their focus on multiple modes of representation, have the potential to change the nature of the language and literacy class through privileging modes of communication other than spoken and written language; however, such pedagogies only have value if they form an integral part of assessment practices in which each mode is accorded a specific value and the sociocultural diversity of students' local knowledges and modes of representation is valued and privileged in forms of productive diversity.

Conclusion

The political, cultural, and social history of South Africa has been characterized by fracturing, discontinuity, and diversity. The violence and pain of the past seeps into the present. It makes its way into our language and literacy classes through how we choose to act, speak, or remain silent. In this period of profound social change and transformation, critical pedagogies need to take into account not only what students are saying, thinking, and feeling in classrooms, but how they are doing this: in other words, the range of possibilities of representation that are open to these same students for representing their meanings. I have argued that the choice of mode for representation is neither neutral nor benign but inflected with the relations between culture, power, and language that particular communities and institutions have evolved. The educational implications of this claim involve developing pedagogies that provide access to those groups or individuals who wish to represent their meanings and understandings through their preferred modes of communication, which may include, or go beyond, language. Multimodal pedagogies provide a starting point for such possibilities.

Acknowledgments

Grateful thanks to University of the Witwatersrand Human and Social Sciences Research Council, Lynne Slonimsky, and Patti Henderson for their help with this article.

Notes

1. I am grateful to Gerard Bester, who works in African and Western contemporary dance groups, for this explanation.
2. The project at Olifantsvlei Primary School was conducted by two Grade 1 and 2 teachers, Ntsoaki Senja and Tshidi Mamabolo, in collaboration with Thandiwe Mkhabela.

References

Archer, A. (1999). *Curriculum development through a social semiotic analysis of student poster productions: Visual literacy in engineering.* Unpublished manuscript, University of Cape Town, South Africa.

Beynon, A. (in press). Tinker, tailor, teacher, text . . . : Using a multiliteracies approach to remediate reading. In M. Hawkins (Ed.), *Social-cultural approaches to language learning, teaching and teacher-education.* Clevedon, England: Multilingual Matters.

Butler, J. (1990). *Gender trouble: Feminism and the subversion of identity.* London: Routledge.

Cope, B., & Kalantzis, M. (2000). (Eds.). *Multiliteracies: Literacy learning and the design of social futures.* New York: Routledge.

Emanuel, L. (2001). *A multiliteracies project: Designing enterprising futures.* Unpublished master's research report, University of the Witwatersrand, Johannesburg, South Africa.

Freire, P. (1970). *Pedagogy of the oppressed* (M. B. Ramos, Trans.). New York: Continuum Books. (Original work published 1968.)

Grosz, E. (1994). *Volatile bodies: Toward a corporeal feminism.* Indianapolis: Indiana University Press.

Henderson, P. (1999). *Living with fragility: Children in New Crossroads.* Unpublished doctoral dissertation, University of Cape Town, South Africa.

Heugh, K. (2002). The case against bilingual and multilingual education in South Africa: Laying bare the myths. *Perspectives in Education, 20*(1), 171–96.

Hodge, R., & Kress, G. (1988). *Social semiotics.* Cambridge, England: Polity Press.

Hofmeyr, I. (1993). *"We spend our years as a tale that is told": Oral historical narrative in a South African chiefdom.* Johannesburg, South Africa: Witwatersrand University Press.

Jaworski, A., & Sachdev, I. (1998). Beliefs about silence in the classroom. *Language in Education, 12*(4), 273–92.

Kapp, R. (2000). "With English you can go everywhere": An analysis of the role and status of English at a former DET school. *Journal of Education, 25,* 227–59.

Kress, G. (1993). Against arbitrariness: The social production of the sign as a foundational issue in critical discourse analysis. *Discourse and Society, 4*(2), 169–93.

Kress, G. (1997). *Before writing: Rethinking paths into literacy.* London: Routledge.

Kress, G. (2000a). Design and transformation: New theories of meaning. In B. Cope & M. Kalantzis (Eds.), *Multiliteracies: Literacy learning and the design of social futures* (pp. 153–61). New York: Routledge.

Kress, G. (2000b). The Futures of Literacy. *The RaPAL [Research and Practice in Adult Literacy] Bulletin, 42.*

Kress, G. (2000c). Multimodality. In B. Cope & M. Kalantzis (Eds.), *Multiliteracies: Literacy learning and the design of social futures* (pp. 182–202). New York: Routledge.

Kress, G., Jewitt, C., Ogborn, J., & Tsatsarelis, C. (2001). *Multimodal teaching and learning: The rhetorics of the science classroom.* New York: Continuum.

Kress, G., & Van Leeuwen, T. (1996). *Reading images: The grammar of visual design.* New York: Routledge.

Kress, G., & Van Leeuwen, T. (2001). *Multimodal discourse: The modes and media of contemporary communication.* London: Arnold.

Nekwhevha, F. (2000). Education transformation and the African renaissance in a globalising world. *Journal of Education, 25,* 19–48.

New London Group (1996). A pedagogy of multiliteracies: Designing social futures. *Harvard Educational Review, 66*(1), 60–90.

Norton, B., & Stein, P. (2001). Why the "Monkeys Passage" bombed: Tests, genres and teaching. In S. W. Beck & L. N. Olah (Eds.), *Perspectives on language and literacy: Beyond the here and now* (pp. 419–34). Harvard Educational Review Reprint Series, No. 35. Cambridge, MA: President and Fellows of Harvard College.

Pan South African Language Board (PanSALB). (1999). PanSALB's position on the promotion of multilingualism in South Africa: A draft discussion document. *Government Gazette* (No. 20098).

Phelan, P. (1993). *Unmarked: The politics of performance.* New York: Routledge.

Plato. (1952). *Phaedrus* (R. Hackforth, Trans.). Cambridge, England: Cambridge University Press.

Ross, F. C. (2000). *Bearing witness: Women and the South African Truth and Reconciliation Commission.* Unpublished doctoral dissertation, University of Cape Town, South Africa.

Scheub, H. (1975). *The Xhosa Ntsomi.* London: Oxford University Press.

Seremetakis, C. N. (1994). The memory of the senses, Part 1: Marks of the transitory. In C. N. Seremetakis (Ed.), *The senses still: Perception and memory as material culture in modernity* (pp. 1–19). Chicago: University of Chicago Press.

Stein, P. (1999). Drawing the unsayable: Cannibals, sexuality, and multimodality in a Johannesburg classroom. *Perspectives in Education, 18*(2), 61–82.

Thesen, L. (1999). *Access to academic literacy through multimodal text: Rifts in the semiotic landscape?* Retrieved October 1, 2000, from http://education.leeds.ac.uk/AILA/Symposiumthesen.

7 *Subversive identities, pedagogical safe houses, and critical learning*

Suresh Canagarajah

The practice of reserving something of oneself from the clutch of an institution . . . this recalcitrance is not an incidental mechanism of defence but rather an essential constitution of the self. (Goffman, 1961, p. 319)

A Century of English Education, written by John V. Chelliah (1922), a local teacher in my hometown while the British were still governing Sri Lanka, intends to glorify the pedagogy and policies of the colonial educational system. The teaching approaches of the missionaries are presented as very effective in creating a new breed of Sri Lankan Tamils who mastered the knowledge and language of the rulers. In these boarding schools, the missionaries wanted to isolate the students from the vernacular influences of their homes and mold them according to their new set of values. Occasionally, we see references to some unruly students in Chelliah's book. Such students have been dismissed from the school for escaping from the boarding at nights to attend Hindu temple festivals, maintaining secret miniature shrines for Hindu deities in their cupboards or desks, and surreptitiously practicing what are called heathen songs and dances. Though the author is ashamed by the hypocrisy in this behavior and is happy that such acts met with decisive punishment, it is possible to guess that many more of these acts went undiscovered. Those who read Chelliah's book today may have a new sense of respect for these students. It appears that they were trying to negotiate a conflict that was common to other colonized subjects. How could they learn English while also maintaining membership with their vernacular community and culture? While some were obviously prepared to join the new English-speaking community formed by the missionaries and British settlers, these students didn't want to lose their local identities. Perhaps they struggled for a way in which they could maintain dual identities – learning English while also remaining Hindus. Since such hybridity was not permitted in the missionary educational enterprise, they had to resort to indirect and surreptitious ways of living out their unusual identities.

We know today that challenges of such nature are widespread in language learning and that they are, in fact, integral to the language acquisition process. What motivates the learning of a language is the construction of the identities we desire and the communities we want to join in order to engage in communication and social life. How we resolve these conflicts is at the heart of becoming a successful language learner. I am among those who welcome what has come to be known as the *social turn* in language acquisition studies and literacy instruction. From focusing on the abstract grammar system and treating learners as a bundle of psychological reflexes, we have begun to treat learners as complex social beings. Our interest now is to consider how learners negotiate competing subject positions in conflicting discourse communities and how these struggles shape their practices of language learning.

In order to pursue such an orientation profitably, we have had to redefine our understanding of the human subject. We have borrowed constructs from disciplines as diverse as philosophy, rhetoric, literary criticism, and the social sciences. We have adopted different theoretical positions ranging across feminist scholarship, language socialization studies, Bakhtinian semiotics, and Foucauldian poststructuralism. These schools have helped us understand identities as multiple, conflictual, negotiated, and evolving. We have traveled far from the traditional assumption in language studies that identities are static, unitary, discrete, and given.[1] To elaborate, our new realizations are as follows:

1. The Self is shaped considerably by language and discourses.
2. The Self is composed of multiple subjectivities deriving from the heterogeneous codes, registers, and discourses that are found in society.
3. These subjectivities enjoy unequal status and power, deriving differential positioning in socioeconomic terms.
4. Because of these inequalities, there is conflict within and between subjects.
5. In order to find coherence and empowerment, the subject has to negotiate these competing identities and subject positions.
6. Selves are not immutable or innate; they are reconstructed and reconstituted in relation to the changing discursive and material contexts.

Despite the fascinating theoretical advances we have made in this inquiry, I sense a dilemma for researchers when they study learner identities in classroom contexts. Though they are theoretically attuned to representing the resistance of students to unfavorable identities imposed on them, they don't have any evidence for such complex acts of negotiation in their corpi. In many cases, they find that students appear to take on the unitary identities (shaped by notions of deficiency, inferiority, and disadvantage) conferred on them by the dominant discourses. With some disappointment, the researchers promise to look further into their data or continue to do more research on the classrooms and subjects to address ways in which students critically negotiate identities. The purpose of this chapter is to identify some hidden spaces in the classroom where students negotiate identities with positive consequences for their literacy development.

The pedagogical dilemma

Let's look at some cutting edge research that is being conducted currently on classroom identities to consider how students fare in resolving the conflicts they face in language learning. Sandra McKay and Keith Chick (2000) talk about the contradictions between the multicultural discourse of the African National Congress (ANC) and the monolingual policies of schools in their paper, "Positioning Learners in Post Apartheid South African Schools: A Case Study of Selected Multicultural Durban Schools." Examining the power of two dominant discourses – *English-only* and *Declining Standards* – they show how speaking Zulu is associated with being disruptive, deficient, and rude in the school context. Also, not adopting the "Christian middle class ethos" (constituting such values as involvement, work ethic, honesty, and charity) is negatively associated with monolingual working or underclass behavior. The students gradually begin to align themselves with the favored discourses and identities, distancing themselves from the indigenous discourses of the lower classes in their classroom interactions with the teacher.

Though the narrative stops there, we can guess that there is more to the experience of the students than that. How do the students negotiate the conflicts between the multiculturalist policy of the state and the monolingualist policy of the school? Surely, they can sense some of these tensions in their everyday social and educational life? How do they cope with the dual life of participating in the vernacular life *outside* the classroom and the English-based Christian ethos *inside*? We need some way of exploring these less conspicuous issues of student consciousness and agency in our research. McKay and Chick (2000) do sense the need to discover evidence of student resistance and promise to go back to the research site to obtain further data. But the data we need may not be more of the same; we may need data from different sites of student life.

To take another study, consider Eva Lam's (2000) presentation of the Chinese high school student, Almon, in her paper, "L2 Literacy and the Design of the Self: A Case Study of a Teenager Writing on the Internet." The student is frustrated by the negative identities provided for his "broken English" in the classroom. But on the Internet, Almon engages in a variety of discourses – pop culture, religion, therapy, cyberculture – all in English with a range of native and nonnative speakers. He can sense a visible improvement in his proficiency in the language as he engages effectively in these communicative interactions. His ability to distance himself from the language in computer-mediated communication perhaps enables him to be expressive in biographical and narrative writing on his homepage. He is definitely empowered by the new identities he enjoys on the Internet as a friend, knowledgeable fan of Japanese pop music, founder of the fan group for pop singer Ryoko, and owner of an internationally popular homepage. Lam (2000) brings out the ironies effectively when she concludes:

> Whereas classroom English appeared to contribute to Almon's sense of exclusion or marginalization (his inability to speak like a native) which paradoxically contradicts the school's mandate to prepare students for the workplace and civic involvement, the English he controlled on the Internet enabled him to develop a sense of belonging and connectedness to a global English-speaking community. (p. 476)

We are left with the question, What is it about the school that prevents students from negotiating favorable identities? Why is it that Almon has to enjoy these empowering identities outside the walls of the classroom? Are there other sites in the classroom where Almon may practice some of the alternate identities he enjoys or negotiate the conflicts in his selfhood?

To consider a final example that brings me close to the niche I am creating for my study, take Kelleen Toohey's (2000a) "Assigning Marginality: The Case of an 'ESL/Learning Disabled' Student." She discusses how an Indian student, Surjeet, gradually acts according to the learning disabled status assigned by her elementary school teachers in Canada. Ironically, Surjeet fits neither the ESL (English as a second language) nor the learning disabled status. She speaks English at home with her primarily Punjabi-speaking parents and siblings. She displays some interesting skills of social and linguistic negotiation in her off-task interactions in the classroom. But the very anxiety of trying to avoid the learning disabled status influences her to falter. In a case of self-fulfilling prophecy, her teachers' ascription of the learning disabled identity gets solidified as the school years progress and Surjeet gets loaded with more remedial courses. But, here again, we sense that there is more to the story than what we see in the classroom interactions. How does Surjeet explain to herself the contradictions between her life at home and the classroom, between interactions with her teacher and with her friends? How does she negotiate the conflicting roles and identities she plays out in these different settings? In a more extensive discussion of this study in a different context, Toohey (2000b) observes that there is more student agency and resistance displayed in off-task activities away from the teacher. My purpose here is to explore such off-task sites to understand their role in the construction of more complex student identities and the development of critical learning practices.

The politics of safe houses

To understand why students may seek alternate sites in the classroom to construct more complex identities, we have to understand the school as a power-laden site. Students may be so intimidated by the authority and power of the teacher that they desist from presenting identities that are not institutionally desired. Also, examinations, tracking, and other institutional reward systems place subtle restrictions on the extent to which students can resist the subjectivities desired in the school. In interacting with students from a variety of backgrounds (some from more privileged backgrounds), students are under peer pressure to conform to the dominant discourses and identities preferred in the classroom. These are but some of the mechanisms through which the school functions as a medium of ideological and social reproduction. Ironically, even when students flagrantly oppose the identities desired in the classroom, the school has a way of defining them as failures and assigning them socially marginalized positions. Linda Harklau (2000) shows how the immigrant students who are continually being assigned stereotypical "ESL student" identities (as culturally alien and socially handicapped) resist these roles in favor of more complex subjectivities as they become gradually socialized into the new community in the United States. But the more they oppose, the more they earn the displeasure of their teachers and become failures. In the face of power of this nature, students are caught between two bad alternatives – that is, to conform or to fail.

Though students are not always blind to the hidden curriculum in the classroom (Almon, for example, is painfully aware of the negative identities ascribed to him), they don't have the resources or space to negotiate these conflicts favorably. More important, they also need a safe way of adopting alternate identities without being penalized for (what is perceived as) deviant behavior. I wish to present some hidden spaces in the classroom that provide a safe site for students to negotiate identities more critically. It is my contention that if classroom ethnographers and other researchers can go beyond the surface-level interactions between teachers and students (especially in on-task encounters), they can discern the agency of the students in managing the conflicts for their identity in more complex ways.

I call these sites *safe houses*, following Pratt's (1991) theorization of their role in the cultural contact of postcolonial societies. She defines safe houses as "social and intellectual spaces where groups can constitute themselves as horizontal, homogeneous, sovereign communities with high degrees of trust, shared understandings, and temporary protection from legacies of oppression" (p. 40). Though it is Pratt's definition (first introduced in a keynote address at the annual convention of the Modern Language Association) that has influenced recent academic discussions in fields such as composition, literature, and English, I have used the term in ESL contexts (see Canagarajah, 1999). The term is generally used as synonymous with underlife in institutional contexts (as in the sociological studies of Goffman, 1961, and Scott, 1990). I also see connections with studies in ESL, bilingualism, and literacy where researchers have seen students adopting discourses and behaviors that are not authorized or rewarded by teachers (see note 7 for a list of studies in this field).

Safe houses in the academy are, then, sites that are relatively free from surveillance, especially by authority figures, perhaps because these are considered unofficial, off-task, or extrapedagogical. Domains of time, as well as space, may serve as safe houses in educational institutions. The following is a list of spatiotemporal domains I have uncovered as safe houses in my research:

In the classroom: asides between students, passing of notes, small group interactions, peer activities, marginalia in textbooks and notebooks, transition from one teacher to another, before classes begin, after classes are officially over.

Outside the classroom: the canteen, library, dorms, playgrounds, and computer labs.

In cyberspace: e-mail, online discussions/chat.

There is a danger in describing safe houses in such a schematic and structured fashion. Students can make almost any site in the educational environment free of surveillance by colluding in constructing a culture of underlife behavior. They can develop gestures, signs, and symbols that can enable them to interact and communicate in their own terms right under their teacher's nose. In this sense, safe houses are somewhat fluid and mobile.

Before I offer some data on the ways students negotiate conflicting identities in safe houses, let me note the significance of such sites for minority students (who feature in my studies). It appears that minority communities have always collaboratively constructed sites of community underlife wherein they can celebrate suppressed identities and go further to develop subversive discourses that inspire resistance against their domination. In addition to Chelliah's (1922) book cited at the beginning of the chapter, there is further documentation from my own community in Sri Lanka during colonial times when locals adopted a double-faced behavior of pretending to be Christians outwardly, but maintaining a vigorous life as Hindus within the local community in in-group circles (see Wickramasuriya, 1976). They pretended to be Christians to qualify for better jobs and higher education from the British. This surreptitious behavior often led the colonial rulers to call my people lying, inscrutable, undependable, hypocritical, shifty, and cunning. But these are *the weapons of the weak* – to borrow the title of the book by James Scott (1985), who articulates the politics of this strategy through peasants in Southeast Asia. For the disempowered who realize the difficulties of challenging the might of dominant groups directly, these are simple acts in their everyday life for gaining a measure of control over their lives. The acts of stealing, foot dragging, cheating, and noncompliance are partial and safe ways of resisting the power of the master and gaining some relief in material terms for their survival. These are acts through which they also retain their dignity and develop hidden ideologies that explain the injustice of the situation and work out spiritual alternatives that give them hope. Over time, these communities develop a shared understanding of their oppression and ways of coping with the hostile environment. Even the jokes, parody, sarcasm, name calling, and veiled threats are disguised forms of resistance. There is an expanding body of ethnographic literature that shows that there is a well-developed tradition of underlife resistance in minority communities. In Asia, we know of lower caste communities using safe houses against upper caste communities, women against men, serfs against landowners.[2]

Here in North America, we now know that the African American community has a well-developed tradition of safe houses. Slaves had to adopt a double life – appearing to fulfill the expectations of the master, but sharing another level of social life with fellow slaves where they outsmarted the master – as a safe and sometimes the only way of regaining their humanity and dignity. There is an evolving ethnographic literature from slave society that reveals the underlife of the slaves (see Raboteau, 1978). Slave narratives give insight into the ways in which black people organized Sunday schools and literacy classes unknown to the master, where they developed theologies that condemned the injustice and promoted utopias of glorious afterlife for the slaves. Frederick Douglass' (1845) personal path to literacy had to involve surreptitious means – including bribing white kids, using the books of the master's children when the family was away, and cheating school-going kids to make them share their knowledge. Sociolinguist Thomas Kochman (1981) finds contemporary speech acts keeping alive the hidden forms of resistance from slave times. Ambivalent talk, speaking behind the back, or parodying, joking, and satirizing the talk of the dominant communities are an indirect form of opposition. Kochman calls them "fronting" (p. 125).

Apart from such anthropological precedents, there are also sociological explanations for why safe houses are important for all of us – whether from the minority or the dominant social groups – for identity construction. There is an interesting tradition in social psychology, stemming from Goffman's (1961) study of underlife behavior in what he calls "total institutions" (e.g., mental asylums, prisons). While the inmates conform to the restrictive selves demanded by the institution for the official eyes (primary adjustment), they take up a range of alternate practices and identities in the underlife to develop a more qualified or independent conformism (secondary adjustment). Goffman goes on to theorize that it is in the gaps and cracks of institutional life that we develop our independent orientations to identity, although we are expected to display the restrictive selves demanded in public life. My assumption is that all students may construct such safe houses in schools to develop their in-group culture and alternate identities, while minority communities have the additional advantage of drawing from traditions of underlife culture from their communities as they borrow historically well-tested strategies for negotiating conflictual identities.

Safe house styles of negotiation

My examples of the ways safe houses function in helping students negotiate identities come from two different pedagogical contexts that share some similarities – African American students learning academic writing in a southwestern university in the United States and Tamil students learning English for general academic purposes in Sri Lanka.[3] Unlike the Sri Lankan ESL students, the former are learning academic English as a second dialect and not as a second language. I am offering examples from communities that are distant from each other, partly to show how widespread these underlife practices are. In both cases, however, students perceived that their acquisition and use of the standard codes and discourses of academic English would involve taking on identities that were undesirable for them, would complicate their community consciousness or solidarity, and would lead to the denigration of their valued identities. They perceived the academy to be imposing unitary selves that didn't take account of the cultural complexity they brought with them. Still, they adopted the roles and identities demanded for academic success as they were motivated by social mobility and economic well-being. In the safe houses, however, they displayed a more critical negotiation of identities that gave evidence of their agency. I have discussed elsewhere the challenges and conflicts experienced by these students (see Canagarajah, 1993, 1997); here, I'll focus on the ways safe houses helped them construct alternate identities and practice critical literacy.

To begin with, safe houses provided a space where students could adopt more hybrid identities deriving from the heterogeneous discourses they were competent in. These identities could not be displayed in the classroom because the school demanded standardized English codes and discourses. In the Sri Lankan university, there was frequent code-switching in the student underlife interactions. When English-only was the norm for interactions in the ESL class, such mixing of languages in the safe houses is subversive. Note, in the interaction below, how two students (S1, S2) switch to Tamil to unpack the meaning of the comprehension passage being read aloud by the teacher (T) standing at the front of the class:

Text 1:

T: (reads) . . . it is our duty to look after trees and replace them through reforestation. (To class) Reforestation means replanting trees and vegetation. (Continues reading)
S1: Reforestation *enRaal ennappaa?* [What does "reforestation" mean?]
S2: *kaaTaakkam. umakku teriyaataa?* Social science-*ilai paTiccam.* [Don't you know reforestation? We studied about that in Social Science.]
S1: *enna? kaTukalai aLikkiratoo?* [What? Destroying forests?]
S2: *illai appaa. marankalai tirumpa naTukiratu.* [No, man, replanting trees.]

By speaking softly to each other in a private aside, the students are defining this as a safe house interaction. Their use of Tamil in this case enables them to share information from other courses and experiences outside the lesson to collaboratively define a difficult English word. Also this communicative practice is a representation of the bilingual and bicultural life these students live outside the classroom. Similarly, in the case of the African American students, they draw from both the vernacular and the mainstream codes they were proficient in as middle class subjects. Their e-mail and online chat discussions gave evidence of a wide range of speech acts from both traditions, that is, capping, sounding, insult routines, and narratives, interspersed with detached argumentation and textual interpretation. Whereas the public sites of the classroom adopted a narrower range of legitimized discourses and pressured students to adopt uniform identities, safe houses provided a space for the display of more complex discourses and mixed identities.

In fact, in many cases, students celebrated identities that had to be suppressed in the classroom. Some identities and discourses may be construed as deviant or dysfunctional in educational contexts. Consider the insult routine two African American boys, Donnie and Ray, are engaging in below in an e-mail exchange:

Text 2:

From: DONNIE JONES
To: *RAY WRIGHT*
Subject: *HIMSELF 8/09*
PUSSY ASS NIGGA'!!!

Text 3:

From: *RAY WRIGHT*
To: *DONNIE JONES*
Subject: *A PUNK NAMED DONNIE 8/09*
HOMEBOY YA' SLIPPIN. YOU DON'T KNOW WHAT TIME IT IS POPPIN'
THAT WACK BULLSH-T. IT'S TIME I PUT SOME HEAD OUT. DON'T PLAY ME SMALL MONIE!!!

Apart from the profanities and expletives used here, even vernacular speech events like insult routines have to be suppressed in the classroom. Since vernacular discourses are treated as rustic, unsophisticated, and sometimes uncouth by the social mainstream, students wouldn't want to earn these associations by flaunting vernacular speech acts in the public sites of the classroom. Similarly, the Sri Lankan students are engaged in discourses of cinema, Hindu chauvinism, and Tamil political nationalism. These discourses are associated with negative identities by the educated bilinguals in the local community. Tamil cinema is associated with romantic, emotional, and unrealistic approaches to life. The latter two discourses are associated with extremism, divisiveness, and violence; however, these discourses are popular and widely shared by members of the monolingual community. Given the divergent estimations of these discourses, it is understandable that students should seek a hidden space in the classroom to adopt such identities in their in-group.

In some cases, students adopted identities that were oppositional to the pedagogical agendas of the course and may be considered subversive to the objectives of schooling. Though both student groups made positive comments about the curriculum and pedagogy in surveys with the teacher-researcher, the safe houses give a different picture of their attitudes. In the e-mail exchange below, Andrew and Sonny are commenting on the writing assignment that the whole class is busily doing to earn a good final grade in the course:

Text 4:

From: *ANDREW HUBBARD*
To: *ANYBODY*
Subject: *THIS 8/19*
aaaaaaaaaaaahhhhhhhhhhhhhhhhhhhhh, ssssssssssssshhhhhhhhhhhhhhhhiiiiiiiiiittttt!

Text 5:

From: *SONNY TIPPENS*
To: *ANDREW HUBBARD*
Subject: *R) THIS 8/19*

ANDREW
it's AAAAAAAAAHHHHHHHHHHHHHHHHH
  shit!

Though these students ended up writing a fairly good essay and received good grades, it is clear from the e-mail that they hated the topic they wrote on. The textbooks of the Sri Lankan students had graffiti which insulted the teachers, the characters in the textbook, and sometimes the American publishers and authors of their ESL textbooks. Comments like this show that students do adopt a critical orientation to the assignments given to them, though outwardly they fulfill the requirements in order to score good grades. It is easy to guess that any direct criticism of the course would be associated by the teachers with a bad student image. Such images may jeopardize their chances of scoring good grades in the course. Therefore the good, obedient, and disciplined student image we get in the public sites is complicated by the identities in the safe houses.

Furthermore, students experimented with identities with a flexibility and freedom that they didn't experience in the public sites of the classroom. To some extent, they playfully adopted imagined identities that they found desirable or interesting for diverse reasons. In the e-mail exchange below, Sonny and Dexter use motifs from the world of rap music to posture "radical" identities of black militancy and community solidarity. They are using phrases and slogans popularized by the group Public Enemy as they construct these imagined identities for themselves:

Text 6:

From: *SONNY TIPPENS*
To: *DEXTER BOMAR*
Subject: *FIGHT THE POWER 8/10*
stay black, fight the power, support your people.
PEACE HO!

Text 7:

From: DEXTER BOMAR
To: *T.K.*
Subject: *THE BLACK MAN 8/10*
TO STRONG . . . TO BLACK . . . TO STRONG . . . TO BLACK . . .
FFFFF
F
FF
F
F IGHT THE POWER

These discourses would be associated with divisiveness, confrontationalism, and narrow-mindedness in the mainstream circle of the classroom. Although playful and imagined, we mustn't discount the possibility of these identities being inspired by the pressures of cultural reproduction and ideological conformism in the institutional context. At other times, students adopted academic roles playfully. In a peer critique, Donnie adopted the teacher's authoritative tone. Initially, he provided a very balanced and complex feedback on the paper of a colleague:

> Rhonda, this has the potential of being a good paper but it needs a lot of work. This is a research paper yet there isn't any research in the paper except for the interview. You are being too subjective in your writing. It is O.K. to be somewhat subjective but not too much. You are focused in on the subject well but you have seem to lost touch of your audience. Remember that they are social scientists and they require hard facts.

Then, finally, in the space given for "Other Comments," he dropped his mask and exposed his true feelings by saying: "Get real, this is a lousy paper." This very direct statement contrasted with the carefully worded and sensitive statements that preceded it. However, his play-acting was so convincing that one cannot help but admire him for having mastered the academic voice (featuring highly qualified comments, syllabic abstract words, complex syntax, and an authoritative tone).

These acts of identity are not educationally unhelpful. Donnie is getting some practice in the use of the academic register. This ability to style shift is an important communicative competence required in the contemporary world of fluid discourses and the mingling of social groups. The adoption of competing identities – vernacular and academic in this case – would also invite interesting comparisons and a reflexive analysis of these roles. These psychological and educational advantages are also evident from a series of marginal comments by Sri Lankan students in a beginning-level ESL textbook. One student has first written, "I love all of the girls peautiful in the Jaffna University." Under this comment, another has written in different ink, "Reader: I love you. Bleave me." Yet another student – presumably female – has written (in different ink and handwriting), "I do not love you because I do not believe you. You are terrible man." These students are playing at being lovers. They are engaging in a discourse that is usually taboo in local classrooms (coming from a sexually conservative society). These words and clauses have been picked up by the students, themselves, from outside the classroom. But they are being used creatively here as the two initial statements are combined by the third writer to form a complex sentence. This playfulness therefore leads to syntactic and vocabulary development in addition to the psychological benefit of vicariously living out distant (sometimes oppressive) roles and understanding the alien discourses undergirding these identities. Such practices can also encourage a reflexive awareness of the students' own statuses and roles in relation to the imagined identities they are often excluded from.

It should be clear from the examples above that students adopt identities that are more complex, interesting, independent, creative, and sometimes pedagogically oppositional than the ones they display in the public sites of the classroom. We can move further into the data to ask how they explain this dual life to themselves, why they adopt the strategy of safe house negotiations, and what implications these acts of negotiation may have for their larger educational and social life. A consideration along these lines shows that students can move beyond their conflicts to reflect critically on their challenges and construct their own explanations and strategies for dealing with them. We thus see in the safe houses the students' capacity for critical awareness and agency.

Students are aware of the relative benefits safe houses provide in the educational context. They find the public sites of the academy very oppressive and stultifying and desire the detachment provided by the safe houses. Consider the following discussion among some African American students in their online chat forum:

Text 8:

Rhonda: I FEEL A LOT OF PRESSURE HERE TO PERFORM WELL BECAUSE EVERYONE KNOW WHAT HAPPENS IF YOU DON'T. I DON'T THINK THEY SHOULD TREAT US LIKE STATISTICS. THEY PREACH INDIVIDUALITY, SO TREAT US AS INDIVIDUALS AND NOT COMPARE US TO OTHERS

Sonny: (. . .) like Donnie said, you can only be pushed so far on the same track. It seems as if we are all being taught to be exactly like the board of education of the state of (xxx).

Dexter: the univ. is trying to strip us of are identity, beliefs in order to make a world where it comforts them the most. (INT 8/15)[4]

It is clear that students sense the reproductive effects of education. They are clearly under pressure to conform and adopt identities they perceive to be desired by the educational institution. We can also sense the opposition they have for pedagogical identities. Safe houses provide enough detachment from these pressures for students to negotiate their identities in a manner that suits them.

What makes safe houses additionally attractive is that students have the space here to develop a relatively strong sense of solidarity and community against the impositions of the school. Though students lack this sense of solidarity at the beginning of the semester (and thus adopt only safe and conformist identities), they become more daring once trust is established in the safe houses. This supportive atmosphere is important for students to adopt identities that are uncomfortable in the company of those who are alien or antagonistic. This solidarity is also important for students to withstand the onslaughts of dominant discourses and ideologies. So we find messages like the following where students cheer each other up with reminders of their past achievements:

Text 9:

From: *SONNY TIPPENS*
To: *N.O.S. & H.O.S.*[5]
Subject: *SCHOLARSHIP 8/03*
Hey! We're on scholarship!!!

Some messages advise students to stay united as they struggle against the common challenges they face for their identity and values:

Text 10:

From: *SONNY TIPPENS*
To: *ALL*
Subject: *IS BERN GERT*[6] *8/19*
. . . to the PREVIEW posse; stay close to each other.
we are all gonna need help to get through, and i'd like to
say all of us minorities make it. do it for your family,
community, and culture, but most of all do it for yourself.
. . . good luck everyone
and remember, you on scholarshirp!!!!!
Sonny Tippens (T.K!)

Others send reminders to their colleagues not to lose touch with their roots. I call these the "stay black" messages, which pop up in the most unexpected places during discussions and e-mails:

Text 11:

From: *RHONDA NICHOLAS*
To: *ALL*
Subject: *FIGHT THE POWER 8/19*
Hello everyone, this is a reminder to everyone:
"STAY BLACK"
I LOVE YA'LL,
KELLI(MOOKY)

Indirectly, these messages show the pressure students feel to adopt identities they don't desire. Such messages show the need for safe houses for students to collaboratively work out ways of coping with the challenges they face in the academy. Once inside the safe houses, the students adopt many strategies and activities to negotiate identities.

Students do not adopt alternate identities unthinkingly. The safe houses provide a site for reflecting on the differences between divergent discourses and subjectivities. This comparative and critical reflection is important for students to negotiate identities effectively. Such discussions also show evidence of a metadiscursive awareness among students on the challenges for their identity. In the case of African American students, we see them talking in their safe house encounters about the differences between academic discourse and their home discourses and the implications for their identity:

Text 12:

Andrew: The scientist, at the start of his paper, announces his problem. Next, the author procedes to spew data in stuffy scienitific terms that only a well educated or well read scientist would know. The pattern is the same throughout the paper; state scientific data and interpet it for your own argument. Usually, half-way through the paper, the alert reader can predict the conclusion. Anything that is so predictable is not enjoyable to learn from. (INT 8/15)

Though students perform this kind of writing in class activities, here they adopt a critical position toward this discourse. They also discuss often the reasons for their dislike of this discourse:

Text 13:

Sonny: i dont kno about the rest of the black world, but i do kno that i have alot of imagination and feelings, and that is how i write. i guess that is why i dont really like english classes, since you have to stay on topic, and a mind like mine likes to just write and include the topic, understand? (INT 8/15)

Comparisons of this sort show that students have a reflexive awareness of the competing identities and the choices they are left with.

There is evidence that the strategies students adopt to negotiate identities are also well-considered. They have their own reasons why safe houses are a good place to negotiate their conflicts. Students display metasocial awareness on the controversial strategy of compartmentalizing their identities, that is, adopting conformist identities in the public spaces and displaying subversive identities in safe houses:

Text 14:

Rhonda Nicholas: I really don't have much to say because I'm here and I know what it takes to make it. Things haven't changed and it's not likely that they will be soon, so instead of trying to fight the system, I'll just go along with it and perform as expected. It will make my college life a lot more peaceful and enjoyable. Imagine what kind of people and what kind of attitudes we would have if we went around holding grudges toward this university. Do you think they really care? They probably feel the fewer minorities, the better. (INT 8/17)

As minority students sense that their criticism and opposition will only lead to their failure in education, they see it necessary to adopt this dual life of identities. Sonny rationalizes their acts of "fronting" in the following way:

Text 15:

Sonny Tippens: . . . our experience at the university is what we make it, to a certain extent. We don't have to take in everything, and believe it. Just remember it, put it down as the correct answer, and go on with the good grade. Not everything that is heard has to be believed, just recalled for a good grade. (INT 8/17)

This strategy of dual selves is therefore consciously adopted. Students see that the safe houses provide a way in which they can fulfill the expectations of their teachers in order to earn a good grade while retaining their independence and detachment in the hidden spaces of safe houses.

All this shows that students are aware of the challenges facing them and have self-awareness of the need for and objectives of qualified conformity in certain contexts. We mustn't be misled by their outward conformity to think that students are simply passive and complacent. If we only had access to the in-group life and personal reasoning processes of the students, we would appreciate their logic for the need of this controversial approach for negotiating identity conflicts. With the data from the safe houses, we can say that the students are on top of the situation. They display agency in taking stock of the challenges facing them and in working out strategic ways of dealing with them. They have a way of explaining to themselves why they use safe houses to negotiate the conflicts for their identity.

Social and educational implications

Can keeping modes of critical learning to the safe houses and adopting conformist identities for on-task activities be of any educational value? Would this seemingly hypocritical approach be detrimental to the learning experience and social life of these minority students? We can first think of many indirect benefits for language awareness and literacy. An important consideration in critical literacy is that students should be encouraged to go beyond adopting the normative textual conventions or grammar structures in their writing practice. They should learn to negotiate the conventions and grammar to develop a text that favors independent and critical thinking. But students are often tempted by two evils: to either follow slavishly the established rules of writing in a genre or not grapple with the conventions at all so that they can enjoy a freedom of expression. As Foucault (1969/1972) argues, both extremes lead to forms of silencing. The former leads to the suppression of voice in favor of dominant textual structures, while the latter is idealistic in believing that voice is possible without following any conventions whatsoever. We have begun to appreciate now that voice is developed in the interstices of discourses and rules (see Foucault, 1969/1972). The detachment safe houses provide from both dominant academic discourses and the vernacular enables students to position themselves strategically for an independent and creative voice.

Furthermore, the retention of heterogeneous discourses and speech acts – thanks to safe houses that help students keep alive suppressed identities and discourses – helps in the development of multivocal literacies. All this is important at a time when we have come to appreciate that texts are not necessarily constructed in univocal discourses and uniform genres in postmodern practices of communication (see Warschauer, 2000). Texts may contain multiple discourses as long as they are given a creative wholeness by the writers to evoke their hybrid identities. The representation of diverse styles and codes within a single text doesn't necessarily lead to its incoherence. The text is getting redefined in the digital world where multiple texts may be embedded within the same text. There is therefore greater scope now for students to bring in alternate or nonacademic discourses – including the vernacular and even street speech – into academic writing. Safe houses provide important practice in negotiating the terms under which nonacademic discourses can be introduced in academic contexts.

The practice of moving between the safe houses and the public sites of the classroom also develops competencies necessary for crossing discourses and community boundaries. This movement between communicative sites and contexts develops important skills for literacy in contemporary society where students are called upon increasingly to shuttle between genres and discourses of diverse communities in order to be socially functional. Students gain practice in such important multilingual communicative strategies as code switching and style shifting through interactions in the divergent classroom sites. While on-task activities often restrict discourse to the ones officially sanctioned by the school, the safe houses develop competence in nonstandard discourses. Similarly, the ongoing comparison between the vernacular and the mainstream discourses in the relative safety of the underlife helps develop a metadiscursive awareness to engage in these boundary-crossing forms of communication.

In a more direct sense, the safe ways of communicating opposition, practicing suppressed discourses, and adopting controversial identities helps develop strategies of footing. Students are testing out safe and strategic ways of constructing identities desirable to themselves without getting penalized by the academy. These strategies help in academic literacy where students face similar struggles of expressing critical opinions without antagonizing their academic audience. I have presented elsewhere some writing samples of students who bring into their texts some of the strategies they use in safe houses (see Canagarajah, 1997). Donnie, for example, writes a seemingly bland essay filled with quotations from academic sources in his effort to argue that the academy is a racist institution. When one reads the quotations closely, one finds that he has strategically picked these statements from venerable educationists to make allegations against the academy in very direct and expressive terms. This is a safe way of representing Donnie's criticism as he is making his point under the cover of the very academics he is interested in critiquing. Even the tone and style of communication that Donnie prefers are represented through the voice of his sources.

Finally, the practice of safe houses enables certain complex forms of legitimate peripheral participation. Since the classroom as a community of practice involves conflicts and inequalities for minority students (see Toohey, 2000a), they adopt certain detached forms of participation. Though students are slightly detached from the activities of the classroom, they are not completely so. Life in the safe houses has relevance to the pedagogical activities of the classroom. The students are simply orientating to pedagogical matters in different terms. The detachment provided by the safe houses enables them to relate to pedagogical matters in more critical and creative terms – especially from values that matter to them from outside the school. So the safe houses are complementary to the concerns of the school and classroom. The discourses and identities students develop in the safe houses enrich their critical and creative contribution to academic literacies and discourses.

In relation to issues of power, this study enables us to adopt a more complex orientation to micropolitics in society and education. According to traditional ways of looking at it, safe houses may represent an elaborate form of conformism. After all, if students keep their oppositional discourses and identities to the underlife and simply collude with the dominant discourses in their public life, it is possible that the status quo won't be challenged in any way. But James Scott (1990) sees more possibilities in what he calls the "infra politics" of underlife behavior. Safe house politics are *infra* for reasons that they are hidden from the eyes of the others and they represent a form of micropolitics that is not very conspicuous in the impact it has on wider social life. Hidden in the recesses of social spaces are pockets of resistance that have the potential of flowering into something profound and radical. What goes on in the safe houses simply represents a period of strategic mobilization and collaboration for marginalized groups to construct an oppositional culture. In extreme forms of oppression, crisis, or simply with increased confidence among the underprivileged, these hidden cultures may surface. If the tactic of the dominant institutions is to root out any signs of protest or to eliminate any space for the breeding of oppositional ideologies and identities, safe houses represent an outsmarting of the powers that be. The oppressed are collaboratively constructing social spaces that can enable them to form bonds, support each other, develop a critical consciousness, and construct subversive cultures.

We also mustn't discount the possibilities inherent in imagined communities and identities. Though safe houses represent ideal conditions friendly to minorities that don't exist outside, they keep alive a vision of the possibilities. Eventually, students may act out their imagined communities and identities. The very contradiction between both enables them to reflect on the differences and develop a keener sensitivity to what *is* and what *could be*. The imagined communities can, in fact, be very functional as they develop roles, discourses, and values that counter the dominant institutions and prepare the oppressed to adopt these when the time is ready for change. James Scott (1990) cites the examples of many peasant revolts where the seemingly spontaneous struggle for change is soon characterized by very orderly and planned forms of action. He argues that the members are taking on roles and identities that have been gestating in their communal underlife. Similarly, the discourses and identities students adopt in the safe houses – although they are sometimes playful – may, in fact, be very subversive. They nurture the dream of alternate possibilities in educational and social life.

Conclusion

There are other educational researchers who are beginning to discern alternate sites and cultures in the classroom.[7] Though they don't theorize pedagogical safe spaces as I have done here, they show that classroom discourses and cultures are more complex than we have imagined. The objective of this essay is to offer these safe houses and sites of student underlife as opening up interesting possibilities for the study of student agency in the construction of alternate identities. An understanding of student life in these domains can creatively complicate our estimation of the critical thinking and learning potential of our students. By tapping the strategies students display here, teachers may help them engage in critical literacy and language acquisition.

Notes

1. For a comprehensive theoretical review of these definitions, see Smith (1988). For an application to language teaching contexts, see Norton (2000).
2. Consider the following publications for masked forms of resistance in these communities: Abu-Lughod (1986); Adas (1992); Guha (1983); and Khare (1984).
3. A study on the challenges for African American students in academic writing was conducted in the University of Texas at Austin as a classroom ethnography. The subjects were part of an orientation course for minority students in order to increase their retention rates. These were all largely middle class students who were assigned to my class by the usual registration process. As a computer-mediated class, I had access to the e-mails, online discussions, and drafts of essays in a semester-long study. My data also constituted sociolinguistic interviews and classroom observation notes (see Canagarajah, 1997). The study with the Sri Lankan students was conducted at the University of Jaffna. These were largely rural students from the Tamil-speaking ethnic group. This was an ethnographic study on the challenges in learning English for general academic purposes. This group of students was also part of my class and they were grouped according to their placement scores. They were among the weakest groups in the entering batch of students. In this year-long study, I gathered data from pre- and post-course interviews, attitudinal surveys, and classroom observation, in addition to texts of writing and speech. The safe house practices were not the focus of the study; they emerged as significant sites of inquiry on classroom culture during the research process (see Canagarajah, 1993). In both cases, I obtained permission from the students to use the diverse forms of data in my research. In the case of the African American students, they signed consent forms giving me access to the e-mail messages after the course was over. The other texts were permitted for use as the course was in progression.
4. This set of data is from the online discussion of the students. Therefore, the conventions of representing them in the text are different from the mail messages cited earlier (in Texts 2–7). The coding at the end of the text refers to the date on which this Interchange discussion (i.e., INT) took place.
5. It is not clear whom Sonny refers to here as his recipients. It appeared to me that there were cliques among the students, with different acronyms to identify them, but I have not been successful in identifying these groups. In terms of discourse, it is possible that Sonny is using this as a secret language

to confuse the others in the class, especially because this message is sent as an open (i.e., unprotected) e-mail.

6. Sonny often adopts this strategy of violating spelling conventions to parody or mock standard dialect spoken features. Here, he obviously means, "It's been great." Later in this message, he also deliberately misspells *scholarship*. I have generally cited the messages of the students with the spelling and typographical conventions as in the original.
7. For studies that give insight into safe houses, see Brooke (1987); Lucas and Katz (1994); Martin-Jones and Heller (1996); Miller (1998); and Rampton (1995).

References

Abu-Lughod, L. (1986). *Veiled sentiments: Honor and poetry in a Bedouin society*. Berkeley: University of California Press.

Adas, M. (1992). From avoidance to confrontation: Peasant protest in precolonial and colonial Southeast Asia. In N. Dirks (Ed.), *Colonialism and culture* (pp. 89–126). Ann Arbor: University of Michigan Press.

Brooke, R. (1987). Underlife and writing instruction. *College Composition and Communication, 38*(2), 141–53.

Canagarajah, A. S. (1993). Critical ethnography of a Sri Lankan classroom: Ambiguities in opposition to reproduction through ESOL. *TESOL Quarterly, 27*(4), 601–26.

Canagarajah, A. S. (1997). Safe houses in the contact zone: Coping strategies of African-American students in the academy. *College Composition and Communication, 48*(2), 173–96.

Canagarajah, A. S. (1999). *Resisting linguistic imperialism in English teaching*. Oxford: Oxford University Press.

Chelliah, J. V. (1922). *A century of English education*. Vaddukoddai: Jaffna College.

Douglass, F. (1845). *Narrative of the life of Frederick Douglass, An American slave*. Boston: Massachusetts Anti-Slavery Society.

Foucault, M. (1972). The discourse on language. In *The archeology of knowledge* (A. M. Sheridan Smith, Trans.) (pp. 215–37). New York: Pantheon. (Original work published 1969.)

Goffman, E. (1961). *Asylums: Essays on the social situation of mental patients and other inmates*. New York: Anchor.

Guha, R. (1983). *Elementary aspects of peasant insurgency*. New Delhi: Oxford University Press.

Harklau, L. (2000). From the "good kids" to the "worst": Representations of English language learners across educational settings. *TESOL Quarterly, 34*(1), 35–68.

Khare, R. S. (1984). *The Untouchable as himself: Ideology, identity, and pragmatism among the Lucknow Chamars*. Cambridge, England: Cambridge University Press.

Kochman, T. (1981). *Black and white styles in conflict*. Chicago: University of Chicago Press.

Lam, E. W. S. (2000). L2 literacy and the design of the self: A case study of a teenager writing on the internet. *TESOL Quarterly, 34*(3), 457–82.

Lucas, T., & Katz, A. (1994). Reframing the debate: The roles of native languages in English-only programs for language minority students. *TESOL Quarterly, 28*(4), 537–62.

Martin-Jones, M., & Heller, M. (1996). Introduction to the special issues on education in multilingual settings: Discourse, identities, and power, Pt. 1: Constructing legitimacy. *Linguistics and Education, 8*(1), 3–16.

McKay, S., & Chick, K. (2000, March). *Positioning learners in post apartheid South African schools: A case study of selected multicultural Durban schools.* Paper presented at the meeting of the American Association for Applied Linguistics, Vancouver, British Columbia, Canada.

Miller, R. (1998). The arts of complicity: Pragmatism and the culture of schooling. *College English, 61*(1), 10–28.

Norton, B. (2000). *Identity and language learning: Gender, ethnicity and educational change.* London: Pearson Education.

Pratt, M. L. (1991). Arts of the contact zone. *Profession, 91*, 33–40.

Raboteau, A. J. (1978). *Slave religion: The "invisible institution" of the Antebellum South.* New York: Oxford University Press.

Rampton, B. (1995). *Crossing: Language and ethnicity among adolescents.* London: Longman.

Scott, J. C. (1985). *Weapons of the weak: Everyday forms of peasant resistance.* New Haven, CT: Yale University Press.

Scott, J. C. (1990). *Domination and the arts of resistance.* New Haven, CT: Yale University Press.

Smith, P. (1988). *Discerning the subject.* Minneapolis: University of Minnesota Press.

Toohey, K. (2000a, March). *Assigning marginality: The case of an "ESL/learning disabled" student.* Paper presented at the meeting of the American Association for Applied Linguistics, Vancouver, British Columbia, Canada.

Toohey, K. (2000b). *Learning English at school: Identity, social relations, and classroom practice.* Clevedon, England: Multilingual Matters.

Warschauer, M. (2000). The changing global economy and the future of English teaching. *TESOL Quarterly, 34*(3), 511–36.

Wickramasuriya, S. (1976). Strangers in their own land: The radical protest against English education in colonial Ceylon. *Navasilu, 1*, 15–31.

8 *"Why does this feel empowering?": Thesis writing, concordancing, and the corporatizing university*

Sue Starfield

Introduction

In a recent guest editorial in *Discourse and Society*, Billig (2000) argues that those of us who see ourselves as operating within a critical paradigm have a responsibility to continually challenge received orthodoxies, be they in the so-called mainstream, uncritical paradigms or within research and teaching that situates itself within a critical frame. His contention is that in a growing number of contexts, critical work can be seen to be approaching mainstream status as it establishes itself in the academic marketplace, and he proposes a perpetual vigilance in our practices to guard against the complacency that may come with even partial entry into the establishment (p. 292).

It was with these words in mind that I allowed myself to critically consider issues of empowerment, not only in my practice as a teacher of English as a second language (ESL) and academic literacy within what I call the *corporatizing*[1] Australian university, but also from within my own positioning in and by the university and its new discourses. The title of this chapter intertextually speaks to an article that has acquired dominant status within the critical pedagogy community (see next section) and begins to ask whether, in the twenty-first century, our work can be empowering for ourselves and our students even as the sites within which we are working are being fundamentally reshaped by globalization and marketization. Higher education's restructuring not only of institutional identities as more entrepreneurial, but also of the professional identities of university teachers and those of their students through the marketization of public discourse has been highlighted by Fairclough (1995, p. 158). Since Fairclough's article, restructuring has progressed apace. As identities are discursively constructed in social practice (Fairclough, 1992; Gee, Hull, & Lankshear, 1996), so these new discourses – ways of doing, being, saying, and valuing within universities – actively reshape the identities of learners and teachers. But it is the sociocultural construction of identities – which are always plural and multiple – that opens them to contestation (Farell, 2000; Ivanič, 1997; Norton, 2000).

Teachers who feel disempowered by workplace restructuring and learners who experience powerlessness through being positioned as foreign and non-English speaking are, as I argue in this chapter, thus able to challenge their discursive positionings and construct identities that are potentially empowering. In this process, progressive orthodoxies may be challenged and discourses previously dismissed as "technicist" may be explored.

In Australia, substantial federal funding cuts brought about by the implementation of the economic rationalist/neoliberal agenda, which is part of the global restructuring of capitalism, have encouraged the universities to recruit students from the Asian region who generate additional income from the full fees they pay. A recent newspaper article stated that the overseas student industry was worth $3.7 billion (Australian dollars = $7.4 billion U.S.) annually (Boucher, 2001). Students are recruited on the basis of certain IELTS and TOEFL (International English Language Testing System and Test of English as a Foreign Language, respectively) scores or through various other means, with universities' entry levels tending to be set in terms of how our entry levels compare with those of our perceived competitors (other Australian universities) in the marketplace. This may lead to students' experiencing difficulty in completing projects, such as writing a Ph.D. dissertation, that demand highly complex levels of academic language proficiency in English. Equally, teachers may experience difficulty in assisting students with meeting the expectations of the examiners.

It is through an analysis of some aspects of my support work with students who are enrolled in Ph.D. programs in the Faculty of Arts and Social Sciences of my university that I have come to reexamine some of the discourses on student and teacher empowerment that are currently in circulation. I explore a range of areas and practices, including the use of materials based on computer concordancing techniques, as a point of departure for further exploration of issues of power and identity in academic writing. In so doing, I draw on notions of strategic competence from both language pedagogy and management discourse to suggest that we can, through poststructuralist insights, actively reposition ourselves to work "between and within . . . perspectives and paradigms" (Denzin & Lincoln, 1994, p. 2) in ways that can be empowering to students and teachers.

Recontextualizing empowerment discourses

Fairclough (2000) describes recontextualization as a process whereby genres and discourses move from one set of practices to another. For example, a feature of the new global form of capitalism is the recontextualization of discourses and genres of management to many new domains such that, for example, "Total Quality Management" has become pervasive in many areas, including government, schooling, and health. Within the corporatizing university, discourses on quality and management, both separately and jointly, are restructuring the conditions of what is possible. I, myself, am now recast as a *Manager* of the Learning Center, not a traditional academic, and I recently completed a course in "Strategic People Management" – *strategic* being another new capitalist recontextualization of the language of politics and opposition that I shall say more about below.

In the workplaces of the late twentieth and early twenty-first centuries, there is also a great deal of talk about worker empowerment. As Gee et al. (1996) and others (see Fairclough, 2000) have pointed out, recontextualization has happened within the discourse of management itself, with terms such as *empowerment* being recontextualized into the discourses of management and human resources. They situate this as an instance of how in "New Times," or what has also been called late modernity or neoliberalism, new capitalism works to appropriate the language of opposition so that managers now empower workers to feel part of the company through shared ownership, working in apparently nonhierarchical teams, and other processes. They question whether these processes can be seen as empowering or whether they mask new forms of more subtle control.

The notion of empowerment – that pedagogy could be liberatory for the oppressed – was central to early conceptualizations of the possibilities of critical pedagogy. The notion of empowerment lost its innocence, however, when subjected to a singeing critique by feminist and poststructural pedagogies in the early 1990s. Critical pedagogy and the notion of empowerment, in particular, were variously critiqued as being constructions of rationalist and paternalistic Enlightenment discourses in which socially powerful, radical teacher-educators (frequently male) conceived of themselves as "liberating" oppressed students through the transmission of power – conceived of as a property – to their up-until-then disempowered students. Gore (1992) contended that "empowerment pedagogy" was itself a "regime of truth" – as much a set of socially shaped discursive practices as the discourses from which its proponents sought to liberate their students. According to Gore, Foucault's notion of regimes of truth "highlights the potential dangers and normalizing tendencies of all discourses, including those which aim to liberate" (p. 63). Ellsworth's (1992) challenge to critical pedagogy and its repressive myths, against which she argued that "strategies such as student empowerment and dialogue give the illusion of equality while in fact leaving the authoritarian nature of the teacher/student relationship intact" (p. 98), was forcefully titled, "Why doesn't this feel empowering?" It is to this article that the title of my chapter refers, but I argue that we now need to reclaim, through a strategic recontextualization, discursive and pedagogical practices that are empowering to the identities of learners and teachers. It may be that a strategic engagement with technology will assist us in this task. It is this argument that is developed in the remainder of this chapter.

The explicit pedagogies of the genres of power as advocated in Australia have been subjected to a critique along similar lines. One of the clearly articulated intentions of the Australian proponents of genre-based pedagogy was to empower learners, especially those from socioeconomically disadvantaged groups, by providing access to socially powerful genres from which their schooling was perceived to be excluding them (see Cope & Kalantzis, 1993; Hyon, 1996). According to Hyon, genre-based instruction in Australia is "described as a tool for empowering students with linguistic resources for social success" (p. 701). Luke (1996) and others argue, however, that genre pedagogy fails to see that powerful academic genres may themselves be implicated in the maintenance of power, rather than its contestation. Kress (unpublished manuscript) further argues that the promotion of explicit pedagogies of inclusion and access and the genre debates of the 1980s and the early parts of the 1990s are premised on an implicit view of the essential stability of the societies that gave rise to these pedagogies. As these societies become less stable, so genres become less predictable and their forms more obviously heteroglossic as the forces of uncertainty and instability gain in strength. Kress' sociohistorically situated critique can be extended to the critical pedagogy enterprise as critiqued by Ellsworth and Gore, and it becomes legitimate to ask to what extent empowerment pedagogy can now itself be viewed as a product of much more certain times.

Strategic competence

These debates and critiques may appear to constrain and restrict the pedagogical possibilities available to us. However, as Pennycook (2001) reminds us, we need to use "crucial tools" strategically and contextually, and we need forms of analysis that lead to forms of action (p. 73). I take this to mean that particular discourses or positions do not *own* particular notions; we may need to reintroduce (or recontextualize) existing notions into the second language agenda and to use these strategically to alter, through our discursive practices, the unequal power relations that shape students' lives in the university.

In my own practice as an educator, these critiques of critical pedagogy as a regime of truth and a new master narrative had made me wary of considering my practice as having to do with empowering my students. While finding this positioning potentially immobilizing, reflecting on the nature of my work led me in two unexpected directions: one was to work on strategic competence in language learning and teaching and the other to the notion of strategic competence in human resource management.

Strategic competence in second language pedagogy

I turned to Michael Canale's (1983) writings on communicative competence where he identifies strategic competence as a component of communicative competence involving verbal and nonverbal communication strategies that may be called into action to compensate for breakdowns in communication often due to "insufficient competence in one or more . . . areas of communicative competence" (p. 10). Examples of these are paraphrasing, ways of addressing strangers when unsure of their social status, and ways of achieving coherence in texts when unsure of cohesive devices, all considered by Canale to be particularly important in the early stages of learning another language. As an example of how such strategic competencies might be learned in a second language classroom, Canale refers to what he calls "power vocabulary": English words such as *place*, *person*, and *thing*, which learners can use in paraphrase strategies. He further stresses that learners be encouraged to use such strategies rather than remain silent and that they be given opportunities to use them. I shall return to this notion below when I describe how I introduced concordancing into my classroom.

In my view, the notion of strategic competence is potentially much more powerful than the way in which second language pedagogy has typically taken it up to characterize communication strategies as either reduction or achievement oriented (Ellis, 1992), locating it solely within individuals. Surprisingly, perhaps, we can bring a much more social dimension to bear on the concept by looking at how the concept of strategic competence is being used in human resource management.

Strategic competence and knowledge management

In contemporary human resource management, as I discovered when my new position as a manager led me to enroll in the course "Strategic People Management," there is a strand which argues that a company's strategic competencies, or its tacit internalized knowledge, constitutes its greatest advantage in the marketplace. These intangible assets are socially complex, cannot be represented on a balance sheet, and draw, in part, on what has been called *organizational memory*, which is the memory not just of individuals, but of groups of people working in communities of practice in which they, through dialogue, "share tacit knowledge and learn through experimentation" (Tidd, 2000, p. 25). It is through constant engagement in such communities of practice in my own professional life that I feel I have developed the abilities to critique and challenge the given and to seek out – through experimentation – new ways of doing and thinking. Along similar lines, the academic English workshops described below enabled the students to begin to form their own community of international Ph.D. students by building a *community of interaction* – a "knowledge network" that crossed the traditional disciplinary boundaries (Tidd, 2000, p. 24).

Strategies in context

In this section, I describe a particular strategy I have used in my work with international arts and social sciences Ph.D. students at my university, to which they have responded positively. I contend that student empowerment is a possibility, but that it needs to be strategically recontextualized by those of us with an interest in the future of critical ESL pedagogy. The number of international Ph.D. students in the faculty is not large, but they are disproportionately struggling to write their theses and their completion rates are lower than those of the local students. When I started doing this work, I saw students on an individual basis, by appointment, and I would give them detailed feedback on drafts of their thesis chapters in terms of the language, organization, and structure and the extent to which they were meeting the academic literacy demands of the thesis genre. I soon became aware that the students were experiencing many similar difficulties in writing academic English and I started what I call the Academic English Workshop, in which the students and I meet weekly for two hours. In the section below, I describe how the introduction of academic English materials, based on developments made possible by the existence of large corpora of academic English and the use of concordancing software, impacted the progression of the weekly workshops and students' language development.

Concordancing – Developing power vocabulary

I will begin with a brief overview of developments within corpus-based linguistic research focusing on a consideration of their relevance for second language pedagogy. Computer technology has made possible the collection of huge electronic databases or *corpora* of spoken and written language. Concordancing is a technique which can now be carried out on computer by concordancing software and has chiefly been used by lexicographers for dictionary databases and by language researchers.

Concordancing programs can search through millions of words of texts to find every example of a particular word, which will be shown in its immediate textual context. Statistical analyses enable the frequencies of lexical items in the language to be determined as well as common collocations (words that appear within four words of the key word in the concordance) of these items. Its proponents argue that these data-driven approaches to descriptions of English (and of other languages) build a more accurate and real description of language in use (Biber, Conrad, & Reppen, 1998; Sinclair, 1991). For Sinclair, the improved descriptions of language use made possible by corpus-based research furnish us not only with better grammars and dictionaries, but also a sounder basis for selecting which lexical items and grammatical structures to include in language learning syllabi than do current syllabi, which are often based on teachers' intuitions of what needs to be taught rather than on evidence from research.

One of the largest and earliest projects of direct relevance to English language teaching was the "Collins COBUILD English Language Dictionary" project, begun in 1980, which draws on the twenty-million-word COBUILD corpus assembled from recent written and spoken texts in (mostly) standard British English (Sinclair, 1991). Concordancing software and access to existing corpora have facilitated interesting developments in second language pedagogy and research. As Stubbs (1995) pointed out, "exactly how such findings should best be turned into teaching materials and presented to students is a topic which will require long-term experimentation" (p. 255). I shall review a few of these developments to give a flavor of the kinds of approaches now possible and then examine some critiques of corpus-based approaches and concordancing. I shall then discuss in more detail my own use of English for Academic Purposes (EAP) materials based on concordancing.

Course design

Concordancing made possible the *Collins COBUILD English Course* (Willis & Willis, 1988), which is based on a lexical syllabus originating from the 2,500 most frequent English words and phrases. These words led to a syllabus organization that, according to its authors, is radically different to traditional English teaching courses in that it is based not on teacher intuition as to what should be taught, but on authentic data (Willis, 1990). Moreover, the most frequently used words are identified not in isolation, but in their commonly occurring contexts (or collocations) as well.

Flowerdew (1993) describes the development of an English for Specific Purposes (ESP) course through the application of concordancing to a small corpus of spoken lectures and written texts to which students were exposed in their biology studies. He claims that using concordancing as a tool in ESP course design allows for the development of materials based on the selection of the most frequently used vocabulary items in the corpus and for the identification of how these items are "actually used" (p. 237) lexicogrammatically. He maintains that this not only increases the face validity of the course as materials are drawn directly from actual use in the content area, but, furthermore, it may reveal discrepancies between the concordancing-based materials and grammatical descriptions in published courses which are based on "fabricated examples" (p. 239). How the course dealt with language in use above the level of the sentence is not addressed in the article.

Hughes and McCarthy (1998) argue for discourse-based, as opposed to sentence-based, approaches to grammar teaching, drawing on two large electronic corpora of informal written and spoken English to illustrate their claims that discourse-based approaches provide a more "appropriate and accurate" way of teaching language use (p. 280). Certainly, the discourse-based approach they advocate would provide learners with greater access to larger stretches of language and highlight the use of language functions such as the interpersonal and the textual while enabling explanation of aspects of grammar not traditionally amenable to explanation by sentence-level models.

In a more recent study, Weber (2001) advocates a concordance- and genre-based approach to teaching academic essay writing to undergraduate law students from non-English-speaking backgrounds. The students were given a minicorpus of model legal essays written by native English speakers and were encouraged to investigate various generic features and associated lexical items using simple concordancing software such as the *Longman Miniconcordancer* and *WordSmith*. Weber maintains that students were given a firm foundation in both essay writing and legal reasoning. He argues that this approach is highly relevant to teaching essay writing as it allows for the integration of attention to form into a task-based paradigm.

Cobb and Horst (2001) report on an EAP vocabulary course in which students were taught to use specially modified computer concordancing software to build their own learner databases of the target vocabulary. Several researchers (Biber et al., 1998; Flowerdew & Peacock, 2001; Widdowson, 2000) suggest that corpora and concordancing packages have the potential to become a significant language-learning tool for students in the future. Students may be able to generate their own concordance lists and work as language researchers on particular items or they may be able to search large corpora of academic texts to investigate how specific disciplines use particular language or discourse features.

Biber and Conrad (2001) highlight the significance of corpus-based studies for teachers of English to speakers of other languages, particularly in EAP course design, arguing that they allow for a renewed focus on the centrality of register in that they permit a complete analysis of patterns of use within and across registers and also that they demonstrate the unreliability of intuitions about use on which teachers and published materials frequently rely. Another interesting application of concordancing and related techniques in corpus-based linguistic research is in the development of the new academic word list (AWL) (Coxhead, 2000) drawn from an electronic corpus of academic texts of 3.5 million words, which the author maintains could be of use in identifying key vocabulary goals for EAP course design.

A more critical look at corpus-based linguistics

While insights from concordancing and corpus-based linguistics have led to exciting and novel insights into language use and have opened up intriguing new avenues in course design, there are a number of premises that demand greater scrutiny, particularly from a critical perspective. Critiques of the claims of corpus linguistics and concordancing approaches revolve around the claim of authenticity, the criteria used in the selection of the corpus, the limited notion of context employed, claims of appropriateness, and the notion of register.

Widdowson (2000) raises issues of whether the authenticity of the data collected is a guarantee of teachability and learnability. Can simply presenting learners with "real data" that are extracted from their original context and transported into the language classroom – a pedagogic context that is no longer that of the original native speakers – necessarily lead to enhanced language learning? Teachers, in fact, need to devise other local contexts that will "activate the process of learning" (p. 8). He believes the corpus should inform and enrich the pedagogic process and not drive it.

The issue of the context reoccurs in different forms in the critiques of concordancing. One of these has been that it offers instances of language in use that may be representative of specific registers but, nevertheless, remain largely decontextualized instances. It has been argued (see Aston, 1995) that presenting students with concordances of particular expressions in the classroom provides them with data that will allow them to infer or test rules which govern their use. Aston contends that giving students selected lists of essentially decontextualized items in concordances fails to expose them to the broader social processes at work in "negotiating meaning" (p. 260). Discourse and genre-based approaches (see above) may assist in countering some of these issues. McCarthy and Carter (2001) argue, for instance, that the quantitative data (from concordancing) should be supplemented by qualitative data, particularly in the exploration of the expression of interpersonal meanings – in other words, to broaden accounts of social context to include the nature of the relationships between the speakers and the types of encounters involved.

The constitution of the corpus, I would argue, raises broader and more critical questions as to who counts as legitimate speakers of the language and of who has not only the right to speak, but the right to be heard, and under what conditions (Norton, 2000). Hughes and McCarthy (1998) identify one of the potential drawbacks of corpus-based approaches as being the exposure of learners to discourse "belonging linguistically or culturally to an inner circle of language users" (p. 284), which I take to mean the need for a corpus to draw not solely on the speakers of "standard" British English. McCarthy and Carter (2001) reframe this complex issue within the notion of "representativeness" – that is, whose variety of English is collected as authoritative in specific corpora – and how acceptable nonnative speaker varieties are. But, as more critical researchers have argued, the notion of language varieties is itself open to critique:

> In no actual speech community do all members always behave in accordance with a shared sense of which language varieties are appropriate for which contexts and purposes. Yet such a perfectly ordered world is set up as an ideal by those who wish to impose their own social order upon society in the realm of language. (Fairclough, 1992, p. 34)

According to Fairclough (1992), in an appropriateness model of language variation, a basic assumption is that "members of a speech community have a shared and well-defined repertoire of language varieties" and that "each variety can be matched with contexts" (p. 42) leading to a view of language that, although broadly social, sees language education as providing training in sets of "unitary, normative, and determinate practices" (p. 42). Appropriateness, he argues, is an ideological category that reflects struggles within a speech community for hegemony over its sociolinguistic order (i.e., norms, values, discursive practices).

Similarly, the notion of register, which seems fundamental to much of corpus-based research, postulates static, easily identifiable registers without consideration of the sociohistoric construction of the status of the different registers. It would seem possible to apply the critique of genre pedagogy, to which I referred earlier in this chapter, to the concept of register as being premised on more certain, stable times. Moreover, corpus-based linguistics cannot take into account what is absent from the language it samples – i.e., that signs are contested and that discourse is a site of struggle over who controls the right to mean. So, critical researchers and teachers may seek, for example, to investigate what is not said – the silences – or contest dominant meanings.

Introducing concordancing into my workshops

Bearing in mind the various positions outlined above, I decided, for the reasons described below, to try out concordancing-based materials with my students. The materials I used were collected in *Exploring Academic English: A Workbook for Student Essay Writing* (Thurstun & Candlin, 1998b). Drawing on the University Word List cited in Nation (1990) and the *Microconcord Corpus of Academic Texts* – a large database of over a million words taken from books, chapters, and journal articles – the frequency of particular items in academic writing was established (Thurstun & Candlin, 1998a). They focused on a limited set of academic vocabulary or key words but through concordancing were able to provide intensive exposure to the use of these lexical items. Their selection consists of "frequently used words which are common to all fields of academic learning," rather than discipline-specific lexis, as it is claimed that tertiary students do not necessarily find discipline-specific lexis difficult (Thurstun & Candlin, 1998b, p. vi). In aiming to introduce new university students to some of the most important items of the vocabulary of academic English, they categorized the vocabulary in terms of the rhetorical functions it could typically serve in academic texts. Their workbook is therefore divided into six units on topics (rhetorical functions) that range from "Stating the topic," with the key words being *issue*, *factor*, and *concept*, through "Reporting the research of others," with key words *according to*, *claim*, and *suggest*, to "Expressing opinions tentatively," with key words *may*, *possibly*, *unlikely*, and *probably*. Each key word is shown in about thirty different instances of the contexts in which it has been used in an academic text and then students can do a variety of language exercises based on this.

I began using the workbook with the Ph.D. students and although it is explicitly aimed at undergraduates, they responded positively. Most of the students had several years of formal study of English grammar behind them and knew many of the rules, but this knowledge was not helping them with the highly complex language of thesis writing. The concordancing approach, through its integration of grammar and lexis, its stress on collocation, and its use of authentic academic texts, provided them with a fresh take on a done-to-death area. As Thurstun and Candlin (1998a) point out, students can "explore, on the basis of the primary source of the language itself, with no mention of rules or need to resort to pedagogic grammar" (p. 275). I have included an extract from the concordance for the phrase *according to*, a commonly used term in "Reporting the research of others," so that readers can get an idea of what a concordance looks like (see Figure 8.1). The key word appears in bold and the text is arbitrarily cut off by the computer at the end of the line. Students need to pay particular attention to the words to the left

```
till practised in his own day. <p> In time, according to Islamic tradition, mankind had strayed away
of an immaterial substance, a mind or soul. According to Locke, however, the question is 'what makes
  in this case, it is indirect. This stage, according to Morgan and Engels, is marked by the limitin
d escalating repression by the Nazi State - according to one calculation, roughly one in every 1200
eeks. And new hope - 'utopian expectations' according to one report - arose again following the anno
lacial periods over the past 160 000 years, according to recent polar ice-core studies. Total global
e categorical distinctions of our language. According to such a theory, if we, in English, call both
 produce generalisation decrement and thus, according to the account presented above, an overshadowi
             chapter. 8.1 Singularities. <p> According to the general theory of relativity, space-tim
ting Roman dates to those of the Olympiads. According to the historian Polybius, the founding of Rom
of the calendar in AD 1582 (see Ch. 8). <p> According to the Iranian scholar S.H. Taqizadah, a corr
= by virtue of geometry and demonstration'. According to the science of optics, light travelling fro
ry forest. This conclusion is questionable, according to the survey's findings. <p> For one thing, d
on earth, of the chosen people, Israel. <p> According to the theologian O. Cullmann in his book <i>
d interpretation of proactive interference. According to this alternative view, the target associati
  over 7200 kg of oil equivalent per year. According to World Bank figures, each inhabitant of the
```

Figure 8.1 Extract for "according to" concordance from Thurstun and Candlin (1998b, p. 40). Reprinted from Exploring Academic English *by J. Thurstun and C. N. Candlin. Reproduced with permission from the National Centre for English Language Teaching and Research (NCELTR), Australia. © Macquarie University.*

and right of the key word to familiarize themselves with the word's use, its meaning in context, and its grammar (Thurston & Candlin, 1998b). Exercises that follow would include use of prepositions, verbal forms that tend to collocate frequently with certain nouns, meaning in context, modality, and so on.

I need to emphasize that concordancing was a point of departure for our workshops, not an end in itself; one line concordances, although providing instances of authentic use, cannot provide full enough contexts for deducing or inferring meaning. It was, however, through concordancing that the workshops began to look at discourse and genre within academic texts and to consider issues of identity and authority when negotiating with the words of academic authorities. It did begin to provide students with ways of looking at and thinking about language and discourse in more critical and more empowering ways that are particularly helpful when writing a Ph.D. dissertation.

From concordancing to identity and authority issues in thesis writing

Reading the drafts of my students' theses chapters, I could see the effect of their exposure to a limited set of academic English resources – particularly lexically – and the struggles they were experiencing to express the complex meanings arising from their research. How were they to "invent the university" and "appropriate (or be appropriated by) a specialized discourse" (Bartholomae, 1985, p. 135) and appear authoritative? Corson (1997) contends that students, by virtue of their prior sociocultural positioning, have unequal access to the resources of the

Greco-Latin vocabulary that dominate the prestige academic vocabulary of English that is essential to academic success. The ESL students in my workshops kept telling me how hard it was for them to express themselves in written, academic English; their writing was evidence of this and of their limited access to the "lexico-semantic" (Corson, 1997, p. 679) meaning-making systems of academic English. In fact, of the thirteen nouns and verbs used as key words in *Exploring Academic English* (excluding modals and adverbials), all but one have Greco-Latin roots. Concordancing strategies enable students to begin the "difficult and complicated process" that Bakhtin (1981) described as *expropriation* – "forcing it [language] to submit to one's own intentions and accents" – based on Bakhtin's recognition of the fundamentally social nature of language that is "not a neutral medium that passes freely and easily into the private property of the speaker's intentions; it is populated – overpopulated – with the intentions of others" (p. 294).

According to Bourdieu (1982/1991), all speakers will recognize the authorized, prestige language but will have very unequal knowledge of its usage. He points out how the ability to have access to the "language of authority," which he identifies as resources such as rhetorical devices, genres, legitimate styles, authoritative formulations, and good usage, "confers on those who engage in it a power over language and thereby over the ordinary users of language" (p. 58). Bourdieu discerns a sort of "authority effect," which would distinguish legitimate speakers from impostors on the basis that the former group's authority to speak the language of authority has been institutionally endowed. My students, institutionally positioned as second language speakers of English, had very small amounts of "authority capital." Yet, each of the students, by virtue of the intersection of their research project – typically located, at least in part, within their home context – with the Australian university context, is uniquely placed to do original research.

The introduction of concordancing, with its heightened reflexive dimension, into our workshops and where it has led us has enabled the students to expand their linguistic and discursive resources to make more complex meanings, build their arguments, and appear authoritative – to begin to develop identities as academic writers.

I will outline how one such series of sessions developed. We began by reading the concordances in the unit "Reporting the research of others" and worked through the exercises. I then brought along an article by John Flowerdew (2000), from a recent *TESOL Quarterly*, titled "Discourse Community, Legitimate Peripheral Participation, and the Nonnative-English-Speaking Scholar" and asked the students to read the introduction and theoretical sections to identify how he was reporting the research of others. I gave them the worksheet I had developed (see Figure 8.2) to facilitate their task.

Academic English Workshops for Ph.D. Students

Reading and Writing a Literature Review

Study the review section of your article

Underline the verbs, nouns, or expressions which are used to report the research of others.

List these words and phrases below. Include author's name if mentioned.

Verbs	*Nouns*	*Phrases*

Figure 8.2 Academic English Worksheet – Reading and Writing a Literature Review.

This activity led to much animated discussion in the classroom as we were also able to see how Flowerdew was not merely reporting the research of others but how, in so doing, he was, as Swales and Feak (1994) have demonstrated, setting up a niche or gap in which to insert his own research. We had already begun to move beyond concordancing. The topic of the article also resonated with the students as its theme is the struggle of a recent Ph.D. graduate from a non-English-speaking background to publish his research in an academic journal. I then suggested that the students bring to class their own texts that they were reading within their different disciplines and examine how the writers they were reading deployed their linguistic resources to report the research of others. Once again, our point of departure was the worksheet. We began to work strategically – deconstructing these authoritative texts – carving out spaces for students to try out or try on the words and phrases of these authorities. In the workshops, students pooled ideas and we built rich mind maps on the board of overlapping and distinctive ways of saying and doing in and across disciplines. While we had started with *according to*, *suggest*, and *claim*, we soon moved into consideration of the very many different ways in which writers of academic research articles use language to report on the research of others and considered why it is that they might use the words they did – i.e., how they were using these words to build their argument in order to locate their own research within a field or fields. This type of scaffolded activity in which there is much talking about text is, according to Corson (1997), crucial for successful entry into academic discourse communities by students whose lexicosemantic positioning differs from the dominant community's discursive practices: "learners can talk repeatedly about knowledge gained from text, using an acquired metalanguage set against a meaning system used to interpret and extend understanding" (p. 684). They can "talk [their] way inside meaning systems and become active participants within them" (p. 684). As they began to take ownership of these powerful words, they began to challenge the dominant impersonal genres of the scientific research paradigm. We had many discussions about issues such as writing in the first person, the active voice versus the passive voice, and the ways in which quantitative research typically positions researchers versus the ways in which researcher identities are constituted in qualitative research.[2] I would now like to give two examples of how, through individual consultations with the students, I became aware of how they were adopting concordancing strategies to good effect.

Kim, a Korean woman, writing about the explosion of feminist discourses in which she had been involved in Korea, wrote about discourses "blossoming out" – one of the first times in her writing in which she tried to use a phrase which was her own creation. She told me that she had spent about half an hour thinking of the best way of saying what she wanted to, and we had a discussion about whether she should keep the phrase or use *flowered*, *bloomed*, or *blossomed*. I don't know what she will ultimately decide, but what I found exciting was that she was using the concordancing strategy to develop her ability to insert herself into the text she was writing. There was a sense that she was lessening the very unequal relations of power that positioned her as a foreign student with poor English language skills and was beginning to occupy her research space as someone who has a history with its own discourses to bring to the Australian academy.

Similarly, when Aziz, an Iranian student, writing his thesis on traditional Iranian theater, recently wrote about the audience being "nailed up," my initial reaction was to underline it and offer a correction. When we talked through his draft, I became aware that he had wanted to convey a sense of the audience being riveted to their seats or perhaps nailed to their chairs, hence using the terminology, "nailed up." We were then able to talk about the range of resources available to him in English to express the nature of the relationship between Iranian audiences and the actors, which is something very different to what Western audiences know as audience participation.

More recently, I noted a dramatic improvement in Kim's draft, which she brought to our meeting. "Has someone else read this?" I asked, thinking that perhaps she had already had some feedback on the chapter that would account for the improvement. "No," she said, "I've been concordancing." Kim explained to me that while she was reading texts in her field, she had been noting down words and phrases that she thought might be of use to her in her own writing and then "trying them out" as she wrote her chapter. The effect was remarkable – her writing sounded so much more academic and her organization and structure were better, too, as many of the words and phrases she was borrowing were often typical metadiscursive or metatextual markers, which typically help with structuring large amounts of text such as theses (Bunton, 1999). Metadiscourse is central to writers' representations of themselves and to the organization and presentation of their arguments in their texts as it allows them to "engage and influence readers in ways that conform to a discipline's norms, values, and ideology, expressing textual and interpersonal meanings that their audience is likely to accept as credible and convincing" (Hyland, 1999, p. 5). Metadiscourse is therefore clearly implicated in the construction of writers' identities. Phrases such as "my research is also concerned with...," "considerable attention has been paid to...," and "this section attempts to challenge the underlying assumption that..." began to appear in Kim's drafts. Her use of textual metadiscourse via logical connectors (Hyland, 1999, p. 5) also made her writing much more reader-friendly. Not every choice worked seamlessly in the new context, but we could adapt the syntax or lexis or talk about what she had been trying to say with a much greater degree of metalinguistic awareness, which, in turn, enabled us to talk more about writing and the resources she would need in order to express the complex meanings she wished to convey. Her sense of frustration at the limitations imposed on her by her restricted academic English resources also began to lift, and the success of her strategy has boosted her confidence. She is now writing regularly.

These are the beginnings of expropriation: students strategically engaging with the resources of authoritative English. An approach, which may at first sight appear overly technicist, can become a strategy that is empowering for students. Teachers who situate themselves within a critical framework may be reluctant to consider such approaches, but I cannot stress enough how it was the extent to which the students themselves took up the concordancing and did something else with it that made it an empowering tool for them. Concordancing provided us with a point of departure – a way into powerful, potentially exclusionary, discourses – that then took us further than we might have imagined at the outset.

Strategic empowerment – Learners and teachers

I want to suggest that we, too, can recontextualize discourses and reclaim empowerment by linking it to an expanded notion of strategic competence. I see strategic empowerment operating on two related levels. For myself as an educator, within a protean, constantly changing university that seeks to appropriate the language of change and empowerment and manage change, it is important to engage strategically about where and how one's work can still be empowering both for oneself and for students and expropriate a domain in which to work to lessen powerlessness – to take back words, discourses, and social spaces.

What I have been doing is empowering for the students, and I am witnessing growth and development in their writing, but it was through strategies to which I exposed the students and which they chose to try out. Their own sense of powerlessness within an institution that invited them in, without providing them with the grounds for success, is reduced. Pennycook (2001), in his discussion of critical applied linguistics, refers to Spivak's notion of "the strategic use of essentialism" and argues that there are terms that "we cannot not use" (p. 73). Empowerment, I would argue, is one of these, but we need to use it strategically.

Critical academic literacy pedagogies in the corporatizing university, I suggest, will need to engage strategically and recontextualize or expropriate – try out – those aspects of discourses and pedagogies that our students may or may not find powerful. Denzin and Lincoln (1994) conceive of the qualitative researcher as a *bricoleur* (a "professional do-it-yourself person") who uses the "tools of his or her methodological trade, deploying whatever strategies, methods, or empirical materials are at hand" to produce a *bricolage* – a "complex, dense, reflexive, collage-like creation that represents the researcher's images, understandings, and interpretations of the world or phenomenon under analysis" (p. 3). The researcher-as-bricoleur resolves the struggles between paradigms by working "between and within competing and overlapping perspectives and paradigms" (pp. 2–3). We may wish to reflect on this description and begin to think of pedagogy as bricolage as we negotiate the new times in which we find ourselves.

Notes

1. I use the progressive aspect, rather than *corporate,* to signal that the process is not fully accomplished as there is a struggle over this transformation of the university. I define the *corporatizing university* as a site in which, in the global economy, knowledge is marketized as a commodity, where English language degrees are part of the competitive advantage the institution has when competing globally to attract international students and where discourses on quality and flexibility begin to restructure institutional practices and identities.
2. Most students were doing qualitative research projects but were still writing in the objectivist language of traditional research, using categories such as results/findings and an impersonal tenor.

References

Aston, G. (1995). Corpora in language pedagogy: Matching theory and practice. In G. Cook & B. Seidlhoffer (Eds.), *Principles and practice in applied linguistics* (pp. 257–70). Oxford: Oxford University Press.

Bakhtin, M. (1981). *The dialogic imagination: Four essays by M. M. Bakhtin.* Austin: University of Texas Press.

Bartholomae, D. (1985). Inventing the university. In M. Rose (Ed.), *When a writer can't write* (pp. 134–65). New York: Guilford.

Biber, D., & Conrad, S. (2001). Corpus-based research in TESOL. *TESOL Quarterly, 35*(2), 331–36.

Biber, D., Conrad, S., & Reppen, R. (1998). *Corpus linguistics.* Cambridge, England: Cambridge University Press.

Billig, M. (2000). Towards a critique of the critical. *Discourse & Society, 11*(3), 291–2.

Boucher, D. (2001, June 6). No entry under false pretences. *Australian–Higher Education*, p. 33.

Bourdieu, P. (1991). *Language and symbolic power.* (G. Raymond & M. Adamson, Trans.). Cambridge, England: Polity Press. (Original work published 1982)

Bunton, D. (1999). The use of higher level metatext in Ph.D. theses. *English for Specific Purposes, 18,* S41–S56.

Canale, M. (1983). From communicative competence to communicative language pedagogy. In J. C. Richards & R. W. Schmidt (Eds.), *Language and communication* (pp. 2–27). London: Longman.

Cobb, T., & Horst, M. (2001). Reading academic English: Carrying learners across the lexical threshold. In J. Flowerdew & M. Peacock (Eds.), *Research perspectives on English for Academic Purposes* (pp. 315–29). Cambridge, England: Cambridge University Press.

Cope, B., & Kalantzis, M. (Eds.). (1993). *The powers of literacy: A genre approach to teaching writing*. Bristol, England: Falmer Press.

Corson, D. (1997). The learning and use of academic English words. *Language Learning, 47*(4), 671–718.

Coxhead, A. (2000). A new academic word list. *TESOL Quarterly, 35*(2), 213–38.

Denzin, N., & Lincoln, Y. (1994). Introduction: Entering the field of qualitative research. In N. Denzin & Y. Lincoln (Eds.), *Handbook of qualitative research* (pp. 1–17). Newbury Park, CA: Sage.

Ellis, R. (1992). *Second language acquisition and language pedagogy*. Clevedon, England: Multilingual Matters.

Ellsworth, E. (1992). Why doesn't this feel empowering? Working through the repressive myths of critical pedagogy. In C. Luke & J. Gore (Eds.), *Feminisms and critical pedagogy* (pp. 90–119). New York: Routledge.

Fairclough, N. (1992). The appropriacy of appropriateness. In N. Fairclough (Ed.), *Critical language awareness* (pp. 33–56). London: Longman.

Fairclough, N. (1995). *Critical discourse analysis*. London: Longman.

Fairclough, N. (2000). *Language in the new capitalism*. Retrieved June 17, 2001, from http://www.uoc.es/humfil/nlc/LNC-ENG/lnc-eng.html

Farell, L. (2000). Ways of doing, ways of being: Language, education, and "working" identities. *Language and Education, 14*(1), 18–36.

Flowerdew, J. (1993). Concordancing as a tool in course design. *System, 21*(2), 231–44.

Flowerdew, J. (2000). Discourse community, legitimate peripheral participation, and the nonnative-English-speaking scholar. *TESOL Quarterly, 34*(1), 127–50.

Flowerdew, J., & Peacock, M. (2001). The EAP curriculum: Issues, methods, and challenges. In J. Flowerdew & M. Peacock (Eds.), *Research perspectives on English for Academic Purposes* (pp. 177–94). Cambridge, England: Cambridge University Press.

Gee, J. P., Hull, G., & Lankshear, C. (1996). *The new work order*. Sydney: Allen & Unwin.

Gore, J. (1992). What we can do for you! What *can* "we" do for "you"? Struggling over empowerment in critical and feminist pedagogy. In C. Luke & J. Gore (Eds.), *Feminisms and critical pedagogy* (pp. 54–73). New York: Routledge.

Hughes, R., & McCarthy, M. (1998). From sentence to discourse: Discourse, grammar and English language teaching. *TESOL Quarterly, 32*(2), 263–87.

Hyland, K. (1999). Talking to students: Metadiscourse in introductory coursebooks. *English for Specific Purposes, 18*(1), 3–26.

Hyon, S. (1996). Genre in three traditions: Implications for ESL. *TESOL Quarterly, 30*(4), 693–722.

Ivanič, R. (1997). *Writing and identity*. Amsterdam: John Benjamins.

Luke, A. (1996). Genres of power? Literacy education and the production of capital. In R. Hasan & G. Williams (Eds.), *Literacy in society* (pp. 308–38). London: Longman.

McCarthy, M., & Carter, R. (2001). Size isn't everything: Spoken English, corpus, and the classroom. *TESOL Quarterly, 35*(2), 337–40.

Nation, I. (1990). *Teaching and learning vocabulary.* New York: Newbury House.

Norton, B. (2000). *Identity and language learning: Gender, ethnicity, and educational change.* Harlow, England: Pearson Education.

Pennycook, A. (2001). *Critical applied linguistics: A critical introduction.* Mahwah, NJ: Lawrence Erlbaum Associates.

Sinclair, J. (1991). *Corpus, concordance, collocation.* Oxford: Oxford University Press.

Stubbs, M. (1995). Corpus evidence for norms of lexical collocation. In G. Cook & B. Seidlhoffer (Eds.), *Principles and practice in applied linguistics* (pp. 245–56). Oxford: Oxford University Press.

Swales, J., & Feak, C. B. (1994). *Academic writing for graduate students.* Ann Arbor: University of Michigan Press.

Thurstun, J., & Candlin, C. (1998a). Concordancing and the teaching of the vocabulary of academic English. *English for Specific Purposes, 17*(3), 267–80.

Thurstun, J., & Candlin, C. (1998b). *Exploring academic English: A workbook for student essay writing.* Sydney: National Center for English Language Teaching and Research, Macquarie University.

Tidd, J. (2000). The competence cycle: Translating knowledge into new processes, products and services. In J. Tidd (Ed.), *From knowledge management to strategic competence* (pp. 5–25). London: Imperial College Press.

Weber, J. J. (2001). A concordance- and genre-based approach to ESP essay writing. *ELT Journal, 55*(1), 14–9.

Widdowson, H. (2000). On the limitations of linguistics applied. *Applied Linguistics, 21*(1), 3–25.

Willis, D. (1990). *The lexical syllabus.* London: Collins.

Willis, J., & Willis, D. (1988). *The Collins Cobuild English course.* London: William Collins.

9 *Modals and memories: A grammar lesson on the Quebec referendum on sovereignty*

Brian Morgan

Introduction

Like many teachers, I came to understand theory through the back door of pedagogy. Extended graduate study was supported by extensive teaching in adult English as a second language (ESL) community programs. These two worlds meshed nicely. The university offered conceptual details. The community center provided a setting to explore applications – what it might mean, for example, to realize a second language (L2) pronunciation lesson via feminist poststructural notions of *discourse* and *subjectivity* (Morgan, 1997, 1998). With time, I grew less certain of the natural order of things. I began to reflect more upon the human diversity and specialized language practices that came together and shaped identity formation in my classroom and in others like it. These ESL sites – in which close attention to form and meaning were often carefully managed – could not be simply theorized as "disciplinary regimes" (cf. Foucault, 1975/1979) or the relics of a modernist, rationalist epistemology. I came to see these sites as distinct. They seemed to bring subjects into discourse in ways quite unlike the doctoral programs in which most identity theories are conceived and fostered (see Morgan, in press). Subsequently, I started to focus on a notion underpinning this chapter – that as applied linguists, we might see ourselves as contributing unique, language-based insights to the critical theories from which we borrow.

Such contributions are advanced when we take the experiences and observations of ESL practitioners seriously. Empowering pedagogy is not guaranteed by any particular technique or theory; rather, it is the articulation of practices within specific programs and communities that is the most exciting and potentially transformative (see Kumaravadivelu, 2001). Without consulting those closest to developments, the possibilities for innovative pedagogies related to identity are constrained. Moreover, we lose the opportunity to "understand pedagogy as a mode of cultural criticism for questioning the very conditions under which knowledge and identities are produced" (Giroux, 1994, p. 280).

In this chapter, I hope to give some substance to the foundational status of pedagogy as stated by Giroux. To this end, I will describe a lesson on grammar: how it was conceptualized and organized in terms of identity and its implications for poststructural and applied linguistic theories. The lesson is from a unit on the 1995 Quebec referendum on sovereignty. It takes place in downtown Toronto and involves a group of recent Chinese immigrants who were responding to an unexpected crisis in their lives – the possible dismantling of their new home at the same time political change was transforming their place of origin, Hong Kong.

Pedagogical grammar: Conceptual issues

Whereas linguists may argue endlessly over the categories and purposes of grammatical description, teachers must deal with much broader and coinciding sets of issues such as students' prior learning experiences and the demands of standardized curricula. Similarly, whereas linguists may anchor their descriptive schema in claims of scientificity and truth (see Robinson, 1975), teachers tailor their explanations to the "here and now" of classrooms, improvising and elaborating upon a particular description through ongoing dialogue with students (see Johnston & Goettsch, 2000). And perhaps most important, whereas linguists' descriptions may remain immersed in a world of conceptual abstraction, teachers' explanations require reference to worldly affairs in which notions of grammaticality may only have minimal bearing on ESL students' life chances outside the school.

In reflecting on the activity described here, I am reminded of Allen's (1974) prudent advice on the importance of "asserting the independence of methodological decisions from formal linguistic constraints" (p. 68) in pedagogical grammars. As Allen proposed, almost thirty years ago, pedagogical grammars should not be subordinate to the explanatory values governing formal, descriptive grammars: "Whatever statement about grammar 'makes sense' to a student and helps him to achieve a learning task, is in some important sense explanatory" (p. 69).

Recent confirmation of the need for more flexible, teacher-directed approaches to form-focused instruction can be found in Ellis's (1998) discussion of options in grammar teaching. Ellis rightfully argues that the discourses[1] that regulate academic, second language acquisition (SLA) research and the conditions of pedagogy are, in many ways, fundamentally incompatible – a longstanding argument that has had marginal influence on institutional decision making and theory formation in applied linguistics (see Clarke, 1994; Crookes, 1997; Ellis, 1997). Greater collaboration and research options are needed, in Ellis's view, in order to understand both the factors that shape a teacher's instructional choices and the extent to which such choices might be supported by SLA inquiry.

An example of Ellis' proposal can be found in Borg's (1998) comprehensive portrait of one teacher's "personal pedagogical system." The notion of system here is not synonymous with experimental research intent on correlating specific methods with acquisition; rather, Borg seeks to provide insights into individual teacher development and decision making that are initiated by formal preservice training and are subsequently (re)shaped over time through classroom interaction. Similar to Ellis and others (e.g., Johnston & Goettsch, 2000; Varghese, in press), Borg views such personalized accounts as contributing to teacher understanding in ways that are unmet by the provision of prescriptive methods.

Interestingly, and to reiterate Allen's (1974) observations, what made sense or had "explanatory value" in the context of Borg's (1998) report varied at times – and for reasons that I would characterize as inscribed by power–knowledge relations – from the types of concerns normally foregrounded by SLA research. For example, Borg's informant used error analyses in class not only as the basis for designing a student-centered syllabus, but also as a way of satisfying some students' expectations of what constituted a legitimate approach to language instruction. As Borg notes, this teacher's "beliefs about students' expectations had a powerful influence on his behavior here and did in fact emerge in the study as a pervasive influence on his approach to grammar teaching" (p. 16). The components of this teacher's personal pedagogical system "revealed a network of interacting and potentially conflicting beliefs about a wide variety of issues related not only to L2 teaching but also to teaching and learning in general" (p. 28).

In the activity described below, I expand upon the types of extralinguistic variables that Borg identifies. The interacting beliefs and issues he mentions, I would argue, are an integral feature of the pedagogy and the options we might imagine for grammar teaching, especially in the kinds of community-based programs in which the Quebec referendum was discussed. That these variables might, at times, appear marginal or conflicting is a reflection, in part, of the continuing power of SLA to co-opt teachers into prioritizing autonomous, psycholinguistic issues over the dynamic, multifaceted social and ideological contexts that co-occur and interrelate with all aspects of pedagogy (see Ellis, 1997; Norton, 2000).

Pedagogical grammar in a community-based ESL program

In the Chinese community center where the following lessons took place, students' reasons for attending a particular class are often only partially motivated by second language issues, narrowly defined. In contrast to generic ESL programs (Burnaby, 1988, p. 29) typically offered in formal settings such as universities, colleges, and schools, community-based ESL programs often attract students by way of special provisions for childcare, flexible ESL programming, and a wide range of settlement services often provided in a students' first language (L1).

In the center where the Quebec referendum was studied, many newcomers receive information in English, Cantonese, or Mandarin on public services such as healthcare, employment, and education. A women's support group, Chinese language school for children, and a yearly tax consulting service for seniors are also very popular. Many have learned about our ESL classes through attendance at monthly seminars on topics such as the citizenship process, menopause and osteoporosis, and the Employment Standards Act, to name a few. The popularity of services provided has been instrumental in attracting new students to the ESL program, a crucial point given that continued funding for a particular class is contingent upon attendance (e.g., a minimum of fifteen during this lesson).

Also, many students travel several hours a day to attend our classes, even though the class time is relatively short (from 9:30 A.M. to 12:30 P.M. every Tuesday through Friday morning) and closer programs might be available. Moreover, in spite of the fact that Toronto is a city in which almost every conceivable personal and business service can be obtained in Cantonese, some students attend almost every day of the year. Some of them have been in my class, the advanced class in the program, for over eight years. Though I'd like to think that my teaching abilities and interpersonal skills are primary reasons for such loyalties, a better case could be made that at the community center, students feel a sense of belonging that they would not otherwise have in a more formal institution. This sense of belonging, even ownership – many students hold memberships in the center and contribute time and money in all fundraising activities – is based largely on shared identity. A common language and cultural background, age similarities (most are seniors), and a familiar place of origin (most of my class originates from Hong Kong) help form close allegiances to the community agency as well as between fellow students and teachers.

Pedagogy in such settings evolves in ways that mirror the social, cultural, and political contexts of the settlement agency and the local community (see Auerbach, 2000; Morgan, 1998, 2002; Rivera, 1999; Sauvé, 2000). Not only course content, but also teaching styles (e.g., teacher-centered methodologies, extensive use of L1) can reflect the identities and expectations of students. But it is also a two-way street: Unexamined beliefs, which might initially underpin an activity, can become focal points during lessons. Intentionally or not, traditions and norms sometimes undergo critical exploration as students measure the past against the present and (re)evaluate their commonalities and differences in light of how they interpret Canadian life. Identity, in this respect, can be seen as both the *condition* and the *outcome* of what takes place through pedagogy. A teacher's recognition of this process adds an important dimension to his or her personal pedagogical system by expanding the range of teaching options in ways that acknowledge and utilize the fundamental role that language plays in identity formation.

A grammar activity, conceptualized in the community setting I've briefly described, necessarily involves a number of overlapping concerns, reminiscent of Odlin's (1994) description of pedagogical grammar as a "practically oriented hybrid drawing on work in several fields" (p. 11). For the lesson below, practical needs suggested that I focus on providing students with accessible descriptions, clear examples of target structures, and useful practice activities. Yet I also wanted to organize this lesson in ways that reflected the complex social and political contexts influencing my students. I didn't want to present these grammar forms as closed meanings within a graded hierarchy of structures, functions, or tasks. Instead, I wanted to conceptualize this lesson in broader terms, as a *social* practice, one in which meanings are also shaped by the dynamics of a classroom – its personalities, gestures, spaces, collective memories, and power relations. Such dynamics would not be seen as discrete elements outside the parameters attributed to a grammar activity but, rather, as interacting phenomena that collectively structured the range of meanings deemed permissible in the course of an activity.[2]

Grammar, in this hybrid perspective, wouldn't be preoccupied solely with helping students make correct choices. Instead, it might also look at the activity in terms of poststructural identity and *investment* as defined by Norton (1997): "The construct of investment conceives of the language learner as having a complex history and multiple desires. An investment in the target language is also an investment in a learner's own social identity, which changes across time and place" (p. 411). Notions of choice and desire, in this sense, are not entirely our own autonomous creation, but reflect our positioning within the various discourses that shape our lives. Interesting conceptual questions come to mind: How might a pedagogical grammar attempt to articulate and facilitate "complex histor[ies] and multiple desires" of students' lives "changing over time and place" (p. 411)? Or, in other words, how might a lesson in "consciousness-raising" – in its more familiar, grammatical usage (see Yip, 1994) – potentially reach out and initiate a *critical* consciousness of how subjects are constituted through discourse?

I can better elaborate upon these difficult ideas with reference to the Quebec referendum. For my students, the Quebec referendum was being evaluated though China's reacquisition of Hong Kong in 1997. For many, this was a continuous juxtaposition that reflected juxtaposed lives – a diasporic, transnational imaginary, following Appadurai (1996) – sustained by frequent travel back "home" and unlimited access to

Chinese media (e.g., television, movies, music, newspapers), products, and services in the Toronto area.

From the beginning of class in September 1995, speculative statements on Canada–Quebec relations after a potential yes vote were often compared and evaluated in respect to the Basic Law agreement negotiated between China and Britain, which promised to maintain the political and economic status quo in Hong Kong for 50 years. Comments in the class indicated that this was a difficult process. As personal beliefs and predictions regarding one event changed, various emotional and financial commitments pertaining to the other were reconsidered and, in some cases, revised.

Two students had spouses who worked in Hong Kong because of the relatively high incomes and low taxes there, and they were concerned that the benefits of such an arrangement might end with the transition to Beijing's authority. Others worried about property and other financial resources. Would their assets be more secure in Hong Kong, post-1997, or in a postreferendum Canada, destabilized by the separation of Quebec? A degree of bitterness was also evident. Many came to Canada to escape instability only to perceive it as equally present in Canada. In sum, the co-occurrence of the referendum and China's acquisition of Hong Kong seemed to bring out a wide expression of conflicting emotions and loyalties over the course of several months, which reminded me of Norton's (2000) depiction of identity as "multiple and contradictory" and "a site of struggle" (p. 127).

Based on these conditions, two aspects of treatment seemed appropriate to me for the purposes of grammatical consciousness-raising: (a) make the comparative assessment or intertextuality of Hong Kong and Quebec an explicit feature of a direct grammar lesson, and (b) introduce a particular subsystem of grammar through which feelings and meanings of ambivalence, apprehension, and possibility regarding the future are expressed. In terms of the latter, I selected the field of modality, in the dialogic sense defined by Hasan and Perrett (1994), where language functions to express a "speaker's intersubjectivity, whereby relations are created, maintained, and, in time, changed" (p. 207).

Modality, in this latter sense, is intimately bound up with the negotiation of individual and collective identities. It involves the production and reception of statements on what is held to be real or true for those who share a common background.[3] And it makes demands on the receivers of such messages to conform or risk censure from those whose support – be it emotional, spiritual, or financial – often sustains us. It also involves relations of power/knowledge and discourse as meant by Foucault (1975/1979, 1982). Within the discourse of "us," whose voice has greatest authority? Who, among "us," can use softer words than *must* or *will* or *definitely* or *surely* and without diminishing the force of their assertions? (See Janks, 1991, pp. 193–5.) And how is this authority contingently and interpersonally mediated by the signifiers of age, race, or gender, for example, and by the spatial settings where these assertions are made – that is, in a restaurant with close friends as opposed to a classroom grouping among several unfamiliar faces?

These contingent, discursive aspects of modality are rarely taught or examined in ESL settings, yet they are a crucial dimension of the meaning making that takes place through pedagogy. For teachers, a "consciousness of discourse" should be viewed as an integral component of (critical) language awareness (see Corson, 1999; Cummins, 2000, 2001; New London Group, 1996): a way of thinking and responding that is, on the one hand, attendant to forms, (multi)modalities, and their intrinsic properties and, on the other, alert to the social dynamics through which forms (temporarily) attain both dominant and subordinate meanings within particular communities and public spheres.

In the classroom: First lessons on the referendum

The day after the Quebec legislature introduced the referendum question, I brought in an article from a local newspaper (*Toronto Star*) that examined its controversial aspects. The question was, "Do you agree that Quebec should become sovereign, after having made a formal offer to Canada for a new economic and political partnership, within the scope of the bill respecting the future of Quebec and of the agreement signed on June 12, 1995?" (Stewart, 1995). In my classroom, as across Canada that day, people were unsure of what the word *sovereign* meant or what Quebecois were specifically being asked to vote on. Our first lesson focused on examining the terms *sovereignty* and *independence*, the word with which sovereignty was frequently being compared by politicians and pundits. In this activity, students drew upon decompositional strategies and principles of word formation in their L1 as a way of analyzing and potentially understanding the public controversy emerging over the question's wording (see Morgan, 2002, for a detailed discussion).

After the vocabulary activity, we read the *Toronto Star* article (Stewart, 1995), which highlighted specific concerns over the referendum question and included a number of quotes from prominent federal and provincial politicians. The next day, one of my students brought in an article from the local Chinese press ("Will Quebec," 1995), which included a translation of the referendum question and a discussion of the potential ramifications of a yes vote. I had students discuss and compare the two articles and report to me on any important differences between the two. Of note, the Chinese article predicted that the projected annual Quebec deficit of 3.9 billion dollars could rise as high as 15–20 billion after a yes vote. The Chinese article also provided a short background discussion on the previous Quebec sovereignty referendum in 1980.

A grammar lesson

Some students had had problems putting across their thoughts in the activities above. As mentioned above, I decided to organize a lesson around modality forms that might help them convey their ideas and, for some, convey the mixed feelings they were experiencing. To begin the grammar activity, I mentioned to the students that, at times, their expectations and feelings about the referendum were not clear to me. I then reviewed several structures used to express degrees of likelihood, an area of modality related to our prior discussions.[4]

Prior to the referendum, we had already examined several forms of prediction and likelihood in a book called *Communicative Grammar Practice* (Jones, 1992). Jones provides examples of personal (e.g., I'm certain/ I'm sure) and impersonal (e.g., It looks/It sounds as if/There's a chance) forms of attribution as well as degrees of likelihood (im/probability, im/possibility, un/certainty) in the present and past. Following Jones's forms and categories, I placed several examples on the board for discussion. Similar to the teacher described in Borg's (1998) article, my provision of explicit descriptions and model sentences (cf. options in form-focused instruction; Ellis, 1998) was based on my long-term work in this community program and my recognition of the legitimacy that such an approach has with my students. Here are the examples I placed on the blackboard:

Certainty after a NO vote:
1. The Canadian dollar will go up.
2. I'm absolutely sure (that) the Canadian dollar will go up.
3. I'm certain/sure (that) the Canadian economy will improve.

Probability after a YES vote:
4. Many Anglophones will probably leave Quebec.
5. It looks as if Quebecers won't be allowed to keep two passports.
6. Relations between Quebec and Canada are likely to be difficult.

The content matter for these sentences had come from previous classroom discussions. The three variations on certainty and economic issues reflected students' intense interest in such matters, and it provided an opportunity to elaborate on the relative emphases provided. For example, most students easily recognized that the second sentence indicated a slightly stronger position of certainty than the third based on the adverb or modal adjunct *absolutely*. But in the first, the use of *will* to express high likelihood was slightly ambiguous for some because of its overlapping function in expressing future tense (see Lock, 1996, p. 196).

I also talked briefly about strategic differences when choosing between personal (e.g., statements 2, 3) and impersonal attribution. Sentences using declarative mood, and especially statement 5 with its hypothetical "as if" clause and nonreferential subject (i.e., "it"), can allow agents of an action to be hidden or can defer the speaker's personal responsibility for the content of an utterance. But as I reminded the students, in some contexts (e.g., legal and academic settings), sentences that appear impersonal imply that the author has applied greater care and objectivity in formulating a concept or opinion, and the rhetorical influence of facts constructed in this manner can be particularly persuasive in public debates (see Janks, 1991; Lakoff, 1990).

The role of newspapers was also pertinent to this specific activity because several students had mentioned that the major Hong Kong newspapers were "more careful" or "silent" about any negative predictions for the future after China's reacquisition. In retrospect, it would have been interesting to have the students do a contrastive analysis of the forms used to be more careful in Chinese and English. Due to time constraints, however, I used the example to simply reiterate the point that language choices are shaped by larger contexts and power relations.

After the discussion of the model sentences, I placed the class in small groups and asked them to talk about the implications for Canada and Quebec after a yes or no referendum vote using some of the forms described above. I also made predictions of Hong Kong's future after 1997 an option. I told each group to write down any sentences that were similar to the ones on the board and that were interesting for their group. During the activity, I went around the room to listen and make suggestions regarding intentions and choice of forms. Since I was providing corrections and suggestions throughout the group activity, the examples below do not reflect the degree to which my earlier explanations may have contributed to their accuracy. The following examples were produced by students and placed on the board for discussion:

1. We're absolutely sure that China is going to take over Hong Kong in 1997.
2. I'm certain that Hong Kongers won't be able to keep two passports.
3. Quebecers won't be fooled by the duplicity.
4. Some of the Chinese people are likely to leave Quebec.
5. Canada is not likely to treat Quebec as an equal partner in economic and political affairs.
6. After a yes vote, the federalist leaders will probably have a meeting to talk about a new treaty with Quebec.

7. It's likely that the Hong Kong immigration laws will change in 1997.
8. After a yes vote, it's likely that Quebecers won't be allowed to keep a Canadian passport.

In my mind, several aspects of these sentences affirm Hasan and Perrett's (1994) depiction of modality as a site of dialogic engagement "whereby social relations are created, maintained, and, in time, changed" (p. 207). As mentioned earlier, China's 1997 reacquisition of Hong Kong signified the experience through which the Quebec referendum would be evaluated by my students. The interweaving of these two historic events in the lesson, I believe, further encouraged students to explore the meaning potential available through the lexicogrammar system. As well, attention to form should be seen in the context of power relations and Norton's (2000) construct of investment. Whenever a teacher authorizes a language activity, it provides a certain degree of anonymity and deferred attribution for the expression of ideas that potentially challenge the rules regarding what can be said and by whom in the evolving discourse of who we are as Chinese Canadians, as in this particular case. The provision of L2 forms with which to express the subtle degrees of modality enabled students to explore the complexity of their own histories and their emerging and often contradictory desires for the future.

In statement 2, for example, the possibility of keeping Hong Kong passports after 1997 was a topic that students had been reluctant to talk about in English, if at all in Chinese, during this and earlier activities. Again, mixed feelings were abundant on this issue. Maintaining a Hong Kong passport certainly facilitated easier entry for trips back home. But on an emotional level, a Hong Kong passport also enhanced a feeling of still belonging – a transnational identity – and many newcomers in my class were anxious about their future prospects in Canada given its high rate of taxation and unemployment compared to Hong Kong. Thus, the selective and interchangeable use of two passports was a possible means of getting around the legal requirement that landed immigrants spend at least six months a year in Canada in order to qualify for citizenship. Although no one in my class had ever personally claimed doing this, they were certainly aware that others might be doing it and that it contravened Canadian immigration rules.

Another reason, which paralleled the caution of the Hong Kong media mentioned above, was that if someone expressed a desire to hold two passports, he or she would be indicating a lack of confidence in Hong Kong's future under Beijing's direction. While a simple statement in this respect might seem relatively harmless, especially in the context of an ESL classroom in Toronto, a few students remained guarded, uncertain as to the type of government that would soon emerge in Hong Kong and the reach and scope of its authority.

When asked, the student who wrote statement 2 told the class that the Canadian–Quebec debate about passports (Would Quebecers be allowed to keep Canadian passports after a yes vote?) had focused his attention on speculation in the Toronto Chinese press on the same issue related to Hong Kong. From his comments, I inferred that his specific realization of modality could be described as *multifunctional*, simultaneously predictive and pragmatic, the "certainty" of the former function emphasizing the urgency of the latter – the need to act upon this possible development for those who frequently travel and work in both Canada and Hong Kong. Also, in terms of pragmatism, it is interesting to note that the author of this sentence strategically avoids directly identifying or criticizing the government source of this future restriction, which could be characterized as a particularly skillful use of modality forms given the context and mixed feelings present. Modality, in this particular example, and in light of concepts stated by Hasan and Perrett (1994) and Norton (2000), might be seen as a way of negotiating a new political identity; that is, a means of exploring what can be said and what might be insinuated in a new political culture.

Placing these sentences collectively on the board raised other important issues for the class. Statement 3 indicated the integration of new vocabulary (e.g., duplicity) from the *Toronto Star* article we had read earlier. But the sentence also referred to an earlier debate in class. Following the opinions of federal politicians at the time, many students criticized the Parti Québécois (the governing party in Quebec and the author of the referendum question) for intentionally deceiving voters. In fact, some were astounded that the federal government was allowing the referendum to take place. In their opinion, no country can possibly function or continue to exist with the kinds of ongoing pressures that Quebec nationalism poses for Canada. Moreover, a couple of students suggested that the Canadian army should be sent in to stop this and other referenda from ever occurring. However, by having statement 6 on the board, other options promoting compromise and negotiation were circulated in class. Again, several students related this issue to their experiences in China and their concerns for the future. One student mentioned Tiananmen Square and his fear that, one day, the Chinese army would be similarly used in Hong Kong.

For all present, it was a thought-provoking exchange, in terms of both ideas and their implications beyond this particular activity. The analyses (in terms of both accuracy and function) and group discussion of competing views – especially from those who ostensibly share core values based on ethnicity – help prepare students with a range of linguistic and rhetorical skills with which they might better anticipate and promote controversial ideas in public. At the same time, this activity raised students' awareness of the dynamic and discursive nature of identity – that cultural norms (e.g., the "correct" way to govern a nation) are subject to change, especially in contact with the dominant belief systems of a new society.

One final grammar issue should be mentioned. Statement 1 was difficult for me to deal with in the whole-class discussion. I tried to explain that the propositional content of the sentence was a future fact (i.e., China *is* going to take over Hong Kong in 1997), not really an expression of one's feelings of inclination and potentiality. So the use of personal attribution seemed inappropriate to me in this case. I'm not sure my explanation clarified very much. In retrospect, this error might be seen as an example of semantic overlapping between modality and future tense indicators caused by auxiliaries such as *will* and *be going to*. But reflecting on this sentence, I also see an interesting point to make in the context of critical language awareness (CLA). The appearance of personal attribution – taking credit for something – implies some form of agency has occurred or is in process, either in terms of doing something or taking a particular ideational stance in regard to an issue. But if the propositional content includes phenomena in the natural and social world that are clearly not or are unlikely to be subject to agency, then the sentence is misleading or intentionally deceptive. What comes to mind is the time-honored political activity of claiming to do much more than is actually accomplished or possible under the circumstances. In the future, this might be an interesting area of CLA to explore in class.

In sum, the examples and discussion above indicate how conventional ESL activities, such as a grammar lesson, can be organized in ways that take advantage of the reconceptualizations of identity and culture now current in the ESL literature (see Cummins, 2001; Harklau, 1999; Ibrahim, 1999; Kramsch, 2000; Kubota, 1999; Lin et al., 2002; McKay & Wong, 1996; Nelson, 1999; Norton, 1997, 2000; Pavlenko & Lantolf, 2000; Toohey, 2000; Vandrick, 1997). Once we recognize language as a vehicle through which identities are continuously negotiated – rather than a linguistic repository of innate or naturalistic elements – the transformative possibilities of pedagogy increase accordingly. This grammar lesson did not just describe preexisting states and thoughts. Nor did it develop in an insular and predetermined way. As the title of this chapter indicates, modals evoked memories, but classroom organization (e.g., space, seating), form-focused techniques, and interpersonal relations all combined to shape how these memories would be understood. Through such articulations – some direct and observable, others indirect and introspective – pedagogy can be seen as initiating and facilitating emergent understandings of what might or might not be possible for oneself and one's community in the Canadian context. As Simon (1992) eloquently states, "When we teach, we are always implicated in the construction of a horizon of possibility for ourselves, our students and our communities" (p. 56).

Conclusions: Toward constructive dialogue

In this final section, I want to revisit a couple of points introducing this chapter: the relative uniqueness of our profession and the need to see ourselves as contributors, as well as borrowers, in the development of identity theories across the social sciences. The relevance of such efforts, especially in educational contexts, will be enhanced if we pay greater attention to the conditions of pedagogy and the insights of ESL/EFL (English as a foreign language) practitioners. In this respect, the determination of what counts as valid knowledge about identity should not be based on theoretical foundations alone, but also on pedagogical outcomes and a genuine dialogue with teachers.

The grammar activity in this chapter serves as an example. At the level of theory, my discussion of modality forms might seem incompatible with poststructural views on subjectivity. My classroom treatment, which maps out several correspondences between particular forms and their ideational and/or social functions, would be characterized as overly deterministic, a critique often directed toward the Hallidayan, systemic-functionalist approach to language that partially underpins my conceptualization of grammar in a community-based ESL program. Halliday's theory seeks to provide a systematic account of how social experience, interpersonal relationships, and language intentions are embedded within and can be abstracted from the sentence and clausal level of language (cf. Halliday's notion of *register* – Halliday & Hasan, 1985; Hasan & Perrett, 1994; Hyon, 1996). Every sentence is described in terms of its multifunctionality and co-occurrence in varied conceptual fields: "We do not look separately at its different parts; rather we look at the whole thing simultaneously from a number of different angles, each perspective contributing towards the total interpretation" (Halliday & Hasan, 1985, p. 23). This layered perspective is further enhanced by a "continuity of description" (Kress, 1976, p. xi) whereby the smallest linguistic units are explained in relation to the largest contextual units to reflect the various functions that language is intended to serve in a given situation.

From a poststructural perspective (see Cherryholmes, 1988; Shea, 1998; Weedon, 1987), the authenticity of such social mappings would be highly problematic. Quite likely, dominant notions of identity and society would be descriptively formalized; the meanings that privileged groups attach to particular forms would be made to appear *natural* ("that's the way it is for everyone who speaks the language"), whereas important complexities, contradictions, and differences – other ways of knowing and being in society – would be diminished or erased. Drawing from Foucault (1975/1979, 1982), the concern here wouldn't just be over the relative accuracy of such representations, but rather their *effects*, how they bring others into discourse, and the new forms of subjectivization that are produced as a consequence. The point is more than academic: When forms of social representation (e.g., grammars, histories, ethnographies) become normalized, minorities who have been so represented often come to fashion themselves – even in terms of their *otherness* and the forms of resistance they might develop – through the positions that a dominant discourse establishes.

Given the inherent dangers of representation, would it not be prudent to avoid all kinds of form-function modeling in class altogether? Certainly, there are strands of postmodern and poststructural thought that would advocate this response (see Rosenau, 1992; Shea, 1998). In her portrait of what she terms "skeptical postmodernists," Rosenau describes their stance as a profound doubt toward

> ever authentically representing anything. They suggest focusing not on the generalizable, the unified, what is common to the modern world, but rather on all that difference implies, what can never be represented. This calls for a nonrepresentational methodology or none at all. (p. 97)

A comparable category is provided by Shea (1998) in her survey of the literature (cf. "nihilistic deconstructive postmodernism," pp. 341–2). *Deconstructionism*, as noted by Shea and others (Cherryholmes, 1988; Norris 1982, 1987; Weedon, 1987), is a method or strategy that is especially characteristic of this line of thought, of which Derrida's (1972/1982) concept of *différance* is foundational – if such a thing can be said in an area of inquiry that eschews foundations, universals, and metanarratives. *Différance* builds upon Saussure's structuralist principles, particularly its relational semantics in which the meanings of words and signs are produced *within* language through differences between other signs in a self-regulating language system. Derrida radicalizes this conception: "In a language, in the *system* of language, there are only differences. . . . On the one hand, these differences *play*: in language. . . . On the other hand, these differences are themselves *effects*" (p. 11).

A fundamental indeterminacy is the paramount value here. There is no natural or nonsocial guarantor for the meanings we attach to words. Deconstruction applies this play of differences to broader conceptualizations of texts – not only books, but also events and experiences, even the categories and discourses that shape identity. Texts are read against themselves, revealing their inconsistencies, assumptions, and "aporias" (i.e., self-generated paradoxes). In this way, texts become much more and often much less than they appear to be.

Much has been written about the limits and possibilities for deconstructive analyses. Does deconstruction open up or reduce the parameters for interpretive critique? On the positive side, Terdiman (1985) sees deconstruction as providing poststructuralism with "conceptual substance and coherence to that image of culture as a 'field of struggle'" (p. 33). In contrast, Foucault, according to Norris (1987), views "deconstruction as a mere rhetorical bag of tricks, a neat little 'pedagogy' secure in its knowledge that nothing exists outside the text" (p. 216). And it is this latter position that compels us to examine the ethical dimensions of textualization and deconstruction when such techniques are applied to identity. To what extent can we, or should we, read people's intentions, thoughts, and acts as if they were potentially works of fiction, open to any number of equally valid interpretations, or more specifically, from the perspective of another discursive formation. As Pennycook (2001) notes in a discussion of the politics of texts, "poststructuralism may be criticized on a number of grounds including its inability to deal with the 'real,' its tendency to slide back into forms of determinism (we are all products of discourses), and its apparent relativism" (p. 108).

While acknowledging such critiques, we should also guard against conflating a plurality of views and possible applications within a singularized term such as poststructuralism. Many educators, whose teaching and research are indebted to the critical theories named here, would agree that methods in support of nonrepresentation (e.g., deconstruction and critical introspection) are insufficient in terms of bringing about meaningful social, political, or environmental changes (see Benesch, 2001; Gore, 1993; O'Sullivan, 1999; Pennycook, 2001). Also required are more politically engaged critiques of power in everyday life, communities, and institutions, followed by the provision of constructive alternatives and concrete plans of action. Opposing representation, as a general principle, is therefore not the most productive option for teaching purposes. Instead, what we might explore are better forms and ways of doing it (see Canagarajah, 1996).

This latter strategy – exploring better forms of representation – seems more relevant to me, most of all because it concurs with my own assumptions about the engaged, participatory nature of pedagogy. Moreover, I think that it is a goal toward which applied linguists and ESL practitioners might contribute unique and insightful perspectives, opening up dimensions of constructive dialogue and theoretical hybridity not previously considered. This has been the spirit behind my efforts in this chapter. I have tried to give a detailed account of my own personal pedagogical system, informed by discursive elements of both poststructuralism and applied linguistics and grounded in the conditions of a community-based ESL program. In this respect, I have conceptualized a grammar lesson as not only a site of identity *representation*, but also a site of identity *creation* – the former drawing on Halliday's social-semiotic perspective, the latter inspired by notions of discourse and poststructural subjectivity, especially through the work of Norton (2000).

Drawing on my experiences in ESL classrooms, I would contend that if we, as critical practitioners, avoid formal models of sociocontextual representation (based on their theoretical or foundational inadequacies), we may be ignoring one of the central experiences of L2 learners' subjectivities. Given the prior development of a metalanguage, ESL students are favorably predisposed – in contrast to monolingual students – toward making abstractions and generalizations that link the microstructures of texts to the discursive macrostructures of society (see Cope & Kalantzis, 1993; New London Group, 1996). Similarly, Janks (1991) notes that "discourse is, amongst other things, a linguistic construction" (p. 192). If, as Fairclough (1989) states, "being constrained is a precondition of being enabled" (p. 39), then the types of cognitive–analytical/semiotic–multimodal experiences that L2 students have acquired warrant serious consideration. These experiences are not only salient features of identity formation, they are also important resources with which to shape counterdiscursive practices in ESL classrooms.[5] Such a view is also strongly supported by the work of Jim Cummins (2000, 2001) and his linguistic interdependence principle, in which sustained academic exposure in both L1 and L2 furthers a common underlying proficiency with significant advantages for the development of critical literacy skills.

Janks' work in critical language awareness exemplifies this approach. For example, note what she says regarding the function of agentless passives in the naturalization of existing social relations: "It goes without saying that students are not in a position to find or interpret agentless passives, unless they understand the structural forms of the passive voice. The critical approach provides students with a reason for mastering the forms" (Janks, 1991, p. 196). Consistent throughout her work, Janks uses categories for critical text analyses that are familiar to the ESL classroom and are derived from Halliday's approach to grammar. Examples would be direct and reported speech (Janks, 1998), the article system (Janks, 1991), lexicalization (Janks, 1997), and choices of mood, modality, or polarity (Janks, 1997).

Janks is also sensitive to the critique made against systemic-functionalists and the tendency for some to deploy form–function relationships reductively and normatively in the classroom. Drawing on Fairclough's (1989, 1995) three-dimensional model of discourse, Janks (1997) emphasizes that critical text analyses must always be related dialectically to the processes of their social production and interpretation and always within the larger societal and institutional discourses in which they circulate. Also of note, issues of identity formation (e.g., race, gender) and their discursive construction in the South African context, where Janks lives and works, figure prominently in many of her analyses (see Janks, 1991, 1997). Most important, by making L2 students' metalinguistic experiences central to CLA, Janks' approach is especially responsive to their experiences of difference and power/knowledge relations.

It is not my intention in this chapter to suggest that all critical teachers become grammarians. But I do believe that those of us inspired by contemporary critical theories might learn from, and quite possibly advance, our aspirations for social justice by way of engaging seriously with the experiences of pedagogical grammarians. As I found in the lessons on the Quebec referendum, awareness of the formal properties of language can contribute to developing critical citizenship skills – perhaps not for all L2 students, but certainly for some.

Regarding identity formation, we might also explore more seriously the degree to which classroom instruction in an L2 constitutes different ways of being and knowing in the world. In so doing, we might reflect on what Rey Chow (1998) observes as the current tendency among "the community of intellectuals, East and West" – to be "complacent about our ability to criticize the racist and sexist blunders inherent in the stereotypical representations of our cultural 'others'" (p. 74). Part of this complacency could be redressed through constructive engagement with pedagogy as a legitimate site of identity formation and knowledge production – hence, our understanding of others.

Notes

1. Discourse is a term I use frequently in this chapter. Variously interpreted (see Kumaravadivelu, 1999; Pennycook, 1994), my usage reflects my understanding of Foucault (1975/1979, 1982). Discourses regulate and ascribe social values to all forms of human interaction – oral and written texts, gestures, images, and spaces – of which language is one important modality. In Foucault's provocative terminology, discourses are systems of *power/knowledge*, operating on and through people in their everyday lives. An ESL teacher, for example, would understand his or her professional role through the particular subject position offered by the type of SLA discourse inferred by Ellis. The insights that he or she might have gained from pedagogy would then be viewed as merely anecdotal and not relevant to theory formation. Moreover, this teacher would not be acknowledged as an "expert" on language and thus would be relatively powerless in the decision-making processes that determined his or her professional life. Such effects of discourse are not incontestable, however. Access to other discourses, through self-study or colleagues, might assist a teacher in challenging the marginal subject position offered here through SLA (see Norton, 2000).
2. The influence of spatial organization on identity first came to my attention through Foucault's *Discipline and Punish: The Birth of the Prison* (1975/1979), in which he traces the emergence of architecturally enhanced forms of power. Benthem's "panopticon," emblematic of the modern prison, was only one manifestation of a discursive shift toward the perpetual management and surveillance of populations through new techniques of observation and measurement. Recently, Kelleen Toohey's (1998, 2000) work has alerted

me to the significance of classroom seating arrangements in the identity formation of primary school kids. In her study of a Grade 1 classroom combining both L2 learners and anglophones, L2 learners are seated close to the teacher, enabling sustained observation and normalization of the behaviors and values deemed necessary for schools and society. Toohey describes how both students' conformity and their instances of resistance are transformed over time to reflect these arrangements. Similar to Foucault, Toohey's microanalysis illuminates the expansion of neo-liberalism into every facet of our lives. Liberalism is not simply an economic set of principles. Values regarding individualism, utility, private ownership of ideas and things, and so forth are inculcated at a very early age and reinforced by a complex set of verbal, gestural, and spatial resources.

3. Expressions of modality also pertain to images that are measured against cultural assumptions regarding reality and naturalism. In our society, "the dominant standard by which we judge visual realism and hence visual modality, remains for the moment, naturalism as conventionally understood, 'photorealism'" (Kress & van Leeuwen, 1996, p. 163).
4. As noted by Lock (1996), "expressions of likelihood can include: modal auxiliaries (e.g., *might, may*, and *should*), modal adjuncts (e.g., *definitely* and *probably*), attributive clauses (e.g., *I'm certain, It's likely*, and *I'm sure*), [and] mental process clauses of cognition (e.g., *I think* and *I doubt*)" (p. 194).
5. A comparable argument comes from Poynton (1993): "There is a need for the recuperation in poststructuralist theory of certain kinds of linguistic knowledge, considered as technologies for understanding how the representations constituting discourses are actually constructed and the linguistic means by which subjects come to be constituted in specific power/knowledge relations" (p. 2). Similar to my own perspective, Poynton sees the grammatics of systemic functionalism as potentially advantageous for poststructuralism.

References

Allen, J. P. B. (1974). Pedagogic grammar. In J. P. B. Allen & S. P. Corder (Eds.), *The Edinburgh course in applied linguistics, Vol. 3: Techniques in applied linguistics* (pp. 59–92). London: Oxford University Press.

Appadurai, A. (1996). *Modernity at large: Cultural dimensions of globalization.* Minneapolis: University of Minnesota Press.

Auerbach, E. R. (2000). Creating participatory learning communities: Paradoxes and possibilities. In J. K. Hall & W. G. Eggington (Eds.), *The sociopolitics of English language teaching* (pp. 143–64). Clevedon, England: Multilingual Matters.

Benesch, S. (2001). *Critical English for academic purposes.* Mahwah, NJ: Lawrence Erlbaum Associates.

Borg, S. (1998). Teachers' pedagogical systems and grammar teaching: A qualitative study. *TESOL Quarterly, 32*, 9–38.

Burnaby, B. (1988). Community based ESL: An assessment of a federal pilot initiative. *TESL Canada Journal, 6*, 27–39.

Canagarajah, A. S. (1996). From critical research practice to critical research reporting. *TESOL Quarterly, 30*, 321–31.

Cherryholmes, C. (1988). *Power and criticism: Poststructuralist investigations in education.* New York: Teachers College Press.

Chow, R. (1998). *Ethics after idealism*. Indianapolis: Indiana University Press.
Clarke, M. (1994). The dysfunctions of the theory/practice discourse. *TESOL Quarterly, 28*, 9–26.
Cope, B., & Kalantzis, M. (1993). *The powers of literacy: A genre approach to teaching writing*. London: Falmer Press.
Corson, D. (1999). *Language policy in schools*. Mahwah, NJ: Lawrence Erlbaum Associates.
Crookes, G. (1997). SLA and language pedagogy: A socioeducational perspective. *Studies in Second Language Acquisition, 19*, 93–116.
Cummins, J. (2000). *Language, power and pedagogy: Bilingual children in the crossfire*. Clevedon, England: Multilingual Matters.
Cummins, J. (2001). *Negotiating identities: Education for empowerment in a diverse society* (2nd ed.). Ontario, CA: California Association of Bilingual Education.
Derrida, J. (1982). *Margins of philosophy* (A. Bass, Trans.). Chicago: University of Chicago Press. (Original work published 1972.)
Ellis, R. (1997). SLA and language pedagogy: An educational perspective. *Studies in Second Language Acquisition, 19*, 69–92.
Ellis, R. (1998). Teaching and research: Options in grammar teaching. *TESOL Quarterly, 32*, 39–60.
Fairclough, N. (1989). *Language and power*. London: Longman.
Fairclough, N. (1995). *Critical discourse analysis*. London: Longman.
Foucault, M. (1979). *Discipline and punish: The birth of the prison* (A. Sheridan, Trans.). New York: Vantage Books. (Original work published 1975.)
Foucault, M. (1982). The subject and power. In H. Dreyfus & P. Rabinow (Eds.), *Beyond structuralism* (pp. 208–26). Chicago: University of Chicago Press.
Giroux, H. (1994). Doing cultural studies: Youth and the challenge of pedagogy. *Harvard Educational Review, 64*, 278–308.
Gore, J. (1993). *The struggle for pedagogies: Critical and feminist pedagogies as regimes of truth*. London: Routledge.
Halliday, M. A. K., & Hasan, R. (1985). *Language, context, and text: Aspects of language in a social-semiotic perspective*. Oxford, England: Oxford University Press.
Harklau, L. (1999). Representing culture in the ESL classroom. In E. Hinkel (Ed.), *Culture in second language teaching and learning* (pp. 109–30). Cambridge, England: Cambridge University Press.
Hasan, R., & Perrett, G. (1994). Learning to function with the other tongue: A systematic functional perspective on second language teaching. In T. Odlin (Ed.), *Perspectives on pedagogical grammar* (pp. 179–226). Cambridge, England: Cambridge University Press.
Hyon, S. (1996). Genre in three traditions: Implications for ESL. *TESOL Quarterly, 30*, 693–722.
Ibrahim, A. (1999). Becoming black: Rap and hip hop, race, gender, identity and the politics of ESL learning. *TESOL Quarterly, 33*, 349–70.
Janks, H. (1991). A critical approach to the teaching of language. *Educational Review, 43*, 191–199.
Janks, H. (1997). Critical discourse analysis as a research tool. *Discourse, 18*, 329–42.
Janks, H. (1998). Reading "womanpower." *Pretexts, 7*, 195–212.

Johnston, B., & Goettsch, K. (2000). In search of the knowledge base of language teaching: Explanations by experienced teachers. *Canadian Modern Language Review*, 437–68.

Jones, L. (1992). *Communicative grammar practice*. Cambridge, England: Cambridge University Press.

Kramsch, C. (2000). Social discursive constructions of self in L2 learning. In J. Lantolf (Ed.), *Sociocultural theory and second language learning* (pp. 133–53). New York: Cambridge University Press.

Kress, G. (1976). Introduction. In G. Kress (Ed.), *Halliday: System and function in language* (pp. vii–xxi). London: Oxford University Press.

Kress, G., & van Leeuwen, T. (1996). *Reading images: The grammar of visual design*. New York: Routledge.

Kubota, R. (1999). Japanese culture constructed by discourses: Implications for applied linguistics research and ELT. *TESOL Quarterly, 33*, 9–35.

Kumaravadivelu, B. (1999). Critical classroom discourse analysis. *TESOL Quarterly, 33*, 453–84.

Kumaravadivelu, B. (2001). Toward a postmethod pedagogy. *TESOL Quarterly, 35*, 537–60.

Lakoff, R. (1990). *Talking power: The politics of language*. New York: Basic Books.

Lin, A., Wang, W., Akamatsu, N., & Riazi, A. M. (2002). Appropriating English, expanding identities, and re-visioning the field: From TESOL to teaching English for globalized communication (TEGCOM). *Journal of Language, Identity, and Education, 1*(4), 295–316.

Lock, G. (1996). *Functional English grammar*. Cambridge, England: Cambridge University Press.

McKay, S. L., & Wong, S. C. (1996). Multiple discourses, multiple identities: Investment and agency in second language learning among Chinese adolescent immigrant students. *Harvard Educational Review, 3*, 577–608.

Morgan, B. (1997). Identity and intonation: Linking dynamic processes in an ESL classroom. *TESOL Quarterly, 31*, 431–50.

Morgan, B. (1998). *The ESL classroom: Teaching, critical practice, and community development*. Toronto, Ontario, Canada: University of Toronto Press.

Morgan, B. (2002). Critical practice in community-based ESL programs: A Canadian perspective. *Journal of Language, Identity, and Education, 1*, 141–62.

Morgan, B. (in press). Teacher identity as pedagogy: Towards a field-internal conceptualization in bilingual and second language education. *International Journal of Bilingual Education and Bilingualism.*

Nelson, C. (1999). Sexual identities in ESL: Queer theory and classroom inquiry. *TESOL Quarterly, 33*, 371–91.

New London Group. (1996). A pedagogy of multiliteracies. *Harvard Educational Review, 66*, 60–92.

Norris, C. (1982). *Deconstruction: Theory and practice*. New York: Methuen.

Norris, C. (1987). *Derrida*. Cambridge, MA: Harvard University Press.

Norton, B. (Ed.). (1997). Language, identity, and the ownership of English. *TESOL Quarterly, 31*, 409–29.

Norton, B. (2000). *Identity and language learning: Gender, ethnicity and educational change*. Harlow, England: Pearson Education.

Odlin, T. (1994). Introduction. In T. Odlin (Ed.), *Perspectives on pedagogical grammar* (pp. 1–21). Cambridge, England: Cambridge University Press.

O'Sullivan, E. (1999). *Transformative learning: Educational vision for the 21st century*. London: Zed Books.
Pavlenko, A., & Lantolf, J. P. (2000). Second language learning as participation and the (re)construction of selves. In J. P. Lantolf (Ed.), *Sociocultural theory and second language learning* (pp. 155–77). New York: Oxford University Press.
Pennycook, A. (1994). Incommensurable discourses? *Applied Linguistics, 15*, 115–38.
Pennycook, A. (2001). *Critical applied linguistics: A critical introduction*. Mahwah, NJ: Lawrence Erlbaum Associates.
Poynton, C. (1993). Grammar, language and the social: Poststructuralism and systemic-functional linguistics. *Social Semiotics, 3*, 1–21.
Rivera, K. (1999). Popular research and social transformation: A community-based approach to critical pedagogy. *TESOL Quarterly, 33*, 485–500.
Robinson, I. (1975). *The new grammarians' funeral: A critique of Noam Chomsky's linguistics*. Cambridge, England: Cambridge University Press.
Rosenau, P. M. (1992). *Postmodernism and the social sciences: Insights, inroads, and intrusions*. Princeton, NJ: Princeton University Press.
Sauvé, V. L. (2000). *Issues, challenges and alternatives in teaching adult ESL*. Don Mills, Ontario, Canada: Oxford University Press.
Shea, C. M. (1998). Critical and constructive postmodernism: The transformative power of holistic education. In H. S. Shapiro & D. E. Purpel (Eds.), *Critical social issues in American education: Transformation in a postmodern world* (2nd ed.) (pp. 337–54). Mahwah, NJ: Lawrence Erlbaum Associates.
Simon, R. (1992). *Teaching against the grain*. Toronto, Ontario, Canada: OISE Press.
Stewart, E. (1995, September 8). Parizeau "lacks courage" federalist leaders insist. *The Toronto Star*, p. A12.
Terdiman, R. (1985). *Discourse/Counter-Discourse*. Ithaca, NY: Cornell University Press.
Toohey, K. (1998). "Breaking them up, taking them away": ESL students in grade 1. *TESOL Quarterly, 32*, 61–84.
Toohey, K. (2000). *Learning English at school: Identity, social relations and classroom practice*. Clevedon, England: Multilingual Matters.
Vandrick, S. (1997). The role of hidden identities in the postsecondary ESL classroom. *TESOL Quarterly, 31*, 153–7.
Varghese, M. (in press). Professional development for bilingual teachers in the United States: A site for articulating and contesting professional roles. *International Journal of Bilingual Education and Bilingualism*.
Weedon, C. (1987). *Feminist practice & poststructuralist theory*. New York: Basil Blackwell.
Will Quebec separate from the Canadian federal system? (1995, September 15). *Tsing Dao Newspaper*, p. C14.
Yip, V. (1994). Grammatical consciousness-raising and learnability. In T. Odlin (Ed.), *Perspectives on pedagogical grammar* (pp. 123–39). Cambridge, England: Cambridge University Press.

PART III: RESEARCHING CRITICAL PRACTICES

10 *The logic of nonstandard teaching: A course in Cape Verdean language, culture, and history*

Inês Brito
Ambrizeth Lima
Elsa Auerbach

Cape Verdean students in the United States are all but invisible in educational literature and practice; although these students have a rich cultural and linguistic tradition, their language and culture have been understudied by researchers and ignored even in areas where there are large concentrations of students whose first language is Cape Verdean (CVL). In their homeland, an archipelago off the west coast of Africa, the language of schooling is still Portuguese, the language of Cape Verde's former colonizers. The rationale for this choice is that Portuguese is a world language with a greater body of written text and that Cape Verdean is a local language that does not provide access to economic or social status. In the United States, to the extent that Cape Verdeans are taught bilingually, the medium of instruction is often Portuguese as well. Thus, Cape Verdean students are largely schooled in a language that is associated with the history of colonialism and, in the United States, may be immersed in two school languages, neither of which is their home language. Often, their literacy and academic development are impeded by these linguistic influences and policies.

This chapter describes one course in the Boston area which aimed to demonstrate the benefits of teaching in CVL for Cape Verdean students. The class, an elective called Cape Verdean Language, Culture, and History (CVLCH), took place in a high school (hereafter called Hope High School [HHS]) where approximately thirty percent of the student population is Cape Verdean. It integrated the teaching of Cape Verdean language, culture, and history, providing a context for students to gain academic skills through the medium of their first language. A significant goal of this work was to address the stigma associated with CVL on the part of both students and the Cape Verdean community in general. The development of this course was informed by a critical ideological perspective that views language pedagogy as integrally intertwined with issues of power and status in the broader social order. Principles which informed the course included

- promoting the appreciation of CVL as a critical basis for student learning;
- fostering awareness of the interaction of language, culture, history, and power;
- constructing the classroom as a shared terrain – a site for the practice of participatory democracy;
- valorizing family experience and knowledge;
- drawing curriculum content from students' lives; and
- gearing learning toward action for change in schools and community.

In this chapter, we describe a collaborative inquiry project centered on the CVLCH class and its contexts, rationale, curriculum, assessment processes, challenges, and implications for future work.

The collaboration: "I decided to learn to democratize my teaching"

The decision to engage in a reflective inquiry project had its roots in a graduate course which the teacher of the CVLCH class, Inês Brito (hereafter called Nézi), took with Elsa Auerbach. Through their interaction in that course, Elsa and Nézi recognized that they had a strong political affinity; the bond was tightened when Nézi discovered that Elsa had been an activist in support of the liberation of the Portuguese colonies in the seventies while Nézi had been a militant for the PAIGC (Partido Africano de Independencia de Guiné e Cabo Verde – African Party for Guinea Bissau and Cape Verde Independence). Elsa met Ambrizeth Lima, another Cape Verdean teacher at HHS, after Ambrizeth delivered an inspiring speech about the role of advocacy in bilingual education at Harvard University (Lima, 2000). Our shared ideology as activists, citizens, and women motivated us to work together.

We did not frame our collaboration as formal research: We had no a priori research question, hypothesis, or product in mind; we never expected to publish anything; and our work was not funded. This gave us the freedom to let the process develop in its own way. Thus, not only was the curriculum emergent – the project itself was.

Our process, quite simply, was that Elsa and Ambrizeth observed the CVLCH class for one period a week (about seventy minutes) over the course of a semester, took notes, and conferenced with Nézi afterward. Because of our shared perspective, working together was, as Nézi said, just fun. Ambrizeth and Elsa acted as sounding boards for Nézi, mainly listening as Nézi talked about what she was doing, the students' reactions, her thoughts on how things were going, and her plans. The mere fact of

Elsa and Ambrizeth's presence without specific intervention turned out to be useful to Nézi; as she said,

> I didn't feel you were judging me, but I felt conscious that I couldn't fail regarding the principles we shared; I felt safer to take risks with your support. It wasn't just me; now it was a team. I decided to learn to democratize my teaching. The feeling of trust gave me the confidence to try.

The contexts: "Political independence didn't bring linguistic independence"

It is important to understand the historical and linguistic contexts in which the course was situated since they generated the content of the course. The community and institutional contexts, likewise, shaped students' engagement with it. In each of these contexts, the status of Cape Verdean language and culture has been contested and this fact deeply affected the learning process. It is not possible to talk about the language education of Cape Verdean children without discussing issues of power, oppression, and resistance.

The historical context

Cape Verde, a tiny archipelago of ten islands in the Atlantic Ocean off the west coast of Africa (350 miles from Senegal), was part of the Portuguese colonial empire for five hundred years. It gained independence in 1975 after decades of struggle for liberation under the leadership of the PAIGC, founded by Amilcar Cabral and his comrades.

For many centuries, this small nation has suffered drought, famine, and the massive exodus of its people. Cape Verdeans have been immigrating to the United States since the eighteenth century when American whaling ships went to the archipelago to recruit crewmen. At first, the crewmen would come to the United States and then return to Cape Verde. Soon, however, they began to bring their families, who settled in Southeastern Massachusetts (see Meitel, 1979, 1984). By 1990, the population of Cape Verde was a little more than 340,000, and it is said that about 400,000 Cape Verdeans live in the United States. Cape Verdean immigrants maintain close ties to their homeland through family, culture, and most of all, language.

The linguistic context

The linguistic context is very much a reflection of the historical and political realities in Cape Verde. Because of colonialism, the official language of Cape Verde has been Portuguese for five hundred years. However, the native language, the language of the people, is CVL. It is not only the language they use every day, but the language in which they love, they work, they sing, they mourn. In the diaspora, there is no doubt that CVL is the language that unites Cape Verdeans and brings to them images of home and feelings of *sodade* [longing] and *morabeza* [loving kindness].

The Portuguese colonial government, by prohibiting the use of CVL in schools and in all official transactions, fomented the notion that CVL was inferior to Portuguese. This unequal status contributed to the devaluation of CVL. Because Cape Verdeans were told that CVL was a dialect (not a language) for hundreds of years, those who spoke Portuguese to their children at home usually were considered of higher status in society. During the years of struggle against colonialism, when nationalism was linked to liberation ideology, CVL was considered to be a weapon for independence and was thus further denigrated by the Portuguese.

Even after independence, Portuguese has continued to be used in schools and government offices. While many countries have more than one official language, Cape Verde has yet to make CVL an official language. Thus, political independence didn't bring linguistic independence. Given that Portuguese is the only language used to teach Cape Verdean children and that most of these children only speak CVL from birth, it is not surprising that this linguistic discontinuity would lead to pedagogical problems.

The community context in Boston

The parents of Cape Verdean students in Boston, driven by severe economic conditions in their homeland, came searching for a better life in the United States. Most are from rural areas of Cape Verde where they were farmers, fishermen, and domestics. Despite the fact that schooling is a core value for Cape Verdeans, often children in these families could not attend high school due to their economic situation. Some, lured by the prospect of emigrating to the United States, abandoned school all together.

Once in Boston, Cape Verdean families soon realize that finding a "better life" is not easy; many have more than one job – working during the day at one and at another in the evenings, or sometimes two full-time jobs. The high-school-age children reenter school, seeing education as part of the route to a better life; they often work after school to contribute to the family resources. With both children and parents working, there is little time for them to spend with each other. It is often difficult for parents to find ways to support their children's education. Further, many of the children have been sent here to live with relatives; as with many immigrant groups, parents and children are separated by the legal processes associated with immigration. Thus, many Cape Verdean children have no one to aid them in their transition to this society, not knowing where they fit in as immigrants and people of color. Many attempt to assimilate into what they consider American culture, but experience frustration if they are not accepted.

Compounding these problems, although Cape Verdeans have been a relatively obscure community in the United States, they have experienced an onslaught of negative media attention in recent years; the two major newspapers in Boston have written extensively on the involvement of Cape Verdean youth in criminal activities. What has enraged the community is the fact that their success stories rarely become public.

In addition to family, community, and school influences, societal forces shape how Cape Verdean students see themselves. They often see themselves "mirrored" (Suárez-Orozco, 2000) in the eyes of society as being troublemakers and criminals. Many times, they do not have a positive image of what it is to be Cape Verdean. Furthermore, they get conflicting messages of what constitutes being Cape Verdean or what Cape Verdean culture is. This ambivalence is exemplified by community attitudes toward the use of CVL in schooling. Some of the strongest opposition comes from Cape Verdeans themselves with many parents and teachers still saying that CVL is not a viable language of instruction. Therefore, if at home, at school, and in the community children are hearing that CVL is not a language, and if language is inexorably connected to culture, the message they get is that Cape Verdean culture is of no importance. For these reasons, many Cape Verdean educators and activists feel that the school must take on the responsibility to teach the students how to navigate their Cape Verdean and American worlds. As they begin to read and write their language, CVL, they can begin to read their own world (Freire & Macedo, 1987) and begin to understand who they are as Cape Verdeans and members of American society.

The institutional context

The institutional context, as well, has been shaped by ambivalence and struggle relating to Cape Verdean language, culture, and identity. The school where this study took place is situated in the heart of an urban area with a large immigrant and African American population. The majority of the school population is African American, but the second significant group is Cape Verdean. Cape Verdeans are important in this school not only because of their numbers, but also due to their high academic achievement. In 1999, for example, the largest number of students on the honor roll, the first place entrants in the school science fair, and the school valedictorian were Cape Verdean. At the same time, however, there are ways in which Cape Verdeans are outsiders even at this school. Here, the struggle for dominance is between African Americans and other minorities. Thus, despite the efforts of supportive staff, sometimes these students who are marginalized outside of school experience the same marginalization in school.

Language education is an important arena where issues about the status of Cape Verdeans have come to the fore. State laws on transitional bilingual education (TBE) mandate that groups of children who cannot perform in English medium classes due to language barriers must receive instruction in their native language and learn about the history and culture of their country of origin.[1] The rationale for TBE comes, in part, from research suggesting that students learn a second language more easily when they have a basis in their first; this proficiency can then be transferred to the second language as well (Cummins, 1981). In accordance with these laws, transitional CVL bilingual programs were initiated in Boston in 1973. Since then, according to Georgette Gonsalves (1999), a leading advocate for CVL bilingual education in Boston, "the program . . . evolved from one with only four children and a teacher in a small elementary school to one of 690 students in Grades K–12 in seven schools across the city" (p. 20).

By the mid-nineties, HHS had a large CVL bilingual program with almost two hundred students and ten teachers either certified in bilingual education or in the process of becoming so. Cape Verdean students took content courses (math, science, social studies, etc.) in CVL as well as English as a second language (ESL) courses. However, because of interrupted or ineffective prior schooling, many did not have the literacy skills necessary to function successfully in their bilingual program. Until the CVLCH course was offered in 1996, there was no CVL language arts program in which students could study their own language; the assumption was that they would acquire the necessary reading and writing skills in content area courses. The only mandated CVL language-focused course was a CVL literacy program for fifteen students per year with minimal prior schooling.

System-wide writing prompts given to students as part of formative assessment revealed problems which arose from the lack of CVL instruction. The Cape Verdean students were given open-ended questions in three languages (English, Portuguese, and CVL) and were asked to respond in the language of their choice. Most attempted to respond in Portuguese, the language of their prior schooling; however, their responses reflected a kind of hybrid language that was neither CVL nor Portuguese. When several Cape Verdean teachers at HHS suggested that the bilingual department offer a CVL language arts course to address this problem, there was some initial resistance. This resistance demonstrated the hegemony of English as the desirable language to learn. Just as the students were told in Cape Verde that Portuguese was the important language to learn, here in the United States, they were told that English was the only language worth learning. While teachers promoting the CVL language arts course never lost sight of the fact that learning English is of utmost importance for their students, they argued that language acquisition is a long process, taking place in stages. After extensive dialogue, the department decided to offer one CVL course, as an elective, to eighteen students per semester. This was how the CVLCH course was born.

The classroom context

The teachers in the Cape Verdean bilingual program understand that, at school, they are the students' educational parents. They work hard to make their classrooms become harbors for these students who are teetering between two cultures and languages. One of the ways they do this is by translating or creating materials in CVL that will not only help students acquire content knowledge, but also enhance pride in their own culture and language. The walls of the bilingual teachers' classrooms reverberate with the twin messages of cultural pride and political struggle; there are posters of Amilcar Cabral, Rosa Parks, Martin Luther King, Malcolm X, Gandhi, Cesaria Evora, the Kennedy brothers, and the tanks in Tiananmen Square. There are quotes from Paulo Freire, photos of Cape Verde, a great deal of student work, maps of the United States and Cape Verde, as well as official materials (about writing rubrics, etc.). Students and teachers laugh, joke, dance, and play music with each other; there is affectionate teasing and much hugging. Students talk to their teachers about what is happening in their lives outside of class and have a strong sense of ownership of the classroom. It's their space. They stay late after class and work on their own in the classroom; they sit around reading or working on the computer before and after class. They take responsibility for physical aspects of the class, bring food for parties, and ask the teacher if she needs help during lunch.

Teachers in the CVL bilingual program at HHS have also built a strong community of their own; they have made a lunchroom for themselves, bought a microwave, and eat lunch together every day. They share food and use lunchtime to talk about what's happening with individual students and the program. They socialize outside of school as well as working on professional and community events together; they are organizing a Cape Verdean educators' association.

The rationale and principles: "I didn't choose language and power as a theme – It was just my life"

For Nézi, the formation of the CVLCH project is a continuation of her own process of liberating herself. The principles that inform her practice are rooted in a process that began with the work she was immersed in during and after the anticolonial struggle. The course design is shaped by the history which she lived. She narrates this history here:

> The fact that I lived under colonial oppression is very important to my thinking about teaching. I have two levels of awareness: on the one hand, I have a conscious belief that people should have their own space, their rights; at the same time, I have the understanding that struggling to liberate the Cape Verdean society implies that I also have to struggle to decolonize myself. So my principle is that if you want to liberate your country, you have to liberate yourself; and if you want to keep your country liberated, you need to liberate the youth. It was living under colonial oppression that started the process of my own liberation.
>
> I had been educated in a colonial system where the teacher's role is authoritarian; nothing from students was considered valuable. During my adolescence, there were three censors that shaped me: the school, the church, and my parents' values. I wanted to be a good student and please my parents. Then at age 16, in my last year of high school, I stopped going to church. Church didn't answer all my questions and I became involved with social issues. When I realized that they could only be addressed through political means, I began working with the PAIGC. I was in Portugal during the time of the revolution (1974), and while there, I was trained in the Freirean literacy approach. At 20, I started teaching in a literacy program with Cape Verdean workers, reading with them and talking about independence and unions.
>
> Back in Cape Verde, while working with the PAIGC, I had meetings with women and young people, drawing out their experiences. This was teaching – political work was seamless with teaching. The whole process of becoming ideological evolved through struggle; I didn't start with an ideology and move toward action. Likewise, literacy training wasn't separate from other political work: all militants went to workshops for literacy, first aid, etc. In the eighties, we wanted to introduce CVL in the literacy program, with literacy linked to people's lives, attached to projects (e.g., people raising pigs would learn to write a report about raising pigs). Some of the principles of that work were the basis of the CVLCH project in Boston: literacy should be linked to learners' lives; the context should generate the content; the emphasis should be working as a group for a common goal. . . .
>
> So by the time I came to the United States, I was ripe – had all the elements in my experience to move to a different pedagogy. I was looking for a program that would give me the tools to defend my language. Here, my hope just blossomed. I didn't make this happen: I didn't choose language and power as a theme for the CVLCH course – it was just my life.

All three of us had been strongly influenced by the work of Paulo Freire (see Auerbach, 1992; Lima, 2000). We shared the principles outlined at the beginning of the chapter: that pedagogical processes must be democratic, with all participants working as a group for a common goal; that everyone's knowledge counts; that content should come from the context of students' lives and issues that are important to them; that family and community knowledge should be drawn in and valued; that students should develop a critical consciousness of who they are and what their language represents by examining questions of language, culture, and history through the lens of power; that the study of Cape Verdean history should include a focus on linguistic mechanisms that perpetuate colonialism; and that learning should also entail action for change. The rationale for the course was not just a matter of ideology, but also of research-based evidence regarding language and literacy acquisition. Studies suggesting that first language (L1) literacy facilitates second language (L2) acquisition under specific conditions are abundant (see Garcia, 1999). Further, research indicates that certain groups benefit most from first language and bilingual approaches, namely subordinated minority language groups and those with limited L1 literacy and schooling backgrounds (Cummins, 1981). This research suggests that relations of power and their affective consequences are implicated in language acquisition: Acquiring an L2 is, to some extent, contingent on the societally determined value attributed to the L1. Moreover, denying L1 literacy to subordinated language groups may virtually ensure that they remain marginalized academically and, ultimately, economically (Skutnabb-Kangas, 1988). Thus, research suggests that Cape Verdean students are exactly the kind of students most likely to benefit from L1 literacy education as a basis for English literacy and academic achievement.

The emergent curriculum: "We didn't tell them the facts; they discovered them"

One of the key principles of the CVLCH course was that teacher, students, and families should participate in coconstructing the class through a process of negotiation. Thus, rather than predetermining course content as she had done previously, Nézi embarked on an experiment in developing an emergent curriculum. The following identifies features of this process and examples of how it evolved.

Make students' knowledge, attitudes, and experiences the starting point

Because students had been assigned to the CVLCH class based on their writing prompt responses (rather than the students self-selecting it), for many, the first question was "What am I doing in this course? Why am I learning in CVL? I wasn't taught in CVL in my country. Here I need to learn English." Nézi asked them to individually write and present orally their hopes and expectations concerning the course. The class then summarized main themes, and the questions generated by students became a draft for the content and objectives of the course. Some of their questions (translated here from CVL) were, What was Cape Verde like from the fifteenth century until independence? How has Cape Verdean culture been shaped by foreign influences? How is Cape Verdean culture viewed in a global context? Other topics students wanted to study were the process of colonialism, slavery in Cape Verde, dialect variations in different islands, the relationship between Portuguese and CVL, the standardization of CVL, and Cape Verdean literature.

What emerged from this exercise was a wide range of attitudes and knowledge. Nézi had anticipated more overt resistance to CVL than she got at the beginning, but she noted that there were two levels of resistance: conscious and unconscious. Some students openly questioned the value of studying in the language they knew best. Nézi found that these students were thinking the way that some parents still think twenty-five years after independence – that Portuguese is more legitimate than CVL (one father, for example, wrote a note requesting that his son be taken out of the CVL class). Others had an open mind on a conscious level, but showed internalized resistance with comments like, "I understand why I should learn CVL, but I feel like I'm losing time when I could be studying English or Portuguese because I already know my language very well."

It also became clear that the students were more interested in culture and history than in structural aspects of language. For this reason, Nézi decided to start with culture as a strategy to draw students in and examine history in the context of culture. The students' responses also led Nézi to approach the study of CVL from an ethnographic and sociolinguistic, rather than a linguistic, point of view.

Involve students in pedagogical decisions and make the emergent curriculum process explicit

For Nézi, part of the process of democratizing the classroom was sharing decision making with students. On the first day of class, she explained that they would build the class together, saying, "This is not a traditional classroom." She reminded students that she, as a teacher, was a learner too: "This format is not just new for you; it's new for me, too." Nézi then asked students to establish ground rules for the class; these rules included the following: show each other respect, be on time, and *Djunta mon* [join hands] – show solidarity. Nézi's way of introducing Elsa into the classroom illustrates her power-sharing strategies. When, on her first day of observation, Elsa went to sit at the back of the room, Nézi asked, "Why are you sitting there? You have to ask the students where they want you to sit." The students told Elsa to sit in front, next to Nézi so they could see her. From then on, Elsa not only observed but participated with the group, asking questions and sometimes even conferencing with students using gestures and her rudimentary understanding of CVL.

The seating arrangements in the class also fostered a sense of dialogical participation; students often sat in a circle with Nézi, or, at other times, they were clustered in groups so that they could work together. By the end of the semester, students moved freely around the class, getting up to help each other as needed.

Draw in families' perspectives and build support for the curriculum at home

After the preliminary discussion, Nézi asked students to investigate, through interviews, what their families knew and believed about CVL. The data from these interviews became a basis for dialogue: Students discussed similarities, differences, and common areas of interest. Students discovered that many of the parents were happy to discuss this topic and had a great deal to say. One student whose mother only had an elementary education reported that she said, "It is nice that you're learning in your language; I could have done better in school if I'd had this chance." Students also discussed variations in attitudes toward CVL based on the age of the person interviewed; they discovered that older people (e.g., grandparents) had different attitudes than those who had been involved in the anticolonial struggle – that their historical place influenced their views.

Invite students to become researchers of language use

In order to delve more deeply into the role of CVL in their lives, Nézi asked students to investigate their oral and written uses of both CVL and Portuguese. As homework, they took notes on "when, how, where do you use your language? Portuguese?" This revealed to them the discontinuity between their beliefs and their actual usage; many thought that they used Portuguese most of the time and were surprised to discover that they were predominantly users of CVL.

As students' awareness grew, they discussed why Portuguese was the language of education in Cape Verde. They also talked about strategies for democratic action, including petitions, letters, and demonstrations. They decided to write a letter to the Cape Verdean government about their ideas. Nézi asked them to make posters with slogans representing the essence of their opinions and to defend their slogans in front of the class. Slogans (translated from CVL here) included: "I am my language!" "My language is Cape Verdean!" "My language is my identity!" "Listen to the people!" They then posted the slogans on the walls, provoking debate and responses like "Portuguese is my language!" from a student in another class. Thus, the discussion of the status of CVL spilled out into the wider school community.

Connect the community outside the classroom with learning inside the classroom

As the debate about CVL evolved, Nézi invited in other HHS teachers who were advocates for, and experts on, CVL and culture. A guidance counselor who had been a leading advocate for the CVL bilingual program came to the class to discuss the history of that struggle. Other teachers made presentations on Cape Verdean music and festivals. Guests from the community were also invited, including elders who belonged to a group called Pilon Colá that gives after-school workshops on Cape Verdean storytelling, drumming, and singing; a group which involves students in community-based mural painting; and a renowned Cape Verdean poet and novelist who writes in CVL and Portuguese. Throughout this process, students participated in decision making; for example, they discussed whether to get involved in the mural project – six students decided to do so.

Students also participated in events outside of the classroom. They attended a conference to commemorate the anniversary of Amilcar Cabral's assassination and a Cape Verdean festival sponsored by the Boston Center for the Arts. Through these activities, students came to see the work they were doing inside the classroom as connected to dialogue and action in wider school and community contexts.

Value students' skills, knowledge, and cultural expertise

A key strategy in Nézi's class was drawing on students' own "funds of knowledge" (Moll, 1992). It was clear early on that students were most engaged when they were talking about issues and experiences that were familiar to them (e.g., when they were comparing festivals on their respective islands). In addition to the ongoing inclusion of students' experiences and data from their investigations, students did final research projects focusing on familiar aspects of Cape Verdean culture that they wanted to investigate further. The purpose of this project was for each student to apply academic and research skills in becoming an expert on a self-selected cultural practice and then to teach classmates about it. For example, one student whose father was a drum expert chose to do his project on drum making and drumming (*tanbor y tokâ tanbor*) while others compared festivals of the popular saints (*Féstas di Santus Pupular*) or studied *tabanka*.[2]

Integrate the learning of academic skills with content

For every topic that the class explored, Nézi focused on specific cognitive skills. For example, oral presentations on the slogans taught argumentation, and discussions of dialect differences between the islands or of contexts for the use of Portuguese versus CVL reinforced comparison skills. Nézi often used graphic organizers to facilitate this process. She scaffolded organizational skills with writing prompts like the following: "What would be the cultural, social, economic, and political consequences if the Cape Verdean government decided to make Cape Verde a monolingual Portuguese country?" Nézi then typed students' responses as a composite text for further discussion and analysis. Excerpts from this text (translated from CVL) include the following:

> *Culturally*, they would kill our oral production and the originality of our oral language. For example, Nasía Gomes [a popular traditional singer] couldn't express herself as she does in CVL. Language as an element of identity cannot be replaced because it would disturb every other element of culture.
>
> *Socially*, it would maintain the inequality of success. People who had the chance to learn Portuguese would advance more than others.
>
> *Politically*, the role of the language is very important for the exercise of democracy. Democracy is a regime that allows people to participate and express freely what they think and they believe. Therefore if you take away people's native language, you are going to shut their mouths. You reduce their ability to participate easily without effort so this would make democracy in Cape Verde poor.

Nézi taught reading strategies using teacher- and student-generated texts as well as authentic texts (e.g., articles from Cape Verdean academic journals on the history of CVL, poetry). Since these texts were not simplified or geared toward high school students, Nézi modeled strategies like previewing and asking questions of texts. Ambrizeth taught a lesson on how to deal with unknown vocabulary.

Promote metacognitive awareness as a means of fostering control over learning

Throughout the semester, Nézi gave students tools to take on responsibility for their own learning. Part of this involved developing a discourse for talking about the learning process. They spent considerable time exploring questions like, What's a strategy? What's an objective? What are goals? In addition, Nézi frequently invited students to reflect on their own learning processes with questions like, Why was this reading difficult? How did you read it? What did you do when you got to hard words? What questions does this text raise? She engaged them in ongoing evaluation and asked for their feedback with questions like, "Write about what you learned, how you learned, and what you would have liked to learn. Don't forget to give your input or suggestions." She made the criteria for evaluating work explicit and then handed students responsibility for evaluating their own and each other's work.

Nézi often invited students to participate in devising assignments. For the final research project at the end of the term, she posed questions like, What sources can you use to find out about *tabanka*? How do you do an interview? Who do you ask; who is your informant? What is important to know about your informant (age, schooling, gender)? How do informant factors shape the response? How do you analyze the data? The class debated how to set up their projects and established a framework together. One student suggested doing projects in teams and many of the students followed this suggestion.

Infuse all work with critical analysis

Nézi began with the assumption that her students were capable of critical analysis and thus treated them like thinkers. She constantly asked probing questions like, "Why is CVL still not the language of Cape Verde even though colonialism has ended?" She insisted that students explain reasons for statements and defend their positions. Elsa was struck by the fact that students often discussed topics similar to those addressed in her graduate courses (the relationship between language and identity, the consequences of being denied mother tongue education, and the processes of internalizing colonialism).

Throughout the course, Nézi infused the analysis of power into the curriculum, making it the axis around which themes of culture, history, and language were addressed. Through dialogue, students posed questions like, "Why was *tabanka* forbidden during the colonialist period? Has independence freed us and our culture also?" They discovered that cultural forms like *tabanka*, *batuku*, and *funana* had their origins on the most Africanized of the islands, Santiago, but, since they were forbidden, were practiced primarily in the interior or countryside; all of them became forms of cultural resistance to colonialism.[3] They learned that it was only after independence that these forms came to be recognized and appreciated nationally.

Assessing student learning

In order to understand the learning that was taking place, there was ongoing assessment using a range of tools (writing prompts, self-assessment, peer assessment, student portfolios, written and oral project presentations, observation of classroom participation). No single measure or tool could capture the complexity of the learning. From the first day of class, students knew that they were part of the assessment process. They participated in assessing each other and themselves through ongoing feedback, using a range of criteria and rubrics. It is not surprising that, in this complex process, performance varied depending on the tool being used.

Furthermore, some aspects of the curriculum yielded greater change than others.

For example, Nézi had high expectations for students' final projects; however, the products of the students' work (their written reports and oral presentations) did not live up to these expectations. If student learning had been assessed solely on the basis of these products, much of what they had learned during the semester would have been obscured. An analysis of the process of doing the projects, however, revealed a range of learnings that did not show up in the final products. Further, when students were asked to reflect on their learning, their responses revealed less visible, but quite dramatic, changes in thinking and attitudes.

Our observations and Nézi's notes indicated that student engagement at the beginning and middle of the research process was strong. Through class discussions, they demonstrated acquisition of a range of academic skills: how to choose a topic, evaluate its feasibility, and plan research. They integrated terms like *research design*, *methodology*, *informants*, and *objectives* into their discourse. They suggested not just books, but individuals within their communities as sources (demonstrating their valuing of community knowledge). However, it became clear that difficulties in their final projects arose precisely because they had gone beyond traditional schoolwork and were taking on the challenge of fieldwork. Some had problems transcribing, organizing, and analyzing interview data; others didn't know how to generalize from their findings. Students who relied on traditional sources (books and articles) had more information. Of course, other factors also intervened (e.g., students had work for other classes due at the same time). Nézi's conclusion was that she had to be more available to work with them outside of the classroom. They needed more guidance on fieldwork skills. Her reflection suggested not a weakness in the overall approach, but the need for some fine-tuning in terms of implementation.

Further, students' commentaries on each others' final projects demonstrated their capacity for critical evaluation. They were able to differentiate various kinds of strengths and weaknesses in each other's work. They noted that one student had sharpness in his analysis but didn't do the necessary work to back it up. They commended another student for his oral presentation, but criticized his written work. Their final course assessments were particularly revealing. Students did not just say that they learned a lot, but listed what they had learned. One student wrote that she had learned how to analyze and ask questions about a text. Another said that she sees her culture differently now. Some students commented on the ways their families were impacted. One reported that her brother, who is in a Portuguese bilingual program at another high school, had made fun of her for being in a CVL class at the beginning of the term, but now wants to learn CVL too.

Student self-assessments also showed changes in their sense of responsibility about their own learning. For example, at the end of the semester, one student who did not follow through on his work acknowledged his own role in this. When asked, "What should be changed about this class?" many students focused not on what they did or did not like about the teacher, but on what they should change about themselves. Framing their responses as "I need to . . ." showed that they saw themselves as agents in their own learning.

Another important kind of change which did not show up in any "product" relates to classroom dynamics, patterns of participation, and kinds of participation. For example, at the beginning of the term, the girls rarely took the initiative in discussions or spoke unless called on. By the end of the term, many of them participated actively, volunteered information, and, in some cases, took on leadership roles. They argued their positions, spoke at length, and even sang in front of the class. There was a visible increase in cooperation between students as well. They helped each other more, gave each other feedback, and contributed to the community of the class. There were intangible changes in terms of the students' air of confidence and sense of their own expertise.

Taken together, our findings suggest that many kinds of learning occurred in this course which are not traditionally valued in schooling. They reinforce the notion that learning should not be equated only with measurable outcomes and that assessment should not be tied to one product or tool.

Challenges: "But what am I going to read in CVL?"

A number of challenges and constraints influenced the outcome of the course. First was the fact that it was only a one-semester course. This is not enough time to go deeply into reading strategies, linguistic aspects of language, cohesion in writing, and so on while at the same time exploring content. Another facet of this issue relates to the chicken-and-egg dilemma of integrating the teaching of content and language; students need literacy and linguistic knowledge to access historical and cultural content, but they need historical and cultural content to motivate them to study language. Because of her concern that students might resist the study of linguistic aspects of CVL, Nézi started by focusing on sociolinguistic aspects (language use and attitudes). As a result, she felt that structural aspects were shortchanged.

Compounding this dilemma is the paucity of appropriate materials in CVL. The fact that there are so few pedagogical materials available forces the use of either authentic materials which may be too difficult or of student- or teacher-produced materials. However students need many genres in language learning. Students, too, recognize this dilemma and it can undermine their desire to study CVL. One student, for example, said, "It's nice to study CVL but what am I going to read in it? If I learn Portuguese, I know I'll have something to read." The broader questions that these problems raise are, Does learning CVL just have an ideological function? Is it just for self-affirmation? Or does it have a more concrete function for students?

Additional constraints coming from outside the classroom shaped students' learning; these included not living with their parents, facing an anti–Cape Verdean climate in Boston, and needing to work after school. These factors raise the following questions: Is it the way we teach the students or is it the circumstances of their lives which determines their engagement? To what extent are the results that we see shaped by our teaching versus other social factors?

Implications: "Teaching CVL is part of a democratic ethos"

This project is an unfinished piece of work. Nézi teaches the CVLCH course every semester and a different curriculum emerges with each group of students. These differences reinforce the point that the essence of the course is not a particular body of knowledge or skills but, rather, a set of underlying principles enacted through the process of reflective inquiry. This chapter describes the enactment of these principles within the constraints of everyday teaching as opposed to presenting a model or a set of best practices. Thus, rather than concluding with prescriptions, claims for success, or quantifiable outcomes, we want to talk about what each of us has taken from the project as well as its broader implications for critical pedagogy and the education of Cape Verdean youth. In the spirit of our collaboration, we will do this by weaving together our separate and collective voices.

Nézi:
Teaching is a learning process. I am not a teacher: I'm in the process of becoming a teacher. I am not a critical pedagogue: I am on my way to becoming one. It is a long process – it's not a natural behavior. I'm naturally a strict person, predisposed to being more of an authoritarian teacher than a facilitator. However, being strict and making space for student input do not have to contradict each other. The context and conditions in this country give you space to teach as a facilitator. I have shifted from being authoritarian to being more of a facilitator; I give students more time and space. Having colleagues to collaborate with in this process was a good feeling. It's nice to observe together. I am now a person who thinks about teaching. I don't see myself as a teacher; I see myself as someone who thinks about teaching. I am always the observer of my own teaching.

Elsa:
For me, this project was a lesson in humility. I was amazed at how much I imposed my own cultural assumptions where they didn't fit: for example, I interpreted gender dynamics through a North American feminist lens, lumping all the girls together, but learned that the varying ways girls interacted reflected differences in how they had been socialized on different islands. I couldn't understand Nézi's strategies just by observing her: I had to talk with her to understand why she did specific things. For example, I thought she was unconsciously calling on a few boys more than other students; she explained that she did this intentionally because they often said something provocative which then elicited dialogue from others. I had to let go of my assumptions and my urge to mentor. The project mentored me. I was able to witness the evolution of a work of art – the dynamic interaction of an amazing teacher and an amazing group of kids.

Ambrizeth:
This work taught me that I have a responsibility as an educator and as a member of a community. Therefore, I see this project as a way of bringing to the surface a people, an ethnic group, that has existed in obscurity although it has contributed a great deal in the educational and research fields – as much as other groups which have achieved more prominence in society and benefit from resources put into their education and adaptation. We Cape Verdean educators have an understanding of our kids and should have a say about their education. It's about time we started writing about our kids. If we don't write about our work, we're not taking action.

Nézi and Ambrizeth:
Writing this chapter serves the function of lifting an unspoken taboo about the value of CVL. After more than twenty years of struggle, CVL is still not seen as a legitimate medium of education; many educators are afraid of talking about the question of Portuguese versus CVL. It is time that CVL comes out of the closet as a viable and important educational language; we hope that this chapter contributes to the process of emancipation of our native language and the promotion of bilingual education. Teaching CVL is part of a democratic ethos.

All of us see this chapter as a call to action for greater parity for Cape Verdeans with other language groups. It has implications for policy makers, scholars, and most important, students. We hope that policy makers and administrators will recognize the importance of demonstrating to Cape Verdean students that their language and culture are valued by the broader societal institutions. This means offering CVL language arts courses not just as one-semester electives for a few students, but institutionalizing them so that they are available for all Cape Verdean students. In terms of implications for scholarship, we have endeavored, as teacher-researchers, to uncover the logic of one teacher's nonstandard teaching. Our work has the strongest implications, though, for the Cape Verdean students. If these students see themselves on paper not as social problems or at-risk youth but as experts and producers of knowledge, they will feel greater pride. As they gain strength from knowing who they are, we hope that they will liberate themselves from the marginalization they experience inside and outside the schools. Our hope is that they will be able to transform their own lives by knowing where they fit in the larger society and by knowing that who they are is not determined by others but by what they bring with them as human beings and as Cape Verdeans.

Notes

1. Since the manuscript was written, this law has changed: bilingual education has been outlawed in Massachusetts.
2. *Tabanka* is a self-help association, which incorporates a range of cultural forms.
3. *Batuku* is a kind of celebration with singing, dancing, and entertainment that takes place when many people gather to prepare a feast for a wedding or other celebration. *Funana* is a kind of music and dance which originated in Santiago and later became a national cultural form.

References

Auerbach, E. (1992). *Making meaning, making change: Participatory curriculum development for adult ESL/literacy*. Washington, DC: Center for Applied Linguistics & Delta Systems.

Cummins, J. (1981). The role of primary language development in promoting educational success for language minority students. In California State Department of Education (Ed.), *Schooling and language minority students: A theoretical framework* (pp. 3–49). Los Angeles: California State University.

Freire, P., & Macedo, D. (1987). *Literacy: Reading the word and the world.* Westport, CT: Bergin and Garvey.

Garcia, G. E. (1999). Bilingual children's reading: An overview of recent research. *ERIC/CLL News Bulletin, 23*(1), 1–5.

Gonsalves, G. (1999, Spring). Cape Verdean bilingual education: The Boston experience since 1973. *Cimboa: Revista Kabuverdianu Di Literatura, Arti y Studu/A Journal of Letters, Arts, and Studies, 7*, 18–21.

Lima, A. (2000). Voices from the basement: Breaking through the pedagogy of indifference. In Z. Beykont (Ed.), *Lifting every voice: Pedagogy and politics of bilingualism* (pp. 221–32). Cambridge, MA: Harvard Educational.

Meitel, D. (1979). *Cape Verdean-Americans: Their cultural and historical background.* Unpublished doctoral dissertation, Brown University, Providence, RI.

Meitel, D. (1984). *Race, culture, and Portuguese colonialism in Cabo Verde.* Monograph. Syracuse, NY: Foreign Comparative Studies Program, Syracuse University.

Moll, L. (1992). Bilingual classroom studies and community analysis: Some recent trends. *Educational Researcher, 21*(2), 20–4.

Skutnabb-Kangas, T. (1988). Multilingualism and the education of minority children. In T. Skutnabb-Kangas & J. Cummins (Eds.), *Minority education:*

From struggle to shame (pp. 9–44). Clevedon, England: Multilingual Matters.

Suárez-Orozco, C. (2000). Identities under siege: Immigration stress and social mirroring among the children of immigrants. In A. C. G. M. Robben & M. M. Suárez-Orozco (Eds.), *Cultures under siege: Collective violence and trauma* (pp. 194–221). Cambridge, England: Cambridge University Press.

11 *Comic book culture and second language learners*

Bonny Norton
Karen Vanderheyden

Extract 1: Karen and Joong-ha, an English language learner

Karen: When did you come to Canada?
Joong-ha: Two years ago.
Karen: Did you speak English in Korea?
Joong-ha: No.
Karen: So you've learned all your English in the last two years?
Joong-ha: Yes.
Karen: That's amazing. That's fantastic. Has it been easy for you to learn English?
Joong-ha: No.
Karen: What has helped you to learn English?
Joong-ha: Reading comics.
Karen: Seriously?
Joong-ha: Yeah, I read a comic every day. I read Calvin and Hobbes and Archies and adventure things.

Extract 2: Karen and Dylan, a native speaker of English

Karen: I want to find out one more thing. You've got ESL [English as a second language] kids and a lot of them hang out with their own group of friends. Then you've got English-speaking friends and they hang out together. Is popular culture like Archie a good way of bringing kids together?
Dylan: Well, yes because I know that one reason most of the kids with English problems and kids with good English don't relate is because the English kids seem to think that either they are stupid because they can't speak English which is totally a misconception or they're not like them and they're kind of pushed away by that.
Karen: So that's what you think, that it's a good way 'cause they can talk to each other?
Dylan: 'Cause it would give them something to realize that these kids like some things that they like, that they are kids who like things that other kids like, which is a way of bringing them together.

Introductions

Joong-ha, who is eleven, and Dylan, who is twelve, both attend a Vancouver school in which many of the students speak English as a second, third, or fourth language. While Joong-ha, from Korea, describes the remarkable achievement he has made in English language learning, Canadian-born Dylan reflects on the complex relationship between these newcomers, defined by Dylan as "kids with English problems," and their anglophone peers. Although Dylan recognizes that "it's a total misconception" to think that people who don't speak English are "stupid," his comment highlights the struggles for acceptance and respect that many young language learners face in English-dominant schools in North America and beyond (see, for example, Duff, 2002; McKay & Wong, 1996; Miller, 2003; Tosi & Leung, 1999). He notes further that friendship groups among anglophones are developed among students who are "like them" and share similar interests. What both boys have in common is their positive evaluation of comic books. While Joong-ha finds them useful for the purpose of language learning, Dylan notes that they serve as a common interest among English language learners and native speakers.

Joong-ha and Dylan are both participating in a study on a topic that is of interest to them and intriguing to us: the appeal of Archie comics. The Archie comic, unique in maintaining its popularity for over fifty years (see Robbins, 1999), has monthly sales of approximately one million and a Web site (www.archiecomics.com) that attracts thirteen to fourteen million hits a month. It is for these reasons that Norton began a program of research on Archie comics in 1997. She found that these comics have attracted the attention of millions of primarily preadolescent children, not only in North America, but in diverse countries around the world. Indeed, on a visit to Pakistan in October 2000, Norton was intrigued to find dozens of Archie comics on magazine racks in Karachi markets and, upon further investigation, found that many young Pakistanis were avid readers of these texts. Similarly, another student in the study, Namisha, commented that a friend of hers who had visited Thailand had ready access to Archie comics.

While Norton's research has addressed a range of questions about the appeal of Archie comics (see Norton, in press), this chapter focuses on one particular aspect of the research, conducted with Karen Vanderheyden, which addresses the appeal of Archie comics for English language learners. In this regard, Krashen's (1993) work in the area of free voluntary reading serves as a starting point for this research. He suggests that comic books, as a form of light reading, could be viewed as an incentive for children to read, citing Archie comics, specifically, as one of the comics that could be used in language classrooms. The appeal of Archie comics, he contends, stems mainly from its high interest content (high school context) and its accessibility (Grade 2 level of writing). In this chapter, however, we move beyond Krashen's claims to investigate the multiple ways in which English language learners engage with Archie comics in both classrooms and communities. Thus, we are interested not only in the ways in which Archie comics facilitate language learning and the development of literacy in English, but how popular culture can serve to engage second language learners in the culture of their peers as well as in the wider target-language culture. In this spirit, as Luke and Elkins (1998) have argued, we are interested in literacy as more than the process of reading and writing; we conceive of literacy as a social practice that must be understood in the context of wider social and institutional relationships.

For the uninitiated, an introduction to Archie comics is appropriate. Archie comics describe the lives of a group of teenagers living in a suburban area called Riverdale, in a temperate coastal region of the United States. The main characters in the stories are Archie, the classic boy-next-door; Betty and Veronica, two best friends; Jughead, an eccentric who is constantly eating (but never gets fat!); Reggie, the local rich boy; and various parents and teachers. The girls generally wear fashionable clothing, and beach scenes are common. The stories are often humorous and there is much play on words. Any given comic book has about twenty short stories of varying length addressing a variety of themes about friendship, schooling, dating, and family life. The comic is published in the form of a small booklet and costs about $4 Canadian ($2.60 U.S.). It is popular among both girls and boys, with ages ranging from approximately nine to twelve years old.

Comics, critical literacy, and popular culture

Almost two decades before Krashen's work on free voluntary reading, Wright (1976) had already made the case that the type of visuals found in comic books contributes positively to second language reading (p. 37). He argues that visual materials are an invaluable part of the construction of meaning for language learners and advocates the use of comics in all areas of the language curriculum. Furthermore, he makes the case that comics can also support writing as a nonverbal prompt to composition. He cites an example of a cartoon strip activity that was created by students for a classroom activity that entailed cutting up a comic, remounting the drawings, and having the students either write their text and dialogue on the strip or in their books.

Notwithstanding Wright and Krashen's enthusiasm for the use of comics in the second language classroom, there has, in fact, been little research on this topic. One of the few studies in the literature is that of Elley and Mangubhai (1983), who conducted research using nontraditional literature with Fijian elementary students. They were particularly interested in the impact these materials had on second language literacy skills. Using the shared book experience method developed by Holdaway in 1979, the teachers were able to engage the English language learners in lively group discussions around the comic books presented. The teachers also encouraged the use of comic books during sustained silent reading periods in the classroom. After eight months, the researchers found that students exposed to high-interest stories progressed in reading and listening comprehension at twice the normal rate. Furthermore, after twenty months, they found that the increase was even more dramatic and began to have a beneficial effect on other language skills, including writing and speaking.

While the literature on comics and second language learning is limited, there is a growing body of research in the areas of critical literacy and popular culture that brings insight to our study of Archie comics and language learning. Educators who are interested in critical literacy are interested in studying texts as sites of struggle, negotiation, and change (see, for example, Kress, 1997, 2000; Luke, 1995, 1997; New London Group, 1996; Norton Peirce & Stein, 1995). Such educators argue that texts are not restricted to the written word, but include oral, visual, and graphic representations of meaning. In this view, the meaning of such texts is not stable, but is constructed within the context of a variety of social and institutional relationships and assumes diverse identities on the part of readers. Such readers use texts to make sense of the world even as readers, themselves, are positioned in particular ways by different kinds of texts. Changing forms of literate behavior have become the central interest of the work of the New London Group (1996), who, through groundbreaking research, address the multiple ways in which technology is transforming literacy practices. The group takes the position that literacy pedagogy should account for the increasing variety of text forms associated with information and multimedia technologies, including an understanding of the way visual images relate to the written word.

Likewise, the emerging literature on popular culture and educational practice seeks a more complex appreciation of the role of popular culture in schooling than hitherto conceived (see Alvermann, Moon, & Hagood, 1999; Buckingham, 1998; Dyson, 1997; Finders, 1997; Giroux & Simon, 1988, 1989; Hilton, 1996; Lewis, 1998; Norton, 2001). These scholars take the position that if educators do not take seriously the social and cultural texts that are authorized by youth – which may simultaneously empower and disempower them – they run the risk of negating and silencing their students. Much of this research locates the study of popular culture within the context of a critical pedagogy that seeks to validate the knowledge that students bring with them to the classroom, knowledge that is constructed within the practices of students' everyday lives outside the classroom. In this view, popular cultural texts provide an important window on the activities and investments of students outside schools.

While popular culture has received little attention in the second language literature, a recent study by Duff (2001, 2002) suggests that, at least in some K–12 classrooms, references to popular culture are integral to classroom practice. In her Canadian study in a multilingual secondary school classroom, she found that references to such TV shows as *Ally McBeal*, *The Simpsons*, *Seinfeld*, and *Friends* were common and that English language learners were unable to enter into discussions that assumed such cultural knowledge. Duff (2002) quotes the following comment made by Sue, an anglophone Canadian. It is an eerie echo of the comment made by eleven-year-old Dylan, quoted at the beginning of this chapter:

> Most of the [ESL] students in this class don't sit down and read the paper or anything . . . for the popular culture aspect, like the movies and even things like the radio songs and stuff. Different types of radio. They're missing a lot. And I think that might be one of the spots where the segregation starts between ESL students and us because they don't have the same radio stations, and they don't watch the same movies and they're not as absorbed by the same pop culture that we are. (p. 485)

In Norton's (2000) research with immigrant adult women, she found that references to popular culture were also common in conversational banter in the workplace. She cites the case of Eva, a language learner from Poland, who felt silenced and disempowered when her coworker, Gail, berated her for having no knowledge of the TV show, *The Simpsons*.

Given such changing perspectives on literacy and popular culture, it is timely to revisit debates on the comic book and second language education. Since the 1950s, when texts such as Wertham's (1955) classic, *Seduction of the Innocent*, were published, there has been much controversy about the value of comic books within educational practice. These debates have frequently been related to prevailing conceptions of the text, the reader, and the process of reading. While Wertham might dismiss comic books as trash, Haugaard (1973) believes they deserve a better press. Meek (1988, 1992), more recently, argues that comic books have unique characteristics that call for thoughtful analysis and expresses surprise that educators "have ignored for so long the reading skills they taught our readers" (Meek, 1988, p. 25).

What, indeed, have Archie comics taught our readers, and do they have a place in the multilingual language classroom? Given the multimodal features of Archie comics, which include pictures, dialogues, and narrative text, they might be conceived of as a classic multimodal text. However, as Stein (2000) argues, incorporating multimodal texts in the classroom, whether they be photographs, drawings, television shows, dramatic exercises, or computer graphics, requires nothing less than a reconceptualization of representation in the classroom. Fundamental to the theory she cites is the principle that semiotic modes serve as *resources* that do different kinds of work and produce different kinds of effects. Such theory is relevant to the Archie research because comics represent a particular kind of multimodal resource that produces different effects among children, teachers, and parents. Such effects, in turn, have a significant impact on the perceived legitimacy of comics within the context of schooling, more generally, and second language education, more specifically.

Because we are interested in English language learning among preadolescent children, we have also been drawn to sociocultural research which investigates the social relationships between English language learners and their first language peers within the context of the multilingual K–12 classroom. The research of Duff (2001, 2002), Gunderson (2000), Harklau (1994, 2000), McKay and Wong (1996), Miller (2003), Toohey (1998, 2000), and Tosi and Leung (1999) is particularly relevant here. While language learners in Gunderson's Canadian study reported overwhelmingly that practicing English with native English speakers was essential for language development, opportunities for interaction were rare. Researchers have found that a major challenge for school-aged language learners is gaining access to the social networks of their first language peers that will, in turn, provide opportunities for interaction and English language development. Harklau (1994), for example, drawing on a longitudinal study in an American secondary school, notes the following: "Perhaps the most salient aspect of observations of ESL students in mainstream classes was their reticence and lack of interaction with native-speaking peers." Likewise, Duff (2001, 2002) refers to the lack of confidence of the ESL students in her study, noting that if language learners wish to become active members of the classroom discourse community, their cultural knowledge may be as important as their academic proficiency.

The research is not uniformly bleak, however. McKay and Wong (1996) cite the case of Michael Lee, who, as a result of his prowess at sports, was not only successful in accessing peer relationships with first language speakers in his American secondary school, but also made great progress in his development of oral skills in English. Toohey's (2000) work with elementary school children in Canada is another case in point. Those students, such as Julie, who made effective use of allies were able to access first language friendship networks and make great progress in language learning. Of particular interest to this study is Toohey's observation that the lending and borrowing rituals within elementary classrooms provide a window into social relations and learning opportunities within the classroom. In our study, we were particularly interested in the extent to which Archie comics were traded, exchanged, and borrowed among our preteen readers and the impact this may have had on learning opportunities for second language students.

A study of Archie comic readers

The study in which Joong-ha, Dylan, and Namisha participated was conducted at Mountain Elementary School, in the city of Vancouver, from May 1998 to May 1999. This site was selected for its culturally diverse student population as well as its large second language population. The study included fifty-five elementary students in Grades 5, 6, and 7, twenty-five of whom were English language learners – defined as those students who speak a language other than English at home. There were approximately equal numbers of male (thirteen) and female (twelve) students in the second language group, thirteen of whom were Archie readers (six male and seven female). This chapter will focus on the contributions of the thirteen Archie readers, whose language backgrounds include Korean, Swedish, Mandarin, Bengali, Farsi, and Cantonese. For the purposes of confidentiality, pseudonyms are used for both the site and the following participants in this research: Guofang, Jonas, Liming, Nancy, and Ping from China; Diane, Dustin, Joong-ha, and Sook from Korea; Badar and Mohammed from Iran; Namisha from India; and Eva from Sweden.

In October 1998, a three-part questionnaire was distributed to elementary students in Grades 5, 6, and 7. For the purposes of this chapter, we focus on the third part of the questionnaire which targeted our Archie readers only. The questionnaire was designed to gain insight into the appeal of Archie comics, the literacy development of the Archie reader, and the social network of Archie readers. Such questions included the following:

- Why do you like reading Archie comics?
- How old were you when you started reading Archie comics?
- How did you find out about Archie comics?
- Do your friends like reading Archie comics?
- Which world would you rather live in – your world or Archie's world?

Following an analysis of the questionnaires, we interviewed ten of the second language Archie readers on a chilly day in February 1999. The interviews took place in the nurse's station at the school, where we could catch glimpses of students and teachers scurrying in the corridors and hear the distant sound of intercom announcements. In the interviews, which were tape-recorded and lasted approximately thirty minutes each, we asked students to elaborate on comments they had made in the questionnaire and to respond to a variety of prompts, including the following:

- Do you think Archie comics are helpful in learning English?
- Do you read comics in your home language?
- Should you be allowed to read Archie comics during silent reading?
- Do you talk about Archie comics with your friends?
- Do Archie comics tell you anything about Canadian society?

After much animated discussion, each student left the room brandishing a copy of the latest Archie comic we could find in our local grocery store. In May 1999, we returned to the school and presented some of the major findings from the study to groups of elementary students and their teachers.

Insights from Archie comic readers

In this section, we will present and discuss our findings with respect to three related questions we were investigating for the purposes of this chapter:

1. What is the appeal of Archie comics for English language learners?
2. To what extent can the reading of Archie comics promote literacy development?
3. Do Archie comics foster social interaction between English language learners and their anglophone peers?

The appeal of Archie comics

Like many of their anglophone peers, the English language learners in our study found Archie comics appealing because they are humorous and engaging to read. Out of a total of thirteen language learners who responded to the question, "Why do you like reading Archie comics?" eleven cited humor as central to the appeal of these texts, using the adjectives "fun," "funny," and "humorous" to characterize the Archie appeal. This was a sober reminder that the pursuit of pleasure and enjoyment is no less important for second language learners than for their native-speaking classmates. Namisha, for example, explained how the Archie comic hooks the reader:

> 'cause it's funny and it's like interesting 'cause most – like novels – in the beginning it hooks you but then it gets boring, right? Archie comics don't really because you want to know what happens at the end without all that boring detail.

Mohammed, in a similar spirit to that of Namisha, highlights the entertainment value of Archie comics. In response to the question, "Do you think you should be allowed to read Archie comics during silent reading?" Mohammed replied:

> Yes! I don't really know what my teacher would care, but like, I would love it. I would love not wasting time working – just reading Archie books. . . . I'd like to do Archie books for entertainment. So it would be just like having entertainment at school.

The humor and entertainment value of Archie comics should not be dismissed as trivial. Meek (1988, p. 19), in arguing that "a joke is often the best reading test," notes that while children learn very quickly the rules for both behavior and for reading, they also learn, likewise, that rules can be broken and subverted. The puns, the humor, and the twists in Archie stories presuppose sophistication on the part of readers and are a source of great delight for preadolescent children, whether English language learners or anglophone readers.

The pleasure principle was not the only source of the Archie comic appeal, however. Children new to North America who are struggling to understand the sociocultural practices of their new society find in comic books like Archie images of popular activities among young people. In this regard, the students made little distinction between popular activities in the United States and those in Canada, agreeing, as Liming noted, "they're pretty much the same." In response to the question, "Do Archie comics tell you anything about Canadian society?" some of the students felt that Archie comics were appealing because they could help students learn about their new society. In his interview with Norton, Dustin illustrates this point:

> Bonny: Do you think that Archie comics teach you about Canadian society? I mean, you know you come from Korea right?
> Dustin: Yeah, it does.
> Bonny: Oh, it does? Oh like what, Dustin?
> Dustin: Like when they go to the swimming pool or restaurant and – not a lot, but a little about swimming pools – I mean the beach. There's like all these ah – it tells a little bit.
> Bonny: So you said "the beach" and um "the swimming pools" and things like that – like the events that people spend time, their leisure activities. Yeah.
> Dustin: In Korea (laughs), they don't like spend time a lot um – going to the beach or something because they're like busy or they got like a lot of work to do.
> Bonny: You mean like even the children?
> Dustin: Children they have to study till midnight to get their homework done, but there's like not much homework here.

Guofang explained that her mother suggested that she lend her immigrant cousin some of her Archie comics to help him acquire his new language as well as knowledge about Canadian society. She offered the following insights in her interview:

Guofang: I'm lending some of them [Archie comics] to my cousin. He just came here from China and like then the words he can't understand and then he could learn about the society here.
Bonny: And he's learning?
Guofang: He's learning.
Bonny: So did you think when he came here, "Oh, Archie comics will help my cousin." Did you think that?
Guofang: First, it's like my mom gave me a suggestion to give, lending them to my cousin – Well, first she just said it's kind of easy to understand and he could learn more.

We explored, in some depth, the question of whether students thought that Archie comics would give them insight into their future lives as teenagers. Of the eleven language learners who responded to the question, "Do you think Archie comics tell you what your life will be like as a teenager?" there was a mixed reaction. Six of the students said no, four said yes, and one was uncertain. Of those who said no, they explained, for example, that some stories are "impossible" and that comics are "just stories." Of those who said yes, students explained, for example, that "you should be ready for some bimbo to steal your boyfriend" and that "whatever I do I'm going to be a teenager." The student who was uncertain added, "Well, some of them will, but not all of them."

While students indicated that Archie comics gave them some insight into what life might be like as a teenager, how friends relate to one another, and what leisure activities are popular among young people in North America, they recognized that Archie comics are not "real life." Joong-ha, for example, said that characters "never die," Sook said that Archie comics are "cartoony," and Ping noted, with reference to what she called the "fictional" Archie story used in the study, "how can [Betty] go into fairytale land and go and talk to people and tell them to switch their ways and stuff like that?"

While the English language learners found aspects of the Archie world appealing, most agreed that they would not trade their world with the Archie world. In answer to the question, "Which world would you rather live in – your world or Archie's world?" only two students, Guofang and Mohammed, indicated a preference for Archie's world. Guofang made the point that teenagers in Archie's world seldom got into trouble, while in her world, "if you're a teenager, you've got lots of problems to solve." Mohammed indicated that in Archie's world, students had greater freedom than in his culture in which there were "lots of rules." Thus, contrary to what some teachers and parents might think, the students had no difficulty distinguishing between the reality of their lives and the fantasy of the Archie world.

Archie comics and literacy development

When asked if the reading of Archie comics would be helpful for people learning English, nine of the ten English language learners interviewed responded affirmatively. Most students agreed that the simplified vocabulary of Archie comics makes them accessible to language learners, rendering them, as Mohammed said, "perfect" for instructional purposes. Liming made the point that the acquisition of vocabulary is a developmental process and that the simplified vocabulary of Archie comics helps to scaffold language learning: "Because they use quite easy words that you could learn that could help you, and as you grow older, you can learn harder words by yourself."

Even more appealing for the students, however, are the visuals and pictures in Archie comics. As Liming explained, "When the author draws and when I read it, it makes me laugh." For many learners, however, the visuals are not only a source of humor, they are important signposts for events in the Archie stories. As Guofang explained, "Well, they got picture, can help them, colorful pictures can help the reader to understand like how, what is happening, going on." Namisha elaborated on this point, noting, "Well, sometimes when it's normally written, there's like not much pictures, right? But here it's showing you who's saying it with those little bubbles." Eva's strategy was even more proactive than Guofang's and Namisha's. "The stuff that I did," she said, "was that I first looked at the pictures and then I made up my own words."

While many teachers consider visuals and pictures a distraction in the reading process, Meek's (1988) response is more textured. She makes the case that the comic book demands that the reader make two interpretations simultaneously: one of pictures and another of text. The multiple forms of representation, including balloon dialogues, inset sketches, the drawing of asides, together with the reader's impulse to keep the story going, are not only challenging for readers, but illustrate convincingly that the reader assumes two identities in the reading process: the identity of the teller and that of the told. This dual identity is one that is rarely taught, she argues, except in those instances when an adult might substitute for the author by reading out loud to a child. In comic book reading, however, a child cannot rely on an adult to assume the author's voice as visuals and icons cannot be easily interpreted. It is the young reader, alone, who assumes the identity of the teller and the told in the construction of meaning. When Eva "made up [her] own words," she was following the dictates of the genre.

Ownership over meaning making is clearly one of the appealing facets of comic book reading, and Archie readers in the study were very astute at using multiple strategies to engage with the comic book. Not only did they closely examine the pictures, study the dialogues, and make up their own words, but they also felt at liberty to move nonsequentially through the text, from one section to another. As Mohammed explained, in response to the question, "Why do you like reading Archie comic books?",

> A regular book is just like completely one story and wherever you go, if you like get from somewhere – like if you're in the middle of the book, and you don't want to read it, and you just want to go forward, you won't know the middle – so there's no point to the book. But with Archie, you can just go to another complete section.

Thus, the structure of Archie comics provides the reader with diverse strategies for negotiating the text, much as the more contemporary World Wide Web offers choice and variety for readers. As Kress (1997, p. 161) argues, "The sequentiality and linearity of former textual structures is replaced by a web, which can be entered at any point of my choosing and explored with neither a pre-given point of entry nor a pre-given point of departure."

While the focus of our study was on literacy development with reference to Archie comics, we discovered that the students in our study found other English language comics, such as Calvin and Hobbes, equally entertaining. Perhaps more significantly, we also collected interesting data pertaining to comic book reading and literacy development in the mother tongue. In answer to the interview question, "Do you read comics in your home language?," six out of ten students indicated that they read comics in their first language as well as in English. One student, in fact, began reading comics in English *before* he began to read comics in his first language. Such data supports Gunderson's (2000) finding that the reading of comic books in the mother tongue was common among the students in his large-scale study.

It is intriguing to consider whether mother tongue maintenance could be promoted by encouraging second language learners to read comics books in the mother tongue. The study suggests that comic books in the mother tongue may provide an important connection to the preimmigration life of young language learners. First language loss is often a devastating consequence of immigration of young people (Kouritzin, 2000; Norton, 2000) as children seek acceptance among target-language speakers in their classrooms and communities. If children read comic books in the mother tongue and find connection to their home language through popular culture, they may engage more actively with their histories and identities. Indeed, as Stein (2000, p. 336) would argue, such students would be "re-sourcing resources" – that is, "taking invisible, taken-for-granted resources to a new context of situation to produce new meanings." Consider the following extract:

Karen: Now you've talked about reading comics in Korean, that you read some Korean comics. So I'm really interested in that. What kind of comics do you read in Korean?
Joong-ha: They're like fighting things.
Karen: How do they compare to Archie comics?
Joong-ha: This is like new life and that's old life.

The data suggest further that students make cultural distinctions between the comics they read in their first language and Archie comics, noting, in general, that Archie comics are more about real life than other comics they have encountered. Liming noted, for example, that Pokémon Power, a favorite Japanese–Chinese comic, focuses on adventure, while Archie comics focus on what he referred to as "our lives in the future." Dustin described his enjoyment of the Korean comic, Dragonball and, in answer to the question, "So how is Dragonball different from the Archie comics?" responded as follows:

Like Korea doesn't make any comics like this [Archie comics]. Um – this is based on environment – I mean nature. But Dragonball and stuff it's like – um – it's like a place that's not real. It's fake, it's all fake. All the stuff in there is fake in there but it's all real in here [Archie comics]. Like swimming and beach and all those stuff are real, but in Dragonball it's fighting.

With the exception of Guofang's mother, however, data from the study suggest that both teachers and parents were, at best, ambivalent about comics – at worst, completely dismissive. Data to support this view were generated by the following key question: "Should you be allowed to read Archie comics during silent reading?" While many of the students thought Archie comics could be helpful in language learning, many of the same students said that their teachers would not find Archie comics acceptable in the classroom, especially during silent reading. Joong-ha, for example, said his teacher would think it was "bad," explaining that, "I think they think that there's few words and a lot of pictures." A similar sentiment was expressed by Namisha who, in response to the same question, answered as follows:

Um I mean you read and stuff, right. Well, there are some comics, some popular comics that people were allowed to read like in my old school, but they're not allowed to read Archie comics for some reason. There's like no swearing or anything so we could probably but teachers say that it's like not challenging.

In addition, some of the students interviewed mentioned that their parents did not approve of their reading of Archie comics as comics were seen as a distraction from the child's school work or a waste of time. As Ping said:

Ping: My mom just doesn't want me to read comics anymore –
Bonny: So why do you think your mom doesn't like you to read comics?
Ping: She said it's like I'm wasting my time like I could do something better, like instead of reading comics, like actually doing homework.
Bonny: Now um do you think teachers think the same way about comic books?
Ping: Yeah, probably, but not always but usually they do because they want you to focus on your homework.

Such comments from Joong-ha, Namisha, and Ping suggest that although children derive great pleasure from their Archie comics and are clearly actively engaged in meaning making, this practice is considered an unchallenging waste of time and is consequently not authorized by teachers and parents.

In his classic text, *Schooling as a Ritual Performance*, McLaren's (1986) insights about the nature and function of rituals within schooling are important for understanding why novels and chapter books, rather than comic books, are privileged during silent reading and homework activities. His argument is that rituals symbolically transmit societal and cultural ideologies, which are best understood in the context of competing claims to power. In the context of schooling, the teacher's power is derived from familiarity with chapter books, extended prose, classic texts, and teachers' guides. As Gunderson (2000) argues:

> The study of literature, the "classics," is viewed as essential to the development of literate human beings. Central to the study is the notion that a particular body of literature is the canon, like Shakespeare and Chaucer, and to be truly "literate" one must study it. This view ignores the substantial oral and written contributions of most of the cultures of the world. (p. 701)

Within such a context, the humble comic book, with its cheap paper, extensive pictures, and bubble dialogues, is no match for the powerful canon.

Archie comics and a community of readers

Drawing on the data from our study, we have examined, thus far, the appeal of Archie comics in terms of their humor and their teenage content, we have discussed their accessibility with reference to vocabulary and visual representation, and we have suggested that their dismissal by some teachers and parents may not be in the best interests of language learning and mother tongue maintenance. As discussed earlier, however, we are concerned not only with literacy as a process of reading and writing; in this study, we are also addressing literacy as a social practice. As Barton, Hamilton, and Ivanič (2000) argue, all uses of written language can be seen as located in particular times and places, positioned in relation to the social institutions and power relations which sustain them. Given this perspective, we would like to argue that the community of readers associated with Archie comics is important for both the development of orality in English and for social relationships between English language learners and their anglophone peers.

In our study, we found that comics, in general, and Archie comics, in particular, constitute part of what Finders (1997, p. 25) would argue is the "literate underlife" of preadolescent children. In support of this view is data collected in response to the question, "How did you find out about Archie comics?" Eight out of thirteen language learners said a friend told them about the comics, and another two said they found out about Archie comics because of a sister. In addition, a majority of the Archie readers interviewed (seven out of ten) said that their friends also enjoyed reading Archie comics. What is significant about these data is the suggestion that students learn about Archie comics predominantly from peers or siblings – not from teachers or other adults. Thus, the network of Archie readers is one that is developed and nurtured by the peer group. As Badar said, "Well, lots of people in our class, last year they were reading it so I thought it's good to borrow it from my friends and started reading it." Further, when students were asked the following question, "Do you talk about Archie comics with your friends?" eight out of ten said that they discussed Archie comics with their friends on a regular basis:

Bonny: Do they [all your friends] read Archie comics?
Guofang: Yeah. We go to each others' houses like after school time and then, and we sometimes talk about characters, about their personality and stuff.
Bonny: So how did you get to read Archie comics, who introduced you to Archie comics?
Guofang: My friend.

Like Guofang, Dustin explained that he has a Korean friend who reads Archie comics, and "when I go over to his house, I read his comics, and when he comes, he reads my comics."

It was evident from the data that Archie readers, and the girls in particular, constituted an informal and loosely connected reading community in which students borrowed comics from one another, went to one another's houses to swap comics, and talked about the stories on a regular basis. In this regard, two findings were of particular significance: First, we found that the talk which Archie comics generated was usually conducted in English, and, second, we found that the rituals of swapping and borrowing crossed ethnic and linguistic lines. As Ping (1) and Joong-ha (2) said:

(1)

Ping: When I started reading it [Archie comics] when I was reading it I used to always talk about it with my friends who had them and we used to switch and read them –
Bonny: But that you did in English?
Ping: Yeah, even like with most of my Chinese friends.

(2)

Karen: Now when you trade, are you trading with other Korean kids or are you trading with Canadian kids? Or, who are you trading with?
Joong-ha: Both.
Karen: So some of your Korean friends read Archie also? Now when you trade with your Korean friends, do you speak in Korean with them about Archie, or is it in English?
Joong-ha: English. Well sometimes Korean.

Given the rich use of English generated by the reading of comic books, it is perhaps not surprising that Elley and Mangubhai (1983), quoted earlier in the chapter, found that the use of comic books had a beneficial effect on other language skills, including writing and speaking.

Further, perhaps more important, is the possibility that the literate underlife we associate with comic books and popular culture has much potential for building relationships among students of different linguistic backgrounds. In this regard, as Toohey (1998, 2000) would argue, the borrowing and lending practices of Archie comic readers are significant. Toohey has demonstrated that rituals of lending and borrowing among school children are intricate practices which engage the identities of students in complex ways. In her study of a multilingual elementary school classroom, Toohey found that children would engage in borrowing and lending rituals even when a student may have had little need of the borrowed item. Among other purposes of borrowing was the desire to enter into social interaction with other students – a practice that carried attendant risks. Lenders were in a powerful position vis-à-vis borrowers in that it was up to the lender to decide if the item could be shared and if conversations with the borrower were welcome. For example, while the initiatives of one language learner, Surjeet, were often rebuffed by classmates, other language learners, like Amy, were more successful at borrowing practices and would engage the lender in short conversations. As Toohey (1998, p. 75) concluded, "it seems evident that borrowing and lending practices in this classroom were reflective of the social relations of the children therein."

In follow-up research, Toohey and Day (1999) have analyzed those practices in elementary classrooms which facilitate access of second language students to community resources, of which English as a linguistic resource is a prime example. They note that playful activities, in which the identities of students are protected and community knowledge appears accessible to all, help to transform the classroom participation of second language learners from minimal to full. For many students at Mountain Elementary School – and perhaps in other multilingual elementary schools – Archie comics could become another resource that not only promotes interaction between language learners and their anglophone peers, but helps build precisely the kind of community that Toohey and Day envisage. To this end, pedagogical practices would need to extend beyond the "cut and paste" methods discussed by Wright (1976) or the silent reading exercises promoted by Elley and Mangubhai (1983). Teachers would need to provide structured opportunities for the borrowing and lending of Archie comics, for discussion among students, and for input from parents. Language learners would be encouraged to bring their mother-tongue comics to the classroom, to share different stories, and to compare comic book genres. In this way, a comic book culture, which includes comics in both English and other languages, might enrich the literacy practices in the elementary classroom and promote community relationships in which diversity is celebrated.

Some concluding comments

In her Canadian study, Duff (2001, 2002) observed that teachers and anglophone students in the Grade 10 humanities class made frequent reference to aspects of North American popular culture, including Hollywood-produced television series and movies. She concluded that the English language learners in the class, besides needing academic literacy skills, also needed a more general popular culture literacy, characteristic of teen magazines, youth-oriented radio stations, and other media. While the language learners in her study showed little familiarity with such aspects of popular culture and were consequently marginal to many classroom discussions, we found that many language learners at Mountain Elementary, along with their anglophone peers, found Archie comics accessible and engaging. The students noted that the colorful pictures, contextualized vocabulary, and interesting content provided a compelling hook into reading. Further, we found that both language learners and their anglophone peers engaged in rich oral discussion about Archie comics and that the community of Archie readers crossed ethnic and linguistic boundaries. We noted, finally, that the reading of comic books in the mother tongue may be important for mother-tongue maintenance.

Teachers and parents might find it reassuring that the students did not necessarily embrace all the activities depicted in Archie comics. Even those students who said that Archie comics could provide insight into their lives as teenagers qualified their comments in a number of ways. Further, while students gained a great deal of pleasure from Archie comics, they were almost unanimous in stating that they would rather live in their world than the Archie world. What attracted students to the comics was the humor, the variety, the action, the social relationships, and the fact that they could work out meanings and understandings for themselves. For learners struggling to understand academic texts in a second language, the comic book represents an exciting opportunity to engage with text from a position of strength rather than weakness. There is no right answer to ferret out of the text, and there are multiple cues to meaning making.

Nevertheless, we believe it is highly significant that these young language learners had accepted the dominant view that comics, in general, and Archie comics, in particular, do not constitute "real reading" and hence have little educational value. It is clear that children are learning from a young age that "good reading" is associated with chapter books that are challenging, include lots of print, and have no pictures. When "good reading" is equated with "difficult reading," the second language learner is particularly disadvantaged. We believe the scaffolding function of comic books in literacy development for second language learners has been underestimated. Further, it is possible to argue that while the use of chapter books, novels, and extended prose can have important pedagogical consequences for language learners, many teachers and parents may have shifted the focus of literacy instruction from meaning making to ritual.

As scholars in critical literacy would argue, there is much controversy among parents, teachers, and students about what constitutes literacy and how literacy should be promoted in the classroom. It is possible that the emerging research and theory on multiliteracies may begin to have an impact on the way texts such as comics are perceived in the multilingual classroom. Members of the New London Group would argue that the multimodal text is a legitimate genre, that the visual medium is here to stay, and that "surfing" an Archie comic is consistent with changing literacy practices on the Web. Perhaps both teachers and parents need to rethink their conceptions of literacy in a changing technological and social world. Notwithstanding the fact that many teachers and parents often think our influence on children is limited, the study suggests that what adults think can have a powerful influence on student perceptions of literacy. If we recognize that literacy references not only words on the printed page, but social relationships and community practices, we may yet find a place for Archie comics in the multilingual classroom.

Acknowledgments

We would like to thank students and teachers at Mountain Elementary School for their generous participation in this study. We would also like to thank Patsy Duff for her thoughtful comments on an earlier draft of this chapter. We gratefully acknowledge the support of a Hampton Grant from the University of British Columbia, as well as a grant from the Social Sciences and Humanities Research Council of Canada.

References

Alvermann, D., Moon, J. S., & Hagood, M. C. (1999). *Popular culture in the classroom: Teaching and researching critical media literacy*. Newark, DE: International Reading Association.

Barton, D., Hamilton, M., & Ivanič, R. (2000). *Situated literacies: Reading and writing in context*. London: Routledge.

Buckingham, D. (Ed). (1998). *Teaching popular culture*. London: University College London Press.

Duff, P. (2001). Language, literacy, content, and (pop) culture: Challenges for ESL students in mainstream courses. *Canadian Modern Language Review, 58*(1), 103–32.

Duff, P. (2002). Pop culture and ESL students: Intertextuality, identity, and participation in classroom discussion. *Journal of Adolescent and Adult Literacy, 45*(6), 482–7.

Dyson, A. (1997). *Writing superheroes: Contemporary childhood, popular culture, and classroom literacy*. New York: Teachers College Press.

Elley, W. B., & Mangubhai, F. (1983). The impact of reading on second language learning. *Reading Research Quarterly, 19*(1), 53–67.

Finders, M. (1997). *Just girls: Hidden literacies and life in junior high*. New York: Teachers College Press.

Giroux, H., & Simon, R. (1988). Schooling, popular culture, and a pedagogy of possibility. *Journal of Education, 170*(1), 9–26.

Giroux, H., & Simon, R. (1989). *Popular culture: Schooling and everyday life*. Toronto, Ontario, Canada: OISE Press.

Gunderson, L. (2000). Voices of the teenage diasporas. *Journal of Adolescent and Adult Literacy, 43*(8), 692–706.

Harklau, L. (1994). ESL versus mainstream classes: Contrasting L2 learning environments. *TESOL Quarterly, 28*(2), 241–72.

Harklau, L. (2000). From the "good kids" to the "worst": Representations of English language learners across educational settings. *TESOL Quarterly, 34*, 35–67.

Haugaard, K. (1973). Comic books: Conduits to culture? *Reading Teacher, 27*, 54–5.

Hilton, M. (Ed). (1996). *Potent fictions: Children's literacy and the challenge of popular culture*. London: Routledge.

Kouritzin, S. (2000). *Face(t)s of language loss*. Mahwah, NJ: Lawrence Erlbaum Associates.

Krashen, S. (1993). *The power of reading: Insights from the research*. Englewood, CO: Libraries Unlimited.

Kress, G. (1997). *Before writing: Rethinking the paths to literacy*. London: Routledge.

Kress, G. (2000). Multimodality. In B. Cope & M. Kalantzis (Eds.), *Multiliteracies: Literacy learning and the design of social futures* (pp. 182–202). London: Routledge.

Lewis, C. (1998). Rock 'n' roll and horror stories: Students, teachers, and popular culture. *Journal of Adolescent and Adult Literacy, 42*(2), 116–20.

Luke, A. (1995). Text and discourse in education: An introduction to critical discourse analysis. In M. W. Apple (Ed.), *Review of research in education,* (*Vol. 21,* pp. 3–48). Washington, DC: American Educational Research Association.

Luke, A. (1997). Critical approaches to literacy. In V. Edwards & D. Corson (Eds.), *Encyclopedia of language and education, Vol. 2: Literacy* (pp. 143–52). Amsterdam: Kluwer Academic.

Luke, A., & Elkins, J. (1998). Reinventing literacy in "New Times." *Journal of Adolescent and Adult Literacy, 42*(1), 4–8.

McKay, S. L., & Wong, S. C. (1996). Multiple discourses, multiple identities: Investment and agency in second language learning among Chinese adolescent immigrant students. *Harvard Educational Review, 66*(3), 577–608.

McLaren, P. (1986). *Schooling as a ritual performance*. London: Routledge.

Meek, M. (1988). *How texts teach what readers learn*. Avonset, England: Thimble Press.

Meek, M. (1992). *On being literate*. Portsmouth, NH: Heinemann Educational Books.

Miller, J. (2003). *Audible difference: ESL and social identity in schools*. Clevedon, England: Multilingual Matters.

New London Group. (1996). A pedagogy of social multiliteracies: Designing social futures. *Harvard Educational Review, 66*(1), 60–92.

Norton, B. (2000). *Identity and language learning: Gender, ethnicity and educational change*. Harlow, England: Pearson Education.

Norton, B. (2001). When is a teen magazine not a teen magazine? *Journal of Adolescent and Adult Literacy, 45*(4), 296–9.

Norton, B. (in press). The fantastic motivating power of comic books: Insights from Archie comic readers. *Reading Teacher*.

Norton Peirce, B., & Stein, P. (1995). Why the "Monkeys Passage" bombed: Tests, genres, and teaching. *Harvard Educational Review, 65*(1), 50–65.

Robbins, T. (1999). *From girls to grrrlz: A history of women's comics from teens to zines*. San Francisco: Chronicle Books.

Stein, P. (2000). Rethinking resources: Multimodal pedagogies in the ESL classroom. *TESOL Quarterly, 34*(2), 333–6.

Toohey, K. (1998). "Breaking them up, taking them away": Constructing ESL students in Grade 1. *TESOL Quarterly, 32*(1), 61–84.

Toohey, K. (2000). *Learning English at school: Identity, social relations, and classroom practice*. Clevedon, England: Multilingual Matters.

Toohey, K., & Day, E. (1999). Language-learning: The importance of access to community. *TESL Canada Journal, 17*(1), 40–53.

Tosi, A., & Leung, C. (1999). *Rethinking language education: From a monolingual to a multilingual perspective*. London: Centre for Information on Language Teaching.

Wertham, F. (1955). *Seduction of the innocent*. New York: Rinehart.

Wright, A. (1976). *Visual materials for the language teacher*. London: Longman.

12 *Classroom interaction, gender, and foreign language learning*

Jane Sunderland

At least since the early 1970s, education in relation to all curricular subjects and at all levels has been subject to widespread feminist critique along with (though less prevalently) suggested strategies for transformation (see, for example, Acker, 1994; Arnot & Weiner, 1987; Burchell & Millman, 1989; Deem, 1978; Frith & Mahony, 1994; Gaskell, 1992; Measor & Sikes, 1992; Spender, 1980, 1982; Walkerdine, 1989; Weiner, 1994; Wolpe, 1988). Monographs and edited collections in the area have tended not to be curricular-subject specific (though for exceptions, see Walkerdine [1989], Whyld [1983]; for work specifically on foreign language classrooms, see Clark [1998], Powell [1986], Sunderland [1994]). In language education, however, gender has been the topic of numerous articles. Much of this work has tended to focus on gender difference rather than gender disadvantage and thus has not engaged as thoroughly with justice, equality, and opportunity as it might. In this chapter, I survey gender research in education and in language education in particular, describe a recent study of gender and interaction in the language classroom (Sunderland, 1996), and consider how some concepts of critical discourse analysis might point us in productive directions for future research.

Alastair Pennycook inscribes gender into his work on critical pedagogy and language education (1989, 1990, 1999), and the *TESOL Quarterly* 1999 special issue devoted to critical pedagogy (and edited by Pennycook) contains a range of work that refers directly or indirectly to gender (Frye, 1999; Ibrahim, 1999; Mackie, 1999; Nelson, 1999). However, while critical pedagogy sits well with feminist pedagogy, and gender sits well with language education, the critical pedagogy–gender–language education triad has worked less well. Mainstream language educators have tended to show an unawareness of or lack of interest in critical pedagogy or have felt uncomfortable with the notion. Stephanie Vandrick (1999) speculates that many language teachers find critical and feminist pedagogies too political and see them as imposing the teacher's political views on students. She finds this somewhat ironic considering that

> Many of the tenets and practices of [critical pedagogy and feminist pedagogy] are those which many ESL [English as a second language] teachers would agree with if they were presented without the labels. For example, critical . . . pedagogies and ESL share a concern for social justice issues, especially regarding the minority students found in most ESL classes. (p. 9)

This "concern for social justice," which would include notions of gender equality, is certainly something that most ESL teachers would recognize in themselves and their colleagues – though for some, it may, indeed, be something new, an effect of the job and of getting to know their students and their backgrounds and histories. Yet a belief in social justice is by no means the same as the practice of, or even an interest in, critical pedagogy. The barriers between the two consist of, inter alia, curricular constraints, institutional expectations, and, crucially, teacher beliefs about the purpose of (language) education and the role of the teacher – put crudely, is she a language instructor or an educator in a wider sense (Branca Fabricio, personal communication)? Additionally, women and girls are widely perceived as being good at languages and language learning, performing better than men and boys in public and school examinations in many countries (Arnot, David, & Weiner, 1996; Arnot et al., 1998), and, in addition, are often more likely to elect to continue with languages when they have the choice (Wikeley & Stables, 1999). Together, these mean that gender is simply not seen as a problem for the language classroom (certainly not for women and girls) by many teachers. Because of this, much work otherwise of value on gender and language education has not been *critical* – in any sense (see Sunderland, 2000a, for a review of relevant work).

The aspect of language education that has been most commonly critiqued in relation to gender by language educators working at the chalkface is that of representation in language textbooks (and other teaching materials). Numerous such studies published in the 1970s and 1980s and into the early 1990s in the form of content analyses reported poor representation of female characters in terms of visibility and gender stereotyping. This, however, is not the subject of this paper (but again, see Sunderland, 2000a, for a review).[1]

A second, more muted, area of broadly critical research in gender and language education has been that of gendered classroom interaction – who talks most, to whom, and says what. The critical focus of this, especially in the late 1970s and 1980s when the dominance paradigm of language and gender was paramount, was to identify manifestations of male dominance in the two senses of male students being more verbose than females in whole-class talk and pair or group work and of the teacher paying more attention to the male than to the female students. The assumption, usually implicit (and, in retrospect, somewhat problematic), was that such male dominance would automatically advantage male students in terms of learning opportunities and learning itself and would disadvantage female students. These studies, on the whole, provided fairly superficial snapshots of classroom interaction and have been critiqued for their inadequate consideration of complexities of meanings and understandings created in classroom interaction.

Early studies of gender and classroom interaction in nonlanguage classrooms

Many studies of teacher talk in mixed-sex nonlanguage classrooms (in different curricular subjects) in the 1970s and 1980s did, indeed, find that not only did teachers talk more than their students, they talked far more to the male students. Dale Spender (1982) famously audiorecorded her own lessons and noted that, in contradiction to her intention and her perception that she had spent more time with the girls, "the maximum time I spent interacting with girls was 42% and on average 38%, and the minimum time with boys 58%" (p. 56). Spender has been criticized for not being explicit about her methodology, but her findings were echoed elsewhere (see Croll, 1985; Dart & Clarke, 1988; Howe, 1997). A meta-analysis of eighty-one such studies found this phenomenon to be widespread, operating "across all subjects in the curriculum" (Kelly, 1988, p. 20).

Research that examined the nature of teacher attention (as well as its amount) with respect to the gender of students found that male students seemed to have an advantage. Good, Sykes, and Brophy (1973) found that boys received more response opportunities in the form of a range of question types addressed to them by the teacher. Gore and Roumagoux (1983) documented significant differences in wait-time in mathematics classes, with boys being given longer to answer questions. Sadker and Sadker (1985) found in a study of Language Arts (first language [L1]) lessons that teachers reprimanded girls for calling out more than boys who did the same. Swann and Graddol (1988), working in a British primary school, identified differences in types of questions asked: in particular, girls were asked "challenging and open" questions less often than boys. Swann and Graddol also found a tendency for the teacher's gaze to be directed toward the boys at critical points, such as when a question was to be answered, thus inviting "self-selection" (see also Hammersley, 1990; Swann, 1988; Swann & Graddol, 1988). In her meta-analysis, Kelly (1988) concluded that boys get "more instructional contacts, more high-level questions, more academic criticism and slightly more praise than girls" (p. 29) – all of which would seem potentially valuable in terms of facilitating learning. However, importantly, she found that the discrepancy was *most* marked for behavioral criticism (see also Dart & Clarke, 1988; Merrett & Wheldall, 1992; Stanworth, 1983; Swann, 1992) – that is, the greatest gender-related difference lay in the fact that boys were told off more than were girls, something that she speculated was unlikely to contribute positively to learning.

Studies of student talk to the teacher in different subject classrooms found evidence of male verbosity in the form of boys talking more than girls to the teacher (e.g., French & French, 1984; Sadker & Sadker, 1985; Spender, 1982; Swann & Graddol, 1988; Whyte, 1984). In her meta-analysis, Kelly concluded, "Girls are just as likely as boys to volunteer answers in class, but boys are much more likely to call out the answers" (1988, p. 29). Some studies, however, found different patterns, including, at the tertiary level, no gender differences (e.g., Boersma, Gay, Jones, Morrison, & Remick, 1981). At the secondary level, Dart and Clarke (1988) found that girls in Year 8 science classes initiated *more* interactions with the teacher than did boys – though this was not significant statistically. Grant (1985), looking at race as well as gender, found weak support for an interaction effect: that boys, especially black boys, approached teachers less often than most girls and that white girls approached most often. Male students were more likely to challenge the teacher, but "white males challenged statements of fact.... black males more typically challenged application of rules, or... the teacher's right to impose rules" (pp. 69–70).

Though such studies were critically motivated, the locus of critique was often unclear. Researchers were unwilling to blame the teacher and his or her discursive practices – rightly so since teachers giving male students more attention than females is unlikely to be intentional, rather the result of a collaborative, unrecognized process between teacher and students (Swann & Graddol, 1988). Good et al. (1973) similarly note that "teachers are primarily *reactive* to the different pressures that boys and girls present" (p. 85). Such teacher talk is accordingly best referred to as "differential teacher treatment by gender" rather than discrimination or favoritism.

Interaction studies in the language classroom

The findings of these studies may have parallels in, and implications for, foreign language classrooms. Yet, partly because these are settings in which women and girls frequently do well (Arnot et al., 1996, 1998), questions about differential teacher treatment or male verbosity and the particular relationship of these asymmetries with language learning have been relatively unexplored. There have been very few such studies in the language classroom, particularly of teacher talk to students (but see Holmes, 1989a, 1989b). Further, findings have not always been conclusive. (I will not be concerned here with gendered student–student talk in pair and group work in the language classroom, but see Alcón, 1994; Gass & Varonis, 1986; Holmes, 1994; Kasanga, 1996; Provo, 1991).

Studying teachers of adult learners in ESL classrooms, Yepez (1994), in a small-scale study, found that most "showed equitable behavior" to male and female students. Regarding student talk to the teacher, findings mirror those of studies of nonlanguage classrooms. In a study by Alcón (1994), who looked at Spanish secondary school learners of English as a foreign language (EFL), the boys used significantly more solicits (language aimed at getting the teacher to say or do something) than did the girls. Batters (1986) similarly found that male secondary school students studying modern foreign languages were dominant in "oral and participatory activities" – including speaking to the teacher in the target language. Losey (1995) observed that Mexican American men contributed four times the amount expected in a mixed monolingual and bilingual Spanish–English class, whereas Mexican American women contributed half as much as expected.

Retrospectively (and all studies are products of their time), these studies can all be seen as having investigated gender and classroom interaction through a limited "critical classroom discourse analysis" – limited in not considering fully the wider social context and social practices these classroom practices operated within and drew on. They thus tended to identify female disadvantage in a rather straightforward and unproblematized way. They were also limited in having had a primarily descriptive function without an additional transformative one (Kumaravadivelu, 1999; Pennycook, 1999) – though see Holmes (1994) for some pedagogic (and thus potentially transformative) suggestions arising from a study of gendered talk in language classroom group work.

Three problems are apparent in the studies described so far. First, influenced by a gender differences paradigm, gender differences were made salient while similarities may have been overlooked. Second, these studies were notably general in terms of gendered talk, not actually ignoring, but downplaying, the possible role of gendered *individuals*. Third, the language classroom studies were largely nonlanguage-classroom specific in their research questions (inter alia, they did not really take into consideration the fact that, typically, more than one language is spoken in the language classroom). My own (Sunderland, 1996) study was intended to address these issues – from a limited critical perspective. I will present the findings and will then consider to what extent such a study addresses questions of social justice, opportunity, and equality in relation to the language classroom.

Gender and classroom interaction in a secondary school German as a foreign language classroom

The two original overarching research questions for this 1996 study were as follows:

1. Does the teacher use more or different language to or about boys and to or about girls?
2. Do boys and girls use more or different language from each other when addressing the teacher?

Specifically, I focused on

- teacher solicits (i.e., verbal attempts to get someone to say or do something);
- student solicits;
- teacher responses to student solicits;
- student responses to teacher solicits;
- teacher feedback to students' responses to the teacher's academic solicits;
- student feedback to teacher responses to their solicits;
- teacher comments;
- student comments;
- the amount of teacher talk *addressed to each* student; and
- the amount of student talk *produced by each* student.

(The last two were formulated after the initial formulation of the overarching questions.) I was specifically interested in how the gendered nature of the language classroom language might be special. Partly in relation to this, a distinction was made between use of the L1 and use of the target language (German) throughout the analysis.

This range of questions acknowledged that while the teacher might give more attention to boys in some respects, she might give more to girls in others, and that while boys might indeed dominate the classroom verbally with their own talk in some ways, girls might do so in others. I was, of course, interested in and open to the possibility of gender similarities as well as differences – indeed, as a teacher interested in equity, I hoped to find relatively few differences.

I arranged to carry out my research in a British secondary school classroom with approximately equal numbers of boys and girls, this last in order to obviate the possibility of an apparent gender effect being, in actuality, a majority group or minority group effect. The class in which I observed and collected data was a first year ("Year 7" – students aged eleven and twelve) group. This meant they had not been "setted" into subject-specific ability groups. There was an approximately even gender balance: fourteen boys and thirteen girls. With the exception of two boys of Chinese descent, the children were all white and from a monolingual (English) background. Since the classroom was in a comprehensive school, students came from a range of socioeconomic backgrounds.

Under the British National Curriculum, at this level, students must study two languages (these students' other language was French). The class had two fifty-minute German lessons each week. I started the observation in Term 2 of the academic year, so the students had settled into their new school and class and were not yet nearing the "endgame" of Term 3, with exams and thoughts of the summer break. I observed the class for ten weeks, attending both German lessons almost every week, observing nineteen lessons in all (for more details, see Sunderland, 1996). The majority of lessons were audiorecorded and the audiotapes transcribed. In the event, I used the first twelve of these transcripts as my data for the analysis.

The findings

TEACHER-TO-STUDENT TALK

The findings painted a complex picture of teacher talk. On the one hand, there was the familiar picture of the teacher paying more attention to the boys. This was certainly true in terms of number of words used in solicits (*solicit words* – significant at the 5 percent level) and the proportion of nonacademic solicits (approaching significance at the 5 percent level). As in Kelly's (1988) meta-analysis, many of the nonacademic solicits were disciplinary, meaning that the attention the boys were getting was partly due to the fact that they were being reprimanded. On most measures, however – including quantity and quality of feedback (positive and negative) to students' responses to the teacher's questions and teacher responses to the students' questions – there was no or only statistically nonsignificant evidence of differential teacher treatment. Similarities were thus the norm.

Two interesting findings were that the girls were asked a greater proportion of academic solicits to which they were expected to respond in German than were boys (approaching significance at the 5 percent level) and a greater proportion of questions which required an answer of more than one word (significant at the 5 percent level). While boys may have dominated this classroom in the sense of being the recipients of more of some types of teacher attention, the girls seemed to have been faring better – quantitatively and, arguably, in terms of learning opportunities – than the boys in other ways (see also Sunderland, 2000a), since these

TABLE 12.1 AMOUNT OF TEACHER TALK ADDRESSED TO EACH STUDENT

Girls	*Number of mentions of name*	*Boys*	*Number of mentions of name*
Kay	63	Gus	119
Lia	42	Len	100
May (1)	39.5	Ken	65
May (2)	39.5	Dan	35
Ann	36	Don	34
Lyn (1)	22	Bob (1)	25
Lyn (2)	22	Bob (2)	25
Bea	21	Pip	23
Ros	21	Sam	17
Una	18	Ray (1)	16.5
Sue	15	Ray (2)	16.5
Eve	10	Jim	15
Liz	11	Max	10
		Guy	11
Totals	360		512
Mean	27.69		36.57

latter findings suggest that the teacher was actually treating – or, arguably, *constructing* – the girls as the more academic students.

A study of teacher talk to *individuals* in this class was also instructive. Table 12.1 shows the amount of teacher attention given to each student, as measured by the frequency with which each student's name was mentioned.[2]

Clearly, it is two boys, Gus and Len, who get a disproportionate amount of teacher attention and who are responsible for raising the mean for the boys. If Gus and Len are excluded from the figures, the collective means for mentions of boys' names versus girls' names become far more comparable (24.42 and 27.69, respectively). As observed elsewhere, the greater part of teacher attention given to the boys is likely to be to a small subset of boys (French & French, 1984; Swann & Graddol, 1988).

STUDENT-TO-TEACHER TALK

Again, gender similarity in student-to-teacher talk was most evident with any gender differences tending to be statistically insignificant. This was true for numbers of solicits, proportions of academic and nonacademic solicits, and, on the whole, discoursal functions of solicits.

Male dominance in regard to verbosity was, however, evident in the statistically significant difference that the average girl produced shorter academic solicits than the average boy. It was also evident in the fact that though boys were only nonsignificantly proportionately more likely to

TABLE 12.2 AMOUNT OF STUDENT TALK PRODUCED BY EACH STUDENT

Girls	*Number of utterances*	*Boys*	*Number of utterances*
Kay	264	Gus	245
Lia	109	Len	78
Lyn (1)	117.5	Dan	74
Lyn (2)	117.5	Ken	51
May (1)	93	Don	50
May (2)	93	Ray (1)	46.5
Sue	92	Ray (2)	46.5
Ros	53	Sam	45
Bea	52	Bob (1)	37.5
Ann	49	Bob (2)	37.5
Eve	32	Jim	36
Liz	30	Max	31
Una	15	Guy	30
		Pip	15
Totals	1117		823
Mean	85.92		58.79

give feedback to the teacher after her response to their academic solicits than were girls, there was a significant gender difference in the greater proportion of the boys' feedback to these teacher responses taking the form of yet another solicit than those of the girls.

However, the average girl was verbally active in several important ways. She produced significantly more solicit words than the boys as well as a significantly greater proportion of unsolicited solicits (i.e., solicits that did not take place within an ongoing teacher–student exchange). Furthermore, when the teacher asked a question without naming a student to answer it, the average girl volunteered significantly more answers in German than did the average boy. She also followed up teacher responses to her academic solicits more than to her nonacademic solicits, whereas the reverse was true for the average boy (this difference approaching statistical significance at the 5 percent level).

It is, again, possible to read these gendered patterns of student–teacher talk as suggesting that, despite evidence of relative male verbosity in some discoursal areas of classroom life, the girls were actively constructing themselves as the more academic students – in the same way as they could be seen as being constructed as the more academic students by the teacher (see also Sunderland, 1998). Certainly, they did not appear as passive victims of verbal male dominance.

An examination of the amount of talk produced by individuals and addressed to the teacher over the twelve lessons was again enlightening (perhaps more so than the figures for teacher talk addressed to individuals – see Table 12.2).

The mean for the girls was far higher than that for the boys. Interestingly, in comparison with the analysis of teacher talk to individual students, this was *not* just due to a small subset of girls since seven of the thirteen girls in the class produced more solicits than all the boys (the exception being Gus). It is thus possible to argue that student talk in this classroom was more gendered than was teacher talk (see also Sunderland, 2000b).

The relevance and limitations of this study

The findings of this study are interesting for both their specificity and the fact that (with the benefit of hindsight) they challenge some of the generalities of previous classroom interaction studies. Of particular interest is the apparent assertiveness and academic approach of the girls and the differential teacher treatment by gender in which boys may have received more attention, but girls more academically useful attention. As the observably more active language learners, the girls had more language learning opportunities in terms of speaking practice in German. Volunteering more answers in German would have enabled them to practice their German and test their hypotheses about the language, in particular about the pronunciation of German words and the syntactic patterning of German words and phrases, since these answers usually resulted in teacher feedback. By speaking more, they would also have been able to show the teacher if and where they needed help.

The range of these research findings showed statistically significant or near-significant gender differences and cases of differential teacher treatment in only a few cases as well as a great number of nonsignificant differences and indeed gender similarities. The analysis of the talk of, and addressed to, individuals demonstrated empirically (if this needs demonstrating) that neither boys nor girls can be treated *only* as members of a particular social group. Neither should they be seen as members of only *one* such group. Importantly, gender coexists with other identities (see Norton, 2000). Good et al. (1973), for example, found that the teacher of a mixed-sex class gave the most attention to high-achieving boys and the least to low-achieving boys. This has implications for the interpretation of studies of gender in the classroom in which findings apparently about gender may, in fact, be findings about something else, such as proficiency, age, or ethnicity, which are, for some reason for the class in question, factors closely associated with gender (see Swann, 2002). A teacher may then relate to girls in a particular way not because they are girls, but because they are, on the whole, more proficient than the boys in the class. This is a real possibility since girls' achievement in foreign language learning is frequently higher than that of boys, leading teachers sometimes to conclude that girls are better language learners. However, Good et al.'s findings do suggest that although (perceived) achievement may have been a factor in the teacher's behavior, so may gender. As with the study of gendered talk and individuals in the German classroom, it would seem important, while always keeping multiple identities in sight, not to lose sight of gender altogether.

Classroom interaction studies that found evidence of male dominance and concluded that this was bad news for women's and girls' learning in nonlanguage classrooms did not sit well with evidence of females' often superior achievements in, and keenness to continue with, foreign languages (though it is possible to argue that, logically, without such male dominance, girls and women would do even better!). But this does not mean that we should see my findings of classroom interaction showing girls doing, on the whole, rather well interactionally as pointing straightforwardly in the same direction as, being on the same dimension as, or even being relevant to gendered patterns in foreign language achievement and subject choice.

It is unclear how representative this classroom is, though the school itself was an unexceptional British example of its kind. However, for the purposes of this paper, I am using this study here not to generalize to a wider sample, but rather to illustrate that male dominance does not necessarily surface in the language classroom (and indeed there are reasons why it should not), and that if it does, it is likely to do so in a complex way with nonevident implications for language learning. Clearly, this study warns against global, unsituated generalizations about gender and classroom talk and, in particular, about male dominance since here, at least, while boys dominated the classroom in terms of the amount of some types of teacher attention they received, girls dominated it in terms of the academic nature of their actual contributions.[3]

The study can be seen as an important one for both gender and language education and for the study of classroom interaction. It identifies important subtleties and language classroom specificities, helps us qualify claims, and, in some sense, rescues girls from a representational victimhood. Future studies might be aimed at further critical identification and description of how social disadvantage may be gendered in, and by, the language classroom and should, in particular, investigate how transformation of this might be achieved. Future work also needs to address issues of verbal dominance as different possible individual and collective meanings of "dominance" obtain. As well, when some form of male dominance does surface, observers will have to assess its relevance for learning. Still underexplored is the relationship between public classroom talk and language learning (or, at least, uptake; see studies by Allwright,

1984; Kebede, 1998; and Slimani, 1987, for an indication of some of the complexities here). Particularly relevant is whether, if opportunities are denied to women and girls (and indeed some men and boys), those women and girls create other opportunities for themselves. Arnot et al. (1998) claim that the relevance of gender differences in classroom interaction (in general) to achievement is *not* self-evident, adding "there is . . . some evidence that girls adopt effective 'compensatory strategies' . . . to ensure that their questions are answered and their needs are met" (pp. 26–7). They cite compensatory communication strategies such as approaching the teacher individually or asking questions after the lesson. Compensatory cognitive strategies for girls may be getting and assimilating useful input from boys' talk and attending to the teachers' responses to boys' questions (Dick Allwright, personal communication). While talk in the language classroom, in which speaking is often seen as a skill to be acquired (not just a means to understanding), may have a special importance, and while Allwright's (1984) and Arnot et al.'s (1998) alternative discursive classroom practices are, of course, only possible within certain systems of social relations (e.g., how accessible is the teacher?), it is important not to overstate the role of classroom interaction in learning in what is arguably an already gendered site.

What I am suggesting is that language classroom interaction is probably not a particularly relevant epistemological site for the investigation and identification of injustice, inequality, and opportunity in language education. Language classroom interaction would appear to be an interesting, but essentially limited, focus of critique, that is, one ring of the onion near the center when the locus should be all the leaves around it.

The most salient gendered issue in the United Kingdom, at least in foreign language learning, is probably differential achievement (girls do better) and subject choice (girls choose languages more). Seeing classroom interaction, however patterned, as a major factor in achievement and choice seems counterintuitive. But does this mean that girls are *not* disadvantaged by masculine verbosity as and when this occurs? Not necessarily. Writing on school literacy, in general, and the sometime acceptance that boys talk rather than read and write, White (1990) claims "the trade-off between oral and written language serves not merely to excuse boys' indifference to school standards of literacy, but actually operates to ensure a different kind of success and power in the dynamics of the classroom" (p. 185).

Writing on out-of-school or postschool dividends, Baxter (1999) observes how although boys' talk might be seen as disruptive (as we have seen, much teacher attention to boys is disciplinary in intent) and may not equate with academic success, boys' talk may nevertheless develop their confidence to "seize and hold the 'floor,' to control topics . . . and, obliquely, to prepare them for the skills of competitive, public speaking"

(p. 86). This, however, points to a need to look beyond classroom discursive practices to social practices and nonlinguistic practices associated with talk outside educational spheres. These include the wider notions of masculinity, and indeed of gender relations, operating outside, as well as inside, the classroom.

Critical pedagogy and critical discourse analysis

My 1996 study and others like it suggest that gender studies of classroom interaction must necessarily be concerned with aspects of the social context in which classrooms are located. Critiques which aim at an explanation of classroom interactions may have to go beyond classrooms to other orders or dimensions of life. I will illustrate this with reference to critical discourse analysis and will draw on Fairclough's now familiar "3-dimensional concept of discourse" (1992).

Critical discourse analysis may help us identify an appropriate locus for research and critical practice (Sunderland, 2001). While the gendered patterns of classroom interaction can certainly be seen as discursive practice (though they have not usually been conceptualized as such), explanation through close examination of discursive practices by gender in classrooms may be unfruitful. It may be that explanation lies in social practices existing *outside* the classroom. With respect to gender, we need to consider the possibility, for example, that social practices outside the classroom (together with their associated social attitudes) might in fact nullify, render irrelevant, or at least lessen any advantages there may be for men and boys for male dominance in the classroom. (Of course, there may not be male dominance in a given classroom; even if there is, this may *not* carry advantages.)

To return to the question, "Why do relatively few boys and young men choose languages?" a relevant further question might be, "What is perceived as masculine?" Gender can be seen as both relational and oppositional – masculinity and femininity being defined and defining themselves in part according to what the other is not. In some (Western) cultures, however, though what is seen as masculine may be the opposite of what is associated with being feminine, this may be less true for the converse and the penalty for women's and girls' transgression of feminine gender boundaries less severe. So, to give two simple examples, boys don't normally wear skirts, whereas girls do wear trousers; women are less likely to receive negative comments for drinking pints of beer than are men for drinking Babycham (a mock champagne drink in a small bottle). The boundaries of femininity in some cultural contexts would appear to be more fluid than those of masculinity (Chodorow, 1978; Phillips, 1994; Sunderland, 2000b) – masculinity and femininity appearing not to be mirror images of each other. Identity may be crucial here – if gender is seen as a binary opposition by boys (i.e., if masculinity is seen as what femininity is not), then the mixed-sex language classroom may be an already-gendered site from which boys try to escape as soon as possible in order to distance themselves from the femininity by which they see it characterized. Certainly, in the United Kingdom, considerably more boys in single-sex boys' schools choose to continue with languages or indeed start new ones, when they have the chance, than do boys in mixed schools (Arnot et al., 1998). One reason for this is arguably that in single-sex boys' schools, languages are less obviously perceived as feminine simply because there are no girls around to take them.

There is likely to be a relationship between choosing to study a language and achieving in that language: Those boys who choose to study a foreign language up to A-level in the United Kingdom (taken normally at age eighteen, in the last year of school) actually perform very slightly better than their female peers. In the widely taken national General Certificate of Secondary Education examinations, which most school students sit at around age sixteen and for which one foreign language is compulsory, fewer foreign language examinations are taken by boys, and boys do worse than girls (Arnot et al., 1998).

Part of the explanation for boys' low level of achievement in languages relative to girls at school, at least in the United Kingdom, may be to do with the culture of school education itself: Boys in the United Kingdom currently perform less well than girls in *most* subjects at all levels. (The gap is, in fact, small, and smaller than that for both physics and social studies [Arnot et al., 1998, p. 13].) Several years ago, the investigative BBC TV program, *Panorama*, featured the issue of gender differential achievement. At one point, the interviewer asked a boy of around eight or nine, "What do you think about boys who work hard?" The response was, "They're not boys." While this clearly does not constitute any form of proof, this tiny exchange may be illuminating. The *Times'* report (2000) of Becky Francis' recent study of "laddishness" in schools read, "Pupils told [Dr. Francis] that there was considerable pressure to appear macho and that boys did not want to appear studious to gain acceptance." In relation, boys who choose to continue with languages may do so because they like other subjects *even less* – in which case we should not expect the boys who do choose languages to do particularly well. One explanation for their poor performance comes from my own male undergraduate students who suggest that adolescence is precisely the time when boys find it most difficult and embarrassing to produce unfamiliar sounds in front of girls – and indeed their own male peers, who are likely to make fun of them (Krista Court, personal communication). It may be precisely this negative experience that prevents boys from learning (and, hence, wanting to continue with) foreign languages.

While this insight begs the question (essentially about gender relations) of why adolescent boys are affected by this more than adolescent girls, it does correspond to the fact that in cultures where males underachieve in foreign languages, this tends to be predominantly at secondary mixed-sex schools.

Might there then be a case for saying that boys and men are the ones who are disadvantaged in the language classroom – receiving a lot of teacher attention of a disciplinary nature, in many cultural contexts opting out as soon as they can, and, most notably, performing less well? Perhaps so. More important, however, I would like to suggest that boys' apparent disadvantage in the language classroom may not only be a disadvantage for them, but also for the girls who seem to be doing relatively well. The first point here is what might be seen as a traditional "1970s feminist" one – that "different and/but (or: therefore) equal" rarely applies in practice: given two apparently different but "equivalent" sets of attributes, one set soon becomes privileged over the other. Any and all gender differences in achievement, then, have the potential to backfire, on the higher as well as lower achievers, if only in a general way. As Johnson (1997) puts it, *vive la différence* is "the most misogynistic adage of all" (p. 16). And, of course, being good at something does not mean it is valued.

In relation to this last point, women and girls may do better in foreign languages than men and boys in the United Kingdom, but the gender gap in wages and salaries remains. So while one feminist response might be "don't worry about the boys, they do all right in other areas, let the girls excel at languages," another might be "the girls are being channeled into 'easier' areas which do not serve them as well as they could in their careers." The HMSO/EOC [4] report of 1996 observes that "relatively few young women are taking A-level courses which are wholly mathematical, scientific or technological, thereby denying themselves some career opportunities in science, engineering and technology" (p. 13). Similar observations have been made about girls' apparently superior achievements in L1 literacy (White, 1990).[5]

Conclusion

Gender and language classroom interaction has never been explored to the extent that gender representation in language textbooks has. This may not, however, be an area in which more research is needed since, despite the possibility of male dominance in some shape or form, classroom interaction may not be a key epistemological site for examining injustice, inequality, and (lack of) opportunity in relation to language education. This does not mean that gender asymmetries are to be condoned; rather, they should be recognized as complex, to the extent that what looks like advantage should be looked at as signaling a potential form of disadvantage. Language education is not obviously a site of injustice for female students – many would see it as an area in which women and girls have succeeded. But if it is to be seen as a site that can limit, as well as further, the lives and careers of women and girls, investigation and critique need to go beyond what can be observed and recorded to what is expected and what is not.

Notes

1. More recent work has tended to include linguistic analysis (e.g., Carroll & Kowitz, 1994; Jones, Kitetu, & Sunderland, 1997; Poulou, 1997).
2. All names have been fictionalized. Two pairs of boys shared a name, as did two pairs of girls; this is reflected in the tables.
3. With the wisdom of hindsight, the analytical concept of male dominance itself has now been widely critiqued. Though it was intended to identify and expose previously unrecognized linguistic manifestations of gender inequality as they adversely affected women and girls, including in the classroom, the (male) dominance model of language and gender (characteristic of the 1970s and early 1980s) is now often seen as positioning females, in general (and female students by implication), as passive – even as victims – with little agency of their own. Though this model of language and gender was soon supplemented with (though not entirely replaced by) the cultural difference model (e.g., Coates, 1993, 1996 – which, inter alia, emphasized *strengths* of women's and girls' talk), *both* of these models were concerned with gender differences (rather than similarities) and some work tended to see language use as a reflection of gender (rather than one of the things which constructed it).
4. Her Majesty's Stationary Office/Equal Opportunities Commission.
5. White (1990) comments critically on "the abiding tension between schools' official criteria for excellence in literacy, and the dispensability of these practices for many rewarding professions in the world outside" (p. 184). Ironically, women with A-levels in language may not even be filling positions in industry which need their linguistic knowledge (Thomas, 1990, p. 6).

References

Acker, S. (1994). *Gendered Education*. Buckingham: Open University Press.

Alcón, E. (1994). The role of participation and gender in non-native speakers' classroom interaction. *Working Papers on Language, Gender, and Sexism, 4*(1), 51–68.

Allwright, R. L. (1984). Why don't learners learn what teachers teach? The interaction hypothesis. In D. M. Singleton & D. Little (Eds.), *Language learning in formal and informal contexts* (pp. 3–18). Dublin: Irish Association for Applied Linguistics.

Arnot, M., David, M., & Weiner, G. (1996). *Educational reforms and gender equality in schools* (Research discussion series No. 17). Manchester, England: Equal Opportunities Commission.

Arnot, M., Gray, J., James, M., & Ruddock, J. (with Duveen, G.). (1998). *Recent research on gender and educational performance.* London: Office for Standards in Education.

Arnot, M., & Weiner, G. (Eds.). (1987). *Gender and the politics of schooling.* London: Unwin Hyman.

Batters, J. (1986). Do boys really think languages are just girl-talk? *Modern Languages, 67*(2), 75–9.

Baxter, J. (1999). Teaching girls to speak out: The female voice in public contexts. *Language and Education, 13*(2), 81–98.

Boersma, P. D., Gay, D., Jones, R., Morrison, L., & Remick, H. (1981). Sex differences in college student-teacher interactions: Fact or fantasy? *Sex Roles, 7*, 775–84.

Burchell, H., & Millman, V. (Eds.). (1989). *Changing perspectives of gender: New initiatives in secondary education.* Milton Keynes, England: Open University Press.

Carroll, D., & Kowitz, J. (1994). Using concordancing techniques to study gender stereotyping in ELT textbooks. In J. Sunderland (Ed.), *Exploring gender: Questions and implications for English language education* (pp. 73–82). Hemel Hempstead, England: Prentice Hall.

Chodorow, N. (1978). *The reproduction of mothering.* Berkeley: University of California Press.

Clark, A. (1998). *Gender on the agenda: Factors motivating boys and girls in MFLs.* London: Center for Information on Language Teaching and Research.

Coates, J. (1993). *Women, men, and language: A sociolinguistic account of gender differences in language* (2nd ed.). London: Longman.

Coates, J. (1996). *Women talk.* Oxford: Blackwell.

Croll, P. (1985). Teacher interaction with individual male and female pupils in junior age classrooms. *Educational Research, 27*(3), 220–3.

Dart, B., & Clarke, J. (1988). Sexism in schools: A new look. *Educational Review, 40*(1), 41–9.

Deem, R. (1978). *Women and schooling.* London: Routledge and Kegan Paul.

Fairclough, N. (1992). *Discourse and social change.* Cambridge, England: Polity Press.

French, J., & French, P. (1984). Gender imbalances in the primary classroom: An interactional account. *Educational Research, 26*(2), 127–36.

Frith, R., & Mahony, P. (Eds.). (1994). *Promoting quality and equality in schools.* London: David Fulton.

Frye, D. (1999). Participatory education as a critical framework for immigrant women's ESL class. *TESOL Quarterly, 33*(3), 501–13.

Gaskell, J. (1992). *Gender matters from school to work.* Milton Keynes, England: Open University Press.

Gass, S., & Varonis, E. (1986). Sex differences in nonnative speaker-nonnative speaker interactions. In R. Day (Ed.), *Talking to learn: Conversation in second language acquisition* (pp. 327–51). New York: Newbury House.

Good, T., Sykes, N., & Brophy, J. (1973). Effects of teacher sex and student sex on classroom interaction. *Journal of Educational Psychology, 65*, 74–87.

Gore, D., & Roumagoux, D. (1983). Wait time as a variable in sex-related differences during fourth grade mathematics instruction. *Journal of Educational Research, 76*(5), 273–5.

Grant, L. (1985). Race-gender status, classroom interaction, and children's socialization in elementary school. In L. C. Wilkinson & C. Marrett (Eds.), *Gender influences in classroom interaction* (pp. 57–77). New York: Academic Press.

Hammersley, M. (1990). An evaluation of two studies in gender imbalance in primary classrooms. *British Educational Research Journal, 16*(2), 125–43.

Her Majesty's Stationary Office/Equal Opportunities Commission (HMSO/EOC). (1996). *The gender divide: Performance differences between boys and girls at school.* London: HMSO.

Holmes, J. (1989a). Is sex relevant in the ESL classroom? *Language Issues, 3*(1), 14–8.

Holmes, J. (1989b). Sex differences and interaction: Problems for the language learner. In P. Meara (Ed.), *Beyond words* (pp. 38–57). London: CILT/British Studies in Applied Linguistics.

Holmes, J. (1994). Improving the lot of female language learners. In J. Sunderland (Ed.), *Exploring gender: Questions and implications for English language education* (pp. 156–62). Hemel Hempstead, England: Prentice Hall.

Howe, C. (1997). *Gender and classroom interaction: a research review.* Edinburgh, Scotland: Scottish Council for Research in Education (SCRE).

Ibrahim, A. (1999). Becoming black: Rap and hip hop, race, gender, identity and the politics of ESL learning. *TESOL Quarterly, 33*(3), 349–70.

Johnson, S. (1997). Theorizing language and masculinity: a feminist perspective. In S. Johnson & U. Meinhof (Eds.), *Language and masculinity* (pp. 8–26). Oxford: Blackwell.

Jones, M., Kitetu, C., & Sunderland, J. (1997). Discourse roles, gender and language textbook dialogues: Who learns what from John and Sally? *Gender and Education, 9*(4), 469–90.

Kasanga, L. A. (1996). Effect of gender on the rate of interaction: Some implications for second language acquisition and classroom practice. *ITL Review of Applied Linguistics, 111/112*, 155–92.

Kebede, S. (1998). *The relationship between uptake and questioning* (Center for Research in Language Education (CRILE), Working Paper 32). Lancaster, England: Dept. of Linguistics and Modern English Language, Lancaster University.

Kelly, A. (1988). Gender-differences in teacher-pupil interactions: A meta-analytic review. *Research in Education, 39*, 1–23.

Kumaravadivelu, B. (1999). Critical classroom discourse analysis. *TESOL Quarterly, 33*(3), 453–84.

Losey, K. (1995). Gender and ethnicity as factors in the development of verbal skills in bilingual Mexican American women. *TESOL Quarterly, 29*(4), 635–61.

Mackie, A. (1999). Possibilities for feminism in ESL education and research. *TESOL Quarterly, 33*(3), 566–73.

Measor, L., & Sikes, P. (1992). *Gender and schools.* London: Cassell.

Merrett, F., & Wheldall, K. (1992). Teachers' use of praise and reprimands to boys and girls. *Education Review, 44*(1), 73–9.

Nelson, C. (1999). Sexual identities in ESL: Queer theory and classroom inquiry. *TESOL Quarterly, 33*(3), 371–91.

Norton, B. (2000). *Identity and language learning: Gender, ethnicity, and educational change*. London: Pearson Education.
Pennycook, A. (1989). The concept of method, interested knowledge, and the politics of language teaching. *TESOL Quarterly, 23*(4), 589–618.
Pennycook, A. (1990). Critical pedagogy and second language education. *System, 18*(3), 303–14.
Pennycook, A. (1999). Introduction: critical approaches to TESOL. *TESOL Quarterly, 33*(3), 329–48.
Phillips, A. (1994). *The trouble with boys*. London: Pandora.
Poulou, S. (1997). Sexism in the discourse roles of textbook dialogues. *Language Learning Journal, 15*, 68–73.
Powell, R. (1986). *Boys, girls, and languages in school*. London: Center for Information on Language Teaching.
Provo, J. (1991). Sex differences in nonnative speaker interaction. *Language Teacher, 15*(7), 25–8.
Sadker, M., & Sadker, D. (1985, March). Sexism in the schoolroom of the '80s. *Psychology Today*, 54–7.
Slimani, A. (1987). *The teaching/learning relationship: Learning opportunities and learning outcomes. An Algerian case study.* Unpublished doctoral dissertation, Lancaster University, Lancaster, England.
Spender, D. (1980). Talking in class. In D. Spender & E. Sarah (Eds.), *Learning to lose* (pp. 148–54). London: The Women's Press.
Spender, D. (1982). *Invisible women: The schooling scandal*. London: The Women's Press.
Stanworth, M. (1983). *Gender and schooling*. London: Hutchinson.
Sunderland, J. (Ed.). (1994). *Exploring gender: Questions and implications for English language education*. Hemel Hempstead, England: Prentice Hall.
Sunderland, J. (1996). *Gendered discourse in the foreign language classroom: Teacher-student and student-teacher talk, and the social construction of children's femininities and masculinities*. Unpublished doctoral dissertation, Lancaster University, Lancaster, England.
Sunderland, J. (1998). Girls being quiet: A problem for foreign language classrooms? *Language Teaching Research, 2*(1), 48–62.
Sunderland, J. (2000a). Issues of language and gender in second and foreign language education. *Language Teaching, 33*(4), 203–23.
Sunderland, J. (2000b). New understandings of gender and language classroom research: Texts, teacher talk and student talk. *Language Teaching Research, 4*(2), 149–73.
Sunderland, J. (2001). Critical pedagogy in language classrooms. In R. Long, K. Lane, M. Swanson, & G. van Troyer (Eds.), *Towards the New Millennium: Proceedings of the 26th Annual International Conference of the Japanese Association for Language Teaching. PAC Journal, 1*(1).
Swann, J. (1988). Talk control: An illustration from the classroom of problems in analyzing male dominance of conversation. In J. Coates & D. Cameron (Eds.), *Women in their speech communities* (pp. 141–57). London: Longman.
Swann, J. (1992). *Girls, boys and language*. Oxford: Basil Blackwell.
Swann, J. (2002). Yes, but is it gender? In L. Litosseliti & J. Sunderland (Eds.), *Gender identity and discourse analysis* (pp. 43–67). Amsterdam: John Benjamins.

Swann, J., & Graddol, D. (1988). Gender inequalities in classroom talk. *English in Education, 22*(1), 48–65.

Teachers "reinforce laddish behaviour." (2000, September 28). *The Times,* p. 15.

Thomas, K. (1990). *Gender and subject in higher education.* Buckingham: Society for Research into Higher Education/Open University Press.

Vandrick, S. (1999). Who's afraid of critical feminist pedagogies? *TESOL Matters, 9*(1), 9.

Walkerdine, V. (1989). *Counting girls out.* London: Virago.

Weiner, G. (1994). *Feminisms in education.* Buckingham: Open University Press.

White, J. (1990). On literacy and gender. In R. Carter (Ed.), *Knowledge about language and the curriculum* (pp. 181–96). London: Hodder and Stoughton.

Whyld, J. (1983). *Sexism in the secondary curriculum.* New York: Harper and Row.

Whyte, J. (1984). Observing sex-stereotypes and interactions in the school lab and workshop. *Educational Review, 36*(1), 75–86.

Wikeley, F., & Stables, A. (1999). Changes in school students' approaches to subject option choices: A study of pupils in the West of England in 1984 and 1996. *Educational Research, 41*(3), 287–99.

Wolpe, A. (1988). *Within school walls.* London: Routledge.

Yepez, M. (1994). An observation of gender-specific teacher behavior in the ESL classroom. *Sex Roles, 30*(1/2), 121–33.

13 *Living with inelegance in qualitative research on task-based learning*

Constant Leung
Roxy Harris
Ben Rampton

Introduction

Within the field of second language acquisition (SLA), there has been some sustained theoretical and methodological discussion on the different research approaches and paradigms. One of the recurring themes of this discussion turns to the differences between, broadly speaking, quantitative and interpretative approaches. The former is often associated with a tendency to work with psychological or psycholinguistic paradigms and statistical data analyses; the latter, the main focus of our attention here, is likely to draw on, inter alia, some form of qualitative methodology or discourse analysis (for a discussion, see Davis, 1995; Kumaravadivelu, 1999). This chapter sets out to discuss some of the issues concerned with the use of interactional discourse data germane to classroom-based SLA research. First, we will provide a brief account of the context of the data gathering that generated the theoretical and research issues that we wish to discuss in this chapter and highlight some of these issues with reference to some classroom data. It is our view that working with naturally occurring data is inevitably a messy enterprise, but one that many researchers find difficult to fully acknowledge or account for in the presentation of their research data. Noteworthy exceptions are, for instance, Bloome (1994); Candela (1999); Gutierrez, Rymes, and Larson (1995); and Kamberelis (2001). After that, we will attempt to relate our concerns and observations to wider debates on the epistemologies and practices of different research traditions and perspectives. It is our contention that, at this particular juncture, there is a hitherto relatively underexplored area of epistemic turbulence in qualitative research within SLA that centers on the eternal research question of what constitutes reality or the representation of reality; we suggest that this is the source of the inelegance alluded to in the title of this chapter. In the final part, we will discuss some of the possible ways of achieving a better understanding of, and working with, the messiness and inelegance we have found.

Theoretical and methodological context of research

Perhaps it would be useful to start by saying something about the intellectual orientations of the two researchers directly involved in the gathering of the classroom data used in this discussion. Leung and Teasdale were trained in linguistics and have worked for a long period in English language education in a variety of contexts.[1] They were familiar with the mainstream English language teaching (ELT) literature and applied linguistic literature on second language acquisition. They had used both quantitative and qualitative methods in their previous work. In the particular empirical study from which the data for this discussion are drawn, they were interested in the kinds of talk students in a linguistically diverse classroom used when they were engaged in curriculum tasks.

The concept of task-based language teaching and learning is well-established in both the SLA research literature and the ELT literature, particularly within the subfield of teaching English as a foreign language (EFL). The notion of task has a long tradition going back at least as far as John Dewey's seminal concept of education as an introduction to the activities of the community (see Mohan, 1986 [pp. 44–9] for a discussion). More recently, the term *task*, itself, has been the focus of some discussion (see Coughlan & Duff, 1994; Crookes & Gass, 1993a, 1993b; Donato, 1994; Kumaravadivelu, 1993; Long & Crookes, 1992; Nunan, 1989; Skehan, 1996, 1998). Skehan (1998) argues that

> a task is an activity in which meaning is primary; there is some communication problem to solve; there is some sort of relationship to comparable real-world activities; task completion has some priority; the assessment of the task is in terms of outcome. (p. 95)

Nunan (1989) suggests that a task is "a piece of classroom work which involves pupils in comprehending, manipulating, producing or interacting in the target language while their attention is principally focused on meaning rather than on form" (p. 10). Mainly, task is often taken to mean a learning activity organized around a topic or curriculum area that requires interaction with others.

Summarizing the development of the concept of task from a largely psycholinguistic-cognitive perspective, Crookes and Gass (1993b) suggest that the value of task as a pedagogic concept is associated with two arguments (pp. 1–2). The first is concerned with the role played by interaction in SLA; it is argued that interaction offers learners an opportunity to use and work out meaning even when the actual language forms encountered may be beyond their current level of linguistic competence. In other words, the opportunity for negotiation of meaning is provided, and this kind of active engagement with language in use contributes to language acquisition. Social interaction tends to be treated as a necessary part of the process, but it, in itself, does not constitute a focus of attention (although cf. Pica, Kanagy, & Falodun, 1993). The second is concerned with attentiveness and involvement. "It is involvement which facilitates acquisition in that it 'charges' the input, allowing it to 'penetrate'" (Crookes & Gass, 1993b, pp. 1–2). Put differently, when learners are attending to language use through active engagement with others in the doing of tasks, language form may be noticed and this is beneficial to learning. In a sense, both the individual learner and the social interaction are abstracted; individual cases are investigated as part of broader universal patterns. The literature in this field would suggest that this is the dominant view underpinning much of the research in task-based language pedagogy.

There are other views on, and approaches to, SLA; for instance, there is a corpus of work within Vygotskian perspectives (see Lantolf [2000]; Lantolf & Appel [1994] for a collection) and ethnographic perspectives (for example, Coughlan & Duff, 1994; Harklau, 1994; Norton, 2000; Toohey, 2000). In the more specific area of task-based research, the theoretical concerns of these particular perspectives tend to direct a research focus on (a) the individual participants' perceptions and motives when they are engaged in tasks in specific contexts, and/or (b) the social process of internalizing new information by learners when they are scaffolded by more knowledgeable participants in the task (Donato, 1994). So, unlike the psycholinguistic-cognitive approach, research within these approaches prioritizes the analysis of the process of interaction and the actual engagement of individuals.

Irrespective of the approach or perspective, it is customarily the case that research data have been used to illustrate an analytical category or support an argument. So, for instance, if a researcher wishes to discuss the manifestation of the use of a particular syntactical form or peer scaffolding in doing a task, segments of discourse data may be presented to illustrate the point. These segments, or more accurately, fragments, tend to be very short and to the point. This practice of selection is so commonplace that it would be invidious to cite any individual examples. Yet, we know that there must be a great deal more surrounding data that are not reported. In other words, "irrelevant" data are not shown. A key question here is, What constitutes "relevant" or "irrelevant" data? A further question is, Is it possible that the so-called irrelevant data may also be inconvenient in that it complicates, complexifies, or even undermines the arguments or points of view being advanced by the researcher concerned? The questions of how to present data and how much data to present in qualitative research are a subject of some very interesting debate that raises issues of adequacy, representativeness, and trustworthiness (see Seale, 1999). Here, we are concerned with the question of not just how much, but which data should be shown. We shall take up these central issues concerning the "which" and the "how much" again later in this chapter.

Context of data gathering

The data that will be presented in this discussion are drawn from a small-scale exploratory study of the kinds of talk students in linguistically diverse classrooms in urban English settings used when they were engaged in curriculum tasks. One of the assumptions the researchers made was that the naturally occurring data would provide helpful information to shed some light on how the concept of task influences language use in mainstream classrooms. A great deal of the discussion and research centered on task-based language learning tends to be related to adult or university-level language classrooms. The application of the concept of task-based pedagogy in the context of linguistic minority students learning English in the mainstream elementary classroom in English-medium schools in England, however, has been relatively little studied, although the term task, itself, is sometimes used in curriculum documents and by teachers in a nonspecialist way.[2]

The data were collected from three Year 4 classes (nine- or ten-year-olds) in three different elementary schools in the outskirts of West London.[3] The data used in this discussion were drawn from a History class. The teacher and the pupils were informed, as were all other teachers and pupils involved in the other schools, that the purpose of the research was to study the way language was used during lessons and when teachers and pupils were working together. The researchers did not impose criteria for the selection of focal students, but the teachers were asked to assist by identifying the occasions when collaborative group tasks were scheduled and by identifying a group of students in their class who tended to work together and who were at various stages of English (as a second) language development.[4] In the event, the teacher put six pupils together in the focal group. He suggested that the membership fairly reflected the composition of the class as a whole in terms of gender, English language proficiency, and experience of schooling in England.[5]

Classroom data: Four consecutive segments

The pupils had been studying ancient invaders and settlers in Britain. In this particular lesson, the topic was the Anglo-Saxons. The task, as planned by the class teacher, involved the pupils working in collaborative groups to read a text and to decide on the key information in the text. In this sense, the task can be seen as concerned with choice and evaluation (Mohan, 1986). The pupils were each given a photocopy of the reading text that had some pictures and eight short paragraphs of text. They were asked by the teacher to sit in assigned groups and to discuss the reading paragraph by paragraph. When they had decided collaboratively on the key information in each of the paragraphs, they were to underline the "most important" sentence(s) on their own photocopied sheets.

The data presented here were collected by means of video (one camera) and audio (four radio microphones) recording, supplemented by field notes where appropriate. The four segments shown here are drawn from an unbroken sequence of approximately fourteen minutes of classroom activities. We have decided to select and present these fourteen minutes of classroom data in this discussion because we feel that they can help illustrate the methodological issues we wish to highlight.

We have deliberately split the fourteen minutes into four segments and use each of the segments to pose rhetorical questions concerning the stance we would take toward accounting for "inconvenient" data. In each instance, we ask questions such as, "Would we excise, or include and account for, the significance of these data as a part of the classroom 'reality' being represented?"

Segment 1

The transcript begins at about the fourteenth minute from the start of the lesson (see Table 13.1). The teacher has explained the task to the whole class. The pupils have been given their reading materials and their exercise books. The different work groups are sitting together (see Figure 13.1) and the teacher is acting as a mobile resource and a monitor circulating around the room to provide guidance and assistance.

Given the focus of our discussion, we will confine our main comments to the questions of selection and presentation of the collected data. However, it can be seen that, even at a relatively quick glance, the general nature and the direction of the exchanges in this segment between the participants are task related even though some may find the strong teacher domination not quite in the spirit of the task-based language learning approach and the attention paid to spelling a deviation from the main task. We could, in the established tradition of reporting data, use this segment to discuss a whole range of task-related language issues such as the use of (teacher) initiation–(student) response–(teacher) feedback (IRF) sequences in the participation pattern,[6] the teacher-led redefining of subtasks within the main task, and discourse functions.

TABLE 13.1 SEGMENT 1 TRANSCRIPT

Turn	*Participant*	*Utterance*	*Context information*
1	Teacher	have you got anywhere?	CAMERA ON WHOLE GROUP Teacher arrives at group and sits at one end of group table, Haroon to his left and Nafisa to his right
2	Haroon	I'm using a black (pen)	Haroon holding up a pen to show Teacher
3	Teacher	fine, good, so have you got a sheet each?	
4	Students	yes yes	Students respond in chorus
5	Haroon	what's the title?	Haroon asks Teacher
6	Teacher	well, we haven't got one have we?	
7	Ahmed	make one up	
8	Teacher	what would you suggest?	
9	Ahmed	er Anglo-Saxon villages	
10	Teacher	oh, it's good, is it about Anglo-Saxon villages?	Teacher praises Ahmed but presses on with his point
11	Ahmed	yes	
12	Teacher	what did I ask you to find?	
13	Kalsoon	er, important, er, important sentences	
14	Teacher	important sentences	
15	Haroon	and important things	
16	Teacher	important things, right, now, who can spell important? can you Saffia? I know you can, I know you can, I asked Saffia	Nafisa signals that she wants to answer; Teacher turning to Nafisa then to Kalsoon to show appreciation and to stop them from answering

(*continued*)

Note

Key:
, = brief pause
? = question
(.) = pause of longer than one second
CAPITAL LETTERS = spelling of words by participants
(transcription) = uncertain transcription, may be inaccurate
(unclear) = data cannot be transcribed, poor quality sound
/IPA symbols/ = phonemic transcription
{ = overlapping speech
italics = language other than English, translated into English

TABLE 13.1 (*continued*)

Turn	*Participant*	*Utterance*	*Context information*
17	Haroon	I, M, P, O, R	
18	Teacher	ssh, how do you start, Saffia?	
19	Saffia	P	
20	Kalsoon	No, no, no, no, no	others at table make laughing sounds
21	Teacher	/im/ (.) /im/ go on Kalsoon, give her a clue	no further response from Saffia
22	Kalsoon	you start it at I	Kalsoon tries to help spell it for Saffia
23	Saffia	N	
24	Teacher	you try Naseem	Teacher passing task to Naseem
25	Naseem	I M	
26	Teacher	have you got a seat, use it	Naseem was standing and leaning forward on the desk while talking; Teacher telling Naseem to sit down properly
27	Saffia	I M	
28	Haroon	P	
29	Teacher	go on	
30	Haroon	O R	
31	Teacher	yeah well done	
32	Kalsoon	T A N T	
33	Haroon	T A N T important	
34	Teacher	right, so you've all got a title now, I M	Teacher sets up an incomplete propositional frame for students to fill in
35	Haroon	/tənt/	
36	Teacher	P O R, who remembers the end?	Teacher presses on with teaching point, ignoring Haroon's contribution
37	Ahmed	T A N T	
38	Nafisa	T A N T	
39	Teacher	T A N T and then either "things" or "facts," which word do you want to use?	
40	Nafisa	important facts	

TABLE 13.1 *(continued)*

Turn	*Participant*	*Utterance*	*Context information*
41	Teacher	important facts, you're gonna use facts, you're gonna use things, I think, because you thought of it, can you spell things?	Teacher looking at Haroon and directs the last part of utterance at him
42	Haroon	T H I N G S	
43	Teacher	good, I'll be back in a minute and then we'll see which one you've chosen.	Teacher moving way
44 45	Teacher	you've underlined, you've done that first, right, try the next one	Teacher looks at Naseem's reading sheet, talks to her as he moves away
46 47	Saffia	I've done this one	Saffia appears to want to engage Teacher as he's moving away
48	Teacher	good, Saffia	Teacher leaves group

Segment 2

At the start of the second segment, the students are at their table (see Figure 13.1). The teacher is elsewhere attending to other students in the room.

Here, in this segment, we see something quite interesting (Table 13.2). The segment begins with one half of the group apparently not engaged or not being able to engage with the task. Haroon and Ahmed are chatting and Naseem is asking for help (turns 49–64). Kalsoon, sitting across the table, provides some support in the form of ready answers. When the teacher returns to the group, his first task-oriented question effectively dislodges everybody else except Kalsoon and Nafisa. Ahmed is brought into the frame by the teacher, but, at this time, the immediate task appears to be reading out loud. Ahmed's struggle through the text is assisted by Kalsoon, Nafisa, and Saffia (turns 70–107). At this moment, some of the students are offering help to a particular group member, but there is no collaboration in the sense of everyone in the group being actively involved in the completion of a common task. For much of this time, Haroon appears to be nonengaged; he is singing a repetitive tune for some of the time (turns 84–104). Naseem does not seem to have chimed in with Ahmed's reading effort, and, for reasons of camera angle, it is hard to say what Saffia might have been doing during the first moments of this segment when Kalsoon was offering help to Naseem across the table.

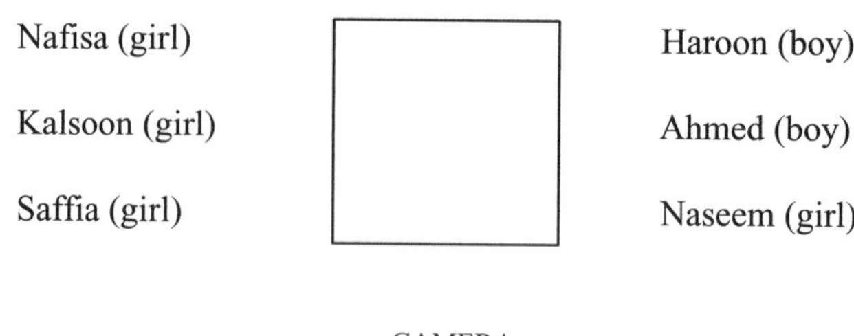

Figure 13.1 Illustration of focus table which has six children.

We are beginning to see a degree of messiness in the data. It would seem that not everyone in the group is attending to the task at hand. There is singing or repetitive chanting by Haroon. Would we use this segment in the "normal" way in a research report on task-based pedagogy? The issue here is that classroom data are not usually presented to explore the full range of use of language when students are supposed to be engaged in task-based work. If we chose not to include this segment, would the omission constitute an active misrepresentation of the reality claim underpinning the whole of this particular classroom research enterprise?

Segment 3

At the beginning of the third segment (see Table 13.3), the members of the group are at the table by themselves. The teacher is elsewhere in the room.

This segment begins with Kalsoon providing some support for Ahmed and possibly the others. It is interesting to note that once the teacher returns to the group and redirects the focus on the text, only Kalsoon seems to be able to actively engage with the recursive IRF sequences (from turn 114 onward). Throughout this segment, Saffia seems to be working on her own or seeking to find clues by looking over Kalsoon's work. She seems to be working in the sense that she is doing something, but it is difficult to say whether she understands the work. Ahmed's and Haroon's contributions suggest that they are trying to stay with the talk between the teacher and Kalsoon without much understanding. Nafisa appears to be working with Kalsoon; it is, however, difficult to work out whether she has followed the discussion with the teacher. Our difficulty in knowing what is going on with some members of the group points to one of the perennial problems of data collection: We know that we cannot cover all events and contingencies in a naturally occurring classroom situation, but how do we report the limitation of our data?

TABLE 13.2 SEGMENT 2 TRANSCRIPT

Turn	*Participant*	*Utterance*	*Context information*
49	Ahmed	what shall I write first?	At this point Saffia, Kalsoon, and Nafisa (all on same side of table) all appear to be reading or organizing their papers; on the other side, Haroon and Ahmed are chatting using mainly their first language (L1), a variety of Punjabi known as Parhari; Ahmed seems to want to pay some attention to work; Naseem is by herself looking at her papers; this moment lasts several seconds
50	Haroon	(important) you know something (unclear)	
51	Ahmed	what shall we do it? A B C?	Haroon and Ahmed laughing
52	Haroon	(something is being recorded)	Haroon and Ahmed continuing to chat to each other in L1 intermittently
53	Haroon	write A B C D E F G	
54	Ahmed	what? do we have to stop from the D? (.) shall I write that down? Is yours like mine?	At this point, Naseem shows Ahmed her worksheet and he starts humming and looking at a blank page in his exercise book
55	Naseem	which one is the second one?	Naseem is asking Kalsoon across the table
56	Kalsoon	I think it's this one	Kalsoon is sitting across the table; Naseem cannot see Kalsoon's reading text
57	Naseem	where's the second one	
58	Kalsoon	this one	Kalsoon moves her reading text to the middle of the table so that Naseem can see it; Kalsoon is out of direct camera shot at this moment (middle of table in frame)
59	Naseem	shall I underline that?	Naseem appears to start writing on her reading text

(*continued*)

TABLE 13.2 (*continued*)

Turn	*Participant*	*Utterance*	*Context information*
60	Kalsoon	yeah	Haroon and Ahmed are turning and looking at blank pages in their exercise books; chatting in L1
61	Ahmed	(it's all empty)	Haroon and Ahmed chatting in L1
62	Naseem	I think this one (and you)?	Naseem and Kalsoon talk across the table
63	Kalsoon	yeah	Naseem and Kalsoon talk across the table
64	Naseem	that was the first	Naseem and Kalsoon talk across the table
65	Teacher	right, just seen the other group finished, they've finished, they've decided, so let's see if you can do that, you catch up, who's read the second paragraph?	Teacher returns to group and stands just behind Naseem and Ahmed; Naseem puts up her hand to signal she has done the reading; the other side of the table not in camera frame; her bid isn't taken up by Teacher
66	Teacher	you've read it, have you? what do you think is the most important sentence?	Teacher opens the floor and invites answers; he also points to a place on Naseem's page – possibly signaling to Naseem where he is referring to
67	Kalsoon	the top one	Kalsoon answers from across the table
68	Teacher	right, they came to steal and burn first then they decided to stay (.) okay, right, who's looked at the third one?	
69	Nafisa	we're looking at it now	Nafisa answers from across the table
70	Teacher	you're looking now, yes, listen to Ahmed read, you read it out, no, we've done that one some	Teacher gives task to Ahmed; Ahmed starts to read (at wrong place); Teacher stands behind Ahmed and points to a place on Ahmed's reading sheet with his finger and shows him where to read[7]

TABLE 13.2 (*continued*)

Turn	*Participant*	*Utterance*	*Context information*
71	Ahmed	some of the Britons did (.) fight back (.) among the the (.)	Ahmed reading slowly and with help from teacher
72	Teacher	chiefs	
73	Ahmed	chiefs chiefs who won	
74	Kalsoon	won	Kalsoon seems to be taking over the helping role temporarily
75	Ahmed	won victories over the /æn/ /æn/	Haroon is tapping on his exercise book with his pen, making a loud noise; others appear to be looking at or reading their papers
76	Teacher	who are we studying? (.) Anglo	Haroon continuing with tapping
77	Ahmed	er, Anglo-Saxons	Haroon continuing with tapping
78	Teacher	good	Haroon continuing with tapping
79	Ahmed	was one called (.) Arto	Ahmed continues with reading
80	Teacher	Artos	
81	Ahmed	Artos or Arthur, we do not know very much about him but he (.) he had come down in (.)	Teacher walks away from Ahmed and the group; Ahmed carries on reading, possibly not knowing Teacher has left their table
82	Kalsoon	legend	
83	Ahmed	legend, king (.)	
84	Haroon	{/lɒ/ /riː/ /eɪ/ /iː/	Haroon turning to Ahmed and sings a tune, increasing in volume; the tune appears to contain the lyrics "a lorry will come" in L1
85	Ahmed	{Arthur King Arthur	Naseem taps Ahmed on the shoulder; Ahmed turns and looks at Naseem; Haroon continuing to make the same sounds
86	Haroon	{/lɒ/ /riː/ /eɪ/ /iː/	
87	Saffia	{King Arthur	Saffia offers assistance from across the table; Haroon continuing to make the same sounds
88	Haroon	{/lɒ/ /riː/ /eɪ/ /iː/	

(*continued*)

TABLE 13.2 (*continued*)

Turn	*Participant*	*Utterance*	*Context information*
89	Ahmed	{King Arthur	Haroon continuing to make the same sounds
90	Haroon	{/lɒ/ /riː/ /eɪ/ /iː/	
91	Saffia	{King Arthur	Saffia appears not to have heard Ahmed; Haroon continuing to make the same sounds
92	Haroon	{/lɒ/ /riː/ /eɪ/ /iː/	
93	Ahmed	{King Arthur	Haroon continuing to make the same sounds
94	Haroon	{/lɒ/ /riː/ /eɪ/ /iː/	
95	Saffia	{King Arthur	Haroon continuing to make the same sounds
96	Haroon	{/lɒ/ /riː/ /eɪ/ /iː/	
97	Ahmed	{King Arthur, and he was	Haroon continuing to make the same sounds
98	Haroon	{/lɒ/ /riː/ /eɪ/ /iː/	Nafisa offers assistance from across the table; Haroon continuing to make the same sounds
99	Nafisa	{(supposed)	
100	Haroon	{/lɒ/ /riː/ /eɪ/ /iː/	
101	Ahmed	{(from pose)	Haroon continuing to make the same sounds
102	Haroon	{/lɒ/ /riː/ /eɪ/ /iː/	
103	Nafisa	{(supposed)	Haroon continuing to make the same sounds
104	Haroon	{/lɒ/ /riː/ /eɪ/ /iː/	
105	Ahmed	(supposed) (demands to have) a kingdom somewhere in the west	
106	Kalsoon	a kingdom somewhere in the West country	
107	Ahmed	country	an unusual classroom event is taking place nearby and the group turns and looks for a few seconds

In this segment, we can see that in terms of direct teacher–student task-oriented interaction, only one student, Kalsoon, is engaged in meaningful exchange. Rhetorically we ask again, Would we use this segment in the normal way in a research report on task-based pedagogy? And how would we account for our inability to describe Saffia's actions more informatively, given that Saffia is a constitutive part of the reality of this group's engagement with tasks?

Segment 4

At the start of this segment, the teacher is talking to a group next to our focal students (see Table 13.4). Haroon seems to have been listening

TABLE 13.3 SEGMENT 3 TRANSCRIPT

Turn	*Participant*	*Utterance*	*Context information*
108	Kalsoon	that he has come down in legend, let's do this one	CAMERA ON SAFFIA, KALSOON, AND NAFISA (ON ONE SIDE) Kalsoon continues from where Ahmed stopped; camera now on the three girls, Saffia, Kalsoon, and Nafisa
109	Ahmed	this one?	Ahmed is off camera, on the other side of the table
110	Kalsoon	yes	
111	Ahmed	what's in the third one?	
112	Kalsoon	er, some of the Britons tried to fight back, they pushed and pushed and took most of the East and the South	Kalsoon and Nafisa start working together; Saffia appears to be working by herself and, from time to time, she seems to be looking over and copying Kalsoon's work
113	Saffia	(unclear)	Saffia's utterance appears to be directed at Kalsoon; Kalsoon has turned to her left toward Nafisa and doesn't respond to Saffia
114	Teacher	now, have you finished? what have you decided?	Teacher returns to group
115	Kalsoon	the Britons	
116	Teacher	what's the most important sentence?	
117	Kalsoon	fight back	
118	Teacher	er some of the Britons fight back, or do you think there's a more important fact?	
119	Kalsoon	yes yes	
120	Teacher	what, who's it about?	
121	Kalsoon	King Arthur	
122	Teacher	King Arthur, do you think he's important?	
123	Students	yes yes	Students respond in chorus
124	Teacher	right, why is he important?	
125	Kalsoon	because he is king	

(*continued*)

TABLE 13.3 (*continued*)

Turn	*Participant*	*Utterance*	*Context information*
126	Teacher	no, what did he do that was so, that's become legendary?	CAMERA ON WHOLE GROUP
127	Nafisa	he ruled the kingdom	
128	Ahmed	he ruled the kingdom	
129	Teacher	he ruled the kingdom, doesn't it say that there though, he was a king, he ruled a kingdom	Saffia and Naseem are not part of this exchange, working independently
130	Ahmed	West Country	Ahmed's contribution isn't taken up
131	Teacher	why was he famous? what did he do that was so good?	
132	Kalsoon	er I know, he won over the Anglo-Saxons	
133	Haroon	out of East	
134	Teacher	no, you've jumped a bit, listen to Kalsoon	Teacher addressing Haroon
135	Kalsoon	er he he er er won over the Britons, over the Anglo-Saxons	
136	Teacher	yes, he fought the Anglo-Saxons and he won, he beat them	Teacher is called away again; Saffia gets up and leans over to look at Kalsoon's worksheet; Naseem working alone; boys chatting, not looking at reading text

to what is being said at that table. He seems to be commenting on the slower rate of progress of the group at the table next to Ahmed. The teacher presently returns to the focal group.

The first part of this segment (from turn 138 onward) shows that, again, only Kalsoon seems to be able to directly engage with the teacher's questions. When Naseem and Ahmed seek help (turns 155–161), Kalsoon and Nafisa refuse to help. Saffia appears to want to be seen to be capable of helping (turn 164), even when she has not been asked. But it is not clear to what extent Naseem and Ahmed regard Saffia as a source of help because they do not seem to have taken up her offer. Here, one of the basic assumptions of the task-based language pedagogy – that students engage in more or less collaborative interaction – is flouted. We are seeing overt

TABLE 13.4 SEGMENT 4 TRANSCRIPT

Turn	*Participant*	*Utterance*	*Context information*
137	Haroon	they still on the first paragraph	a few seconds later, Haroon turning to Ahmed having overheard Teacher at next table
138	Kalsoon	gradually the Anglo-Saxons pushed them back and back, I think that one, that must be the most important thing	Kalsoon is reading to Nafisa
139	Teacher	oh, you think there are two important things?	CAMERA ON SAFFIA, KALSOON, AND NAFISA Teacher returns to group, leaning over Saffia and looking at her underlined text
140	Saffia	no	Saffia shakes her head, smiles, and starts erasing something with an eraser
141	Nafisa	(unclear speech)	Nafisa taps Teacher's arm and says something
142	Teacher	right, let's have a look at this one, gradually the Saxon invaders pushed the Britons into the hills of Wales {and Cornwall	Teacher leaning over and reading from Nafisa's sheet; Saffia leans forward, turns to Kalsoon on her left, and tries to look at Kalsoon's sheet
143	Kalsoon	{and Cornwall	Kalsoon might have been shadowing reading
144	Teacher	so you think that's the important part	
145	Nafisa	yes	nodding
146	Teacher	why's it more important than the other part that tells you where they, they took most of the East and the South and the Midlands and they called their new country Anglo land or England, why do you think it's more important than the Britons went to Wales or beginning of England?	

(*continued*)

TABLE 13.4 (*continued*)

Turn	*Participant*	*Utterance*	*Context information*
147	Kalsoon	because (.) it tells you how they did it, because where they pushed them	
148	Teacher	right, so you think they it tells how, they pushed them back, do you think they literally pushed them?	All this time, Saffia trying to look at Kalsoon's reading sheet and doing some underlining
149	Kalsoon	no, they	
150	Teacher	they what? what does it mean, they pushed them?	Teacher looking at Nafisa
151	Kalsoon	they made them	
152	Teacher	yes, how?	
153	Kalsoon	like fighting them?	
154	Teacher	yes, fighting them, beating them, you understood that well.	Teacher walks away from the group
155	Ahmed	what's the next one, Kalsoon?	Ahmed asks Kalsoon across the table
156	Kalsoon	I'm not telling (unclear)	CAMERA WANDERS, UNFOCUSED camera wobbles, deputy principal and a student walk past
157	Kalsoon	come on, just do that bit	CAMERA BACK ON SAFFIA, KALSOON, AND NAFISA Kalsoon turning to Nafisa, pointing to a place on the reading text
158	Naseem	(unclear)	Naseem talking to Kalsoon and Nafisa across the table
159	Kalsoon	we're doing the fifth one now,	reading
160	Naseem	what is (unclear) tell us (unclear)	Naseem addressing Nafisa and possibly Kalsoon; Nafisa shakes her head in response; Kalsoon looking at the reading text and not responding to Naseem
161	Kalsoon	they do not understand the Roman ways, (unclear) would not go and move towards (unclear), they knew nothing about the Eastern	Kalsoon continues to read, not attending to Naseem

TABLE 13.4 (*continued*)

Turn	*Participant*	*Utterance*	*Context information*
162	Saffia	I've done it	Saffia talks across the table to Naseem
163	Kalsoon	I think that one's the best, because they show you, because they knew nothing about it, yeah?	Kalsoon talking to Nafisa; Nafisa not listening, looking elsewhere
164	Saffia	wait, wait, wait a minute, I'll come to you	Saffia responding to Naseem; although Naseem initially appeared to have wanted Kalsoon and Nafisa's attention
165	Naseem	(will) you come (back)?	Naseem talks to Saffia across the table
166	Kalsoon	what?	Kalsoon responding to Naseem, her voice and facial expression suggest irritation
167	Saffia	I'll tell you, wait, wait, wait	Saffia doing something with her pencil case; Kalsoon underlining; Nafisa looking across the table
168	Ahmed	What's the next one?	Ahmed not in camera shot; he appears to be asking for help
169	Saffia	(unclear), they won't tell you	Saffia addressing Naseem, possibly also Ahmed and everyone else
170	Ahmed	is this the next?	Ahmed not in camera frame
171	Saffia	ah no no	
172	Kalsoon	you can't copy us	Naseem turning to Ahmed, possibly also to Haroon; at this point, Saffia gets up and hands over her reading sheet to Naseem across the table

refusal to assist others by Nafisa and Kalsoon (turns 160–161, turns 168–172). Saffia's volunteering to offer help and her utterances (particularly turn 169) also seem to indicate that at least she knows Nafisa and Kalsoon are not behaving in a totally novel way.

In view of the general tendency to use data only in ways that are supportive of the arguments being advanced, rhetorically we ask again, would we use this segment? Classroom ethnographers and discourse analysts routinely support claims to be representing reality in the classroom by reference to huge quantities of empirical data in the form of audio and video recordings and notes obtained from extended sojourns in specific classrooms. Would the excision of this or any other inconvenient segment require the quantitative presentation, over the research as a whole, of the ratio of inconvenient to convenient utterances surrounding tasks?

Discussion

The data we have seen, if shown in full, do not elegantly and neatly fit in with the theoretical construct of task-based language use. The participants messily engage with the task, sometimes attentively and, at other times, perfunctorily. At some moments, some members of the group appear to be dealing with other matters. They appear to work together sometimes and not at all at other times. There seems to be varying degrees of engagement and involvement with the task collectively and individually; in short, there is a continuum of "on-taskness." This lack of fit between data and theoretical construct could be dismissed in terms of inappropriate choice of tasks, insufficient support for task-based activities, learners not being ready to engage in tasks, and so on. As researchers, we could switch our attention to other sequences of data that fit in more easily with the theoretical construct.

Naturally occurring data of the kind that we have seen do not lend themselves to easy representations of classroom reality. As stated earlier, pedagogic tasks are meant to generate participation and engagement, which, in turn, creates opportunities for meaningful language use and language development. Non- or partial engagement is not generally discussed. However, to dismiss or to ignore the messiness is, ironically, to do what some see as a problem in experimental psycholinguistic research. Roebuck (2000) argues that it is a characteristic of experimental psycholinguistic research to sideline or ignore the messiness or inelegance of data:

> Natural science-based methodologies effectively allow researchers to marginalize subjects by eliminating those who show intentionality or failing to recognize the intentionality and individuality of others. (p. 79)
>
> In second language research it is often deemed necessary, for the purpose of the experiment, to assume that subjects are homogeneous individuals engaged in the same activity (i.e., doing the same thing) in compliance with the wishes of the researchers. Often the suggestion that this may not be the case threatens the supposed validity of the test instrument and the experiment itself, or causes certain subjects to be removed from the study. (p. 84)

We would argue that what we identified earlier as a qualitative or discourse analysis approach to classroom research has tended to offer itself as an alternative to this tendency and to position itself as offering a closer and more sensitive take on classroom reality. Of course, we are aware that this debate of qualitative versus quantitative research is situated within a wider debate in the field of qualitative research concerning the constitution and representation of reality. Guba and Lincoln (1994) make the important and subtle point that "both qualitative and quantitative research methods may be used appropriately with any research paradigm." In their view, "questions of method are secondary to questions of paradigm, which we define as the basic belief system or worldview that guides the investigator, not only in choices of method but in ontologically and epistemologically fundamental ways" (p. 195).

Guba and Lincoln argue that what they call the ontological question asks "What is the form and nature of reality and, therefore, what is there that can be known about it?" (p. 201). It is this question that we seek to place at the heart of the following points of discussion on the treatment and use of data and the relationship between reality, theory, and data.

In our experience, the representational choices and selections we make from our collected research data unavoidably involve us in making direct or indirect statements of our interests and our view of reality. This question of the researcher's interests and choices manifests itself at several levels. At the level of representing talk, it is understood that there is no natural or neutral way of transcribing speech (Atkinson, 1992; Hammersley, 1998; Ochs, 1979). Roberts (1997) argues that

> If talk is a social act, then so is transcription. As transcribers fix the fleeting moment of words as marks on the page, they call up the social roles and relations constituted in language and rely on their own social evaluations of speech in deciding how to write it. . . . Transcribers bring their own language ideology to the task. In other words, all transcription is representation. . . . The more complex the data, for example, video as opposed to audio recording, the more reduction is going on and the more decisions transcribers have to make about fixing sound and vision on the page. (pp. 167–68)

It is customary that, in research or academic papers, we present transcribed classroom talk as data to illustrate an argument or evidence of a theoretical construct. In the process of so doing, our interest can lead to a narrowing of attention to only those aspects of the data that best serve our purpose. In the case of the History lesson data under discussion, for instance, because the focus has been on the content meaning of the talk in terms of the task, the orthographic transcription does not attend to the prosodic features of the utterances in any great detail. This focus on task-oriented talk has also led researchers to adopt the conventions of a traditional linear transcript. This way of presenting data gives the powerful impression that, as Green, Franquiz, and Dixon (1997) argue, the talk is contiguous, when, in reality, this may not be the case. (Overlaps and instances of other noncontiguous talk can, of course, be marked on a linear transcript; but the point here is that the linear format, itself, signals a particular quality.) This kind of selective representation can be argued to be, in some sense, inevitable (we cannot deal with everything!). However, selection at this level can serve the purpose of creating a better fit between data and theoretical concern. For instance, in Segment 2 (turns 84, 86, 88, 90, 92, 94, 96, 98, 100, 102, 104), Haroon's singing could have been omitted on the grounds of its irrelevance to the concurrent on-task interaction and talk between the other students; its elimination would remove some of the messiness from the data. To do so would, however, raise a serious epistemological question of what counts as data.

In fact, the question of what counts as data also raises a large number of issues concerned with contextual information. First, there is a decision to be made on whether to supply contextual information at all. Second, if the decision is to provide contextual information, then we have to decide what information and how much? Hammersley (1998) suggests that "descriptions are always selective: they focus on some aspects of phenomena and omit others" (p. 26). In other words, our decisions on what to selectively include in a contextual description are informed by a variety of theoretical and analytical concerns. Some of these concerns may be more or less consciously oriented toward the researcher's interpretation of the research purpose; others may be related to a more general paradigmatic and epistemological position on language, human action, and social interaction. Segment 2 of the History lesson transcript can be used to illustrate these points. If the decision had been to exclude contextual information, then the transcript would have given the impression that all participants were engaged in contiguous talk. Since contextual information was felt to be important and should be supplied, this decision signaled the researchers' epistemological orientation – that any action performed by the members of the focal group during the task time at the work table was germane to the description and analysis. However, the inclusion of information such as students looking at blank pages and tapping on the table (lines 87–9 and 122–4) adds a messy dimension to the data that can lead to potentially awkward questions about the "relatability" of the theoretical constructs of task-based language pedagogy to the actual conditions of teaching and learning in this particular classroom context.

Another issue of representation is concerned with which and how much data should be used. Green et al. (1997) argue

> The act of choosing a segment of life to transcribe implies decisions about the significance of the strip of talk or the speech event, which, in turn, implies that the talk or event has been interpreted from some point of view. (p. 173)

As we have shown earlier, the fourteen minutes of video data can be divided into four segments. Arguably, Segment 1 has the best fit with the constructs of the task-based pedagogy. Segments 2 and 3 show instances of inattention, engagement with other activities, and copying as a way of accomplishing the task. Segment 4, particularly the sequence showing some of the students refusing to work together, is ill-fitting. We could excise the ill-fitting segments, but to do so would be tantamount to a form of data cleansing. It may well be axiomatic, given the arguments presented above, that all research involves *some* cleansing when turning raw material into data. The key questions here are: How much cleansing and what kinds of claims do we make for the "truth" of our work? Another way of putting this is, assuming that we are trying to avoid cleansing data for theoretical and analytical convenience and that we wish to stay close to the classroom realities in our research, what are we to make of all this messiness?

Living with messiness and inelegance

The honest answer is that it is difficult to provide ready answers to the difficult problems we have pointed to in the present short discussion. It would seem that there are at least two ways of responding and they are not mutually exclusive. One way is to seek a conceptual framework that acknowledges, rather than obscures, the messiness of the data while nevertheless still holding fast to the analytic agenda set in advance. For instance, in this particular case of investigating task-based pedagogy, one may turn to the work in a particular strand of the Vygotskian tradition. Coughlan and Duff (1994) argue that there is a difference between *task* and *activity*. A task is a "behavioral blueprint" conceived and defined by researchers; "an activity, by comparison, comprises the behavior that is actually produced when an individual (or group) performs a task" (p. 175). Participants in a task may orient toward a task differently according to their knowledge, perception, and interests. Seen in this light, we could probably accommodate at least some of the messy data, arguing that they show a variety of student engagements with the set task. This way, we are implicitly saying that pedagogically oriented research, even in the qualitative approach, can attend to only those aspects of naturalistic data that are within touching distance of a preset analytic agenda. Teachers will have to apply this kind of research-generated knowledge in combination with other kinds of professional knowledge and skill in their classroom work (for a discussion, see Leung & Teasdale, 1999a). Teachers, as professionals, know that knowledge from textbooks and research does not necessarily address all aspects of classroom contingencies; in their daily work, they have to call on relevant experience and their own problem-solving capacity to deal with real-life issues and demands (Eraut, 1994).

However, in terms of working as closely as possible to actual real life phenomena in our research, it may be quite interesting to see what else we, as researchers, might do. Another way to respond to the messiness is, therefore, to pay attention to it and to explore the meaning of some of the apparently autonomous activities such as singing or nonverbal noises, drumming or tapping on tables, non-task-related gazes, and non-task-related interactions. At a technical level, one approach might be to present, in the notes to any research presentation, a fuller, nonlinear transcript of the extracted discourse sequence used in the main body of the argument.[8] Another approach, suggested by Coffey, Holbrook, and Atkinson (1996) in relation to ethnographic work, might be to utilize the now commonplace available computer and digital technologies such as hypertext and hypermedia to at least complement the customary linear printed restrictions so that "the simultaneous availability of written text (including the researcher's own interpretations and commentary), visual and sound data will permit the reader to explore alternative, and complementary modes of representation" that would create "room for representations that are more open and complex than are conventional ethnographic texts" (pp. 11–12).

At a theoretical level, we might begin to acknowledge that educationally oriented research should use messy qualitative research data to question the empirical basis of theoretical constructs. In the case of task-based language pedagogy, the central assumptions are that tasks can promote social interaction between the participants in a task and that social interaction can provide the opportunities for task-related language use and acquisition. The data presented in this discussion suggest that interaction cannot be regarded as an on- or off-task binary. It is a multifaceted phenomenon coproduced by the participants locally. Matters such as institutional authority, friendship, social power, personal interests, and language all seem to have a part to play. The messy data provide additional clues as to the areas that we need to study if we are to understand how task-based pedagogy in the mainstream multilingual and multiethnic elementary school classroom may work. As Brumfit (1984) argues, if one is attempting to research language pedagogy without jettisoning the classroom teacher's perspective, then a key requirement is to ensure that "generalizations and principles must be capable of being related directly to existing teaching conditions" (p. 1).

Notes

1. For a sample of the collaborative work of Leung and Teasdale, see Leung and Teasdale (1999a) and Teasdale and Leung (2000).

2. It is worth noting that the general idea of learning and, by extension, ESL or EAL (English as an additional language) learning through talk while doing shared curriculum tasks is often regarded as good practice in mainstream schooling. For a detailed discussion, see Leung (2001). It should be pointed out, though, that this pedagogic view has not grown out of a specifically SLA perspective and, unlike in the international EFL field, the applicability of this "talking to learn" view to ESL in the mainstream classroom context has not been supported by a great deal of sustained research.
3. These data had been previously studied with a view to, inter alia, identify and analyze the relationship between task-based language as specified or expected by teachers and the actual instances of student language use. Some of this work was presented by Leung and Teasdale (1999b).
4. As a matter of standard practice, ESL students are integrated into their mainstream classes as soon as possible when they arrive at school; some schools offer short-term English induction courses, but full-time ESL programs are not supported. See Leung (2001) for a discussion.
5. The two boys in the focal group were recent arrivals and had been in school in Britain for less than one year. The others ranged between two and four years.
6. The IRF sequence is also sometimes known as initiation–response–evaluation (IRE). For a discussion, see Mehan (1979).
7. The reading passage: Some of the Britons did fight back. Among the chiefs who won victories over the Anglo Saxons was one called Arthur. We do not know much about him. He had come down in legend. He was supposed to have a kingdom somewhere in the West.
8. The standard layout of transcript data creates an impression that there is a connected sequence. A column layout, which presents the interlocuters' turns in separate vertical columns, reflects more accurately speaking turns that do not follow one from another. For a discussion on alternative forms of presentation of transcript data, see Swann (1994).

References

Atkinson, P. A. (1992). *Understanding ethnographic texts.* London: Sage.

Bloome, D. (1994). Reading as a social process in a middle school classroom. In D. Graddol, J. Maybin, & B. Stierer (Eds.), *Researching language and literacy in social context* (pp. 100–130). Clevedon, England: Multilingual Matters.

Brumfit, C. (1984). *Communicative methodology in language teaching.* Cambridge, England: Cambridge University Press.

Candela, A. (1999). Students' power in classroom discourse. *Linguistics and Education, 10*(2), 139–63.

Coffey, A., Holbrook, B., & Atkinson, P. (1996, March 29). Qualitative data analysis: Technologies and representations. *Sociological Research Online, 1*(1), Article 4. Retrieved December 21, 1999, from http://www.socresonline.org.uk/socresonline/1/1/4.html

Coughlan, P., & Duff, P. A. (1994). Same task, different activities: Analysis of a SLA task from an activity theory perspective. In J. P. Lantolf & G. Appel (Eds.), *Vygotskian approaches to second language research* (pp. 173–93). Norwood, NJ: Ablex.

Crookes, G., & Gass, S. M. (Eds.). (1993a). *Tasks and language learning.* Clevedon, England: Multilingual Matters.

Crookes, G., & Gass, S. M. (Eds.). (1993b). *Tasks in a pedagogical context: Integrating theory and practice.* Clevedon, England: Multilingual Matters.

Davis, K. (1995). Qualitative theory and methods in applied linguistic research. *TESOL Quarterly, 29*(3), 427–53.

Donato, R. (1994). Collective scaffolding in second language learning. In J. P. Lantolf & G. Appel (Eds.), *Vygotskian approaches to second language research* (pp. 33–56). Norwood, NJ: Ablex.

Eraut, M. (1994). *Developing professional knowledge and competence.* London: Falmer Press.

Green, J., Franquiz, M., & Dixon, C. (1997). The myth of the objective transcript: Transcribing as a situated act. *TESOL Quarterly, 31*(1), 172–6.

Guba, E., & Lincoln, Y. (1994). Competing paradigms in qualitative research. In N. Denzin & Y. Lincoln (Eds.), *The landscape of qualitative research: Theories and issues: Vol. 1. Handbook of qualitative research* (pp. 105–17). London: Sage.

Gutierrez, K., Rymes, B., & Larson, J. (1995). Script, counterscript and underlife in the classroom: James Brown versus *Brown v. Board of Education. Harvard Educational Review, 65*(3), 445–71.

Hammersley, M. (1998). *Reading ethnographic research: A critical guide* (2nd ed.). London: Longman.

Harklau, L. (1994). ESL versus mainstream classes: Contrasting L2 learning environments. *TESOL Quarterly, 28*(2), 241–72.

Kamberelis, G. (2001). Producing heteroglossic classroom (micro)cultures through hybrid discourse practice. *Linguistics and Education, 12*(1), 85–125.

Kumaravadivelu, B. (1993). The name of the task and the task of naming: Methodological aspects of task-based pedagogy. In G. Crookes & S. M. Gass (Eds.), *Tasks and language learning* (pp. 69–89). Clevedon, England: Multilingual Matters.

Kumaravadivelu, B. (1999). Critical classroom discourse analysis. *TESOL Quarterly, 33*(3), 453–84.

Lantolf, J. P. (Ed.). (2000). *Sociocultural theory and second language learning.* Oxford: Oxford University Press.

Lantolf, J. P., & Appel, G. (Eds.). (1994). *Vygotskian approaches to second language research.* Norwood, NJ: Ablex.

Leung, C. (2001). English as an additional language: Distinct language focus or diffused curriculum concerns? *Language and Education, 15*(1), 33–55.

Leung, C., & Teasdale, A. (1999a). ESL teacher competence: Professional education and the nature of professional knowledge. In H. Trappes-Lomax & I. McGrath (Eds.), *Theory in language teacher education* (pp. 56–69). Essex, England: Longman (in association with the British Council).

Leung, C., & Teasdale, A. (1999b, March). *Task-oriented language use: An empirical investigation in the mainstream classroom.* Paper presented at the annual meeting of the American Association for Applied Linguistics (AAAL), Stamford, Connecticut.

Long, M. H., & Crookes, G. (1992). Three approaches to task-based syllabus design. *TESOL Quarterly, 26*(1), 27–56.

Mehan, H. (1979). *Learning lessons: social organization in the classroom.* Cambridge, MA: Harvard University Press.
Mohan, B. (1986). *Language and content.* Rowley, MA: Addison-Wesley.
Norton, B. (2000). *Identity and language learning: Gender, ethnicity and educational change.* Harlow, England: Pearson Education.
Nunan, D. (1989). *Designing tasks for a communicative classroom.* Cambridge, England: Cambridge University Press.
Ochs, E. (1979). Transcription as theory. In E. Ochs & B. B. Schiefflin (Eds.), *Developmental pragmatics* (pp. 43–72). New York: Academic Press.
Pica, T., Kanagy, R., & Falodun, J. (1993). Choosing and using communicative tasks for second language instructions. In G. Crookes & S. M. Gass (Eds.), *Tasks and language learning* (pp. 9–34). Clevedon, England: Multilingual Matters.
Roberts, C. (1997). Transcribing talk: Issues of representation. *TESOL Quarterly, 31*(1), 167–72.
Roebuck, R. (2000). Subjects speak out: How learners position themselves in a psycholinguistic task. In J. P. Lantolf (Ed.), *Sociocultural theory and second language learning* (pp. 79–95). Oxford: Oxford University Press.
Seale, C. (1999). *The quality of qualitative research.* London: Sage.
Skehan, P. (1996). A framework for the implementation of task-based instruction. *Applied Linguistics, 17*(1), 38–62.
Skehan, P. (1998). *A cognitive approach to language learning.* Oxford: Oxford University Press.
Swann, J. (1994). Observing and recording talk in educational settings. In D. Graddol, J. Maybin, & B. Stierer (Eds.), *Researching language and literacy in social context* (pp. 26–48). Clevedon, England: Multilingual Matters and Open University.
Teasdale, A., & Leung, C. (2000). Teacher assessment and psychometric theory: A case of paradigm crossing. *Language Testing, 17*(2), 163–84.
Toohey, K. (2000). *Learning English at school: Identity, social relations, and classroom practice.* Clevedon, England: Multilingual Matters.

PART IV: EDUCATING TEACHERS FOR CHANGE

14 *Introducing a critical pedagogical curriculum: A feminist reflexive account*

Angel M. Y. Lin

Introduction

The body of this chapter is divided into three main parts. In the first part, I describe a teacher-educator's (my own) attempt to develop a Master of Arts in Teaching English as a Second Language (MATESL) course with the aim to introduce critical pedagogical practices to a group of in-service primary and secondary school English teachers in Hong Kong. In the second part, I look back at the course and at what seems to have transpired during the course and reflexively analyze and discuss the difficulties and frustrations as well as some instances of success experienced. In the third part, I discuss some inherent contradictions of critical pedagogy as delineated in the poststructuralist feminist literature and echoed in my own experience and explore future possibilities and ways of doing critical pedagogies without assuming universal, foundational subject positions.

Part I
Naming and introducing critical courses into an MATESL program: Sites of negotiation and strategic compromise

Like most MATESL programs elsewhere, the existing structure of the MATESL program at the City University of Hong Kong does not have critical pedagogy explicitly laid out as one of its aims or core components. Last year, however, a few colleagues started to propose and build critical elements into a Year 1 core course. In program committee meetings, colleagues debated the name of the course and decided to give it a broader, more general name – *Understanding Classroom Practices* – although it was understood that the course would also have as one of its aims the raising of students' critical consciousness about antiracist, -sexist, and -classist issues in teaching of English to speakers of other languages. I can understand why many of my colleagues consider a general, mainstream name to be safer and more acceptable; both staff and students have concerns about possible misunderstandings that can be induced by a nonmainstream name in the Hong Kong context, where critical pedagogy is a seldom-heard-of term and where few teacher-educators and students seem to know what it means apart from some radical connotations (and some unease, given the local cultural traditions)[1] that the word *critical* seems to carry. A telling piece of evidence can be seen in a staff–student consultative meeting. When this new proposed course was discussed, a student representative misunderstood *critical* as behaving in an impolite and difficult way and remarked that her classmates might not want to do such a course. While Elizabeth Ellsworth (1992) succeeded in naming the political agenda behind her course by naming it Media and Anti-Racist Pedagogies, it seems that in the Hong Kong context, any culturally dirty word (e.g., *critical*, often taken to mean disturbing harmony by creating dissent) has to be strategically concealed under a mainstream, *neutral* or instrumental, technical name (e.g., Understanding Classroom Practices) so as to be acceptable and not scare students away.

Since the Year 2 students would not have a chance to take the abovementioned new Year 1 course, and because it so happened that fifteen Year 2 students signed up for my Year 2 elective course, Language, Culture, and Education, I decided to try to develop a critical pedagogical curriculum in this course. While one might charge that I tried to smuggle in critical pedagogical elements into an otherwise ordinary MATESL course, I would rather describe the situation in a somewhat different manner. Traditional ways of dealing with issues of language, culture, and education tend to reproduce dominant cultural, linguistic, and educational notions and practices as neutral and unproblematic and, in this way, conceal relations of domination and subordination in the schooling system and the pedagogy of language teaching. I saw a course on language, culture, and education as an ideal site for interrogating our commonsensical notions about language, culture, and education, as well as their interrelations. To me, at the time, I set out to attempt to do what Freire (1968, 1973) called "conscientization" and "re-experiencing the ordinary"; what Michael Apple (1999) called "interruption of common sense," "relational analysis," and "destabilization of authoritative discourse"; what Giroux (as cited in Gore, 1993, p. 35) advocated – "to both constitute and reorder the nature of our experiences and the objects of our concerns so as to both enhance and further empower the ideological conditions for a radical democracy" – or what Dean called "the restive problematization of the given" (as cited in Pennycook, 1999, p. 343).

The teachers in the course were from a cohort of twenty-three second-year students in a two-year part-time evening program titled MATESL at the City University of Hong Kong. In the first semester of their second (and final) year, they had to take one compulsory core course (Assessment in TESL) and two elective courses. A list of elective courses are put up every year, and if more than eight students sign up for a course, then the course will likely be offered. The courses with the highest student enrollment which were therefore offered this year were Activating Creative Texts, English for Specific Purposes, and Language, Culture, and Education.

In the first meeting of the course, I asked the students why they had signed up for this course and what their expectations for this course were. Many said that they had not read the course description and had just guessed from the course title, Language, Culture, and Education, that the course was about these three topics that they were interested in. Some said that they thought it was similar to the core course I taught in the immediately preceding semester, The Social Context of Language Teaching, and felt that they would want to do something along similar lines. Because they could still change their electives within the first two weeks of the semester, I felt that I needed to make it explicit to them what this course was about so that they could decide whether they still wanted to take the course or not. I distributed and explained the course outline, detailing the course objectives, weekly topics and readings, basic texts, and types of assignments for the course (see Appendix for excerpts from the course outline). I explicitly stressed that they should change to another elective if the course was not what they were interested in or expected. I did so because I felt that for the course to be successful, some matching of students' and instructor's expectations was crucial, especially in the Hong Kong context where chances are that my students had never before come across any course which required them to critically interrogate long-accepted, taken-for-granted notions about language, culture, and education. It turned out that in the second meeting, five out of fifteen students had changed to another elective, and I was left with ten willing students, all female, in my class. I was pleased to have a smaller group of students, for I felt that the atmosphere would be more cozy and there would be more opportunities and time for each student to speak up in class discussions. The remaining students also seemed to be the ones who seemed to have already developed a trusting relationship with me in the immediately preceding course (The Social Context of Language Teaching). I sensed that they seemed to find me friendly, sincere, and helpful and would feel comfortable working with me.

To be honest, I felt both excited and nervous about setting out to develop a critical pedagogical curriculum in an MATESL course, for this was the first time such a course was ever run in Hong Kong as far as I knew. It would seem from the above paragraphs that I had a good course beginning and that it was likely to run smoothly to its end; however, as reflexively and critically discussed in the next section, I experienced some dilemmas, and the students seemed to have experienced some difficulties. The discussion is based on three main sources of data apart from my reflections: (a) course materials and students' writings, (b) a diary I kept after each meeting, and (c) informal discussion about the course with two students after the end of the course.

Part II
Difficulties, frustrations, and some (limited) successes

In this section, I shall discuss the difficulties, dilemmas, and frustrations experienced in the course under two main themes: (a) brokering the difficult academic language of critical pedagogical texts, and (b) dealing with pessimism and frustration that critical consciousness, alone, cannot overcome. Under each of the headings, I shall also describe some (limited) successes and some possible future strategies to deal with the problems despite the difficulties.

Helping students to cope with the academic language

To develop a critical curriculum around the themes of language, culture, and education, I chose James Paul Gee's book *Social Linguistics and Literacies* (1996) as a basic text for the course for four reasons. First, I felt that his concepts and discourse analytic methods (e.g., notions of primary and secondary discourses, social languages, language as design resources, cultural models, and situated meanings) could offer some useful conceptual tools for a sociopolitical analysis of the language and education situation in Hong Kong. Second, his text covers the themes of language, culture, and education. Third, I had found his text to be the most readable among other critical pedagogical texts, and I felt that the book was intended for use with undergraduate or postgraduate students. Last, no local book of a similar nature is available. I had also thought of using a collection of articles instead of a book; however, I felt that James Gee's theories about language and literacies and his discourse analytic examples could provide my students with a coherent set of initial tools to do their own analysis of the situation in Hong Kong. I therefore felt that understanding and then learning to use his tools would provide a good initial focal point of the course. Given the short duration of the course (only fourteen meetings), I assigned only four main chapters from the book (Chapters 4–7) and supplemented the chapters with two articles, one about Hong Kong English language education by myself (Lin, 1999) and one about the cultural incompatibility of the communicative language teaching approach in China (Ouyang, 2000). Due to limited time toward the end of the course, I found that I had to skip my own article, and thus, the students had altogether read Gee's four chapters and Ouyang's article in *Anthropological and Educational Quarterly*.

In the second meeting, students expressed that they had difficulties reading and understanding Gee's writing. They said his writing was dense and that they could only read it very slowly and still felt that they did not understand much of it, thus making the whole reading process very frustrating. This came as a surprise to me as I had not realized that my students, students at the Master's level, had been out of academia for some time and their previous undergraduate training had not apprenticed them in the specialized academic language of scholars and researchers in my field. Also, since this was the first time they had ever come across Gee's critical concepts about language and literacies, they had little background to help them to crack the new concepts.

I was worried and had some soul-searching reflections after the second meeting. Should I continue to ask them to read Gee's chapters? Should I rewrite Gee's writings to make the concepts more accessible to them – such as doing linguistic and conceptual brokering? I also felt guilty about not having been sensitive enough early on to realize that what I found readable and easy to understand myself was actually quite frustrating for my students who had come from different training backgrounds and positions. I said to myself, "Yes, I believe that introducing Gee's concepts to them is important because it will give them some analytic tools to do their own analysis later on in their critical analysis projects, and I've got to find ways of making Gee's concepts easier to understand and relevant to their daily experiences." I therefore designed some study questions to help them to focus on some key concepts and arguments in each of Gee's chapters. At the beginning of each subsequent meeting, I went through the guiding questions, explaining in advance (i.e., before they went home to do the reading) the key concepts and arguments in that chapter. When I explained Gee's concepts and arguments, I drew on students' familiar experiences in the Hong Kong context to illustrate these concepts.

For instance, to illustrate Gee's notions of *primary and secondary discourses*, I drew on the example of new immigrant students from mainland China and elicited from the class what they had observed about the learning styles, manners, and cultures of these students in their schools. I then asked them to articulate the kinds of learning and speaking styles, manners, and cultures acceptable in their schools. My students could relate to this example easily and were eager to contribute their observations to the discussion. Then I drew their attention to the discrepancies between the indigenous speaking and learning styles of the new immigrant students (e.g., speaking up freely in class without raising their hands to get their teacher's nomination to speak first) and those acceptable to the schools as the discrepancies between the immigrant students' primary discourse and the school's discourse (the secondary discourse) that the new immigrants must pick up to be successful in school. I then asked the class to suggest ways of helping these immigrant students to cross the gap between their primary and secondary discourses without labeling or judging them as poorly behaved students, as some Hong Kong teachers had. I was relieved to see that the class discussion was animated by these examples drawn from their familiar contexts.

From that time onward, I tried my best to find examples from the local context to explain and illustrate Gee's concepts in his chapters. I could see my students' lit-up facial expressions and verbal responses whenever I engaged them in discussions involving local, familiar examples. In my diary after each class, I revisited the concepts and my ways of explaining them and tried to think of better examples and ways of explaining them if I were to do this again. In my informal discussions with two students after the end of the course, both of them said that using the study questions and explaining the concepts in advance had helped them to read and understand Gee's chapters.

Critically reflecting on this experience in the class, I started to realize what Apple (1999) meant about how critical pedagogues have established their own field and own capital. For instance, to publish (and to survive in universities) one has to use the specialized language of that field. Critical pedagogues who are adept in this academic game might find it difficult to shift between registers when talking to schoolteachers, and, thus, their theories run the risk of "talking over their heads." The institutional job appraisal requirements and constraints imposed on academics and teacher-educators often make it an unrewarded (i.e., not to say it is unrewarding, but just that it is often not rewarded by tertiary institutes) extra effort on the part of even critical pedagogic academics to develop a nonacademic, teacher-friendly language to relay their theories to teachers to whom their theories purport to be important. This explains why it is difficult to find a critical pedagogy book which is intended for, and written in a language accessible to, schoolteachers. Moreover, teacher-educators working outside of North American academic circles need to further contextualize the critical pedagogy theories in their respective local contexts. I realize that if I am to run the course again next year, I have to develop and write my own course readings for my students to arouse their interest in critical pedagogy (and I will need to find extra time to do this while being fully aware that this effort will not be rewarded by my institute in my annual appraisal as this does not count toward my journal publications). Although I can continue to do linguistic and conceptual brokering in class (i.e., annotating foreign texts with local examples), much more valuable class time can be saved for discussions if the readings are more accessible to the teachers so that the teachers can come to class already familiar with the concepts and analytic tools. I must also hurry, after writing the above, to point out that I am not academia bashing, but I think academics need to be more reflexive and recognize the different language games we are engaged in, like it or not. We need to realize that our own critical pedagogic writings are themselves situated in a political institutional context.

There might be a counter-argument that we must not encourage teachers to be anti-intellectual and so we need to encourage schoolteachers to read original critical texts and to learn the academic language to train their minds to be more critical; however, I think that such an argument runs the risk of naturalizing academic texts, claiming that they embody some universally superior forms of rationality or ways of knowing (and that such forms really exist). Schoolteachers, unlike academics, are situated in a different social field where different kinds of capital count (e.g., the ability to use daily life examples to explain concepts). Academic language is just one way of knowing and speaking, among others. The discourses of critical pedagogy theorists, like those authoritative discourses that they critique, are themselves likely to run the risk of becoming authoritative discourses themselves in relation to schoolteachers whom they often purport to set out to empower (Ellsworth, 1992). So even as I am writing this chapter now, I am reflexively aware of the difficulty of walking the thin line between academic texts and readable texts intended for in-service or preservice teachers. The reader will notice that I deliberately violate some academic writing conventions – such as using *I* often, adopting a more conversational tone, and even referring to my own personal feelings. I hope, in doing this chapter, to achieve the goal of contesting dominant academic writing conventions, showing that it is possible to address complex theoretical issues using a language familiar to schoolteachers.

However, overcoming the frustrating texts is just a first step. Achieving critical consciousness, albeit advocated by critical theorists as the first step toward liberation, can result in pessimism and helplessness, especially in political and working contexts where the room for democratic contestation and alternative practices is limited. Hong Kong presents an example of such contexts. It is to this topic that I am turning in the next section.

Dealing with pessimism and frustration that critical consciousness, alone, cannot overcome

While achieving a critical consciousness of the relations of domination and reproduction in the schooling system and one's position and implication in it has been a common goal in critical pedagogy, how to move from criticism to substantive vision (Giroux, 1988, as cited in Gore, 1993, p. 34) and from substantive vision to substantive action geared toward change is an unanswered question, at least in contexts where the political system is far from democratic, teachers' unions are underdeveloped, and labor relations in the schools are lopsidedly unfavorable to teachers, such as in the situation of Hong Kong.

For instance, at the beginning of the third meeting of the course, I noticed that some students were sighing and groaning to one another about the oppressive administrative measures they experienced in their respective schools. I therefore started the class by asking the students to talk about their difficulties. One after another, they complained about the arbitrary and absolute power of their school principals, how teachers were treated with disrespect, how they were asked to perform duties which they found abhorrent (e.g., in one school, teachers are asked by the school principal to check students' uniforms at the school entrance), how they were monitored (e.g., their marked compositions are checked to see if they have made any errors and whether they have marked each single mistake in students' compositions), how little autonomy they had about what to teach, and how the school principals were only concerned about putting up a superficial good school image to the public (e.g., the parents) and do not really care about the education of students. And when it came to Emily's[2] turn to talk about her school, she was so full of grievances that soon she switched to Cantonese (from English) to pour out more freely what she had to say about her school. She seemed to have wanted sympathetic ears to her grievances for a long, long time. She sighed and talked about how her school had imported a management and quality assurance system from the business sector. In order to meet the standard of the ISO (International Standardization Organization), the school had implemented a number of quality assurance procedures to make sure that the teaching staff's performance was up to an objectively defined standard. The procedure operates in terms of quantification of work (e.g., setting a minimum number of different types of assignments each week) and regular inspection of teachers' marked assignments. There are also frequent seminars and discussion meetings. Although Emily thought that these should have been good for the teachers, too many of them added to the workload of teachers, who simply found it difficult to cope with all these activities and requirements of the schools' management system.

I tried to relate Emily's school situation to the notion of the colonization of education by capitalist, globalized business, and management discourses. Capitalizing on the example of Emily's school, I tried to illustrate how contemporary education is under the risk of colonization by business ideologies which make teachers' lives unnecessarily difficult without actually improving the quality of students' education. While this theoretical delineation might seem elegant to me, my students did not seem to be particularly interested in the theories. They seemed to be totally consumed by a sense of frustration and helplessness as they stand to lose their jobs if anyone dared to speak up against the management. In the context of Hong Kong, school principals have great power over teachers, who have little bargaining power, and any effective unionization has so far been unsuccessful (partly due to the acquired helplessness of many teachers and partly due to the fact that school principals do have the power to find excuses to fire teachers who are active in unionizing or organizing any collective contestation). At that moment, I felt a strong sense of frustration myself as I felt that I failed to connect a critical analysis of their situation to any substantive vision or action strategies that might work toward changing their situation. While James Gee's analytic tools of discourses might help them to do a social analysis of their situation, it seems to fall short of helping them to see any practical way out.

What the teachers in my class and, in fact, in Hong Kong, face is a situation similar to that of the intensification of teachers' work and the centralization of the curriculum in the United States described by Apple (1999). The capitalist, globalized management discourses of *value-addedness*, *quality assurance*, and *standardization* have inserted themselves into Hong Kong's education discourses and have justified or intensified the dehumanizing, deprofessionalizing, and deskilling working conditions for teachers, the majority of whom are females who often also have their families to take care of apart from their jobs. While Emily's school administration takes pride in getting the status of "ISO" – an indicator of objectified quality assurance – for their school, the school's teachers are overworked and cannot see how the quality of education is linked to such management practices.[3]

After the third meeting, I could not help feeling frustrated and unconvinced about the potential usefulness of critical pedagogy and critical sociological analysis, and I recorded in my diary that while the theories I cited might have helped the teachers to see the sources of their oppression under the current school administration system, they remain just that. This reminded me of what Carrington and Luke (1997) discussed of the need to go beyond critical pedagogy to have a broader "public pedagogy":

> the challenges of convincing employers, politicians and the public of the persistent need for the equitable distribution of resources, nondiscriminatory access and fairness in the social institutions of work, government and community life [remain]. Such a project would need to be part of a broader "public pedagogy"... incumbent on us all. (p. 110)

However, in the context of Hong Kong, where a democratic political system is not yet in place and where civil disobedience as a way of contesting socially unjust policies and pushing for more democracy is often met with police disciplinary actions and prosecutions, teachers are, in general, silenced and have acquired a sense of helplessness and sometimes even indifference. Doing critical pedagogy in such a context is frustrating, and doing public pedagogy might put oneself in danger.

To be honest, I was caught up in this sense of frustration and helplessness myself, and, for some time, I could not continue the writing of this chapter because merely reflecting on how ineffective my critical curriculum was in the face of teachers' sufferings agonized and almost paralyzed me. What rescued me from such a depressing mode of thinking and helped me to see the value (albeit limited) of the critical curriculum I put into the course was the publication of the teachers' writings (i.e., their critical project reports in my course) in *TESL-HK* (a newsletter for English language teaching professionals in Hong Kong) and some of my students dropping by my office telling me how proud and happy they felt about the publication of their writings and the opportunity to voice their views and share them with other English teachers in Hong Kong. Below, I shall give the reader some background of the *TESL-HK* project and how I integrated the course assignments with this project to provide an avenue for the teachers' voices to be heard in the local school community in Hong Kong.

In 1997, some colleagues and I started the publication of *TESL-HK* with a small teaching enhancement fund obtained from our university. This was the first nonprofit professional newsletter devoted to secondary school English teachers in Hong Kong (over 5000 copies were sent to all secondary school English departments in Hong Kong). We also obtained some funding to develop a parallel Web site where one can download past and current issues of *TESL-HK* (http://www.tesl-hk.org – the interested reader can go to this Web site to see the sixth issue, which contains articles written by students in the course). Over the years, we have been struggling with funding, but we were able to publish the sixth issue in June 2001. Honestly, we do not know whether we can continue the publication under the current atmosphere of government budget cutting imposed on the universities and our own university's recently shifting emphasis on research more than community outreach; however, in my Language, Culture, and Education course, doing a critical analysis project and writing an article for *TESL-HK* based on the project were made into a major assignment (see Appendix for assignment structures). Three students in the course did a critical analysis of the sexist, racist, and classist stereotypes in English textbooks in Hong Kong. Another two students did a survey of teachers on teacher stress and their working conditions in schools. Other students did some interesting critical projects as well, but, due to the length of their reports, I could not include all of them in the sixth issue of *TESL-HK*. It is my hope that I will obtain funding in the future to publish all their reports in a book for Hong Kong teachers.

In the first meeting of the course, I explained to the students why I deviated from the traditional course assignment pattern, asking students to write for a wider audience (i.e., other Hong Kong English teachers) apart from the course instructor. I explained to the class that I hoped the course would produce some useful products that could be shared with other Hong Kong teachers and explained that the aim of doing the assignments was not just intellectual training or an exercise, but making an impact on the local school community through our intellectual, analytic work.

It is true that just helping teachers to get their voices heard is still far from any substantive change in the oppressive system that teachers are still faced with in their everyday school life; however, it did give me hope when my students came back to say how happy they felt about seeing their articles reaching a wider audience. In their faces, which radiated with assertive pride, confidence, and agency, I could see the value in introducing a critical curriculum in an MATESL course and connecting the assignments of that course to a community publication project. If, as academics, we are best with our words (not to say that we should not also be engaged in other forms of social movements and advocacy work), then I can see some hope in a critical and public pedagogy project that connects teachers' production of words in an academic course to the production of active, defiant, assertive subject positions through their writings for a wider audience in the local education community. On this rare occasion, for the first time, I witnessed the empowering effect of words produced by teachers, themselves, as agents analyzing their own situations and voicing their own views about the oppressive system in which they are caught and in which they have, for so long, felt so helpless. If more and more teachers can find their own ways of recreating their own subject positions (e.g., by substituting the helpless subject positions produced for them by the school system with new, confident, assertive subject positions that they, themselves, produced by drawing on some of the critical sociological analytic tools that a critical discourse might be able to provide them with), then I think there might be some value to such a discourse. I must also hurry to say that the above example is just one possible way among many, and it would be arrogant to assume that using critical sociological tools advocated in critical pedagogy (and critical discourses) will always be the best way (Pennycook, 1999). It depends a lot on the local strategic work of social actors in specific contexts, not on a totalizing grand theory of liberation that critical pedagogy provides (Glass, 2001). This issue is connected to some of the theoretical problems of critical pedagogy – a discussion of which I am turning to below.

Amid the limited successes experienced, there were nevertheless some troubling issues which resonate with some of the fundamental theoretical problems of critical pedagogy that poststructuralist feminist educators

(Gore, 1993; Luke & Gore, 1992) pointed out nearly a decade ago. In the next section, I shall share with the reader my critical reflexive account of my own struggles and blunders in the course and what I have learned from the process that might point to some possible ways of doing critical pedagogy without committing the errors of assuming universal, foundational subject positions or privileging certain forms of rationality and practices as necessarily always higher or more liberating than others.

Part III
Some contradictions in critical pedagogy: Poststructuralist feminist perspectives

In this section, I shall organize my discussion along two issues: (a) dealing with the institutional power relations enacted and reproduced in the classroom, and (b) coping with the working conditions of female junior education workers – that is, heavy daily workloads outside of the course on the part of both the instructor and the students.

Dealing with the institutional power relations enacted and reproduced in the classroom

I ran the course in the same way I had run other courses in the past five years as a teacher-educator. Reflecting on what transpired in the course, I realized that I had not been self-reflexive enough to realize that I had simply reproduced the traditional forms of disciplinary power that I, myself, experienced as a student and then picked up and imposed on my students when I became a teacher and, later, a teacher-educator. To me, for all these years, that was just a taken-for-granted way of being a liberal teacher. My teaching style resembles that of many middle-class liberal teachers. While I do not explicitly discipline students in class, I use indirect, equally coercive technologies of disciplinary power that many Chinese teachers have traditionally used (largely unreflectively because that was the way they were treated as students). These include producing arguments (or forms of discourse-knowledge) that have the power to impose "self-shame" that students internalize and exercise upon themselves when they violate the behavioral norms constructed in the arguments and discourse-knowledge (similar to Foucault's [1997] notion of "technologies of the self"). The agonizing irony is that the entire time I was thinking of introducing a critical curriculum and providing my students with social analytic tools to critique forms of domination and subordination in the schooling system of Hong Kong, I had never for a moment during the course used those tools reflexively to critique my own implication in the reproduction of institutional power relations in my own classroom. I had not, in critical pedagogic terms, interrogated my own common sense regarding acceptable teaching styles – not until one of my students told me after the course in an informal chat about their feelings toward some aspects of my teaching style.

Tammy dropped by my office one day and I asked her to give me feedback on the course I taught in the previous semester. She told me quite candidly that although she and her classmates could understand my good intentions for them, they found some of my expectations rather unacceptable for mature students like them. For instance, I expected them to be punctual for my class. Tammy said that although they were teachers themselves and knew the importance of punctuality, they hoped that I would be more understanding since they had full-time jobs during the day, and sometimes it was difficult for them to make it to the class on time. Another source of their unease was with my expectation that they would do the assigned reading before coming to class. For one thing, Tammy said, they were overworked at school and, for another, they felt that James Gee's book chapters were too lengthy and they often could not find time to finish reading the whole assigned chapter. She suggested that I should assign a short excerpt as a core reading and let the rest of the chapter be an optional reading. Tammy also said that many of her classmates were afraid of my questioning them about the concepts of the assigned readings. She said if they had not managed to finish reading it and were unable to answer my questions, they would feel very embarrassed. Tammy said that these aspects of my teaching style were too much like those of secondary school teaching – which they felt uncomfortable being subjected to as they were not secondary school students.

I thanked Tammy for letting me know her classmates' and her own feelings toward my teaching style, of which I was so uncritical all along. I began to realize that I had, myself, long internalized these technologies of the self; I had always expected every student (whether secondary, undergraduate, or postgraduate students, and including myself) to live up to those norms of traditional Chinese teachers – that is, to be punctual, to do the assigned readings so as to be able to benefit from the class, to answer the teacher's questions about the readings so that the teacher can find out which concepts they have problems with, and so on. I had reproduced the traditional institutional forms of disciplinary power in my own "critical" classroom.

I was agonized to learn of these blind spots in myself and it took me some time to resolve the conflicts between my students' perspectives and my own. On the one hand, I truly believed what I did was good for my students (but good only from my own perspective and according to the regime of truth I imposed – e.g., imposing all those expectations of self-disciplining mentioned by Tammy). On the other hand, Tammy and her classmates did have a valid point; they wanted to be treated as mature, responsible adults who were agents of their own learning and who could determine their own ways of learning. They had every right to resist being put into subject positions which were subordinate to my disciplinary power, like children who are subjected to their parents' disciplinary power. For some time, I had been so confused and agonized that I could not carry on with the writing of this chapter until I came across Gore's (1993) discussion on a similar topic. She pointed out that critical pedagogy (just like any other traditional or even progressive pedagogy) runs the risk of constituting a regime of truth and seems to lack a self-reflexive awareness of the hierarchical institutional power relations reproduced in the critical pedagogic classroom. Gore made the following suggestion:

> If indeed the institutionalization of pedagogy in schools and universities constrains attempts at radical pedagogies, then investigations of disciplinary power in various institutionalized and non-institutionalized pedagogical sites might identify specific alternative pedagogical practices which teacher-educators could attempt to integrate. Pedagogical sites outside of schooling institutions, such as voluntary women's groups and parenting, might successfully employ different practices and, at the same time, avoid effects of domination. (p. 148)

I would add that teacher-educators can openly invite their students to discuss and negotiate aspects of their teaching style. For instance, if I had the reflexive awareness to ask my students early on to discuss my ways of teaching in an open, receptive, and sincere manner, I might have been able to codevelop alternative ways of teaching and learning with my students. This might not always resolve all conflicts of perspectives between instructor and students; nevertheless, this will help to open up some discursive space in which ruptures of the current pedagogy (e.g., as embodied by the instructor) can be induced and new locally effective pedagogies can have a chance to develop. As Gore (1993) suggests, drawing on Foucault's notion of spaces of freedom:

> Foucault (1988) wanted to identify "spaces of freedom" we can still enjoy. According to Foucault's analyses, there will always be regimes of truth and technologies of the self. The point of identifying spaces of freedom is not to escape all regimes and technologies, only current ones; to increase awareness of current regimes and technologies; to recognize that current regimes need not be as they are; to continually identify and squeeze into those spaces of freedom. . . . I would argue that a Foucauldian perspective establishes the instructional practices of pedagogy as an important site of investigation for radical educators, points to ways out of the pessimism often associated with poststructuralist positions (especially vis-à-vis its focus on specific power relations and technologies of the self in local contexts), and (despite arguments

to the contrary) does not mandate rejecting visions of different societies, but proposes that *they get worked out locally* [italics added]. (p. 156)

Gore's emphasis on the importance of working out, in local contexts, critical visions of alternative practices is echoed by Glass (2001) in a recent article:

The aim is to retain the liberatory power of the critique of dehumanization while recognizing the malleability and contradictions of identity, embracing the uncertainties and varieties of reason in knowledge, and respecting the plural compelling conceptions of the good that can shape a just, democratic society. (p. 22)

While the above remarks sound like workable strategies, the constraining aspects of the working conditions of both myself (at the time, a junior female university academic) and my students (junior female education workers in the schools) often leave little space for both instructor and students to have room for doing critical readings of, and reflections on, our own teaching and learning practices. The hectic day-to-day work of the semester often leaves us just enough time to stick to the daily routines to survive the working day without much room left for critical conscientization or self-interrogation. It is to a discussion of these dilemmas that I shall turn in the next section.

The working conditions of junior female academics and education workers

During that semester, I had fifteen contact hours of teaching per week plus over twenty school visits to do over the term for supervision of students' practicums; I had over two hundred lesson plans to read and give feedback on, and I had three postgraduate research degree students and three undergraduate final-year projects to supervise. I also was Deputy Program Leader of the Bachelor of Arts in Teaching English as a Second Language Program and had administrative duties. Of course, I still had my ongoing research projects to manage and research reports and articles to write. I was under constant institutional pressure to produce research publications in high-ranking international (i.e., in reality, U.S.) journals that have acceptance rates of only 15–17 percent and that have, until recently, been interested in publishing research studies situated mainly in North America. I had long working days and when my students came to my 6:30 P.M. classes after their full day's work in their schools, both the students and I were exhausted. Most of them had not had supper yet. I sometimes couldn't help wondering how critical we could afford to be when we had to keep our bodies awake and functioning even amid all the work that we had for the day. The intensification of teachers' work and the deskilling of teachers due to this intensification (e.g., because teachers are so busy, they have to rely on routines and standardized textbooks) that Apple (1999) addresses ring very true in Hong Kong, not only at the secondary school level but also at the university level; however, what is often neglected in the critical pedagogy literature is the gendered pattern of the division of education labor.

At the university, the administration- and labor-intensive practice-oriented front-line courses such as Practice Teaching (the supervision of students' practicums in schools) are coordinated and taught mainly by local female Chinese–English bilingual faculty members. The theory-oriented education courses are taught mainly by male, expatriate, English, monolingual faculty members. There is a gendered division between theory and practice resulting in the local female faculty members having to bridge the gaps between the imported theories taught by their male expatriate colleagues and the local classroom realities that they have to help their students to deal with. Similarly, in the case of my students, they were largely female junior education workers in their respective schools working under the quantifying quality assurance management style with which their male school principals operate. Under such working conditions, both my students and myself found it difficult to engage in self-reflective journal diary-keeping, which is usually encouraged in critical courses.

To deal with the fatigue factor, I used a tape recorder to record my immediate reflections after each meeting as I was too physically exhausted to write. During the semester, I did not even have time to revisit my audiotaped diaries. As for the assignments for the course, early on my students asked me to reduce the number of assignments, which I did because I empathized with their difficulties. In the course, I also assigned an autobiography of one's language learning and teaching journey. I had not realized how difficult it was for busy teachers to sit down and to have some extended period of time to reflect on their language learning and teaching journey until, one day, a student dropped by my office and shared with me her feelings. She said she simply could not get her mind to wind down and have some quiet time to think and write about her past as a learner and teacher.

It seems extremely difficult for women to have the resources (e.g., time, energy, peace of mind, privacy free from interruption of family duties) to engage in critical pedagogic practices. This important aspect of reality faced daily by female education workers, whether in schools or in universities, has been a seldom-talked-of aspect in the critical pedagogy literature. By pointing out these difficulties faced by women in doing critical pedagogies, I hope to raise awareness among the academic circles of the gendered patterns of inequalities in the school as well as in university institutions. I also want to point out that simply producing a critical pedagogic academic literature without also finding ways to address and redress institutionalized gendered forms of domination in which critical pedagogy is implicated and embedded is a very big blind spot that needs to be overcome in the field.

Coda

In this last section of the chapter, I would like to share with the reader some of the psychological difficulties I experienced in writing up this critical reflexive account. I want to problematize my own personal experiences in critical reflexive work and I hope to arrive at some principled understanding of the intimate relation between knowledge and human interests and desires (Habermas, 1987).

Contrary to my past experience in writing academic papers (which are largely nonreflexive – i.e., I researched and analyzed others, not myself), this time I felt an enormous amount of psychological negativities that almost paralyzed me and caused me to suspend writing for long periods of time to deal with them. Exposing one's own mistakes, conflicts, confusions, and dilemmas to the public through writing this critical reflexive account is not only an intellectual task, but also a political action, full of psychological and social risks; however, through learning from my mistakes and explorations in organizing a critical curriculum in an MATESL course, I hope to invite other teacher-educators and teachers to join in the journey of reimagining and working out, at their respective local sites, critical pedagogies specific to, and suitable for, each of our respective contexts.

Appendix: EN6486 language, culture, and education

Course objectives

This course is designed to introduce you to some theoretical concepts and methodological tools in the *anthropology and sociology of education, social linguistics and literacies*, and *ethnography of communication*. The course aims at providing you with a chance to use the concepts and tools learned to critically analyze issues in your own teaching as well as in language education in Hong Kong.

Course materials

Basic Reference Book: Gee, J. P. (1996). *Social linguistics and literacies (2nd Edition)*. London: Taylor & Francis.
A packet of essential readings and weekly lecture handouts and notes.

Course structure

The course is divided into two parts.

Part 1. Background concepts and knowledge (Weeks 1–6)

In the first six weeks of the course, we will focus on five key concepts in James Gee's works. James Gee's works are chosen for this course for the breadth and depth of his discussion of the key topics in language, culture, and education as well as for the useful illustrative examples in his writings. The five key concepts crucial in understanding the inter-relationships of language, culture, and education are laid out as follows:

- language as a set of design resources
- social languages
- situated meanings
- cultural models
- primary and secondary discourses

Intermission: Week 7 – Reading Week/No Classes. You will make use of this time to write an autobiography (approximately 1,500–1,800 words; i.e., 5–6 pages double spaced) of:

- your own language learning experience since childhood, and
- your own journey as a language teacher.

In your autobiography as a language learner and language teacher, *both describe your own experiences and critically reflect on them, drawing on the insights gained from the concepts and knowledge learnt in the previous weeks, as well as your own background and practical knowledge.*

Part 2. Application and Mini-Research Project (Weeks 8–13)

In this part of the course, you will work in pairs, applying the concepts and knowledge learnt, on a self-chosen research topic. The topic can be an issue of interest to you in your own teaching or school, and/or in the language education system in Hong Kong (e.g., critical analysis of textbooks for their hidden perspectives and assumptions regarding gender, race, social class, or other aspects). The instructor will provide some examples of topics to facilitate your thinking, but you are also strongly encouraged to select and develop your own research topic which is of immediate concern and interest to you and your partner. Based on your analysis and findings on your selected topic, *each of you will prepare your own individual project portfolio, which consists of the following two items:*

- Individual *contribution to TESL-HK (A Newsletter for English Language Teaching Professionals in Hong Kong)* – this will be in the format of a nonacademic newsletter article written for other schoolteachers in Hong Kong. You will describe your topic of concern, report on your analysis and findings on the topic, as well as your suggestions and recommendations based on your research insights. Remember to change your academic writing style to a teacher-friendly style and summarize your research findings into a short article for teachers (approximately 900–1,200 words; i.e., 3–4 pages double spaced).

- Individual *letter to the editor* – this will be in the format of a letter to the editor of a major English newspaper in Hong Kong (e.g., South China Morning Post). In the letter, you will describe the issue/problem of concern to you and your views and recommendations based on your analysis/research findings on the topic (300 to 350 words). You can use the newsletter article above as a basis for this letter.

Acknowledgments

I want to thank my students from whom I have learned so much about what it means to maintain a sense of integrity, resilience, and gentle humor under even the most difficult of working conditions. I also want to thank them for kindly allowing me to quote from my conversations with them. Special thanks go to Allan Luke for drawing my attention to the feminist literature. I am also grateful to the editors for allowing me extra time to work on the manuscript. The limitations of this chapter are, however, my own.

Notes

1. Hong Kong people, including teachers and students, seem generally to hold an especially negative notion of politics. To them, political agendas are always dirty and selfish. Their naturalized and technicalized conceptions of education lead them to feel that education should be free of politics (meaning free of political intervention). Educational agendas for promoting social justice and an ethical life are seen as forms of moral education and not political (i.e., not tied to the interests of any political groups, and morality is not seen as political). In this sense, Hong Kong people have developed a special understanding of the word *politics*, one that is different from the way it is used in the critical pedagogy literature. It is in this context that any critical pedagogical courses, to be acceptable to teachers and students, must not have a name that is associated with political actions, although one can include "values education" in the curriculum.
2. All names are pseudonyms.
3. I recently read in the newspaper that teachers in her school have voiced their discontent about being overworked to the Inspectorate of the Education Department of Hong Kong. The news report did not mention any response from the school administration or from the Education Department. My MATESL

course has ended, and I no longer see Emily and cannot find out how the situation is in her school now.

References

Apple, M. W. (1999). *Power, meaning, and identity: Essays in critical educational studies*. New York: Peter Lang.

Carrington, C., & Luke, A. (1997). Literacy and Bourdieu's sociological theory: A reframing. *Language and Education, 11*(2), 96–112.

Ellsworth, E. (1992). Why doesn't this feel empowering? Working through the repressive myths of critical pedagogy. In C. Luke & J. Gore (Eds.), *Feminisms and critical pedagogy* (pp. 90–119). New York: Routledge.

Foucault, M. (1997). *Ethics: Subjectivity and truth*. New York: New Press.

Freire, P. (1968). *Pedagogy of the oppressed* (M. B. Ramos, Trans.). New York: Seabury Press.

Freire, P. (1973). *Education for critical consciousness*. New York: Seabury Press.

Gee, J. P. (1996). *Social linguistics and literacies: Ideology in discourses* (2nd ed.). London: Taylor & Francis.

Glass, R. D. (2001). On Paulo Freire's philosophy of praxis and the foundations of liberal education. *Educational Researcher, 30*(2), 15–25.

Gore, J. M. (1993). *The struggle for pedagogies: Critical and feminist discourses as regimes of truth*. New York: Routledge.

Habermas, J. (1987). *Knowledge and human interests*. Oxford: Polity Press.

Lin, A. M. Y. (1999). Doing-English-lessons in the reproduction or transformation of social worlds? *TESOL Quarterly, 33*(2), 393–412.

Luke, C., & Gore, J. (Eds.). (1992). *Feminisms and critical pedagogy*. New York: Routledge.

Ouyang, H. (2000). One-way ticket: A story of an innovative teacher in Mainland China. *Anthropology and Education Quarterly, 31*(4), 397–425.

Pennycook, A. (1999). Introduction: Critical approaches to TESOL. *TESOL Quarterly, 33*(2), 329–48.

15 Negotiating expertise in an action research community

Kelleen Toohey
Bonnie Waterstone

When teachers talk back to theories, making them "internally persuasive discourse... half ours and half someone else's" (Bakhtin, 1981, pp. 345–346), theories can be dynamic, can lead to productive dialogue and generative reflection. (Ritchie & Wilson, 2000, p. 18)

Introduction

Research collaboration between teachers and academics has recently been advocated not only as a means of producing good educational research, but also as a powerful form of teacher education. In this chapter, we examine some discursive episodes in the research meetings of a group of variously situated educators, a group of which we are members.[1] The group, composed of teachers of children, a video ethnographer, graduate students, and a professor in a faculty of education, is interested in the education of children of diverse language and ability backgrounds. In this chapter, we examine occasions upon which participants in our group talk back to, create, and modify their own and others' theories and knowledge and other occasions that seem to preclude, or at least inhibit, such conversations. In so doing, we hope to understand better how to engage in collaborative research and teacher education in ways that allow for generative dialogue and critical action that leads to classrooms in which children, as well as teachers, are able to talk back and participate in dialogue with their own and others' theories and knowledge.

Collaborative educational research

Including differently situated educators in educational research activities has often been discussed in general educational and, more recently, in second language educational literature (Bailey et al., 1998; Cochran-Smith & Lytle, 1999a, 1999b; Freeman & Johnson, 1998; Nunan, 1992). Teacher and researcher collaborations, for example, have been seen as promoting more complete and nuanced descriptions of classroom events as the perspectives of both teachers and classroom outsiders are available for analysis (Connelly & Clandinin, 1988; Fishman & McCarthy, 2000; Jervis, Carr, Lockhart, & Rogers, 1996; Nunan, 1992; Zeichner & Noffke, 2001). Pappas (1997) argues that collaboration can move teachers from being mere consumers of educational research to becoming participants in knowledge-making about their workplaces, including engagement in dialogue about research methods, agendas, and dissemination. Willinsky (2001) argues that seeing teachers as consumers of educational research has had drastic effects on the quality and accessibility of research knowledge, contributing to the erosion of the public role of research institutions. A more inclusive "public and professional deliberative space" is needed (p. 8), he argues, so that teachers, parents, children, and others might all participate in democratic decision making about schools.

Cochran-Smith and Lytle (1999b) see teacher research as having the potential to undermine the traditional separation "between teachers and researchers, knowers and doers, and experts and novices" (p. 22); they also see such collaborations as taking a critical and political view of education and as committed to a democratic agenda. However, collaborations are often reported as complicated by traditional power/knowledge relations between teachers and university researchers (e.g., Evans, 1998; Moje, 1998). Evans (1998), for example, questions whether equity is possible or even desirable in teacher – researcher collaborations. Even in situations where participants are committed to equity, microanalyses of relationships reveal how power is produced and how it articulates with, and sometimes reinforces, institutional and structural hierarchies (Ilieva & Waterstone, 2001; Moje, 1998).

Critical and political practitioners of teacher–researcher collaboration see their purpose as disrupting business as usual in knowledge-making and school practices, not merely producing a "new canon of best practice" compatible with institutional agendas (Cochran-Smith & Lytle, 1999, p. 21). We align ourselves with those who advocate for teacher–researcher collaborations aimed toward social justice goals and the transformation of knowledge-making practices. While we agree that equity is not simple, we also feel that a pessimism that might close off the possibility for disrupting existing relations is not ethically tenable. Rather than giving up on efforts to create more equitable relationships in classrooms and in research arrangements, we have looked for practices that would allow relationships to be more fluid, rather than becoming static or fixed in one position or another, and for practices that increase the possibilities for diverse participants to share equitably in owning and producing knowledge. This chapter illustrates some of our struggles with that agenda and some of what we are coming to learn about equitable practices in our small knowledge community.

Learning and knowledge communities

Building upon Vygotsky's (1978, 1934/1986) ideas about the sociality of learning, anthropologists Lave and Wenger (1991) argue that "learning, thinking and knowing are relations among people in activity in, with, and arising from the socially and culturally structured world" (p. 51). People in activity with others occupy different positions and many sociocultural theorists and researchers see learning as the appropriation of more expert or old-timer identities within particular communities, with experts and old-timers positioned sometimes by their maturity (adults in relation to children) and sometimes by their experience (Lave & Wenger, 1991; Rogoff, 1990, 1994). Rogoff (1994) writes about a particular educational setting (one using what she terms a "community of learners" approach) in which old-timer or expert identity is less fixed than it might be in more traditional transmissive educational settings. She describes this school as one in which "children learn through participation with adults in community activities" (p. 21) and "both mature members of the community and less mature members... [are] active; no role has all the responsibility for knowing or directing, and no role is by definition passive" (p. 213). In this community of learners, Rogoff argues that such shifting in expertise allows *all* community members to "coordinate with, support and lead others, to become responsible and organized in their management of their own learning, and to be able to build on their inherent interests to learn in new areas and to sustain motivation to learn" (p. 225). From this perspective, when no one has all the responsibility for knowing, when expertise is not static, opportunities for learning seem enhanced.

Jacoby and Gonzalez (1991) also write about a specific community in which expertise is shifting and the relationships between newcomers and novices and old-timers and experts are neither linear nor static. These researchers illustrate in the meetings of a scientific research group how "participants negotiate who is more or less knowing at particular interactional moments" (p. 174). Expert knowledge is assumed by different persons temporarily in ongoing interaction until "some next interactional move either ratifies or rejects [the expertise claimed by any person] in some way" (p. 149). Within the collaborative setting they analyze, the tenured university professor, who is principal investigator of the team's project, sometimes positions himself (and is ratified in this positioning by others) as expert, while at other times (and sometimes even within the same utterance), he positions himself (and is positioned by others) as less knowing, as a novice. Jacoby and Gonzalez query whether our notions of expert–novice relations are sufficiently flexible to account for interactions in such groups:

> Viewing expert-novice as a bipolar dichotomy or as some set of relative statuses to which individuals may be assigned fails to capture both the complexity of what it means to "know things" and the dynamic fluidity of expert-novice relations as they are constituted in unfolding interaction. (p. 152)

This notion of knowing as positioning and as being negotiated dynamically is helpful in understanding much of the data from our research group.

Literary theorist Mikhail Bakhtin (1981) writes explicitly about how participants in discourse position themselves and are positioned by others, and his understandings of discursive positioning are summarized in his dichotomy between *authoritative* and *internally persuasive* discourse. Authoritative discourse, writes Bakhtin, "is indissolubly fused with its authority – with political power, an institution, a person" (p. 343). This type of discourse demands "unconditional allegiance" (p. 342) and talking back to it is difficult. As Bakhtin writes: "One cannot divide it up – agree with one part, accept but not completely another part, reject utterly a third" (p. 343). Nevertheless, argues Bakhtin (p. 345), dispersing and disruptive forces are always present along with authoritative forces, and authoritative discourse is resisted by its opposite, which he terms internally persuasive discourse. Internally persuasive discourse is tentative meaning–exploring dialogue wherein the positioning of interlocutors is flattened, and speakers and listeners are coproducers of, in his words, "ever newer ways to mean" (pp. 345–6).

Jacoby and Gonzalez (1991), Rogoff (1994), and a few others (e.g., Matusov, 1996; Moll, 1992) describe particular communities in which it appears internally persuasive discourse is characteristic, in which expertise seems to shift among participants. In our research group, we have discussed what changes in pedagogical practices would be required so as to keep expertise flowing, rather than fixed, in classrooms so as to meet some of our goals for increasing the equity in those classrooms. In these imagined classrooms, everyone would sometimes have the possibility for participation from a position of *knowing more*, not only those who might be institutionally and culturally positioned as *expert*. Speaking about the (often unrecognized) cultural wealth children of diverse backgrounds bring from their homes and communities, Delpit (1995) argues, "Teachers must . . . learn about the brilliance the students bring with them 'in their blood'" (p. 182). We are similarly interested in students' brilliance and, as a group of differently situated educators, we have taken on the task of recognizing one another's brilliance as well. We hope that by examining how we negotiate expertise within our own adult discursive practices, we might be able to understand better what classroom discursive practices create shifting possibilities for children to occupy and display expertise, thereby creating more equitable learning opportunities for all children (Denos et al., 2001; Waterstone, 2000, 2001, 2003). Bonnie has elsewhere observed that teachers who would teach with the openness, play, and appreciation of ambivalence that characterize internally persuasive discourse need to experience that model themselves (Waterstone, 2001), and in our analysis, here, we aim to understand some of the characteristics of situations that allow adults to talk back and to engage in productive dialogue and generative reflection. Our research group is aimed at providing that experience for ourselves and for self-reflexively analyzing our practices as a community of learners, teachers, and researchers.

The Teacher Action Research Group

The research of this group, the Teacher Action Research Group (TARG), began in September 1999 when Kelleen Toohey invited six teachers and three graduate students to join a group that would be concerned, she then wrote, with "investigating what practices in classrooms might make a difference to the learning of minority language background children." Kelleen knew three of the teachers previously from a course she had taught, and the others were nominated by colleagues she contacted to ask for names of "experienced, interested teachers who had learners of English in their classrooms." Three of the original teachers continued doing directed readings courses with her (through the activities of the group) for the first year of meetings. TARG began with a type of book club format; participants read and discussed several educational research articles and two books (*You Can't Say You Can't Play* by Vivian Paley, 1992, and *Learning English at School: Identity, Social Relations and Classroom Practice* by Kelleen Toohey, 2000). In January 2000, the focus shifted to initiating individual research projects, the data for which the teachers would collect in their individual classrooms. With ethical approvals for observation, the teachers began audiotaping selected activities in their classrooms. In addition, again with ethical approval, an experienced video ethnographer from the university began videotaping in the classrooms and she joined the group as a regular participant in the weekly meetings. Bonnie audiotaped all meetings of the group and transcribed them. She also prepared weekly notes of the highlights of the weekly discussions for subsequent distribution to members of the group.

From January to June 2000, we collaborated on the individual research projects in each classroom. The teachers decided individually to focus on points such as (a) identity practices in schools and in research, (b) power negotiations in classrooms and research, and (c) membership in school and research communities. With respect to identity, the research team examined conflict and affiliation as means children use to exert agency in their positioning. With respect to power, researchers have sought to develop, document, and critically analyze practices of resistance to normalized distribution of resources in the project's classrooms, in part, by trying to shift centers of expertise to provide spaces for children otherwise dominated to become classroom experts. With respect to community membership, the teacher-researchers have asked questions about how classrooms might function as inclusive communities as well as how membership in classroom and school communities might be extended to include families. The team documented and critically analyzed its efforts in this regard.

Videos of classroom interactions were brought to the group and discussed; research problems and dilemmas were talked through and research questions refined. In May of our first year, we gave our first presentation as a group on our research in progress. Over the summer, we met less frequently as a group, but worked in groups of two (graduate student and teacher) to write up the research projects into publishable journal articles. In September 2000, we began with new classrooms and new research plans, building on the previous year's research. Throughout the second year, we continued to meet weekly to develop and discuss individual research projects as well as group presentations.

Over the four years of its existence, TARG has developed its own discursive history of reading and talking about theory; telling stories about our classrooms, personal lives, and research experiences; and thinking together about dilemmas and issues that arise in our research projects. As our conversations interweave issues, stories, and theories, we have a sense of being of use to each other – our differences are valuable. Bonnie described our group as experiencing "shifting centers of expertise" (Waterstone, 2000) as we considered research and classroom issues. Our conversations are respectful and engaging. In one-on-one interviews in September and October 2000, teachers characterized the group as "welcoming and warm" (Donna), "comfortable" and with a "flexible" structure (Kari; Sharon), someplace "I looked forward to going every week" (Marcy), and as an exciting and intense learning experience (Katerina). Laughter is frequent. Participants finish one another's sentences, murmur noises of agreement while others are talking, and have developed a kind of discourse ethic in which problems participants present to the group, whether pedagogical or research oriented, are seriously considered. We have come to see ourselves as a "speaking collective" and see Bakhtin's (1981) description of the social life of such collectives as particularly apt in describing our experience:

> The more intensive, differentiated and highly developed the social life of a speaking collective, the greater is the importance attaching, among other possible subjects of talk, to another's word, another's utterance, since another's word will be the subject of passionate communication, an object of interpretation, discussion, evaluation, rebuttal, support, further development and so on. (p. 337)

As our data will show, our discussions of one another's utterances *are* the subjects of passionate communication. In this chapter, we discuss three episodes of interaction, two in January 2000 and the other in August 2000, in which we focus on conversations that demonstrate how our discursive practices both constrain and enable possibilities for an open negotiation of participants as more or less knowing.

The participants

The members of TARG as of January 2000 were all women, all (except Sharon) over thirty years of age, and all (except Sharon) had more than ten years teaching or university experience. Participants at that time were:

Donna:[2] Elementary school teacher – this year, a Grade 2–3 split class with several special needs children; European heritage, born in Canada
Katerina: English as a second language (ESL) specialist for a school district; European heritage, born in Canada
Kari: Elementary school teacher – this year, a Grade 3 class; Punjabi heritage, born in Canada
Marcy: Elementary school teacher – this year, a kindergarten–Grade 1 split class; European/American heritage, born in the United States
Kelleen: University professor who initiated the group; European heritage, born in Canada
Bonnie: Doctoral student (supervisor: Kelleen); European heritage, born in the United States
Rossi: Doctoral student (supervisor: Kelleen); East European heritage, born in Bulgaria
Sharon: Elementary school teacher – this year, a Grade 2–3 split; Punjabi heritage, born in Canada

The conversations

The first two linked conversations we analyze here took place in January 2000. At this point, we were beginning to think about research questions, about what the teachers would like to investigate in their classrooms. On January 20, 2000, we were talking about Donna's ideas for research in her classroom. Katerina, Donna, Marcy, and Kelleen speak in this conversation; Rossi, Sharon, and Bonnie are listening. Influenced by the autumn's reading and discussion of complex social practices in classroom communities, Donna's research questions center around how to create an inclusive community and what effect her attempts might have. She had brought three pages of writing that described the issues she was concerned with – that is, how she should encourage a community of learners in her classroom "that encompasses those who have been positioned or position themselves on the margins?" She also wondered, "As a teacher, am I getting my message across? Do the children believe in my vision of community?" In the following excerpt, Katerina had just asked Donna to explain more about how she would find out whether the children share her vision of community: "Like are you going to have some discussions around it?"

1.

Donna: Yeah, I think we've done a lot of talking. I think we've done a lot of different discussions. I guess what I, like this is sort of the rough draft, I guess I want to somehow see whether they get it, like it makes sense to them, if it's something that they want as part of their life, if it's something that works for them or if they're just sort of going along with [with the ride

Katerina: (*interjecting*): [What you're saying

Donna: (*continues, talking over*): And not that it's good or bad, I mean everybody has a choice to their own, um, belief system. But whether the discussions that we've had, the things that we've done in the classroom, has had any impact on the way they look at P. [the blind student in her class]. The way they look at other kids in the class. Or whether it's just something you do in the classroom and you sort of let go of it when Mrs. C's not looking. I dunno.

Marcy: So you're looking at the degree to which the discussions that you have with the kids are reflected in their behavior (*pause*) or in what they say

Donna: Yeah

Marcy: [In what they say to each other when you're not listening

Donna: [In what they say (*slowly spoken, covers same time as longer sentence above, then Donna continues*) Yeah, and how they treat, in their discussions with each other.

Kelleen: And to make it sort of technical or la-di-da: have they appropriated this language, like Bakhtin talked about. So that it's not just a ventriloquation of your words, but that it really is part of their perspective. (*Donna saying* "Yeah, yeah" *in background*)

Donna: umhum (*pause, begins to say* "It might" *but Kelleen already talking*)

Kelleen: Yeah, Bakhtin makes it so abstract and you're asking for, you know, can this perspective that I'm trying to develop, can it be appropriated, and what does that mean, what does that look like?

Marcy: (*in background*) What does it involve?
Donna: And if it is, my step further would be, okay what is it that's happening that's making it work. And is that a transferable thing to other groups . . . (*she continues here*)

In this excerpt, Donna is refining her research inquiry. In her words, she will find out if she is "getting her message across," by observing videotapes of what the students say to each other and how they treat each other in peer-mediated discussions. We see Marcy rephrasing Donna's explanation in a way that Donna takes up. In fact, the two teachers speak a phrase in unison. Donna keeps talking about her research interest and doesn't seem to stop to object to or ponder the theoretical language Kelleen offers. Nevertheless, she *is* interested in theory: "What is it that's happening that's making it work. And is that a transferable thing to other groups." As the transcript from next week's talk will show, Donna's response to Kelleen's rephrasing, her "Yeah, yeah" in the background while Kelleen speaks, and her "umhum" do not unambiguously represent acceptance of the rephrase.

A week later, on January 27, 2000, TARG was again discussing ideas for one of the members' research projects: this time, Katerina's ideas. The others who participate in this exchange are Donna, Sharon, Kelleen, and Rossi, listening are Kari and Bonnie. Katerina has presented the idea that she will videotape students in her ESL/Special Needs class talking about this class. She wants them "to be able to articulate what they're doing in the program to visitors. . . . Do they see their classroom as a series of learning centers or areas? . . . I want to look at their language . . . [do they have] the power of language, I don't know."

2.

Donna: Do you want to find out whether the language they use belongs to them, like if it's
Rossi: Appropriated (*softly finishes Donna's sentence*)
Katerina: Well, yeah [but
Donna: [I had an interesting, just driving home last week when we were talking about my question and I don't tend to talk in really academic type language. It was interesting because Kelleen very helpfully reworded what I had said her way. (*Whole group laughs*) Those aren't my words. And yes, it sounded great and wonderful but I won't be using those words now. I might, maybe next year, but right now they are not my words, and it doesn't have
Sharon: You're not connected?
Donna: It doesn't come from my heart. Um, I'm wondering, I think that's the feeling I got with what you're [Katerina] wanting. [*for the kids to explain*] Is this my room? Can I explain it from me?

Katerina: Yes, I want that
Donna: What it is, not just (*Katerina says* "Yes" *in background*) parrot what the adults are saying

Many interactions take place in this small excerpt. First, Donna asks Katerina a question about the purpose of her research to help her focus on what she hopes to gain from it. Donna briefly pauses without finishing her sentence, and two quickly but softly spoken interjections take place. Rossi offers a word to end the sentence, a word from academic language, from the Bakhtinian theory we have occasionally discussed. However, this is perhaps not heard. In any case, Donna goes on to explain further, and "appropriated" does not remain as the final, explanatory word for her. Katerina, who has been explaining her concept for a while, seems to want to continue. Donna has more to say, more to explain, and continues talking over both Rossi's and Katerina's more softly spoken words. What Donna does is tell a story about her own experience in this teacher research group. She refers to last week's discussion (on January 20) when we had all been offering her feedback on her research ideas. She remembers how Kelleen had reworded what she was saying and how she did not feel ownership of the academic language used in Kelleen's translation. Sharon seems to follow what Donna is saying carefully, and when Donna pauses very briefly, she offers a question that seems to indicate she is understanding and agreeing. Donna seems to appreciate this scaffolding from Sharon and is able to state simply "It doesn't come from my heart" and finish there.

In Rossi's softly spoken "appropriated," in Kelleen's original rewording, and also in the "Notes" Bonnie prepared of the January 20 exchange, the three university-based members of the group were ready to offer Bakhtin's words – authoritative discourse – to Donna. The Notes translate what both Donna and Kelleen had said into text and suggest the multiple ways of talking about the issue at hand:

> Donna is interested in whether the children in her class are, in Bakhtin's terms, appropriating or merely ventriloquating a vision of community. Are they performing a script for the teacher, or is their behavior coming from the heart? (TARG Notes, January 20, 2000)

Including this exchange in the Notes and reiterating the Bakhtinian concepts can also be seen as an attempt to scaffold the use of this academic language for the group as a whole. In Donna's story told about her reflection about Kelleen's rephrasing, she rejects the Bakhtinian terminology. She says, "Those aren't my words." However, she continues to pursue the problem of how something (a sense of belonging and community) might become internally persuasive (how might children speak and act "from the heart").[3]

Through the summer of 2000, our focus shifted from collecting and analyzing classroom data to writing up the first year's research projects. Teachers had been bringing memos, drafts of research questions, and ideas in writing throughout the sessions from January to June 2000; however, now our goal changed to producing a particular product. Some of the teachers, Donna among them, were receiving university course credit for this summer writing project.[4] Kelleen believed that the teachers were asking important research questions, that they had collected (with the help of the video ethnographer) high quality video and audiotaped data, and that the analyses they had discussed in the group were sufficiently interesting that the final projects could (and should) be publishable. Two models were presented and discussed in June – an academic article and a professional teacher article. Bonnie and Rossi (doctoral students who have had fairly extensive experience with a variety of research projects, chapter, and paper publication) continued their employment as research assistants to help the teachers with writing these papers as Kelleen felt that scaffolding the writing of these products with the help of the graduate students would be a good way to benefit from the differentiated expertise of the group. Through July, teachers met one-on-one with either Rossi or Bonnie to get assistance with writing their papers. In the half day group meetings on August 3 and August 17, we read and discussed the draft papers as a group. On August 17, Donna brought a second draft of her paper. Rossi, who had had two opportunities to meet with Donna briefly in July, had not seen or commented on this latest draft and was not present. Donna had pulled together a powerful story of the year in her class, asking the questions she had articulated in January – how do inclusive classrooms operate and what makes an ethic of inclusion transferable to other classrooms? After we individually read her paper, the first response was acclaim:

3.

Bonnie: I thought wow! (*whole group laughs*) (*3 second pause*)
Marcy: It's great. I, I, just, from the beginning to the end. And I, I think, um, that the changes in the beginning were really effective. I think when you, um, when you talked about your background in Social Development, it just put the *whole* thing, the whole thing, into perspective and it just made all of it make sense.[5] [*3 second pause*]
Kari: I think when you read it, you want to be in your, *we* want to be in your classroom (*chuckle*)
Marcy: umhum. Umhum, yeah. It's a wonderful picture of a [classroom, you can just feel it
Donna: [umhum

Immediately after this acclaim, Kelleen and Bonnie told Donna how they thought the paper might need to be changed for publication. At this point in the discussion, the two university-based members present took turns, for almost seven minutes (6.6) of talk, offering suggestions:

4.

Bonnie: The details really helped, you added all kinds of details? [*rising intonation*] that really helped. (*unclear*) Like, I noticed that on page 9, you know and there's lots of, lots of places. (*2 second pause, sound of pages turning*) One thing I did notice is, um, some repetition, which I think you can, um you can take out. Umm, what, what seemed to happen is that every now and then we'd go, you know, back to some quotes of stuff? (*rising intonation – her turn is not finished*)
Donna: (*quietly in background*) Right.
Bonnie: And sometimes those were repeating [So that's probably just an
Donna: (*quietly*) [Okay
Bonnie: organizational thing. (*2 second pause*)
Kelleen: I, um, yeah, I really like it too. And I find, I found the ending just works beautifully. (*someone in background, high tone: umhum!*) The story about the kids looking at you defiantly works very nicely. I think now that there's a couple of ways you could go with this, Donna. I'm thinking, in this kind of, like you've woven together the theory and the description and the stories very, very nicely, and beyond a little bit of um, uh, uh, repetition, which as [unclear] I think would be easily cleaned up. It's a little bit of a different structure than a normal, uh, journal article. I really like it the way it is because you know it does, it gives you this really rich picture of some place you wanna be [*chuckles*] and so, you know, so that's one side of my head is saying leave it. You know, it's got this coherence to it that's really, really nice. And then the other side of my head is saying, 'okay for *publication*,
[what you have to have is a problem statement (*list intonation*)
Donna: (*quiet*) [umhum
Kelleen: Theoretical background, a description of the action or the treatment or whatever, and a conclusion. You know, and so you'll pull all the theory into one part and you'll, do you see what I mean?
Donna: Umhum.
Kelleen: And, and I guess, the other thing that you would do then is take some of the evaluative statements you have made about what happens as a result of this activity in the classroom, take that out and put it in the conclusion. Rather than as you're telling the story? (*rising intonation*)
Donna: (*quiet*) Okay.
Kelleen: Well, but I don't know what to do, I don't quite know what to do and I don't know what other people think about that either.
Donna: (*barely audible*) umhum (*2 second pause*)

Kelleen's presentation of herself as uncertain ("but I don't know what to do") and invitation to others to speak was taken up by Bonnie, who then went on to suggest a variety of ways that Donna could revise her paper in line with the suggestions Kelleen had just made. Bonnie offered to go through the paper and sort out which were data statements and which were evaluative statements. Kelleen then suggested that Donna already knew what her problem statement was and that with a "little reorganization, it would look more like a typical journal article."

In this excerpt, the first positive response to Donna's paper as a "wonderful picture of a classroom" seems to get buried in many long minutes of directive suggestions from both Kelleen and Bonnie about changes needed if the paper is to be published. Kelleen presents her suggestions as coming from two different points of view ("one side of my head . . . and then the other"). But since the task has been assigned as writing a publishable article, one might surmise that her experience in this area adds weight to her suggestions. Also, the task is done for credit, and Kelleen can grant or refuse to grant the credit. Bonnie assumes the position of intermediary and attempts to explain how the changes Kelleen has listed could be implemented and adds to the overall effect of a researcher-expertise monologue on improving Donna's paper. Donna's relative silence in this section of the interaction is ambiguous: It could be interpreted as acquiescence to the researchers' assumption of positions of expertise, or it could be seen as resistance. Bonnie then expressed sympathy for the amount of work this might be for Donna and Donna replied with the first sentence since the discussion of her paper started:

5.

Donna: Yeah, I get lost in all the pages and I don't know, I guess it's lack of experience.

Bonnie: Well, but look at how many pages you're dealing with (*Kelleen in background*: Yeah). I mean that's a lot of pages, I mean, I find too when I'm writing a long article it just feels like whoa! (*background, can hear Marcy begin to speak*)

Kelleen: Yeah it's [unclear] long. Marcy?

Marcy: Uh, there were just, (*sound of pages turning*) one was just a comment, oh I just, on page, um, 10. I just was reimpressed over again, and this is what I've, I keep reading this as a teacher and having been involved in training teachers for a long time. I still read things as if I were a student teacher or I was thinking about giving it to a student teacher. And this is what I just keep wanting to hit student teachers over the head with (*pause*), um, that

Katerina: No hitting (*whole group laughs*)

Marcy: Uh, 'that it comes with a true belief' – that's where the difference is. I mean people can read all the methods and strategies in the world, but unless they *really believe* down in their *guts* that each person in the community is valued, and stuff, that's where the difference in somebody's, versus your [Donna's] classroom and somebody else's comes in. It comes in there. And I just, I feel like always underlining that, it's so incredibly important. Um, I found from that perspective, of reading it as a teacher, and someone who's interested in training teachers, that the way it was written in a very personal way is really inspirational. (*Kelleen in background*: Yeah). And um being not a very, there must be some kind of places where you can publish this kind of stuff where, you know, your average run of the mill classroom teacher will read it. (*laughs several voices in background; Kelleen:* Yeah) You know, and be inspired by it and say, yes this is the kind of classroom I wish I had. Um, and if it gets too journalized up then it's not going to be read by those people (*Kelleen*: Yeah, yeah). Um, and I don't know about publications for teachers, I don't, maybe they don't read them, magazines, or I don't know where you get things like that published.

Kelleen: What do you read?

Marcy: You read the, that Teacher thing [magazine] that comes from the BCTF.[6] Umhum. (*pause*) You read it during silent reading usually one day. (*whole group laughter begins at silent reading*)

Donna's comment, "Yeah, I get lost in all the pages and I don't know, I guess it's lack of experience," explicitly names her as a novice in this task. However, after the researcher-expertise monologue (two voices, same theme), Marcy returns to the earlier assessment of Donna's paper as valuable for teachers and advocates for it to remain as is even though she doesn't know where it might be published. As the discussion continues, the problem of a publication venue or how to reach teachers and student teachers is not resolved, with one participant suggesting the group do a presentation for student teachers, Donna saying she will revise the paper with Bonnie's help, the group mulling over the idea of leaving the paper as it is and putting it into a book collection, and so on. No decision was reached.

Discussion

There are myriad examples through the data in which we observe the shifting of expertise, and we continue to observe dynamism in this matter as the group continues to meet. We are particularly interested in the episodes here as examples of interactions in which the issue of expertise seems particularly salient. The episodes analyzed here concern two very different tasks occurring at different times in the group's life. In the January excerpts, the tasks, analyzing classroom dilemmas and developing research questions, directly arise from life in specific classrooms. Teachers whose days are spent in those classrooms and who have the responsibility for framing useful questions about their classrooms have, therefore, acknowledged expertise. Within this activity, Donna speaks with conviction and passion and forcefully talks back, rejecting the theoretical language offered to her. In this situation, Donna does not constitute herself as less knowing – although perhaps as knowing differently.

The Bakhtinian language offered her perhaps does not seem to "do enough." Aoki (2000) reminds us that language is structured so that meanings always remain open, and whether we in the group grapple with Donna's questions using the theoretical word ("appropriated") the plain language words ("from the heart"), the concepts remain complex. Donna says, in effect, that Bakhtin's word, appropriated, is fine, but it's not her word, and she wants to ask more questions that the word does not address: She wants to know if her students believe "in their hearts" in an inclusive classroom, what was it that made them embrace this belief, and can whatever it is that encouraged their acceptance be transferred to other situations?

In the August excerpt, Donna is presenting a written draft – the results of her first year's research, a paper that she has been assigned, with the stakes somewhat higher than for a regular course as this is framed as being a *publishable* paper. In this situation, with this task, the expertise of those more familiar with the production of knowledge for publication in educational journals seemed, for a time, to take precedence. "Publishable" to the university-based researchers meant written in a form intelligible and recognizable as valid within academic discourse communities. Academic discourse can be seen as a heavily policed mode with particular limitations on how and what one can or cannot write (Stein, 1999, p. 62). This writing task also articulated with the institutional power of the university because, despite the flexibility and responsiveness of the course, it fits within the individualizing and ranking system of granting or withholding course credit. In this situation, expertise seems somewhat stuck or fixed in the authority of academic researchers who are affiliated with the university and who can claim membership in a community of "persons who have been published." While the authoritative discourse of distant judges of the worth of one's writing (editors, for example) might be delivered kindly, helpfully, and maybe even tentatively by local interlocutors, nevertheless, the "authoritative word demands that we acknowledge it, that we make it our own; it binds us; the authoritative word is located in a distanced zone" (Bakhtin, 1981, p. 342). As Bakhtin predicts, however, authoritative discourse is resisted. At the same time that TARG members were "speaking as" or "speaking for" editors and university professors who can grant credit, Marcy (who identifies herself twice, as "a teacher and having been involved in training teachers for a long time") advocates for Donna's paper to remain as is, "a wonderful picture of a classroom" that is important for teachers to read. This counter-discourse rests on the affective power of Donna's inspirational story of a year in a classroom and its usefulness for teachers in their practice. Interestingly, in this situation, however, it is not Donna who "talks back," although she shows earlier in the group's life that she *can* talk back, grapple with dilemmas, and raise theoretical questions. In this interaction, her coparticipant, Marcy, does the talking back. Marcy states that if Donna's paper gets "too journalized up" (the direction is interesting), it won't be read by the right people.

Rogoff (1994) and others (Moll, 1992) tell us that well-functioning communities of learners utilize community resources, including differential expertise as well as material resources. We see interactions in such communities as characterized by a flow of internally persuasive discourse that enables multiple kinds of knowing and fluid identifications. We have not already mentioned issues of representation of knowledge, but Marcy's comment about "journalizing" brings this to the fore. Research collaboration between differently situated educators begs the question of how the diverse expertise of differentiated groups might be represented. As we see in the examples, the activities in which participants in a community are involved have a great deal to do with how participants are positioned. When participants are positioned so that their expertise is relevant, then they are able to speak from positions of knowing. Our further question now has to do with how knowing is represented. Our experiences in our group have led us to consider questions like, What should collaborative research groups produce? What difference does it make to produce an educational research journal article as opposed to something else? Should collaborative research groups see the major audience for their work as teachers, or academics, or both?

One tentative answer to these questions might consider how a journal article represents certain kinds of experiences in particular ways, whereas in "something else" perhaps other kinds of experience may be able to be represented in other ways. Pippa Stein (1999), writing from a post-apartheid South African context where the representation of "fear, violation, pain and loss" is integral to a political project of restoring balance, points to the "limits of language in expressing the arc of human experience" (p. 62). Both Donna's refusal to accept Bakhtin's term as encompassing dilemmas arising from her teaching and Marcy's advocacy that Donna's paper not get "too journalized up" suggest that the complexities, the immediacy, and the particularity of teachers' experiences in classrooms may not be easily captured by a traditional academic journal article form and language. Indeed, when we submitted a paper written collaboratively by Kari and Rossi to a call for teacher research, the editors requested revisions that suggested that readers of this genre have different expectations:

> With teacher research it is typical to begin with a classroom story or vignette that represents what set the stage for the inquiry.... The manuscript needs to move between theory and practice more... reflecting on what you believe and

are thinking about theoretically as it relates to these events in your classroom. (T. Smiles, personal communication, May 2, 2001)

Readers of this genre would not be likely to wade through a theory section in the beginning of the article, but to prefer theory to be woven together with stories of classroom events (T. Smiles, personal communication, May 2, 2001). The university-based members of TARG may be limited by our disposition toward (or at least tolerance of) long theoretical passages and our desire to map the field and our place in it through scholarly references. In writing successful articles that artfully blend narrative with analysis, telling dramatic stories of classroom incidents *and* demonstrating theoretical and/or educational policy implications, a collaborative effort that respects both ways of knowing is needed (Fishman & McCarthy, 2000).

Conclusion

What does this analysis tell us about our initial question about how university researchers and teachers might together engage in mutually helpful projects and how research practices might be arranged so that sites of expertise in them shift continually? We now realize that practices within knowledge–research communities such as ours have the potential to restrict or enliven possibilities for shifting sites of expertise. We agree with Evans (1998) that within collaborative work, "power will always exist regardless of equity in relationships. Perhaps the more productive question to ask is, what are we going to do about it?" (p. 23). As we trace the circulation of power within our collaborative group, we note our ethic of equity and "what we do about" power: what practices we engage in that seem to reproduce, affiliate with, or maintain existing hierarchies of knowledge and what practices we engage in seem to allow for different and alternative possibilities.

We have learned through this process that the knowledge-making and knowledge-representing practices in collaborative groups are crucially important in creating dialogic possibilities in them. The question of who can claim the power to speak "research," where, and to whom has branched out into further questions as we realize that such power changes depending on the audiences and purposes of different kinds of research. The university-based members have come to see more clearly our own positions as novices in understanding how to represent knowledge in ways useful to practicing teachers. As more commonly readers of research-oriented literature, we are not as familiar with nor proficient in producing text or knowledge representations that will be internally persuasive to practicing teachers who may have little time to read research literature. Without our efforts to acknowledge multiple sites of expertise and to reflect on how expertise shifts or gets stuck in our collaboration, we might not have realized what we did not understand. By attempting to keep the flow of multiple kinds of expertise sparking between us, we hope to continue to open up to a playful and dynamic interaction where "internally persuasive" discourse "enters into interanimating relationships with new contexts... [revealing] ever newer *ways to mean* (Bakhtin, 1981, pp. 345–6) that draw out the "brilliance" each of us brings to the table from our diverse backgrounds.

Notes

1. A version of this paper was presented at the 2001 meeting of the American Educational Research Association. The research on which it is based is supported by a Standard Research Grant from the Social Sciences and Humanities Research Council of Canada to the first author.
2. All names of participants are pseudonyms except for Kelleen's and Bonnie's.
3. As we were composing this chapter, we discussed these excerpts with Donna. Now a master's student, she added that this was an example of her ongoing struggle with academic discourse.
4. The coursework some of the teachers were engaged in was part of a postbaccalaureate program for teachers offered at the university. These courses are designed to be much more flexible and responsive to practicing teachers' individual needs than regular courses might sometimes be, and they are ungraded – participants either pass or are asked to complete their work differently. The tasks of each course are normally individually negotiated between the professor and the student and were, in this case, negotiated between Kelleen and the group. The teachers' year-long attendance at TARG's meetings and their dedicated contributions to the work of the group were seen by Kelleen as over and above normal coursework requirements. This is a long way of saying that granting credit to these participants for their contributions was never a question, in Kelleen's eyes, at least.
5. Donna had taught for many years in a program in which children who had difficulties in regular classrooms were taught by specialist social development teachers in discrete classrooms. Donna had taught in these classrooms for many years but had recently become convinced that these children would be better served in regular classrooms in their home schools.
6. The British Columbia Teachers Federation.

References

Aoki, D. S. (2000). The thing never speaks for itself: Lacan and the pedagogical politics of clarity. *Harvard Educational Review*, *70*(3), 347–69.

Bailey, K., Hawkins, M., Irujo, S., Larsen-Freeman, D., Rintell, E., & Willett, J. (1998). Language teacher educators collaborative conversations. *TESOL Quarterly*, *32*(2), 536–45.

Bakhtin, M. (1981). *The dialogic imagination: Four essays by M. M. Bakhtin.* Austin: University of Texas Press.

Cochran-Smith, M., & Lytle, S. (1999a). Relationships of knowledge and practice: Teacher learning in communities. *Review of Research in Education, 24*, 251–307. Washington DC: American Educational Research Association.

Cochran-Smith, M., & Lytle, S. (1999b). The teacher research movement: A decade later. *Educational Researcher, 28*(7), 15–25.

Connelley, F. M., & Clandinin, D. J. (1988). *Teachers as curriculum planners: Narratives of experience.* New York: Teachers College Press.

Delpit, L. (1995). *Other people's children: Cultural conflict in the classroom.* New York: New Press.

Denos, C., Hof, L., Ilieva, R., Rowbotham, S., Sandhu, S., Toohey, K., Thompson, J., Tsoukalas, C., & Waterstone, B. (2001, April). *Shifting centers of expertise: Diversity in classroom and research communities.* Symposium conducted at the meeting of the American Educational Research Association, Seattle, WA.

Evans, K. S. (1998, April). *Negotiating roles in collaborative research: Rexamining issues of power and equity.* Paper presented at the meeting of the American Educational Research Association, San Diego, CA.

Fishman, S. M., & McCarthy, L. (2000). *Unplayed tapes: A personal history of collaborative teacher research.* New York: Teachers College Press.

Freeman, D., & Johnson, K. (1998). Reconceptualizing the knowledge-base of language teacher education. *TESOL Quarterly, 32*(3), 397–418.

Ilieva, R., & Waterstone, B. (2001). "Tell us more, don't talk about it": Contradictory economies of immigrant and queer identity performance in academia. *Journal of Curriculum Theorizing, 17*(1), 107–19.

Jacoby, S., & Gonzales, P. (1991). The constitution of expert-novice in scientific discourse. *Issues in Applied Linguistics, 2*(2), 149–81.

Jervis, K., Carr, E., Lockhart, P., & Rogers, J. (1996). Multiple entries to teacher inquiry: Dissolving boundaries between research and teaching. In L. Baker, P. Afflerbach, & D. Reinking (Eds.), *Developing engaged readers in school and home communities* (pp. 247–68). Mahwah, NJ: Lawrence Erlbaum Associates.

Lave, J., & Wenger, E. (1991). *Situated learning: Legitimate peripheral participation.* Cambridge, England: Cambridge University Press.

Matusov, E. (1996). Intersubjectivity without agreement. *Mind, Culture, and Activity, 3*(1), 25–45.

Moje, E. B. (1998, April). *Changing our minds, changing our bodies: Power as embedded in research relations.* Paper presented at the meeting of the American Educational Research Association Annual, San Diego, CA.

Moll, L. (1992). Bilingual classroom studies and community analysis: Some recent trends. *Educational Researcher, 21*, 20–4.

Nunan, D. (1992). *Research methods in language learning.* Cambridge, England: Cambridge University Press.

Paley, V. G. (1992). *You can't say you can't play.* Cambridge, MA: Harvard University Press.

Pappas, C. (1997). Making "collaboration" problematic in collaborative school-university research: Studying with urban teacher researchers to transform literacy curriculum genres. In J. Flood, S. B. Heath, & D. Lapp (Eds.), *Handbook of research on teaching literacy through the communicative and visual arts* (pp. 215–31). London: Macmillan.

Ritchie, J. S., & Wilson, D. E. (2000). *Teacher narrative as critical inquiry: Rewriting the script.* New York: Teachers College Press.

Rogoff, B. (1990). *Apprenticeship in thinking: Cognitive development in social context.* New York: Oxford University Press.

Rogoff, B. (1994). Developing understanding of the idea of communities of learners. *Mind, Culture, and Activity, 1*(4), 209–29.

Stein, P. (1999). Drawing the unsayable: Cannibals, sexuality and multimodality in a Johannesburg classroom. *Perspectives in Education, 18*(2), 61–82.

Toohey, K. (2000). *Learning English at school: Identity, social relations, and classroom practice.* Clevedon, England: Multilingual Matters.

Vygotsky, L. S. (1978). *Mind in society: The development of higher psychological processes.* Cambridge, MA: Harvard University Press.

Vygotsky, L. S. (1986). *Thought and language* (A. Kozulin, Trans.). Cambridge, MA: MIT Press. (Original work published 1934.)

Waterstone, B. (2000, March). *Developing dialogues between practitioners and researchers.* Paper presented at the meeting of Teaching English to Speakers of Other Languages (TESOL), Vancouver, British Columbia, Canada.

Waterstone, B. (2001, February). *More than just "inclusion": The interanimation of difference in Bakhtin's dialogic.* Paper presented at the meeting of the National Council of Teachers of English Assembly for Research, Berkeley, CA.

Waterstone, B. (2003). *Self, genre, community: Negotiating the landscape of a teacher/researcher collaboration.* Unpublished doctoral dissertation, Simon Fraser University, Burnaby, British Columbia, Canada.

Willinsky, J. (2001). The strategic education research program and the public value of research. *Educational Researcher, 30*(1), 5–14.

Zeichner, K. M., & Noffke, S. E. (2001). Practitioner research. In V. Richardson (Ed.), *Handbook of research on teaching* (4th ed.). Washington, DC: American Educational Research Association.

16 *Performed ethnography for critical language teacher education*

Tara Goldstein

Introduction

Conceptualizing and implementing teacher education programming for teachers who work with students who do not use the school's language of instruction as their primary language is a complex task. At the heart of such programming, we usually find a set of courses that examine such topics as the teaching of listening, speaking, reading, and writing skills; content-based language teaching; curriculum planning; classroom management; and evaluation strategies. Increasingly, these methodology courses also include observation of and reflection on language classrooms, peer teaching with feedback, and cooperative learning activities. However, what isn't often discussed is the impact that the arrival of second or other language students has on a school's linguistic, cultural, and learning environment outside the language classroom or the linguistic and racial tensions that sometimes arise as these students attempt to integrate into the school community.

Responding to changes in the school learning environment and linguistic and racial tensions between students is not easy, and school staff members often turn to their language teachers to help them think about effective ways of moving forward. This chapter is about preparing language teachers to respond effectively to the complexities of working across linguistic, cultural, and racial differences in multilingual schools so that they can show leadership around such issues as language choice, linguistic discrimination, and racism. In thinking about how to prepare my own teacher education students for this kind of leadership, I have begun to experiment with ethnographic playwriting and performed ethnography. This has meant writing up some of the ethnographic data I have collected on the issues of language choice and linguistic and racial tensions at school in the form of a play, which is then read or performed by my teacher education students.[1]

I begin this chapter by describing my first critical ethnographic play, "Hong Kong, Canada," and discussing the ways performed ethnography promotes critical teacher development around issues of linguistic difference. "Hong Kong, Canada" is based on findings from a four-year critical ethnographic case study (1996–2000) of an English-speaking Canadian high school that had recently enrolled a large number of immigrant students from Hong Kong.[2] The arrival of these students, many of whom chose to speak Cantonese at the school, had an impact on the school's linguistic and cultural environment and ways teachers and students traditionally worked together. There were a variety of new issues and dilemmas for teachers and students to think through and negotiate, and my play, "Hong Kong, Canada," attempts to represent some of them.[3]

After providing a brief synopsis and several excerpts from the play, I describe several of the pedagogical activities I have used with "Hong Kong, Canada" in my own teacher and community education work. In doing so, I hope to offer something of value to other teacher-educators who want to prepare their students to negotiate linguistic and racial tensions in their own multilingual communities. I conclude the chapter with a short discussion of the ways I plan to move forward in my work with performed ethnography.

"Hong Kong, Canada" – Plot synopsis and excerpts from the play

As mentioned earlier, "Hong Kong, Canada" is an ethnographic play about some of the linguistic and academic issues facing immigrant youth from Hong Kong and their Canadian-born classmates, teachers, and principal. While the characters and plot are fictional, the linguistic and racial conflicts dramatized in the play actually occurred and were documented during my fieldwork.

Set in Pierre Elliot Trudeau Secondary School in Toronto, Canada, "Hong Kong, Canada" tells the story of Wendy Chan, the assistant editor of the student newspaper, as she struggles with the fallout of having published a controversial issue in the school paper. Wendy is a recent immigrant from Hong Kong in a school where more than one third of the student population speaks Cantonese as their primary language. The other Hong Kong-born student who works on the newspaper is Sam, the advertising manager. Joshua Greenberg, the white Jewish editor of the newspaper, is Wendy's love interest. They have become very close even though Joshua knows his family would not approve if they knew he was dating a woman who was not Jewish.

At the beginning of the play, Joshua, Wendy, and Sam face two challenges: they must reduce the newspaper's debt and get more students to read the paper. Joshua searches for a controversial issue to write up. He finds one after his friend Sarah complains about Carol Shen singing in

Cantonese at talent night:

Sarah: Hey . . . were you at the Talent Night on Friday? I didn't see you there.
Joshua: No, I couldn't make it. My cousins from Montreal were in for the weekend and my mother wanted me home for dinner. How was it? I heard it was pretty good.
Sarah: Yeah. Some of it was good. Like, the teachers' band, "P.E.T. School Boys," they were good. And the dance numbers by the Jazz Dance class were great. But, there were so many people who sang songs in Chinese and you couldn't understand a word of them. And all the people who do understand Chinese – most of our school – went crazy. Clapping, whistling. But, like, if you didn't understand any of the words, it was boring. It made me mad.
Joshua: What made you mad?
Sarah: All those songs in Chinese. This isn't Hong Kong. This is Canada. In Canada, people should sing in English. You know what I mean? And I'm not the only one who was mad. Some of the girls from Iran were mad too. Nobody performed in Persian. So how come so many people performed in Chinese?

(Excerpt from Scene 5)

When Wendy also agrees to contribute to a newspaper issue that creates controversy around the uses of languages other than English in school, she and Sam fight about the negative impact her writing might have on Cantonese speakers at the school:

Sam: But Wendy, don't you see the danger of saying in school everybody should only speak English? You don't have the right to make it difficult for people to speak their own language in school.
Wendy: I'm not going to say, "Everybody should only speak English." I am going to say, "In school (*emphasizing*) I only speak English."
Sam: But Wendy, you're Chinese. If you say, "In school I only speak English," people who think that (*emphasizing*) everybody should only speak English, will use what you say to hurt people who want to speak their own language. They'll say, "Even Chinese people think they should only speak English."
Wendy: I don't plan to speak for all people. I plan to speak for myself.
Sam: It's not possible to speak only for yourself. How many other Chinese students from Hong Kong write for the paper? How many other Chinese students can give another point of view? How many?
Wendy: (*Is silent*)
Sam: (*Getting angry*) None. That's how many. None.
Wendy: (*Remains silent*)
Sam: (*Getting angrier*) Do you know what I think? I think that this is more about making Josh happy than it is about you wanting to write about speaking English.
Wendy: (*Remains silent*)

Sam: (*Very angry*) Do you know what else I think? I think you want to act White. You only speak English so you can act White. You need to act White to be Joshua's girlfriend. There's no room in Joshua's life for a Chinese girlfriend who speaks Cantonese…

(Excerpt from Scene 6)

A few nights later, Wendy and Sam are laying out the newspaper for publication (Joshua is not helping as he is attending a family Bat Mitzvah). Sam informs Wendy that he has sold ten ads to customers who want to advertise tutoring services in Chinese. Wendy is uncertain about publishing the Chinese ads, but finally decides to do so. When Joshua finds out about the publication of the ads he is very angry. He and Wendy fight about the choices each has made that evening – Joshua's choice not to invite Wendy to the Bat Mitzvah and Wendy's choice to publish the ads in Chinese. The publication of the Chinese ads provokes Sarah to start a petition for an English-only policy at school. In response, one of the English teachers, Ms. Diamond, decides to hold a school hearing on the issue providing the students with an opportunity to raise dilemmas of linguistic exclusion, assimilation, and discrimination:

Sarah: I strongly support the idea of an English-only policy at Trudeau. A lot of people were angry by the amount of Chinese used at Talent Night. As Joshua Greenberg said in his editorial, "If it is not possible to obtain performers in each and every language represented in our school, then only English should be used because it's the language that we all have in common."

Rita: I am Western African. I would have enjoyed hearing an Ewe song performed at Talent Night. But no one volunteered to perform them. We didn't go for it. Why should those who did go for it be stopped from performing what they want to perform?

Joshua: But I feel left out when people speak Cantonese and I can't understand them. At Talent Night, there were two groups of people: those who understood the Chinese acts and those who didn't. Instead of promoting multiculturalism at our school, the event divided us. This wouldn't have happened if –

Sam: (*Interrupting*) Talent Night did not divide our community. It was Talent Night, not English night. We were there to watch people perform and demonstrate their talent. You can enjoy a performance without understanding every word. It happens at heavy metal concerts all the time.

Sarah: An English-only policy would ensure that when I go to a school event, I would be able to understand every single word that is spoken.

Sam: People who are uncomfortable when they don't understand Chinese are not used to sharing space with people who speak different languages. They want to take away other people's rights so that they don't have to feel uncomfortable, not even for a moment. That's not fair. Toronto –

Sarah: (*Interrupting*) If all acts at Talent Night had been performed in English, it would have assisted those who are learning the language to –

Sam: (*Interrupting*) But Toronto is no longer just an English-speaking city. It is a multilingual city. We all have to share space with people who speak languages we don't understand. We all have to share the discomfort.

Joshua: It's good for people to be forced to speak English at school. They'll learn it faster. Look at people like Wendy Chan. She speaks English really well. And that's because she decided –

Rita: (*Interrupting*) Instead of an English-only policy, we should be offering Cantonese classes during the school day and encouraging as many students as possible to take them. There would be a lot less anger if more people could speak Cantonese.

Joshua: An English-only policy will benefit our Chinese students in the long run. It's a good thing.

Rita: Maybe we should be thinking of making Cantonese classes compulsory for students in this school.

Diamond: (*Scribbling a last few notes*) Thank you all for your contributions. Does anyone else want to say anything? (Carol raises her hand, but Ms. Diamond doesn't see her.) Wendy?

Wendy: (*Stepping forward*) The day after they enrolled me at Trudeau my father and mother left Toronto to go back to Hong Kong. The last words my mother said to me as she went through the security gate at the airport were, "I want you to speak English."
(*In Cantonese*) [To do well in this country you must learn to speak English well.]
(*In English*) My mother wanted all the advantages that were available to Canadian-born students to be available to me. To please her, I decided I would only speak English in school. And speaking English all day did open some doors. I had enough confidence to go on Mr. Wilson's camping trip even though I had never gone camping before and didn't know anyone else who had signed up for the trip. On that trip I met people who were born here and one or two became important friends for a while. But choosing to only speak English also closed some doors. I didn't make any friends with people from Hong Kong.
(*In Cantonese*) [I guess they thought I wasn't interested in being friends with them because I always spoke English.]
(*In English*) Maybe they thought I was Canadian-born, *juk-sin*, a banana, white-washed. I miss speaking Cantonese.
(*In Cantonese*) [I would like to be friends with others from Hong Kong. There are many things we share.]
(*In English*) My mother does not know the discomfort of trying to speak English all day, everyday. She is in Hong Kong where she can speak Cantonese. Some days my mouth, my cheeks, my lips, my throat hurt. When my mother tells me, "I want you to speak English," she thinks only of the doors that might open. Not the doors that close. An English-only policy will close doors for those of us who speak other languages. Unable to say what we would like to say in English, some of us will remain silent. An English-only policy also closes doors for those of us who want to practice speaking other languages with students who already know them well. In the last few weeks, I have learned that the doors we have opened are

> sometimes slammed shut by an unexpected force. It is prudent to keep as many doors open as possible. Thank you...
>
> (Excerpt from Scene 16)

The hearing and the play ends with Ms. Diamond telling the students that she will give the principal and vice principals a report on the hearing so that they can make a decision about a school language policy. The conflict deliberately remains unresolved. This provides my students with an opportunity to write their own endings to the play and "attach what is to what could be" (Fine, 1994). As is illustrated below, the performance of different endings can lead to a rich discussion on ways teachers and principals at Pierre Elliot Trudeau and other schools might move forward; however, before engaging in a discussion of how I have worked with "Hong Kong, Canada," I would like to turn to a discussion on what ethnographic playwriting and performed ethnography have to offer critical teacher education programming.

The possibilities of ethnographic playwriting and performed ethnography

There are a number of reasons why I believe ethnographic playwriting and performed ethnography provide critical teacher-educators with a powerful teaching and learning tool. First, the opportunity to create a number of characters with different racial, ethnic, and linguistic identities provides us with an effective way of exploring the issues associated with identity politics and the complex ways such politics play themselves out in a multilingual school environment. To illustrate, in "Hong Kong, Canada," the characters of Joshua and Sarah represent some of the viewpoints and concerns of monolingual English speakers who, for the first time in their lives, find themselves working and socializing with people who use languages other than English. Similarly, the characters of Sam and Wendy represent some of the dilemmas facing bilingual students from Hong Kong who have to make difficult choices about the languages they will speak in Canada. On one hand, students from Hong Kong know that Cantonese speakers who speak English with other Cantonese-speaking students might be perceived as "show-offs." Speaking English is risky as it might lead to losing the friends they depend upon for companionship and assistance at school.[4] On the other hand, these students also know that some English-speaking teachers and students don't like hearing Cantonese in the school's classrooms and hallways because they feel excluded when people use languages they don't understand. This places the students in a trying linguistic dilemma. If they speak English, they risk being ostracized by the Hong Kong community at school, but if they speak Cantonese, they risk angering teachers and students who don't speak Cantonese. The teacher education students I work with are going to be working in schools with similar identity politics and will face situations that are similar to the ones described in "Hong Kong, Canada." Performing or watching the play allows my students to think about the issues from a comfortable location outside the conflict itself. This gives them an opportunity to think critically about the conflict before finding themselves in the middle of it in their own schools.

Another benefit of ethnographic playwriting is that it allows for the representation of both "comment and speechlessness" (Diamond & Mullen, 1999). It allows us to include what is not said as well as what is said into our ethnographic texts. In several scenes of the play (for example, see Scene 16 above), the character of Carol Shen, the student who sang a Cantonese pop song at Talent Night, is present on stage but remains silent. Because she is usually silent at school, when Carol does indicate a desire to speak, this desire is overlooked and not acknowledged by Ms. Diamond. In "Hong Kong, Canada," Carol's silence represents the "inhibitive silence" that many English as a second or other language (ESOL) students experience at school. The notion of inhibitive silence, conceptualized and theorized by Asian American scholar King-Kok Cheung (1993), is a self-imposed silence that can be attributed to students' fears that their pronunciation and Cantonese-English accent might be laughed at. By representing this modality of silence in the play, I hope to give my students an opportunity to begin learning how to work with issues of silence as well as issues of speech in multilingual schools.[5]

Working with "Hong Kong, Canada"

My teacher education students, as well as others who are interested in working with the play, begin by either reading or performing the entire play aloud. The first time I used the play, a small group of my students rehearsed and performed the play for the rest of the group; however, an entire group of students can be involved in a performance or reading by doubling or tripling up on parts. For example, in one class that worked with the play, half of the group read roles from Scenes 1–7 while the other half read roles from Scenes 8–16. One advantage of this second approach was that everyone was actively involved in the reading. A second advantage was that the students could compare their different interpretations and performances of each character's words, actions, and feelings. Such a comparison can be very important for analyzing and challenging stereotypical performances of the characters that students sometimes create in their reading of the play. To illustrate, my students and I have learned that a performer who plays or reads the role of Joshua Greenberg as confused and uncertain rather than confident and cocky resists representing the character as self-serving and inconsiderate of others (a representation that plays into existing stereotypes about North American Jews). Instead, Joshua becomes a character whose own assimilated, monolingual upbringing has not prepared him to understand the complexities of living a bilingual life as a newcomer to Canada (which is the way I had imagined him when I wrote the play).

Working with emotional responses to the play

After reading or performing "Hong Kong, Canada" aloud, I ask my students to reflect upon their emotional responses to the play. I do this by asking them to answer any of the following questions that appeal to them: What provoked a strong emotional response for you? What made you angry? What made you sad? What made you feel bad? What was satisfying? What was not? What confirmed something you believed about students, teachers, or schools? How did that feel? What challenged something you believed about students, teachers, or schools? How did that feel?

Some of my early work with the play indicated that it was the anger attached to Sam's accusation against Wendy in Scene 6 that helped make the accusation of "acting white" memorable and worthy of additional reflection and analysis for the student playing Wendy. The accusation stayed with her because the anger accompanying the accusation was directed at her during the performance of the play. Asking students to consciously reflect on their emotional responses to the play has allowed me to tap into what has been particularly memorable for them and what they might feel is worthy of additional analysis.

Identifying issues and dilemmas

After our talk of emotional responses to the play (or sometimes during our discussion if a teachable moment presents itself), I ask my students to identify the issues and dilemmas facing each of the characters in the scenes that have just been discussed. In large classes or workshops, students have done this work in small groups. Comparing the lists each person or small group has created has provided us with an analysis of the different issues and dilemmas facing different students and teachers at Trudeau. Understanding the linguistic conflicts and tensions at the school from different perspectives prepares us for the work of writing an ending to the play later on.

As a critical teacher-educator, there are particular discourses or analyses I want my students to engage with during our analytical discussions of the play. If these discourses do not emerge from the discussion the students have begun, then I find a way to bring them forward into our dialogue. One particular discourse that I feel is important to work with when discussing linguistic conflicts and tensions in multilingual schools is the discourse of linguistic privilege.[6]

Talking about linguistic privilege

To engage in the discourse of linguistic privilege, I ask my students to think about how high school students like Joshua and Sarah who speak English as their first language have the privilege of not having to worry about being understood or performing effectively in a second or other language. I note that that they have already acquired what Pierre Bourdieu (1982/1991) has called the linguistic and cultural "capital" needed to succeed academically and socially at school. Students like Wendy and Sam who have not yet accumulated the same kinds of capital need to worry about achieving success in an uneven linguistic playing field. Outside the fictional world of the play, students who are in the same position as Wendy and Sam find that they must use their primary languages as a linguistic resource to pursue academic and social success at school. For example, they need to use Cantonese to solve math problems in a calculus class or sing in Cantonese in order to participate in Talent Night. By talking about the issues and dilemmas that face the characters in "Hong Kong, Canada" in terms of the linguistic privilege accorded to students who use English as their primary language, I hope to increase the possibility that such an analysis will be reflected in the students' writing of the ending of the play.

Like Joshua, many of my students are monolingual English speakers and are unaware of the linguistic privilege they possess in being able to speak the language of schooling as a first language. They don't always understand how difficult it is to work on cognitively and academically challenging problems in a second language. They don't know that sometimes it physically hurts to speak a second or other language. Nor do they know what it's like to have to negotiate the politics of language use and decide which language to speak at school. The characters of Wendy and Sam provide them with an opportunity to witness the experience of those who do. In fact, many of my students have found Wendy's monologue on choosing to speak English in Scene 16 to be very moving and have commented that it has given them new insights into the complexity of the issues ESOL students face and new sympathy for these students' linguistic struggles. Engaging in a discourse of linguistic privilege critically builds on the power of this emotional response of sympathy by asking students to analyze the ways that teachers are implicated in reproducing the linguistic privilege of English speakers when they insist that students only use English in their classrooms.

Even more powerful than discussing linguistic privilege in a teacher education classroom, however, is asking students to research the way it plays out in their own teaching situations. As I have written elsewhere (Goldstein, 2000), the next time I work with the play, I would like to follow up our discussion on linguistic privilege with an activity described by antiracist educator Ruth Olson (1999). The activity asks students to keep a week-long diary of the ways English speakers are privileged in their own school and community settings. Using such an activity as a class assignment, I would like students to undertake the activity individually and, at our next meeting, share their findings with their colleagues.

Writing endings to the play

As mentioned earlier, a third activity my students and I undertake in our work with "Hong Kong, Canada" is writing an ending to the play. In a recent workshop undertaken with undergraduate students studying in an applied theater program at Griffith University in Brisbane, Australia, I asked students to work in four small groups to produce four different endings to "Hong Kong, Canada."[7] I have included one of the scenes that was produced below. It is followed by a brief commentary. In this scene, the principal at Pierre Elliot Trudeau Secondary School addresses the student body with his response to the issues presented at the school hearing:

Principal: Good morning. Today, I would like to address the issue of language conflict in the school. It has come to my attention, through a petition I received, that a number of students want an English-only policy in the school. Others have spoken up against such a policy. I have considered both sides carefully. I understand that some of the English-speaking students may feel uncomfortable and left out when they do not understand all that is said around them. I can also see that the non-English speaking students feel similarly. They feel more comfortable speaking their mother tongue. An English-only policy would be neglecting the needs of the non-English speaking students and may disadvantage them as it could make learning and socializing harder. (*Sarah angrily stamps her foot. A few students look at her. She gets embarrassed.*)

Therefore, I have tried to come up with a solution which is aimed to please and help both sides. I have decided that employing a translator could be the answer. There will be a translator within each class who will ensure that everybody understands each other and that there is more discussion and understanding within the classroom.

Commentary

When working with my students' endings to the play, my role is to ask questions. I am interested in asking my students to what extent and in what ways each of their endings to the play works toward alleviating the racial and linguistic tensions between students like Sarah and Josh and Sam and Wendy. I am also interested in what ways their endings effectively challenge educational linguistic inequities facing ESOL students in multilingual schools like Trudeau. In discussing the scene presented above, the applied theater students and I talked about the way the principal assumed that it was important to ensure that all students in the school felt comfortable. We also noted that in his address to the students, the principal recognized that an English-only policy might disadvantage ESOL students by making learning and socializing harder. Finally, we discussed the way the principal focused on the issue of exclusion as being at the center of the language conflict and the ways that having a translator in each class responded to the discomfort of not understanding what others say. With this group, the discussion on the possibilities of translation ended there; however, in the future, I would like to initiate a discussion about the ways that high school students, themselves, might take on the role of translators and the kinds of classroom agreements or activities that would facilitate the work of such translation.

Future work with "Hong Kong, Canada"

In thinking about ways I might add to my repertoire of critical teacher development activities to accompany "Hong Kong, Canada," I have turned to work undertaken in the field of theater in education. Educators in this field use a combination of presentational theater and participatory drama work to engage participants in active critical learning. Participatory theater work includes the approaches of *forum theater* (e.g., Boal, 1979; O'Connor, 2000) and *process drama* (e.g., Booth, 1994; Heathcoate & Bolton, 1995; O'Neill & Lambert, 1982; Taylor, 2000).

Forum theater refers to a technique made popular by Brazilian drama educator Augusto Boal (e.g., Boal, 1979). It involves replaying a scene from a play or role-play and asking participants to stop the scene and step in themselves to play the scene out differently. For example, in the following excerpt from Scene 6 of "Hong Kong, Canada," Joshua asks Wendy to help him create a controversial issue of the school newspaper by writing an article about her own personal choice to only use English at school. Students could be asked to replay that scene having Wendy challenge, rather than agree to, Joshua's request:

Joshua: . . . Hey, Wen . . . I have a great idea for an editorial for our first issue. It's called, "Multiculturalism: Too much of a good thing?"
Wendy: Too much of a good thing?
Joshua: Yeah. It's about Talent Night on Friday.
Wendy: Talent Night?
(*Sam walks into the newspaper office and sits down on the couch*)
Joshua: Yeah. (*Greeting Sam*) Hey, Sam. Listen to this. Both of you.
(*Reading from his notebook*)
"On stage was a good-looking Oriental girl singing a song in Chinese. Now some people might have looked at this and thought, 'Wow, what a great way to promote multiculturalism. A multilingual event is a great idea.' However, the problem was that P.E.T.'s Talent Night was not multilingual, nor was it multicultural. Songs were available only in English and in Chinese. Is this fair to the rest of P.E.T. students and cultures?"
Wendy: You want to write an editorial about how singing in Chinese is a problem?
Joshua: Yeah. Just listen. I'm not finished.
(*Reading*)
"If Chinese songs were performed, then songs from all of our diverse cultures should have been performed. And if it was not possible to perform songs in each and every language, then only English songs should have been performed."
Wendy: Only English songs?
Sam: (*Standing up and walking to the table, with an edge in his voice*) Why only English songs, Joshua?
Joshua: (*A little defensively*) Because this is Canada. In Canada we speak English. English is the official language of our school.
Sam: (*Getting angry*) When I walk down the halls, I hear a lot of different languages. I don't only hear English. The Iranian guys speak Farsi. Some of the East Indian guys speak Urdu. English is not the only language people speak at this school.
Joshua: (*Also getting angry*) Well, I heard that a lot of people were angry after Talent Night. They thought that Talent Night violated cultural equity.
Sam: I don't believe this.
Joshua: Believe it Sam. I've found our controversy. The first issue of our paper is going to be hot. Everybody will want to read it!
(*Wendy gets up and paces around the room*)
Sam: But Joshua, what about –
Joshua: (*Interrupting*) I've already talked to Sarah about writing an opinion column about her personal reaction to Talent Night and Wendy –
(*Realizing that she's not where he thought she was*)
Wen?
Wendy: (*Quietly*) Yes?
Joshua: What I'd like you to do is write your own opinion column about the language controversy at P.E.T.
Sam: Language controversy at P.E.T.? We don't have a "language controversy" at P.E.T.

Joshua: We do now. And it's going to save our paper. Wendy, do you know what would be really cool? If you wrote about your own decision to only speak English. So you could get better and better at it.

Sam: (*Looking at Wendy in surprise*)
You don't speak in Cantonese? Ever?

Wendy: (*Ignoring Sam, speaking to Joshua*)
You want me to write about myself?

Joshua: Yeah. Your column would give a personal, human touch to the controversy.

Sam: Joshua, there's no humanity in starting a controversy about using Cantonese at school. Do you know what's going to happen?

Joshua: Yeah. I know what's going to happen. We're going to sell lots and lots of newspapers . . . I need to go now. See you later, Wendy. Think about that column!
(*Joshua leaves the newspaper office*)

Working in small groups of three (replaying the roles of Joshua, Wendy, and Sam), students could be asked to replay the scene with Wendy raising concerns about Joshua's plans. The students' replays would then be presented to each other and a discussion comparing the different replays could be pursued. The purpose of this particular forum theater activity would be to provide students with an opportunity to create and rehearse a response to Joshua's understanding that the use of languages other than English "violates cultural equity" at school. Having such a response readily available is important anti-discriminatory work and conflict resolution in multilingual schools.

The second kind of participatory drama work mentioned here, process drama, also uses and manipulates theater forms to provide opportunities for participants to act, reflect on their actions, and transform the status quo. A process drama activity often begins with a story, fable, fairytale, or play that is used as an entry point into drama work. Texts that are most useful for process drama are those that raise questions or suggest "puzzlements" (Taylor, 2000). Drama educator David Booth (1994), who coined the term "storydrama" to describe his own process drama work, has written that such puzzlements might refer to an unsolved problem – a dilemma encountered by a character or a point of intrigue suggested by an action, a stance, or a response. Rather than having students act out plots, storydrama activities ask students to explore a puzzlement through improvisation and role-play. The role of the teacher or teacher-educator in the process drama is that of a facilitator, director, interrogator, or manipulator (Taylor, 2000). To illustrate, after reading and working with the play "Hong Kong, Canada" in the ways described in the first part of this chapter, I could begin a process drama activity by assuming the role of the teacher-adviser at Pierre Elliot Trudeau who has been asked to supervise the students' organization of the school's second Talent Night of the year. Knowing that Carol's performance in

Cantonese created tensions at the school's first Talent Night, my role in the process drama activity would be to ensure that the student organizers of Talent Night find a way of responding to these tensions. Having given my students this task, my own work in character would cease for the moment. The students, themselves, working in groups of three or four, would continue the process drama activity by playing the roles of high school students at Trudeau and strategize how they might effectively organize the second Talent Night. When the strategizing session concluded, the students in each group would share their ideas with the others in the class and we would analyze patterns that emerged from their work. Back in character as the teacher-adviser, my role here would be to question the group on the accuracy of the assumptions underlying their strategizing and raise further issues that might accompany the strategies they have come up with.[8] In playing the role of high school students who are organizing the school's second Talent Night, my students would have the opportunity to brainstorm strategies for dealing with linguistic and racial tensions that might arise in the schools in which they will teach. Once again, having such strategies readily available is helpful for problem solving in multilingual schools.

In this chapter, I have argued that ethnographic playwriting and performed ethnography hold exciting possibilities for preparing language teachers to effectively respond to the complexities of working across linguistic, cultural, and racial differences in multilingual schools. By identifying and working with issues and dilemmas facing fictional but ethnographically developed characters, language teachers have the opportunities to create and rehearse new discourses that will help them engage in conflict resolution and anti-discriminatory education in multilingual schools. Such engagements are vital if we are to create safe, rich, and equitable learning environments for second or other language students.

Notes

1. The project of turning ethnographic data and texts into scripts and dramas that are read and performed before audiences has been taken up by a number of writers and researchers in the disciplines of sociology and anthropology and in the fields of performance studies, theater studies, and arts-based inquiry in education (see Denzin, 1997). My own playwriting work has been informed by the work of playwrights Anna Deavere Smith (1993, 1994), Eve Ensler (1998), Dorinne Kondo (1995), and Jim Mienczacowski (1994, 1995, 1996, 1997).
2. The ethnographic data on which the play is based were collected with the assistance of a three-year Social Sciences and Humanities Research Council of Canada (SSHRCC) grant (1996–9). I wish to acknowledge and thank

SSHRCC for its financial support. I also wish to acknowledge and thank my research collaborator, Cindy Lam, for her assistance and analytical insights during the first two years of the project. For further discussion of this study, see Goldstein (2003).

3. A full version of the play appears in Goldstein (2003) and an edited version of the play appears in Goldstein (2001).
4. For further discussion of the association between the use of English and "showing off," see Goldstein (1997) and "Introduction" in Goldstein (2003).
5. In her book, *Articulate Silences*, Cheung (1993) proposes at least five differing, and often overlapping, modes or tonalities of silences. They are stoic, protective, attentive, inhibitive, and oppressive. For further discussion of the ways these silences impact schooling in multilingual settings, see Pon, Goldstein, and Schecter (2003) and Chapter 3 in Goldstein (2003).
6. Other issues I want my students and I to engage with include accent discrimination and the association many students make between speaking English and showing off or acting white. For further discussion of the ways my students and I engage with these issues, see Chapters 3 and 5 in Goldstein (2003).
7. Students in the applied theater program at Griffith University learn to devise participatory theater work that responds to different social issues in different communities. For example, in a recent project, a team of two student actors and the program director devised a theater piece dealing with issues of domestic violence for high school students living in a housing estate where such violence had been named by the community as a serious problem.
8. For an excellent, fully described example of a process drama activity, see Philip Taylor's (2000) work, "Reinventing the Three Little Pigs: A Drama about Prejudice and Stereotype" (pp. 8–19).

References

Boal, A. (1979). *Theatre of the oppressed*. London: Pluto Press.

Booth, D. (1994). *Story drama: Reading, writing and roleplaying across the curriculum*. Markham, Ontario, Canada: Pembroke.

Bourdieu, P. (1991). *Language and symbolic power* (G. Raymond & M. Adamson, Trans.). Cambridge, England: Polity Press. (Original work published 1982)

Cheung, K. K. (1993). *Articulate silences: Hisaye Yamamoto, Maxine Hong Kingston, Joy Kogawa*. Ithaca, NY: Cornell University Press.

Deavere Smith, A. (1993). *Fires in the mirror*. New York: Anchor Books/Doubleday.

Deavere Smith, A. (1994). *Twilight: Los Angeles, 1992*. New York: Anchor Books/Doubleday.

Denzin, N. (1997). Performance texts. In W. G. Tierney & Y. S. Lincoln (Eds.), *Representation and the text: Re-framing the narrative voice* (pp. 180–217). Albany: State University of New York Press.

Diamond, C. T. P., & Mullen, C. (1999). Art is a part of us: From romance to artful story. In C. T. P. Diamond & C. Mullen (Eds.), *The postmodern educator: Arts-based inquiries and teacher development* (pp. 15–36). New York: Peter Lang.

Ensler, E. (1998). *The vagina monologues*. New York: Villard.

Fine, M. (1994). Dis-stance and other stances: Negotiations of power inside feminist research. In A. Gitlin (Ed.), *Power and method: Political activism and educational research* (pp. 13–55). New York: Routledge.

Goldstein, T. (1997). Bilingual life in a multilingual high school classroom: Teaching and Learning in Cantonese and English. *Canadian Modern Language Review, 53*(2), 356–72.

Goldstein, T. (2000). Hong Kong, Canada: Performed ethnography for anti-racist teacher education. *Teaching Education Journal, 11*(3), 311–26.

Goldstein, T. (2001). *Hong Kong, Canada*: Playwriting as critical ethnography. *Qualitative Inquiry, 7*(3), 279–303.

Goldstein, T. (2003). *Teaching and learning in a multilingual school: Choices, risks and dilemmas*. Mahwah, NJ: Lawrence Erlbaum Associates.

Heathcoate, D., & Bolton, G. (1995). *Drama for learning: Dorothy Heathcote's mantle of the expert approach to education*. Portsmouth, NH: Heinemann.

Kondo, D. (1995). Bad girls: Theater, women of color, and the politics of representation. In R. Behar & D. Gordon (Eds.), *Women writing culture* (pp. 49–82). Berkeley: University of California Press.

Mienczacowski, J. (1994). Theatrical and theoretical experimentation in ethnography. *ND DRAMA, Journal of National Drama, UK, 2*(2), 16–23.

Mienczacowski, J. (1995). Reading and writing research: Ethnographic theatre. *ND DRAMA, Journal of National Drama, UK, 3*(3), 8–12.

Mienczacowski, J. (1996). An ethnographic act: The construction of consensual theatre. In C. Ellis & A. P. Bochner (Eds.), *Composing ethnography: Alternative forms of qualitative writing* (pp. 244–64). New York: Altamira Press.

Mienczacowski, J. (1997). Theatre of change. *Research in Drama Education, 2*(2), 159–71.

O'Connor, P. (2000). Rethinking race relations: New learnings for judges, priests and journalists. In J. O'Toole & M. Lepp (Eds.), *Drama for life: Stories of adult learning and empowerment* (pp. 235–43). Brisbane: Playlab Press.

Olson, R. A. (1999). White privilege in schools. In E. Lee, D. Menkart, & M. Okazawa-Rey (Eds.), *Beyond heroes and holidays: A practical guide to K-12 anti-racist, multicultural education and staff development* (pp. 83–4). Washington, DC: Network of Educators on the Americas.

O'Neill, C., & Lambert, A. (1982). *Drama structures: A practical handbook for beginners*. London: Hutchinson.

Pon, G., Goldstein, T., & Schecter, S. (2003). Interrupted by silences: The contemporary education of Hong Kong-born Chinese-Canadian adolescents. In R. Bayley & S. Schecter (Eds.), *Language socialization and bi-multilingual societies* (pp. 114–27). New York: Multilingual Matters.

Taylor, P. (2000). *The drama classroom: Action, reflection, transformation*. New York: Routledge/Falmer Press.

17 *Critical moments in a TESOL praxicum*

Alastair Pennycook

Departures

The two-level suburban train clanks out of Central Station. Heading away from the city, it's not as crowded as the incoming trains, but I still find myself having to stand by the doors. We creak and rattle across several sets of points before finding our suburban heading, passing through increasingly unfamiliar station names. Outside, it's an achingly clear blue morning; the air is chilly, but the sun is starting to warm the day. It's June, which means the start of winter and the end of the semester just round the corner. Essay marking and clear blue skies. And that end-of-semester exhaustion. It's been another long semester: conferences in Manila, Vancouver, Singapore, Abu Dhabi; I was teaching from 7 to 9 last night; and here I am on a Friday morning, heading off to find a small language school somewhere in the suburbs whose address I fortunately remembered to print off from my e-mail late last night.

The TESOL (teaching English to speakers of other languages) practicum. For many of us involved in teacher education, the teaching practicum holds, I think, a certain ambivalence: It's hard work; it's disruptive; it involves lots of traveling; it's too time consuming; it demands that we show expertise in a domain from which we are often increasingly distanced in our current work. And yet, it's also a welcome break from offices, meetings, seminars, corridors; it takes us back to the classrooms where, in moments of unlikely nostalgia, we often seem to place our happiest and most successful teaching moments; it gives us a chance to engage directly with the "real work" of teaching (the classroom, the "chalkface," the "real world" – all those metaphors that construct both us and the classroom in ways we may want to both acknowledge and avoid), a chance to forget the books, the theories, the papers, the articles, the paradigms, the concepts, the need to keep up. It gives us the chance to get back to something that, at least for those of us who've taught English for many years, we may feel we really know how to do: A dozen or so years of practice and knowledge written onto our teacherly bodies.

The train pauses at another station and I gaze out, trying to remember when I've been through this part of the city before. Nearly all the people on the platform look Southeast Asian. Vietnamese? Chinese? Korean? I find myself trying to catch what people are speaking as they get on the train. Cantonese. Then Vietnamese, I think. Not sure about the next two. Vietnamese again. Another of those complexly mixed suburbs whose daily linguistic and cultural negotiations remain largely a mystery to most of us from mainstream Anglo life. I make a mental note that this looks like an interesting area to come back and explore. But I suspect I won't be back out this way for a while. And I start to wonder about this way of looking at suburbs and the possibility of interesting restaurants and shops. What kind of center-periphery/center-suburbs relationship is this, with its fascination with the suburban high-street display of ethnic difference? The train pulls out of the station and I glance up at the route map above the door. Three more stations to go.

I'm traveling light – a briefcase with some papers for a midday meeting elsewhere slung over my shoulder – but at the same time, as with all journeys, there's a lot of other baggage with me too. The notion of embodied teacher knowledge also makes me feel uncomfortable: I'm not very sure about how my embodied knowledge of teaching relates to the curriculum the students have been following. Embodied knowledge may have an element of conservativism about it. And I haven't been teaching any of the subjects that the students take as part of the foundation for this teaching, the practicum subject itself, or the courses on curriculum design and methodology and language in social context that go with it. Indeed, rather guiltily I realize that I don't really know what's taught in those courses. Do I really know what I'm supposed to be looking for? Will I start to question precisely what this learner teacher has just been taught to do? I recall a practicum observation from last year when I asked the teacher why she didn't make use of the students' languages in the class. She was puzzled. Weren't we supposed to be using only English? But then again, we don't promote an English-only ideology (see Auerbach, 1993) in our courses either, so it's not exactly clear what the relationship is between the curriculum, the practice of each teacher, and the knowledge brought by the observer.[1]

Two more stations to go. In addition to the bag hanging over one shoulder, full of concerns about my own knowledge relative to what this teacher will know and want to know, there is a heavy bag over my other shoulder weighted down with concerns about how I will be able to introduce a critical element into this process. My aim is also to be a bit disruptive. I've been thinking and writing a lot recently about how we can understand the various meanings of the notion "critical" (see Pennycook, 2001), and I run over these ideas as we approach my destination. There's the sense of *critical* used in critical thinking. Unfortunately, this is both the weakest and most common version of the critical in many domains of education. This view of being critical sees the issue as only one of rational questioning procedures, as a way of trying to create objective distance, of identifying bias or lack of logic. This is all very well as far as it goes, but it is what I would call *liberal ostrichism* in that it buries its head in the sands of objectivism (ostrichism) and fails to link its questioning to a broader social agenda (and by so doing, of course, reproduces its own rational and liberal social agendas). Another sense of critical is concerned mainly with making things socially relevant: a reaction to the abstract objectivism (cf. Vološinov, 1973) of many domains of applied linguistics. Such a view is more promising, but without a larger vision of social critique, it remains only a version of the critical that attempts to correlate language with social context.

One more station to go. We pass through an area of brick warehouses and low factories, the drab industrial structures of a passing era. A third approach to being critical is to incorporate explicit social critique and to see one's work as overtly aimed toward trying to change inequitable social conditions and people's understanding of them. This is what I term *emancipatory modernism*. Its strengths are its clearly articulated social critique and explicit agenda for change; its weaknesses are its static assumptions about social and political relations and its belief in awareness of inequality as a step toward rationalist emancipation. It is this version of critical work that has come to dominate critical work in TESOL and applied linguistics, as found in critical discourse analysis (for example, Fairclough, 1995; Wodak, 1996), critical pedagogy (Giroux, 1988; Kanpol, 1994), critical literacy (Clark and Ivanič, 1997), or critical views on language policy (Phillipson, 1992). While crucially putting questions of power, inequality, rights, and injustice to the fore, this focus tends also to reaffirm concepts such as emancipation, awareness, rationality, objectivity, equality, democracy, and transformation, which, from another perspective, may be viewed as products of the same system that gives rise to those very problems that this framework aims to critique. Thus, it both critiques and reproduces at the same time.

The train pulls into the station and I walk down the platform toward the exit sign. It is this dilemma that has given rise to the postmodern, postcolonial, or post-Occidentalist (see Mignolo, 2000) concern that we need not only a critical domain of investigation but also a reappraisal of the frames of knowledge that are applied to those domains. A final way of viewing the notion of critical, then, is as a form of *problematizing practice* (see Dean, 1994; Pennycook, 2001), a perspective that insists on casting far more doubt on the categories we employ to understand the social world and on assumptions about awareness, rationality, emancipation, and so forth. This position has its weaknesses: in particular, its sometimes obfuscatory views on language, discourse, subjectivity, and difference, and its difficulty, because of its constant self-questioning and the resultant pull toward the vortex of relativity, in establishing firm enough ground to be able to articulate any clear political stance. But its strengths are also significant. As Foucault (1980) put it, "the problem is not so much one of defining a political 'position' (which is to choose from a pre-existing set of possibilities) but to imagine and to bring into being new schemas of politicisation" (p. 190). From this perspective, it is then possible to embark on the ethical task not only of seeking to understand different forms of politics but also of provincializing those European frames of knowledge that have come to dominate what counts as the critical (see Chakrabarty, 2000). At the very least, viewing the critical in terms of problematizing practice gives us a way of working in language education that doesn't reduce critical work either to the domain of critical thinking or to crude dialectics between micro and macro relations and, at the same time, keeps questions of language, discourse, power, and identity to the fore.

As I climb the stairs toward the bridge over the tracks, I start to feel weighed down by all this baggage. Hadn't I been told that all I had to do was watch the learner teacher give her lesson, discuss any particular concerns, and give her some comments as a basis for writing in her reflective journal? And yet, there's another sense of the notion critical that seems important here, too: critical as in a critical moment, a point of significance, an instant when things change. It seems to me that in the practicum observation, and, come to think of it, our teaching more generally, this is what we're looking for – those critical moments when we seize the chance to do something different, when we realize that some new understanding is coming about. This is perhaps a rather neglected notion in general approaches to teaching, discussions of teacher education, and critical approaches to education. It is perhaps inevitable that we tend to look at education in terms of the syllabus (the readings, the course materials) and the curriculum more broadly (the teaching methodology, the assignments, the discussions, the activities). But how do we capture those critical moments where something changes, where someone "gets it," where someone throws out a comment that shifts the discourse? A tough question for all teachers is how we manage to pick up on those moments of potential transformation and turn them into critical moments in both senses. And given the limited input I have to this part of the teacher education program, it is this sense of the critical that will, indeed, be critical here.

Destinations

Next to the station, I cut down a small back street to the main road. I'm trying to figure out the area. Certainly Chinese and Korean, but also some Eastern European. There's a bustle of different local businesses that suggests this suburb is doing well enough. Once across the busy main road, I head past a mixed variety of shops until I find the solid dark brick of the church. It stands close to the road, a large imposing structure surrounded by a low wall. Quite strikingly, it is surrounded by notices. One announces in English and Korean its Presbyterian orientation and the times of the services; another asks in English, "What good is it to gain the whole world and lose your soul? (Mark 8: 36)"; three more announce the presence of the English Language School, one claiming, "We can help you speak better English – ENROL NOW," another "Improve your listening, speaking, reading and pronunciation skills." Classes are on Monday, Wednesday and Friday, 9:30–12:30, with "Child care available" ("Women only" has been whited out), or Tuesday and Thursday, 7:00–9:00 P.M. for "Men and women." I start trying to recreate the history behind that white-out and the relationships between these layerings of signs. Part of one of the signs has been covered by a poster – a sign of important local concerns – urging people "It's time to have your say! ON BROTHELS . . . Brothels will affect you, your children, your life. . . ." But the sign I linger over longest, in English and Chinese, announces:

Easy English Church
For New English Speakers
Sundays 9:00 a.m.–9:45 a.m.
Come and join us–Everyone welcome

I'm intrigued by this idea of an "easy English church" and the long history of connections between churches and language teaching. Following Mignolo (2000), we can crudely describe four principal phases of globalization: the Christian mission to convert the world, the European mission to civilize the world, the wealthy nations' mission to develop the world, and the transnational mission to capitalize the world. According to Mignolo, these did not replace each other, but rather can be understood in terms of "the coexistence of successive global designs that are part of the imaginary of the modern/colonial world system" (p. 280). The missionary relationship to different languages has been a complex one and certainly has not been predominantly concerned with promoting European languages. The crucial issue was always getting the knowledge of the Bible to the heathen (along with various other Christian concepts of discipline, order, cleanliness, and decency), and the best way to do that was usually by describing and then translating into local languages. Indeed, the contemporary descendants of missionary zeal may be descriptive linguists rather than English-promoting capitalists. But as global relations shifted through the second, third, and fourth phases, the relationship to European languages, and especially English, shifted. Now English had become a marketable commodity, with Christianity riding on its back. From the waves of born-again teachers from the American Midwest heading off to China and the former Soviet Union as English teacher-missionaries, to the Bible-clutching Seventh Day Adventists offering free English lessons at the corner of Hyde Park in Sydney, English has become the hook (see Pennycook and Coutand-Marin, in press). Easy English Church for New English Speakers. I make a note to find out more about the connections here between English, Presbyterianism, Korea, and China. But I've got enough baggage with me already and I'm almost late, so I hurry round the back of the church to the church hall.

This is old-style community English as a second language (ESL), a long way from the brave new world of whiteboards, colored marker pens, and plastic chairs with fold-down desks. Upstairs in the hall there's a large main room with a couple of tables covered with assorted chipped teacups and chairs gathered in a circle. Leading off from the main room with its worn floorboards, threadbare carpet, high wooden ceiling and tall church windows, there are several smaller rooms that also serve as classrooms. A brief wave of nostalgia comes over me. It's been a while since I was in a place like this, and it reminds me of some of my first teaching jobs twenty years ago. I find Liz, the student teacher, and her cooperating teacher, Barbara, and start talking about the upcoming lesson. How will Liz's lesson today fit into the broader program? What level are the students? What kind of backgrounds? What will the main focus be today? Why? Soon, the students start arriving, so I settle myself in a corner to observe. It's a small class – about ten students – at a lower intermediate level. The majority are under twenty and Korean – apparently, a number of them have come from Korea to stay with relatives here and learn English. Some connection through the church.

The teacher has chosen to do a lesson focusing on practical language for what to do when something is broken at home: vocabulary for describing various problems (my sink is blocked, the fuse has blown, etc.); practice dialogues for talking to plumbers, electricians, and so forth; and ways of asking a landlord/lady to get something fixed for you. There's a good mix of activities: a bit of grammar, plenty of vocabulary, practicing dialogues, doing free dialogues, some reading. The blackboard is used well, there are pictures to elicit and explain vocabulary items, and there's a tape for a short listening activity. It's going to be followed up by a writing task in which they will write a letter requesting for various items to be fixed. The students participate fairly actively: There's clearly quite a variety of levels in this class, but they all seem to find something useful. The main difficulty is a student of Italian background who wants to talk and to keep the teacher's attention. It's fun for a while – he's amusing and very active – but soon it becomes too much – his English is hard to follow and the others tune out when he's talking; he tends to go off on tangents and keeps demanding the teacher's attention. But how to stop him? I make a note – clearly this is something to talk about afterward. But what else? What else can I find that could be deemed critical?

Connections

Afterward, we find a quiet space in another of the small rooms off the central hall and sit down to discuss the lesson. The general process here is for the observer to give the teacher-learner a copy of the notes written during the class and to discuss various points. For the student, one goal is to pick up on a particular point of interest and to write up reflections on that point in the reflective journal, which will later be handed in to the teacher supervising the practicum. This focus on reflection fits closely with current thinking on teacher education. Summarizing recent trends, Freeman and Johnson (1998) point out several emergent reconceptualizations of teacher education in TESOL. Most significant is the recognition that "much of what teachers know about teaching comes from their memories as students, as language learners, and as students of language teaching" (p. 401). Thus, we have to take into account our students' embodied histories of learning and teaching, the memories, pains, and desires that have been written onto their educated bodies. Learning to teach is not just about learning a body of knowledge and techniques; it is also about learning to work in a complex sociopolitical and cultural political space (see Liston & Zeichner, 1991; Pennycook, 2000) and negotiating ways of doing this with our past histories, fears, and desires; our own knowledges and cultures; our students' wishes and preferences; and the institutional constraints and collaborations.

In addition to this broader literature on teacher education, a number of educators have also addressed the teaching practicum in TESOL (Freeman, 1990; Johnson, 1996; Richards & Crookes, 1988). The central focus of this work has been on questions such as how teachers cope with the real world of the classroom or how they start to change and learn to be more independent. Johnson (1996), for example, discusses the mismatch between a student teacher's vision of what teaching should be and her discovery of the realities of high school classrooms. Johnson concludes that preservice teacher education needs to move away from its prepackaged bits of knowledge delivered in a series of courses and instead provide preservice teachers "with realistic expectations about what the practicum teaching experience will be like and what they can expect to gain from it" (p. 48). Others, such as Gebhard (1990), have focused more on the processes of change during the practicum and, in particular, how interactions between participants can be arranged "so that student teachers have opportunities to change their teaching behavior" (p. 129).

My own interest, however, is in how, as educators, we can intervene in the process of the practicum observation in order to bring about potential change. In addition, as already discussed, this concern is constrained by the requirement that such intervention be critical (as defined above) and by the need to work through critical moments. If such interests seem obscure and oddly constrained, I would also suggest (as I have tried to illustrate above) that they emerge from the practical concern from my own context of fitting a practicum observation into an overfull schedule (which is probably not so uncommon) and from a more general interest in how we can seize critical moments. Looking at the process of intervening in the practicum, Freeman (1990) discusses various modes of intervention: the *directive* – where the purpose is to "improve the student teacher's performance according to the educator's criteria" (p. 108); the *alternatives* option, in which the aim is to "develop the student teacher's awareness of the choices involved in deciding what and how to teach, and, more importantly, to develop the ability to establish and articulate the criteria that inform those decisions" (p. 109); and, finally, the *nondirective* option, the purpose of which is to "provide the student teacher with a forum to clarify perceptions of what he or she is doing in teaching and for the educator to fully understand, although not necessarily to accept or agree with, those perceptions" (p. 112).

All of this is well and good as far as it goes. My own conception of finding critical moments fits in with this broad orientation. On the one hand, like Johnson (1996), I do not believe that the teacher practicum should be viewed as a period in which teacher-learners practice the techniques they have learned in their university courses; rather, this is a time for teacher-learners to try to reconcile three competing domains: the knowledge and ideas gained through their formal study; the history, beliefs, and embodied practices they bring with them; and the constraints and possibilities presented by the particular teaching context. For this reason, it is in some ways quite useful that, as an occasional practicum observer, I do not come to the teaching practicum with a checklist of things I want to ensure are being done, though it might also be argued that if practicum observation is no more than setting one set of teacher values and beliefs (my own) against another's (the teacher-learner), we are only dealing here with a clash of potentially incommensurable teacher histories. On the other hand, my approach to teacher education is oriented toward change. For Freeman (1990), the goal of the educator is "to help the student teacher move towards an understanding of effective teaching and independence in teaching" (pp. 116–17). I would describe my own goals, however, more in terms of helping teachers to develop a critical practice in their teaching or "that continuous reflexive integration of thought, desire and action sometimes referred to as 'praxis'" (Simon, 1992, p. 49). Indeed, it might be useful to talk not only of critical praxis but also of the *praxicum*. This might help us think not so much in terms of the practicum, in which teacher-learners get to practice what they have learned in their theory courses, but rather in terms of the praxicum, in which teacher-learners develop the continuous reflexive integration of thought, desire, and action.

The question, then, is how to open up a critical agenda through the pursuit of critical moments. Critical approaches to language education, particularly critical pedagogy, have been critiqued for their bombastic posturing, for creating their own regime of truth, and for developing forms of language and knowledge that do not seem helpful for teachers (see Gore, 1993; Johnston, 1999). At the same time, mainstream approaches to teacher education in TESOL have frequently lacked a social or political dimension that helps locate English and English language teaching within the complex social, cultural, economic, and political environments in which it occurs (Auerbach, 1995; Canagarajah, 1999; Pennycook, 2000). What I'm looking for here, then, is a way of doing critical teacher education that does not put all its eggs in a critical syllabus basket (a critical-directive option) but rather seeks ways of probing, discussing, and negotiating in these moments of teacher reflection. Of course, ideally, the critical education curriculum might work along lines such as those described in Brutt-Griffler and Samimy's (1999) account of a critical teacher education program that used reflective diaries over an extended period to explore the construction of the native–nonnative speaker divide. But my interest here is in the smaller, unplanned micro-moments when possibilities for critical reflection come and go. Rather than a critical-directive framework in which the ideas and issues have been laid out beforehand, then, I am looking for a critical alternatives or a critical nondirective option, one in which other possibilities come to the fore as we discuss choices that were made in the class. This is a search to find alternatives to the *orthopraxy* of the standard practicum and instead to develop a notion of *critical heteropraxy* within a reconceptualized teacher praxicum.[2]

Two other recent practicum observations have provided small examples of this. In the first, I was talking to two teachers, Sarah, whose first language was English, and Christian, for whom English was a second/third language, after their cotaught class. We got onto the topic of grammar and knowledge of language and out of this discussion emerged a shift of power. Whereas the so-called nonnative speaker of English (for a critique and discussion of this concept, see, for example, Brutt-Griffler & Samimy, 1999; Singh, 1998), Christian, had, until then, always been the disadvantaged one of these two teachers – worried about his command of English, deferring to Sarah's judgments, overpreparing materials to compensate for this presumed deficiency – as we talked our way through this, the tide started to turn: Christian was proficient in at least one other language; he had been an extremely successful learner of English; he had traveled, learned languages, engaged with other cultures; and he had, at his fingertips, a broad and formal knowledge of the language and how it worked. As we talked, Sarah, as a monolingual Anglo-teacher, started to become aware of her monolingualism and monoculturalism as well as the fact that it was she who was more out of place in the multilingual, multicultural context of the ESL classroom, not her "nonnative speaker" coteacher. This shift in power and moment for reflection, then, came from a small opening in the feedback session after class.

Soon after this, I was observing Bob, a teacher in a lower intermediate reading class. The text was "Charlie Two Shoes," a simplified newspaper article telling the story of a young Chinese boy who had been exchanging fresh eggs for canned food with U.S. soldiers in Southern China in 1948. Eventually, after establishing a close relationship with them and having been given the name Charlie Two Shoes as the soldiers' closest approximation to his Chinese name, the boy had been left behind when the army pulled out. In the 1980s, one of them had received a letter from Charlie and had invited him to the United States. After various visa problems, he and his family had been granted permission to stay, and thus we see a smiling Charlie Two Shoes now living in Ohio close to his old American friends. Why this text? I wanted to know, when we discussed the lesson afterward. Well, basically, it turned out, because they hadn't done it before. But did Bob have any problems with it?

One of the first things that came up is the problem with the name. Yes, he didn't much like this idea of changing the name. He's always objected to this practice and feels Australians should learn other names. So here we started to touch on an odd disparity between Bob's own beliefs and his use of this text. I kept pushing. Why an American text? How might this text about an immigrant arriving happily in the United States relate to the lives of these students, most of whom were recent arrivals in Australia? What about the war background and the U.S. military (and the silences about what the United States was doing supporting the Guomindang in 1948)? As we talked on, the text, and its potential relationship to these students, and the silences about all of this in the reading lesson (with its nicely presented vocabulary and well-conducted discussion of grammar and meaning) became increasingly problematic. Why were we presenting stories of the happinesses of migration, with the home country only as a place to be left behind and the new country as a friendly accommodating place that will bend visa rules to secure a happy ending (around the same time a recent immigrant to Australia had burned himself to death when he had heard that his family would not be allowed to join him; more recently, Australia has developed a "Pacific Solution" in which potential immigrants are kept in camps on Pacific island and an internal policy in which new arrivals are detained for long periods in appalling conditions in detention camps)? If nothing else, after this long discussion, we walked away from this feedback session very aware that no text is ever innocent.

Ruptures[3]

So we start talking about the class. Liz has got a thirty-minute break between classes, Barbara can join us for the first fifteen minutes, and I have a meeting to get back to. There's never enough time. And the small wooden chairs aren't the most comfortable things to sit on. The most obvious issue was how to manage the one Italian male in the class. He wants to talk; he's happy to fill the space with hard-to-understand Italian English; he wants the teacher's attention and he's not so interested in the other students. And the other students find his English difficult to follow. They tune out and do other things when he's talking. We talk about this for a while; it's clearly the most overtly difficult aspect of the class. And, of course, both Liz and Barbara are very aware of it. They've discussed it before. Perhaps someone needs to talk to him outside the class. But are we being fair? After all, he's an active and motivated student, behaving in what may be a culturally appropriate manner for him. But there are gender politics at play here, too, and cultural appropriacy needs to be negotiated, not just accepted. And his right to behave as he wants clearly impinges on other students' rights. So as we move from a discussion of a student who talks too much to questions of gender, culture, and rights, more critical questions start to emerge. There are bigger issues here than just concerns over an individual student; questions of power have started to emerge. But we've used up almost half the time talking about this one issue. We try and come up with strategies for dealing with him, but I can't see much scope here for further critical exploration. Barbara has to go back to the class.

I take up a couple of other issues with Liz. I liked the practicality of the lesson, the clear focus on helping students to get things done. But I wonder how many people it was relevant for. The younger Korean students are living with relatives and are unlikely to have to call a plumber to get something fixed; others also didn't appear to be relating to the situation easily; few appear to be in rented accommodation where they see themselves as likely to have to deal with these sorts of situations. Though on the other hand, for one woman, parts of the class seemed to be exactly what she wanted; she asked urgent questions, checked answers, brought in other situations, wrote careful notes. To the extent that this sort of language practice may give people more possibilities to get things done and more power in interactions, this lesson certainly might be seen as critical in terms of helping to provide access to domains that are often denied. Perhaps that's enough to justify the lesson. Certainly, the class got some good concentrated language practice and some useful vocabulary. But we discuss ways in which she might tailor it more for the class. I don't want to be too critical here: This sort of contextually relevant language class is exactly what I'd like to see more of. How contextually relevant are we supposed to be?

I want to push the issue of the dialogues. I felt they were too cooperative. There's a long history of this problem in ESL. On the one hand, we might take this up in terms of the debate over authenticity: Should ESL classes aim to be "authentic," or should we accept them as inevitably inauthentic learning spaces? The extremes at either end of this debate seem problematic: classes that try completely to replicate the world outside might be very unproductive learning spaces, but classes that see themselves as wholly separate might be unhelpfully detached. On the other hand, we might take this up in more political terms as reflecting consensual versus conflictual views of society. From a liberal point of view, the social world is generally one in which we have common goals, and although these may at times be in conflict, and although we may need laws, regulations, and police forces to limit "antisocial behavior," civil society should generally be able to proceed as a cooperative venture. From a more critical point of view, however, society is seen as inherently conflictual, riven either by mutually exclusive class interests or by other gender, ethnic, or race divisions. From the one perspective, cooperative dialogues are the norm, and it is only antisocial or other abnormal behaviors that prevent them from happening. From the other perspective, there are no relations without power, and thus any dialogue reproduces relations of power and may be seen as ideologically normalized (see Fairclough, 1995). Given the dominance of liberal ostrichism in applied linguistics (and for a discussion of the problem that sociolinguistics has tended to operate with a liberal view of consensuality, see Williams, 1992), it is not surprising that cooperative dialogues have always been the norm. And it can therefore be argued not only that consensual dialogues are inauthentic, but also that they provide passively cooperative subject positions for language learners.[4]

The students were given semiscripted dialogues into which they were supposed to interject different details. The topic was calling plumbers and electricians to get things fixed. Again, nice contextual work, but I would have liked them to be more conflictual. When I call a plumber, they don't say, "Yes certainly, I'll be there at 6:00." Rather, they're busy for the next few days. They may be able to squeeze it in on Tuesday at 7:00 A.M. on the way to another job. Or, if not, they'll try to come around at lunch on Friday. Will I be home? They'll call if they can make it. Yes, they may be able to send someone today if it's a real emergency, but it'll cost extra. They don't understand what you're talking about: What did you say was broken? Perhaps you should try a builder. They don't do that sort of work. Sure they could come and have a look at it next week, but it sounds like a big job. (In fact, as I write this, I've been putting off calling a plumber for the last two weeks because blockages can be easier to deal with than plumbers.)

I suggest that for these students with their limited English skills, it'll be twice as hard. So they need tougher dialogues. A number of people have developed materials based on a more difficult world than the insipid vision of collaborative ESL texts (see Auerbach and Wallerstein, 1987; Goldstein, 1994). We talk about this possibility for a while and agree that it might be useful to try to make dialogues a bit harder, less collaborative. But I'm also a bit uncomfortable that this has been a bit critical-directive (see above discussion), that I've imposed my own agenda too much. There are some good critical possibilities here that raise questions of language, gender, power, and discrimination. But it's also not clear how relevant it is to most of these students now.

Finally, we move on to a few language points. I ask Liz what she thinks about having accepted "Close the tap" to her question about what to do when water is pouring from a tap. She's surprised. I explain that when a student offered this solution, she took it up: "Yes, you could close the tap, you could close the tap. But what if you can't close the tap?" I ask if this was a strategic move to accept this form; she says she hadn't noticed it. What did she think about having, in a sense, modeled a nonstandard form for the students? This idea worries her. Did it matter? We talk about this some more and consider different ways of understanding it. Modeling this apparently nonstandard form might be considered as (a) an inappropriate act that would have misled the students (but a reasonable knowledge of second language development suggests that we should not be too concerned about such risks), (b) an irrelevant act (we have to make our choices about what to focus on and what not to), and (c) a locally appropriate act, not just in terms of student development, but, more interestingly, in terms of what language forms will get the job done.

While *turn on* and *turn off* are considered more standard, they are also more opaque than *open* and *close*, which are widely used in many varieties of English. According to Platt, Weber, and Ho (1984),

> The use of *open* and *close* for electric switches is common in many of the new Englishes, e.g., East African English, Hawaiian English, Hong Kong English, Malaysian English, Philippine English and Singapore English. It is possible to *open* or *close* lights, fans, radios and the TV. (p. 111)

And, presumably, taps. Perhaps, then, there is a reasonable argument, if not to teach these forms, at the very least to accept them. But as we push on with our discussion of this, another issue emerges. In multilingual cities like Sydney, what is the language background of the plumber likely to be? Of course, there's the whole issue that many communities use services from within that community with the result that a lot of service encounters are done in languages other than English anyway. But just as forms such as open and close are widely used in Englishes around the world, so they also develop within urban Englishes in cities such as Sydney. (I mention a sign I had seen recently in a washroom telling people not to "open the tap" in the sink.) On reflection, open and close may indeed be the best terms to teach. And we might then ask whether the students' use of the terms reflected first language influence, a guessed or generalized term, or was it perhaps a term they had already heard used? This intrigues Liz and we use up our allotted time, and a bit more, talking about the possible Englishes of Sydney.

Reflections

But it's time to go. That's it. Back to the station. Just time for a quick stand-up espresso on the way. What can we learn from this? There's quite a lot to think about on the ride back into the city (the train's fairly empty, and I get a seat). I'd like to find out more about Chinese/Korean/English Presbyterian churches. How does all this fit together? What kind of hybrid cultural mix is this? But that's for another time, another paper. Having finished our talk and wished Liz well in the rest of her teaching, I reflect that we seem to have covered three critical moments: turning the discussion of the difficult student into a broader consideration of gender, culture, power, and rights; looking at how consensual dialogues not only fail to prepare students for the world outside but also potentially construct passive, consensual roles for them in the face of more powerful others; and the notion that it may not be the so-called standard versions of English that are the most common or useful for students. And out of these moments comes a further lesson for me: The first issue might be seen as critical-alternative (adapting Freeman's [1990] categorization of interventions; see above discussion) in that it provided Liz with a forum for clarifying the broader background issues involved in dealing with a difficult student; the second as critical-directive, in that I pushed my own concerns about consensuality and conflict; and the third as a critical-nondirective option in that it helped develop Liz's ability to see potential choices and to become more aware of the politics of language and standardization.

So which mattered most? Which was most critical? I have written this paper in this way in part to point to the very contingency of any answer to this question. This is also related to Canagarajah's (1996) observation that critical work that remains in standard form may reproduce as much as it resists. It is also to try to introduce more time and space and bodies into such texts. We teach and we do our teacher education in particular locations and in particular time frames. I wrote this in this manner not merely as a piece of experimental quasi-ethnography, but also to try to capture the contingencies of the moment that more standard ethnographic writing may start to sanitize.[5] It is akin, in some ways, to Cynthia Nelson's (1999) attempt to describe a moment in a class she was observing in all its complexities and fleeting moments. And it is also a preliminary attempt to take up the challenge posed by Dorothy Smith's (1999) notion of "writing the social" by taking

> one step back before the Cartesian shift that forgets the body. The body isn't forgotten; hence, the actual local site of the body isn't forgotten. Inquiry starts with the knower who is actually located; she is active; she is at work; she is connected up with other people in various ways; she thinks, eats, sleeps, laughs, desires, sorrows, sings, curses, loves, just here; she reads here; she watches television. . . . (p. 4)

I have tried here to recreate the everydayness of doing critical education and the frustration at coming up against that nagging question: Am I being critical (enough)? We can write our grand abstractions about pedagogy, resistance, hidden curricula, multiliteracies, or dialogism, and we can present our examples of the ideal critical lesson, the critical curriculum, the comments from transformed students, the empowerment that came about. But it seems to me that trying to be a critical educator is more often about seeking and seizing small moments to open the door on a more critical perspective. It may be about rethinking the notion of the praxicum, but it is also about all those unplanned moments when possibilities of critical heteropraxy come and go.

Another reason for writing this is to explore a moment of practice that seems to have received little attention. How do we seek out critical moments as an ongoing process of reaction, resistance? And how do we do it on a Friday morning when we're tired? I also decided to include this interlude as an example of neither particular failure nor success. It was a good class. Liz was clearly skilled and innovative. In terms of the different ways of being critical discussed earlier, her agenda would seem to fall into the second type – social relevance. She was trying to teach socially relevant and functionally useful language items for the students. My own agenda might then be seen as trying to move from this second type to the fourth type – problematizing practice. Thus, my interest was not so much in raising "big" critical issues but in working toward a way of questioning some as yet unexplored issues with critical consequences. If we want to be able to make less opaque the practices of critical language education, we can do so by reporting on our successful critical classes or observations of successful classes. But such reporting misses the way in which seeking to be critical is an ongoing, moment-by-moment process of slowly prodding for possibilities. And this, of course, touches on one of the dilemmas of a book such as this: All those moments become packaged and frozen and start to look like solutions rather than contingent possibilities. Being a critical educator, I would suggest, has less to do with the ponderous pronouncements of emancipatory modernism and more to do with the unbearable lightness of problematizing praxis.

And so one of the lessons I have learned here is that while all three modes of intervention – critical-directive, critical-alternatives, critical-nondirective – may be successful, it may have been the latter that was the most important, at least in this instance. Our discussion afterward didn't raise any great moments of enlightenment, empowerment, or emancipation. But the significant lesson for me here was that the potential critical moment needed to emerge not only from the specific context of the class and our jointly constructed understanding of it, but also from Liz's particular interests and concerns. The point that seemed to be of most importance – at least in its potential for further consideration – did not emerge from the agenda I tried to take up, but rather from a seemingly inconsequential issue to do with language form (close the tap). It wasn't something that I would have seen as a critical issue before the class, but it emerged as a point of some significance in our discussion (this is what it seemed to me that Liz got most out of), raising questions about standards and varieties, local norms, and language use.

So the challenge was *to make it critical in that moment*. Underlying this question of language form is a range of issues to do with what forms we model as teachers, how and in whose interests standard varieties are constructed and maintained, what language varieties our students may need, what forms of what varieties may be used in what communities, how language forms may be related to local configurations of power, and how notions of correctness may need to be put on hold. These are small moments of critical language education, critical moments embedded in the process of discussing teaching, and these have affected both Liz's and my own thinking about apparently minor issues in English language teaching. Society hasn't been transformed. Ideological obfuscation hasn't been removed. But in many ways, this is what critical language education is all about. It's the quiet seeking out of potential moments, the results of which we don't always know. It's about the everyday. The train pulls back into Central Station, and I hurry off through the clear sun-filled streets to my midday meeting.

Notes

1. When I discussed some of this in a colloquium at the annual TESOL (Teachers of English to Speakers of Other Languages) conference in 2001 and talked about issues of pedagogical engagement, Sarah Benesch pointed out from the audience that I was lacking institutional engagement here (see Benesch, 2001) and that it was not enough to report this estrangement from parts of

the pedagogical process as if these were inevitable. I take her point, though I would also reply that my point here is to ask what can still be done when the moments of engagement can be so peripheral.

2. I am using the notion of orthopraxy here in a slightly different way than Scott's (1990) conception. For Scott, the important distinction is between orthodoxy – in which we take on hegemonic beliefs – and orthopraxy – in which we act out hegemonic practices without necessarily believing them (a useful distinction, particularly in colonial contexts). I am not, however, suggesting here that orthopraxy implies the acting out of hegemonic teaching techniques without believing in their rationales (though investigating this might be a productive research project), but rather that in a context (teacher education) in which we might be seen to be teaching behaviors as well as ideas, there is a tendency toward orthopractic behaviors as well as orthodox beliefs. My main contrast, therefore, is between orthopraxy and heteropraxy.
3. The observant reader may have noticed the echoes of a well-known English as a foreign language book series in my subtitles up to this point. At a recent conference in the Philippines subtitled "Ruptures and Departures," I speculated briefly on why *Departures*, *Connections*, and *Destinations* were possible book titles but not a more challenging concept such as *Ruptures*. If anyone would like to update that series with the additional *Ruptures* and *Reflections* books, they are welcome to the titles.
4. Of course, it would be dangerous to suggest that such dialogues construct the totality of language and discourse resources of students since clearly many language learners will find resistant ways of dealing with others in conversations. Nevertheless, a good case can be made that such dialogues limit discursive possibilities for students.
5. This paper is what we might call a narrativized quasi-ethnography. Some time sequences and events have been shifted in order to make a cleaner story. Thus, although everything here is based on real events (though certain locations and names have been changed, and pseudonyms have been used), not everything happened quite in this way. For a parallel approach, see Goldstein's (2000) discussion of performed ethnography – writing plays based on ethnographic data (and see also Nelson, 2002). There are, of course, risks with this sort of approach: While I do believe that more experimental writing like this may be useful, it is also worth recalling that, as Watson-Gegeo (1988) pointed out some years ago, the field of TESOL has, for too long, been prepared to accept weak, blitzkrieg ethnographies that caricature rather than characterize. I am therefore wary of some of the problems that arise when attempting new ways to write critically.

References

Auerbach, E. (1993). Reexamining English only in the ESL classroom. *TESOL Quarterly, 27*(1), 9–32.

Auerbach, E. (1995). The politics of the ESL classroom: Issues of power in pedagogical choices. In J. Tollefson (Ed.), *Power and inequality in language education* (pp. 9–33). New York: Cambridge University Press.

Auerbach, E., & Wallerstein, N. (1987). *ESL for action: Problem-posing at work* Reading, MA: Addison Wesley.

Benesch, S. (2001). *Critical English for Academic Purposes: Theory, politics, and practice*. Mahwah, NJ: Lawrence Erlbaum Associates.

Brutt-Griffler, J., & Samimy, K. (1999). Revisiting the colonial in the postcolonial: Critical praxis for nonnative English-speaking teachers in a TESOL program. *TESOL Quarterly, 33*(3), 413–31.

Canagarajah, A. S. (1996). From critical research practice to critical research reporting. *TESOL Quarterly, 30*(2), 321–31.

Canagarajah, A. S. (1999). *Resisting linguistic imperialism in English teaching*. Oxford: Oxford University Press.

Chakrabarty, D. (2000). *Provincializing Europe: Postcolonial thought and historical difference*. Princeton, NJ: Princeton University Press.

Clark, R., & Ivanič, R. (1997). *The politics of writing*. London: Routledge.

Dean, M. (1994). *Critical and effective histories: Foucault's methods and historical sociology*. London: Routledge.

Fairclough, N. (1995). *Critical discourse analysis*. London: Longman.

Foucault, M. (1980). *Power/knowledge: Selected interviews and other writings, 1972–1977*. New York: Pantheon Books.

Freeman, D. (1990). Intervening in practice teaching. In J. Richards & D. Nunan (Eds.), *Second language teacher education* (pp. 103–17). Cambridge, England: Cambridge University Press.

Freeman, D., & Johnson, K. (1998). Reconceptualizing the knowledge-base of language teacher education. *TESOL Quarterly, 32*(3), 397–417.

Gebhard, J. (1990). Interaction in a teaching practicum. In J. Richards & D. Nunan (Eds.), *Second language teacher education* (pp. 118–31). Cambridge, England: Cambridge University Press.

Giroux, H. (1988). *Schooling and the struggle for public life: Critical pedagogy in the modern age*. Minneapolis: University of Minnesota Press.

Goldstein, T. (1994). "We are all sisters, so we don't have to be polite": Language choice and English language training in the multilingual workplace. *TESL Canada, 11*(2), 30–45.

Goldstein, T. (2000). Hong Kong, Canada: Performed ethnography for anti-racist teacher education. *Teaching Education, 11*(3), 311–26.

Gore, J. (1993). *The struggle for pedagogies: Critical and feminist discourses as regimes of truth*. New York: Routledge.

Johnson, K. (1996). The vision vs. the reality: The tensions of the TESOL practicum. In D. Freeman & J. Richards (Eds.), *Teacher learning in language teaching* (pp. 30–49). New York: Cambridge University Press.

Johnston, B. (1999). Putting critical pedagogy in its place: A personal account. *TESOL Quarterly, 33*(3), 557–65.

Kanpol, B. (1994). *Critical pedagogy: An introduction*. Westport, CT: Bergin & Garvey.

Liston, D., & Zeichner, K. (1991). *Teacher education and the social conditions of schooling*. New York: Routledge.

Mignolo, W. (2000). *Local histories/global designs: Coloniality, subaltern knowledges, and border thinking*. Princeton, NJ: Princeton University Press.

Nelson, C. (1999). Sexual identities in ESL: Queer theory and classroom inquiry. *TESOL Quarterly, 33*(3), 371–91.

Nelson, C. (2002, April). *Queer as a second language: Classroom theatre for everyone*. Paper presented at the meeting of Teaching English to Speakers of Other Languages (TESOL), Salt Lake City, UT.

Pennycook, A. (2000). The social politics and the cultural politics of language classrooms. In J. K. Hall & W. Eggington (Eds.), *The sociopolitics of English language teaching* (pp. 89–103). Clevedon, England: Multilingual Matters.
Pennycook, A. (2001). *Critical applied linguistics: A critical introduction*. Mahwah, NJ: Lawrence Erlbaum Associates.
Pennycook, A. & S. Coutand-Marin (in press). Teaching English as a missionary Language. *Discourse: Studies in the Cultural Politics of Education,* 24.
Phillipson, R. (1992). *Linguistic imperialism*. Oxford: Oxford University Press.
Platt, J., Weber, H., & Ho, M. L. (1984). *The new Englishes*. London: Routledge.
Richards, J., & Crookes, G. (1988). The practicum in TESOL. *TESOL Quarterly,* 22(1), 9–27.
Scott, J. (1990) *Domination and the arts of resistance: Hidden transcripts*. New Haven, CT: Yale University Press.
Simon, R. (1992). *Teaching against the grain: Essays towards a pedagogy of possibility*. Boston: Bergin & Garvey.
Singh, R. (Ed.). (1998). *The native speaker: Multilingual perspectives*. New Delhi, India: Sage.
Smith, D. (1999). *Writing the social: Critique, theory, and investigations*. Toronto, Ontario, Canada: University of Toronto Press.
Vološinov, V. N. (1973). *Marxism and the philosophy of language* (L. Mtejka & I. R. Titunik, Trans.). Cambridge, MA: Harvard University Press. (Original work published 1929.)
Watson-Gegeo, K. (1988). Ethnography in ESL: Defining the essentials. *TESOL Quarterly,* 22(4), 575–92.
Williams, G. (1992). *Sociolinguistics: A sociological critique*. London: Routledge.
Wodak, R. (1996). *Disorders of discourse*. London: Longman.

Author Index

Subject Index